The Later Philosophy of Pentti Linkola

Chad A. Haag
Uchakkada, India
2020

Table of Contents

Dedication Page 4

  Part I: The Mind of Nature 6

    Chapter One: Executing the Will of Nature: The Ethics of Deep Ecology 8

    Chapter Two: Nature Does Exist: Linkola's Metaphysics 139

      Part II: The Green Police 254

        Chapter Three: Did Somebody Say Ecofascism? Language and the Failure of Democracy 256

Dedicated to Kaarlo Pentti Linkola

"But if the future is fashioned after a madman's belief in progress and development, delusions and science fictions, the game is most certainly over."
— Pentti Linkola, "Human Nature and History"

Part I
The Mind of Nature

"The guardian of life, the deep ecologist, will not accept progress as the end of evolution and will reject the dominating position man has assumed." – Pentti Linkola, "The Objection Raised by the Deep Ecologist."

Chapter One
Executing the Will of Nature:
The Ethics of Deep Ecology

Green Police at the Gates

One of the strangest political reversals in recent memory lay in the sudden realization, both within the liberal establishment and the social justice left, that "the most dangerous force on the right wing" is no longer to be represented by a lack of ecological awareness, captured by stereotypical images of climate denialism and the anti-environmentalist capitalism it enables; the most dangerous force on the right, they claimed, is rather an *excess* of environmental concern, manifested in burgeoning "ecofascist" movements. Deep Ecology, the philosophy that ecosystems must be maintained in their natural integrity without regard for crass humanistic judgments of value, especially ones rooted in the pursuit of economic wealth or anthropocentric evaluations of utility, is quickly becoming the most forbidden Orwellian thought crime.[1] Even as some academic psychologists are literally working to overturn prejudices against paedophilia by unearthing "new scientific evidence" to prove that this is (supposedly) just one more naturally-occurring sexual difference among all others, we are quickly approaching the point where "having a 'thing' for little girls"[2] will be more socially acceptable than publicly criticizing technological overshoot, needless economic growth, job-killing automation, historically-anomalous lifestyles, or fossil fuel-based pollution.

---

[1] Arne Naess, "Avalanches as Social Constructions," in *Ecology of Wisdom* (London: Penguin, 2008), p. 68.
[2] Ted Kaczynski used this memorable phrase in response to a need for an example of something which even avowed anarchists with no need for conventional morality will still inevitably recognize as intrinsically evil. Ted Kaczynski, "Morality and Revolution," in *Technological Slavery* (Port Townsend: Feral House, 2010), p. 234.

In a 2019 post on his *Ecosophia* blog titled "The Next Twilight of Environmentalism," John Michael Greer warned that the media's growing obsession with attempting to dox "ecofascist" groups was troubling, since their insatiable appetite to dig up dirt on a "fringe of a fringe" movement with arguably less political influence than "the Flat Earth Society" or the "United Church of Bacon" was merely a means to an end to promote a very different cause, one founded on motives which were far from noble.[3] All of this self-righteous sleuthing by the media to turn the public against any non-leftist concern for the environment whatsoever was simply an attempt to lubricate the gears of the technological system by using sheer repetition of propaganda to de-sensitize audiences to the logically-fallacious claim that anyone who believes in ecological limitation "must be racist":

> Over the months ahead, I expect to see many more stories along the same lines all over the leftward end of the media and its associated blogosphere, insisting in increasingly shrill terms that anyone who pays too much attention to the environment—and in particular, anyone who expects celebrity climate change activists to modify their lifestyles to match their loudly proclaimed ideals—is probably an ecofascist. In fact, I would be very surprised if we don't see a series of earnest articles in the media claiming that believing in ecological limits is racist; such claims are already being made in the blogosphere, and their adoption by the mainstream left is, I suspect, merely a matter of time.[4]

The media appears to have made an enormous investment in time and effort to smear anyone who believes ecological limitation is real, simply in order to open the floodgates for unbridled technological and economic excesses to pass as the "only ethical option." Yet even despite this gigantic expenditure of manufactured concern, the media has only managed to find some two authors who

---

[3] John Michael Greer, "The Next Twilight of Environmentalism," *Ecosophia*, 7-8-2019.
[4] Ibid.

are consistently associated with this Orwellian thought crime, a trend reflected even in the official Wikipedia page for the topic of "Ecofascism." Quite predictably, the so-called Unabomber Ted Kaczynski is virtually always paraded out in handcuffs onto the public forum to serve as a rotten tomato target for the raving masses whenever articles of this sort emerge on the internet news cycle. A perceptive reader of such material will have no trouble detecting that behind the media's façade of "moral outrage" and giant crocodile tears at the very mention of the "evil Unabomber," they obviously find Kaczynski's status as a "convicted murderer" something to be gleefully celebrated rather than lamented, simply because his alleged "crimes" provide a little extra ammunition to paint an entire belief system with the same wide brush of shame.

Far less well-known in the general public, however, is Finnish fisherman Kaarlo Pentti Linkola, a figure whom the media has similarly turned to routinely condemning in hit pieces against non-leftist ecological thinkers for his "extreme views" on overpopulation, economic overshoot, pollution, and invasive species' devastation of native animal populations. However, their attempt to hold a monopoly over his exposure to the general public shall go unchallenged no more. The present text will also seek to introduce Linkola to a broader audience, but precisely through refuting the media's roadside puppet show and two-dimensional caricatures of him. Far beyond the cartoon image of a lunatic "eco-extremist" with zero credibility lies one of the greatest thinkers alive today and arguably the single person with the most viable political plan to bail us out of a mess which will certainly end in human extinction if abandoned to its current doomed trajectory. We ignore him only to our own peril.

While Linkola is not the only major thinker to mention that ecological issues such as overpopulation, pollution, and ecosystem disruption are problematic on theoretical grounds, he has distinguished himself as one of the only people with the guts to acknowledge that these ecological crises will *never* be solved through following democratic political procedures. Unthinkable as such an idea might be to the oversocialized and to those with feelings of inferiority,[5] the reasoning behind it becomes all too clear when one considers the simple fact that any candidate who attempted to give people what they actually *need* instead of what they merely *want* would literally have to run a campaign promising a wilfully-engineered economic depression,[6] the destruction of all job-stealing machines,[7] the removal of electricity from every personal home,[8] the violent extermination of minks and other invasive predators,[9] the forced elimination of house cats from most neighbourhoods,[10] the suspension of modern sanitation regulations,[11] as well as restrictions against reproduction which could only be bypassed through receiving a permit from the government to be able to bear children.[12] Linkola has distinguished himself as one of the only thinkers sufficiently faithful to the Will of Nature to explicitly endorse every one of these supremely-controversial though necessary positions over the course of his writings.

Contrary to media caricatures, it would be misplaced to label these stances as "super conservative," since arguably the only issue which every Republican and every Democrat politician can agree on is that economic growth is the sole absolute good in itself, the only universal exception to the ethical code for which the end will always justify even the most horrific of means. It is peculiar for Bernie Bros (seemingly, the most "radical" of all the Democrats) to claim to take environmental issues more seriously than anyone else

---

[5] Kaczynski defined the leftist as a psychological type consisting of these features. Ted Kaczynski, *Industrial Society and Its Future,* in *Technological Slavery* (Scottsdale: Fitch & Madison, 2019), para. 9.
[6] Pentti Linkola, "A Refresher Course in the State of the World", in *Can Life Prevail?* (Kindle Edition).
[7] Pentti Linkola, ""Can We Survive? A Model for a Controlled Future", in *Can Life Prevail?* (Kindle Edition).
[8] Ibid.
[9] Pentti Linkola, "Violence: The Animal Protector as an Apostle of Doom, in *Can Life Prevail?* (Kindle Edition).
[10] Pentti Linkola, "The Suppressed Nightmare of Conservation", in *Can Life Prevail?* (Helsinki: Tammi, 2008).
Pentti Linkola, "Cat Disaster", in *Can Life Prevail?* (Helsinki: Tammi, 2008).
[11] Pentti Linkola, "Humbug", in *Can Life Prevail?* (Helsinki: Tammi, 2008).
[12] Pentti Linkola, ""Can We Survive? A Model for a Controlled Future", in *Can Life Prevail?* (Kindle Edition).

while basically just promising that switching over to questionable "clean energy" sources will produce millions of high-paying jobs and unprecedented leaps in technological progress while simultaneously reversing global warming and converting the entire nation into a universalized "green campus," as a 2016 campaign pamphlet for Sanders explicitly claims:

> If the United States wants to be a leader on climate change— and a leader in new [green] technologies that will bring in billions of dollars over the coming decades— we need a president who understands the magnitude of the issue and is willing to put it front and centre in our nation's political discourse.[13]

On the other hand, in the 50th paragraph of the Unabomber Manifesto, Ted Kaczynski memorably called the conservative politicians of his era "fools" for believing that they could have their cake and eat it too by finding some way to engineer a situation in which everyone can get a high-salary job within the industrial economy while simultaneously preserving traditional religious and family values which are eroded into non-existence precisely by these same technological advances.[14] Needless to say, the Mind of Nature is neither a Republican nor a Democrat, for both of these stances are equally enslaved to Modern Technology and the ecological destruction of which this is a mere euphemism.

In his 1996 essay "What is the Majority and What is the Minority?" Linkola dismissed the illusion of partisan conflict altogether by noting that "the major parties [in Finland] are all the same" insofar as any one of them actually just runs on the same bland agenda of promising economic "development, progress, and money," with no regard whatsoever for the long-term consequences to the Earth.[15] Behind the façade of serious disagreements and

---

[13] Okla Elliott. *Bernie Sanders: The Essential Guide* . Squint Books, Eyewear Publishing LTD. Kindle Edition.
[14] Ted Kaczynski, *Industrial Society and Its Future*, in *Technological Slavery* (Scottsdale: Fitch & Madison, 2019), para. 50.
[15] Pentti Linkola, "What is the Majority and What is the Minority?" in *Can Life*

irreconcilable differences lies the reality of a perfectly unanimous consensus regarding the ecological issues which are, not coincidentally, the only ones which will truly matter in the end.

Nor has this catastrophe come about through an elitist conspiracy to shut out the "common voter" from participating in the process. On the contrary, Linkola notes that it is precisely because "Finland is a democracy" in which "all have the same right to vote" that political parties can reliably count on buying out elections through manipulating the numerical majority's pathological weakness for an ideal of progress founded solely on the crassest standard of materialistic greed.[16] In other words, not only has the concept of a get-rich-quick scheme lost any sense of moral scandal it might have once held; it has even been elevated to become the principle to guide the highest levels of political organization.

By the late 20th Century, Atlantic City and Las Vegas had lost their status as the only places in the United States where gambling was legal, as countless Native American reservations and small towns across the country gave in to the temptation to Las Vegasize themselves in order to cash in on what was once considered a shameful addiction but was progressively coming to be accepted as a harmless pastime. James Howard Kunstler noted in his 1993 book *The Geography of Nowhere: The Rise and Decline of America's Man-Made Landscape*, though, that the moral scandal surrounding gambling in earlier times was not simply religious in nature, something which could not be rationally explained but could only be accepted blindly on grounds of, say, papal infallibility. On the contrary, gambling was rejected for the very specific reason that earlier generations realized that the idea of trying to "get something for nothing" was forbidden by Nature itself.[17] Las Vegas represented something of a Bermuda Triangle in the desert where nothing short of the Laws of Thermodynamics seemed to be temporarily suspended, as pious pilgrims to the holy site of materialistic excess dreamed of circumventing the natural laws

---

Prevail? (Kindle Edition).
[16] Ibid.
[17] James Howard Kunstler, *The Geography of Nowhere: The Rise and Decline of America's Man-Made Landscape* (New York: Touchstone, 1993), p. 232.

which would require one to actually invest a certain amount of hard labour before yielding an economic return from a project. This was a magical site in which one could beseech the gods of greed with the hope of being blessed with the miracle of hitting the jackpot for no reason except sheer luck. The universalization of gambling even into tiny mining towns in the Rocky Mountains such as Cripple Creek, Colorado (population 1,189) could only be explained through a mass psychosis in which the expectation that one can and should get rich without having to work for it had become normalized. It is no exaggeration to say that democracy is simply the Las Vegasization of politics, the mechanism whereby the fate of entire nations is entrusted to the pseudo-logic of gambling and the demand that voters should elect candidates for no reason except that he or she promised them the most free stuff.

This tendency for democratic political procedures to be contaminated by pathological self-interests is not an accidental bug to the System but is a necessary feature, for the simple reason that "democratic engagement" cannot mean anything other than a system in which desire, in the basest Freudian sense, becomes an exploitable resource. In a very real sense, desire has become the new gold, insofar as the winner of an election is simply the candidate who succeeded in mining the largest heap of the stuff from out of the democratic masses in a show of ruthless exploitation which would make Cortes blush.

Under democracy, desire's value cannot avoid being reduced to purely quantitative terms because a raw numerical majority is the sole catalyst necessary to enact even the most far-fetched and self-destructive of proposals. For this reason, candidates have discovered that they actually have a perverse incentive to intentionally provoke voters to generate an excess of this precious material by artificially inducing them to want things they did not know they wanted until they were told to do so. Far from arising out of a natural spontaneity embedded within the deepest layers of the subject's New Age-style "true self," modern political desire has followed the same trajectory as modern sexual desire. In both cases, sheer financial self-interest has driven industrial forces within the System to disseminate a technologically-coordinated fantasy among the indoctrinated masses, knowing full well that a political pornography of "infinite progress" holds as little chance of being actualized in the real world as the most bizarre and shameful Hentai animation would.[18] The following dysfunction at the *elect*-ile level shall prove just as serious as at the *erect*-ile level. The irony of democracy is that the most extreme efforts to "empower the people" only result in a society steeped in political herbivores[19] suffering from the most embarrassing kind of impotence.

What is all too often missed by the media and other casual critics of Linkola is that he defined democracy in exactly these terms, going as far as to categorically dismiss "[a]ny political system based on desire" as "fundamentally flawed."[20] Democracy's "fundamental flaw" is simply that it offers no exit ramp out of this closed feedback loop in which desire self-recursively generates more desire without ever accomplishing a breakthrough to climb up into any higher ideals, let alone reach up to the non-humanistic demands of Nature itself. Linkola is one of the few thinkers sufficiently courageous to note that the Laws of Nature will continue to exist regardless of whether they are acknowledged by humans, or even whether they outright contradict man's arbitrary chimeras of desire. Linkola's stance is nothing short of the ultimate refutation of solipsism and linguistic idealism, insofar as his rejection of democracy is founded on his realization that you cannot simply use the techniques of Habermasian dialogue to "communicate your way" out of accountability to the Laws of Nature.[21]

For this reason, Linkola has explicitly contrasted "individual desire" with "what is good for Nature" by noting that our current "society and [way of] life have been organized" solely on the basis

---

[18] Hentai, or anime porn, is a topic which the reader is not advised to research any further.
[19] In Japan, an herbivore or "grass eater" is a man who has watched so much cartoon pornography that he has lost all interest in human partners of any kind.
[20] Linkola is quoted as saying this in Brett Stevens' 2008 introduction to *Can Life Prevail?*
[21] Linkola's contrast with Habermas shall be explored in much greater detail in the third chapter of the present work.

of the former.[22] This arrangement has proven uniquely catastrophic because of a key ontological difference between the two. Whereas human desires are infinitely flexible and can be manipulated at will to accommodate even the most preposterous of pseudo-forms conjured up during hopelessly-unrealistic daydreams, the demands of Nature are fixed by a level of necessity which the whims of Man shall prove powerless to overcome. Whereas human desires require no deeper foundation than the infinitely-elastic structure of human language, the Mind of Nature's sole frame of accountability lies in the Laws of Ecology.

Linkola has repeatedly contrasted "desire" with "necessity" to communicate this distinction with an even finer level of philosophical clarity. In "The Suppressed Nightmare of Conservation," for example, he defended his controversial proposal that the owner of any cat caught slaughtering a wild animal should be harshly prosecuted by reiterating that one's failure to treat this ongoing catastrophe as an eco-crime worthy of serious punishment would represent a grotesque violation of natural law in favour of humanistic fancy. He admitted, however, that the "utopia" in which the Mind of Nature and the legal code of Man would overlap perfectly continues to be inhibited by the same conflict between desire and necessity which has marred every other serious proposal for a more ecologically-rationalized society: "This, however, is pure utopia — as is always the case with attempts to protect nature which clash with people's ardent desires."[23]

In the essay "Can We Survive: A Model for a Controlled Future," he noted even more explicitly that "[these] two things — desire and necessity — are as far from one another as east and west."[24] In other words, if one is moving in the direction of chasing one of these terms, one is by definition ruled out from pursuing the other, just as one cannot travel eastward and westward at the same time. In the same essay, Linkola went on to note the irony that

---

[22] Ibid.
[23] Pentti Linkola, "The Suppressed Nightmare of Conservation," in *Can Life Prevail?* (Kindle Edition).
[24] Pentti Linkola, "Can We Survive: A Model for a Controlled Future," in *Can Life Prevail?* (Kindle Edition).

allowing humans to coordinate their own political systems on the basis of what they desire defeats its own purpose because it does not even lead them to a satisfying way of life in the long run. Somehow, "what man desires" and "what is best for him" are separated by a vast gulf denominated by a distance which mysteriously expands with each attempt to bridge the gap through leaping into the abyss of self-interest. Human happiness can only ever be achieved through the pathway of nominally rejecting it in favour of natural necessity, an ecological equivalent of the spiritual mystery captured in legends of medieval ascetic mystics' realization that one can only gain one's life if one loses it first.[25] In Farid Al-Din Attar's *Tadhkirat al-Auliya'*, a Medieval Persian collection of Islamic hagiographies, for example, he recounted that Habib al-Ajami was put to the test by a supernatural visitor disguised as a beggar who asked him to give up the two loaves of barley bread and salt which were his sole sustenance for the day. Only after renouncing this simple meal did a supernatural reward materialize for the mystic who was somehow only able to reach the oasis of happiness through wilfully opting for the wilderness of a personal renunciation of his desires.[26]

According to Linkola, personal indulgence is a mirage in the desert which causes its goal of happiness to disappear as soon as one takes the leap of faith to zero in on it. What appears to be the most direct path to seize personal contentment by force is actually the most certain avenue to lose it once and for all:

> [T]he underlying error that is leading us astray is a political system based on indulgence. Our society and ways of life are based on what man desires rather than what is best for him.[27]

---

[25] Matthew 10:39
[26] Farid Al-Din Attar, "Habib al-Ajami" in *Muslim Saints and Mystics: Episodes from the Tadhkirat al-Auliya'* (London: Arkana, 1996), p. 37.
[27] Pentti Linkola, "Can We Survive: A Model for a Controlled Futue," in *Can Life Prevail?* (Kindle Edition).

Despite its admitted obscurity, this counter-intuitive principle has nonetheless found abundant confirmation in the endless failures of modern consumerism to actually make anyone's life better, despite positing "customer satisfaction" as the sole justification for unspeakable levels of ecological devastation and resource waste. Paradoxically, people have become more depressed than ever just as the commodities engineered to maximize their pleasure have exploded in number and technical sophistication while somehow missing the mark more noticeably with each apparent leap in efficiency.

    Nor can one even explain the insanity of allowing humanistic desire to overshadow ecological necessity through pseudo-Darwinist appeals to the "will to survive" as some mysterious force which could be presumed to lie below the surface of any impulse to act, as though even the most reckless desires could be trusted to hold some teleological orientation towards preserving life simply because an organism would be thought to have no other hard-wired instinctual motivations beyond "survival and reproduction." Bronze Age Pervert noted memorably in *Bronze Age Mindset* that reductive claims to explain away all animal behaviour through clichés of reproduction and survival miss the point that cutting to the chase and focusing on reproducing quickly is actually something which stunts an animal's growth and typically indicates some sort of a problem or contradiction of the natural norm. It is peculiar to claim that surviving long enough to "pass one's genes on to the next generation" is the sole purpose for any animal's existence when, in the wrong context, fixating on sexual reproduction is actually more like a roadblock which gets in the way of an animal's true goal of clearing enough personal space to develop its abilities[28] or, as Ted Kaczynski would say, to go through the Power Process.[29] Explaining all activity whatsoever as an encrypted manifestation of a single consistent "will to survive and reproduce" is, paradoxically, not at all a faithful reduction to the Mind of Nature purified of humanistic biases. It is, rather, the

---

[28] Bronze Age Pervert, *Bronze Age Mindset* (Kindle Edition).
[29] Ted Kaczynski, *Industrial Society and Its Future* (Scottsdale: Fitch & Madison, 2019), para. 33.

ultimate humanistic distortion of Nature, fuelled far more by pseudo-scientific Freudian clichés than by any truly serious adherence to the laws of ecological reality.

Linkola has similarly noted the inadequacy of subordinating human desire to the monolithic stereotype of "the will to survive" because he has mentioned the supremely ironic fact that desire will continue circulating stupidly around an impossible object even when one understands explicitly that this will lead to nothing short of death, not only on a personal level but even for the Earth itself. In the "Democracy: The Religion of Death" subsection of the essay "The ABC of the Deep Ecologist – Part Two" he warned that people can be counted on to give in to the pathological temptation to pursue their own ill-founded desires even as "the impending end of the world" looms visibly on the horizon:

> Man has learned almost nothing even when confronted with the impending end of the world. The majority of people continue to make their daily choices on the basis of what they desire and what pleases them.[30]

In contrast with a system in which people are free to make the wrong choices simply because they want to, Linkola has proposed a system in which people are forced to do the right thing regardless of personal fancy. In fact, he was careful to note in the same essay that his proposals for embodying the Mind of Nature in a seemingly-human political institution required him to suspend even *his own* humanistic preferences in order to allow the Will of Nature to speak for itself in the public venue:

> The deep ecologist never confuses human preferences or distastes, whether his own or those of others, with what needs to be done. He will formulate his judgments and establish his guidelines on the basis of what is feasible — without diminishing the possible richness of the biosphere or endangering its continuity.[31]

---

[30] Pentti Linkola, "The ABC of the Deep Ecologist – Part Two," in *Can Life Prevail?* (Kindle Edition).

In fact, in his 1996 essay "Of The Evaluation Of The Book 'Into The Ecological Way Of Life [Ekologiseen Elämäntapaan]'" Linkola explicitly downplayed the idea that any of his proposals were just some ingenious new idea he drafted up as a result of being blessed with the gift of talent or personal creativity. On the contrary, he asserted that he generally "abhors and shirks new thoughts." His reasoning for this aversion to the cult of creative genius was that it is simply another form of materialism in disguise, just as likely as industrial innovations to almost always lead to error. [32]

In his 2004 interview with Virpi Adamsson, Linkola similarly expressed regret that the media had over-sensationalized the name "Linkola" and promoted the caricature of an eccentric ecophilosopher to the point where all too many people within their audience would be tempted to dismiss his warnings with the attitude of "Oh, that's just that [crazy] Linkola again." He noted that this "personalization" of the issues completely misses the point that his motivation is precisely to let the Will of Nature itself speak in public rather than to promote his own "brand."[33]

In the "Democracy: The Religion of Death" subsection of the essay "The ABC of the Deep Ecologist – Part Two", Linkola once again reiterated the tendency for democracy to allow humans to pursue their desires even to the point of self-destruction by warning that democracy causes its inmates to live in what is by definition a "suicidal society," a term he also favoured in his "Can We Survive: A Model for a Controlled Future":[34]

---

[31] Ibid.
[32] Pentti Linkola, "Of The Evaluation Of The Book 'Into The Ecological Way Of Life [Ekologiseen Elämäntapaan],'" in *A Collection of Essays by Pentti Linkola 1993 – 2006*, pp. 144-5.
[33] "Interview with Pentti Linkola 10-2-2004." Available at http://www.penttilinkola.com/pentti_linkola/ecofascism_writings/interview_10-2-2003
[34] "The resources of inland and coastal waters, vastly under-utilised in Suicidal Society, will be put to good use."
Pentti Linkola, "Can We Survive: A Model for a Controlled Future," in *Can Life Prevail?* (Kindle Edition).

> Democracy . . caters to the whims of man: the will of the people. The consequences of this are frightening: what democracy leads to is the kind of suicidal society that we see all around us. Democracy is the most miserable of all known societal systems, the building block of doom. Under such a system of government unmanageable freedom of production and consumption and the passions of the people are not only tolerated, but cherished as the highest values. The most serious environmental disasters occur in democracies.[35]

In his 2011 interview with Francisco Martinez and Larissa Vanamo, Linkola conceded that media accusations that he favours dictatorship over democracy are not hyperbole at all; in fact, he openly admitted that even among dictatorships, "the more draconian" they are, "the better." As controversial as such a claim might be to the politically correct sensibilities of modernity, Linkola explained that his stance towards democracy logically followed from the fact that the only meaning which "freedom" has under democracy is the freedom of consumption and industrial production. This desiring-machine which grants people whatever they want no matter the consequences is so destructive that the only sensible option is to hold people "captive" and forcibly stop them from embarking on this path in the first place, much like how the only options for Odysseus and his crew to survive while sailing past the sirens were for the oarsmen to plug their ears with beeswax to shut out the sirens' song altogether and for Odysseus himself to be tied to the mast so that he could not act out physically after being exposed to their seduction.[36] The height of humanistic hubris is to imagine that we could adopt a less extreme stance towards the ultimate sirens' song of industrial consumerism, one which will lead to nothing short of planetary destruction, a far more horrific conclusion than a single sunk ship in the Mediterranean Sea.

---

[35] Pentti Linkola, "The ABC of the Deep Ecologist – Part Two," in *Can Life Prevail?* (Kindle Edition).
[36] See Francisco Martinez Larissa Vanamo's 2011 interview "A Promenade with Pentti Linkola," http:// www.materialworldblog.com/ 2013/ 03/ invoking-the-apocalypse-a-promenade-with-pentti-linkola/

In stark contrast with the countless would-be revolutionaries and anarchists who tend to wallow in the vaguest of abstractions when describing what sort of positive future might follow after the collapse of the present order, Linkola's proposals for a more ecologically rational society are perfectly specific and highly detailed. The final essay of the collection *Can Life Prevail?*, "Can We Survive: A Model for a Controlled Future," was described by Finnish magazine *Quadrivium* in 2014 as "a seventeen-page instructional essay from nineteen ninety-nine that will probably stand as the final attempt Linkola ever makes to sketch something of a systematic presentation on the improvements that might hinder the climate change and make our environment a feasible place for man to prosper in."[37] In it, he presented an impressively-thorough list of policies which the Green Police would enforce in an ideal society structured solely by the ecological demands of the Mind of Nature.[38]

For example, Linkola has argued that the Will of Nature would mandate a drastic reduction in cereal grain production in favour of a return to a diet consisting of traditional fish sources and nutritious, though unfashionable, wild game such as certain species of rodents. In addition, it would legislate the forced abolition of automation through a coordinated destruction of all job-killing machines. Above all, the problem of mass unemployment would be resolved by reverting to the historical norm of having the majority of people work within the agricultural sector. Anyone who finds this ambition to be hopelessly unrealistic should bear in mind that as recently as 1810, some 84 percent of Americans worked as farmers and that statistical rates in Medieval and Ancient times were arguably even higher. Needless to say, a society in which traditional agricultural practices were restored and artificial technologies were discontinued would also be one in which food could only be eaten in its natural season, a policy which would be

---

[37] Pentti Linkola interview from *Quadrivium* #6 (2014): abridged version. Available at http://qvadrivivm.blogspot.com/2015/12/pentti-linkola-interview-from.html
[38] Pentti Linkola, "Can We Survive: A Model for a Controlled Future," in *Can Life Prevail?* (Kindle Edition).

enforced as much by ecological limitation as by legislative obligation. In addition, Linkola noted that while food preservation would still play a vital role in feeding the population, this would be the responsibility of each household to do on its own rather than have it be outsourced to major corporations which would cut corners with artificial preservatives and other energy-wasting practices.

As one might expect, Linkola argued for the outright criminalization of suburban sprawl and instead proposed that transportation networks should become localized to geographical circumferences which can be traversed with nothing more than human foot-power. In an era where the financial perversion of real estate bubbles is not only normalized but is actively encouraged by government meddling, he shocked audiences by categorically forbidding the "construction of new buildings" unless a set of highly-specific ecological conditions merited an exception to this general rule: "In all cases, ecological balance will be a central factor in evaluating whether to issue a permit."

Linkola's conviction that the tiniest energy waste contradicts the Will of Nature and its ethical code led him to argue that even an eco-crime as seemingly trivial as "sailing against the wind" should be forbidden by law. Needless to say, under these conditions "[a]ll air traffic will cease" and the privilege to own a personal car would be categorically removed, as "walking, skiing, cycling, and paddling" would be mandated as natural alternatives.[39] In the absence of the technical conditions necessary for large-scale transportation networks to continuously function, foreign trade would also drop to a minimum. The one notable exception he reserved was trading for salt, but this was only because of its vital role in food preservation.

These bold proposals fit his underlying logic that the only truly viable way to end pollution is to remove the demand for "plastic and rubber junk" in the first place by fundamentally transforming the underlying economic conditions which currently make these historical anomalies seem so commonplace as to be

---

[39] Ibid.

unavoidable. Put briefly, "most business enterprises will [simply have to] come to an end," with exceptions only reserved for truly necessary manufacturing operations, such as those involving "the production of equipment for public transportation, bicycles, and paper."[40] However, he was careful to note that these industrial operations would be "in the hands of the state" in order to remove the possibility for the temptation to increase profits to pervert private owners into contradicting the ecological demands of Nature by pursuing the chimera of growth for growth's sake.

Contrary to expectation, this prohibition against industrial manufacturing would actually result in a more economically egalitarian society than the supposedly democratic one which we inhabit today. In the absence of Modern Technology, small workshops staffed by skilled tradespeople working with hand tools would make a comeback, as giant factories would lose the competitive advantage which they only temporarily enjoyed as a result of bureaucratic meddling by politicians who rigged the game in their favour in exchange for massive corporate bribes. Linkola himself noted that under these conditions, a large number of people will find meaningful "work in local handcrafting trades" once again.

The benefits of this transition are arguably even more welcome today than when Linkola wrote these words decades ago, as the very concept of a job has all but vanished in the West. Behind the media's slobbering propaganda promising us that the so-called "gig economy" has realized the ultimate democratic fantasy of "letting everyone be their own boss" lies the bleak reality of a coliseum spectacle in which hundreds of online freelance gladiators fight each other to the death over a tiny handful of crumbs from a one-time "job" that will only end up going to some asshole in Pakistan who bid the price all the way down to ten bucks anyway. One could hardly imagine a more humiliating abuse of the modern (non-)worker than this monstrosity of requiring every Tom, Dick, and Harry to go $100,000 in student loan debt only to be thrown to the lions of having to cobble together a living one $20 "gig" at a time afterwards, yet there could be no other outcome to allowing

---

[40] Ibid.

technological overshoot and democracy to run their course than mathematical absurdities of this kind.

In addition to reducing unemployment, Linkola's proposed shift to localized production with traditional tools would simply result in a higher level of customer satisfaction as well. In the absence of Modern Technology, the technical means to produce cheap gimmicks which are hard-wired to break down quickly in order to maximize profits for a handful of highly-centralized corporations would evaporate; on the contrary, "[o]nly sturdy, well-built equipment will be used, which will last several generations."

In addition, strict aversion against resource waste would allow the professional repairperson to make a similar comeback, as throwing away a perfectly salvageable product and ordering a cheap import from China to replace it immediately would cease to be an option at all: "The mending and maintenance of objects will be central to society [once again]." In fact, Linkola went as far as to openly proclaim that "the intentional abandonment of usable objects will be [harshly] punished" by the Green Police, a useful reminder that wasting goods is not only stupid but is also immoral.

In an era in which "weak economic growth" is all but synonymous with "depression," despite the fact that these two things are actually technically opposites, Linkola pulled off the ultimate shocker by promising to engineer nothing short of the Great*est* Depression in history by demanding that "overall consumption in industrial countries would have to be reduced by over ninety percent." Yet his decision to endorse a proposition which would seem flatly impossible to modern sensibilities was grounded in the most bulletproof of ecological foundations, in that he was perfectly specific in his view that this seemingly unthinkable shift would be accomplished through the forced abandonment of fossil fuels. This is arguably the supreme proof of Linkola's commitment to favour ecological comprehension over humanistic prejudice, in that he realized that fossil fuels are the sole natural catalyst sufficiently powerful to make the historically-unprecedented anomaly of continuous, rapid economic growth pass as "normal." He chose not to mince words at all by openly declaring that "[f]ossil fuels, including peat, will be abolished on the first day the programme is implemented."[41]

It is important to acknowledge the unavoidable fact that for the ordinary citizen, this would amount to nothing short of the removal of electricity from every private home. Lacking the luxury of constant access to affordable electrical energy, "[h]ouseholds, as well as businesses, will have to switch to manual labour" to accomplish tasks which are currently taken over by electronic slaves running on autopilot, a luxury which even the poorest households in the West still take for granted. Although the gravity of such changes must not be underestimated, he was careful to note that overall, the effects of doing so would be beneficial rather than harmful. Tempting as the idea of continuing to allow every American to have some 200 fossil fuel energy slaves might be, our loss of agency to machines has been both psychologically damaging and ecologically devastating, a true lose-lose situation. He went as far as to speculate that in the far future, the memory of universal access to electricity will go down in history as "a great misfortune" rather than a source of blissful nostalgia.[42] In his 2011 interview with Francisco Martinez and Larissa Vanamo, in fact, he went as far as to claim that the single worst invention in World History was commercially viable "electricity" in private homes, as well as all the electrical "appliances" that it powered.[43]

In addition, he noted that in the absence of natural gas distribution to personal homes, "[f]irewood will be used in heating," with the additional mandate that all "[f]ireplaces will be made as efficient as possible." In indoor spaces, "bodies will first be warmed by clothing rather than [through artificially heating the] air [with natural gas]." Linkola vehemently warned his readers against the temptation to play games with allowing even the slightest possibility to turn back from these changes in the future by demanding nothing short of the *physical destruction* of the

---

[41] Ibid.
[42] Ibid.
[43] See Francisco Martinez Larissa Vanamo's 2011 interview "A Promenade with Pentti Linkola," http:// www.materialworldblog.com/ 2013/ 03/ invoking-the-apocalypse-a-promenade-with-pentti-linkola/

infrastructure required for mass distribution of fossil fuel energy, much like how a person can only truly break his or her addiction to smoking if he or she is willing to throw away all of the cigarettes left in the house first:[44]

> [Most] power plants will be demolished. The worst kind of plants, energy dams, will be the first to go. Indeed, waterpower has caused the third great ecocatastrophe alongside the clearing of fields and the forest economy: the faltering of our whole marine economy.

Linkola's willingness to contradict politically correct sensibilities by openly endorsing the violent destruction of critical infrastructure as a necessary means to deprive the System of the slightest chance of a "resurrection from the dead" is reminiscent of Kaczynski's similar proposal to destroy factories and burn technical books in the 166th paragraph of his *Industrial Society and Its Future*:

> [The anti-technological] ideology [developed in the Manifesto] will help to assure that, if and when industrial society breaks down, its remnants will be smashed beyond repair, so that the system cannot be reconstituted. The factories should be destroyed, technical books burned, etc.[45]

In a letter written from prison to a figure named A.O., Kaczynski responded to a question regarding news that even the so-called indigenous "primitive people from Mexico" were joining "the values of modern society" as a result of being exposed to television. Apparently, A.O. asked Kaczynski what could possibly make them "go back to the forest." Kaczynski's response lay in reminding the reader that Modern Technology is not a set of disconnected, independent elements so much as it is a highly-complex, tightly-integrated system for which failure in even one

---

[44] When I quit smoking in 2015, I did this myself.
[45] Ted Kaczynski, *Industrial Society and Its Future*, in *Technological Slavery* (Scottsdale: Fitch & Madison, 2019), para. 166.

vital area would disrupt all the others, possibly to the point of death. In other words, the reader must think of the System as an organism:

> You write: "Even some primitive people from Mexico join the values of modern society (because of TV). What could make them go back to the forest?" What could "make them go back to the forest" would be an end to the functioning of the world's industrial centres. The Mexican Indians couldn't use their TV sets if the TV stations were no longer broadcasting. They couldn't use motor vehicles or any internal combustion engines if the refineries were no longer producing fuel. They couldn't use any electrical appliances if the electrical power-plants were no longer producing electricity . . . Thus, if the world's industrial centres stopped functioning, the Mexican Indians would have no choice but to revert to simple, preindustrial methods.[46]

Interestingly, Kaczynski's reasoning regarding which vital organ might be targeted to bring about a full collapse of the System overlaps nearly perfectly with Linkola's conclusion that the power plants must be destroyed if one's overcoming of the System is to be meaningful in a more than symbolic level:

> But what could make the TV stations stop broadcasting, the power-plants stop generating electricity, the refineries stop producing fuel, and the factories stop making parts? If the power-plants stopped producing electricity, then the TV stations would no longer be able to broadcast, the refineries would no longer be able to produce fuel, and the factories would no longer be able to make things. If the refineries stopped producing fuel, then the transportation of goods and people would have to cease, and therefore the factories would no longer be able to make things. If the factories were no longer able to make things, then there would be no more replacement parts to keep the TV stations, power-plants, and

---

[46] Ted Kaczynski, "Letter to A.O.," in *Technological Slavery* (Port Townsend: Feral House, 2010).

petroleum refineries functioning. Moreover, every factory needs things produced by other factories in order to keep operating.

He noted the irony that the technological system's unprecedented scale of complexity actually made it "much easier to kill than a simple organism," something of an Achilles' heel to what would otherwise seem to be an indestructible Titan with godlike immortality:

> [M]odern industrial society can be compared to a complex organism in which every important part is dependent on every other important part. If any one important part of the system stops functioning, then the whole system stops functioning. Or even if the complex and finely-tuned relationship between the various parts of the system is severely disrupted, the system must stop functioning. [47]

In his later fragmentary magnum opus *Anti-Tech Revolution: Why and How*, Kaczynski developed this idea further by arguing that the revolution against the technological system is not at all an unrealistic goal, since it could be accomplished fairly easily if one could just destroy a single vital component of the System. Precisely because Modern Technology is a "highly complex and tightly coupled" self-propagating system for which "the breakdown in one part of the system [would] spread quickly to the other parts," the elimination of even a single one of the vital organs in this vast artificial pseudo-organism would be enough to kill the beast once and for all.[48]

As controversial as Linkola's proposal to destroy power plants might be, it arguably pales in comparison with his willingness to contemplate the ultimate sacrilege by arguing that nothing short of money itself should be discontinued from existence. Rather than allow the sophistry of modern finance, usury,

---

[47] Ibid.
[48] Ted Kaczynski, *Anti-Tech Revolution: Why and How* (Scottsdale: Fitch & Madison, 2016), p. 49.

and quantitative easing to go on unimpeded, he suggested that natural forms of exchange currency could easily replace money in the localized economy of the future: "Products of handicraft, woodwork and foodstuff such as fish and berries will be used as exchange currency."[49] Anyone who argues that no human being could ever possibly survive without the dollar bill (something of a misnomer in a world where cash has basically been outlawed) should bear in mind that until very recent historical times, the average peasant could easily pass an entire lifetime without ever physically handling a single gold coin, as John Michael Greer has repeatedly mentioned in his *Archdruid Report* posts. The following quote from his 2015 classic *After Progress: Reason and Religion at the End of the Industrial Age* explained this point particularly memorably:

> In the aftermath of the Roman collapse, for example, it wasn't just lending at interest that went away. Money itself dropped out of use in most of post-Roman Europe — as late as the twelfth century, it was normal for most people to go from one year to the next without ever handling a coin — and market-based economic exchange, which thrived in the Roman world, was replaced by feudal economies in which most goods were produced by those who consumed them, customary payments in kind took care of nearly all the rest, and a man could expect to hold land from his overlord on the same terms his great-grandfather had known.[50]

Yet it is not only in a Dark Age following the collapse of a complicated civilization that trying to maintain a financial system becomes more trouble than it is worth. Barter is arguably better suited for localized production than money is even in the best of times, since barter intrinsically rules out inflation, usury, fraud, and other forms of financial injustice from occurring. Once again, the

---

[49] Pentti Linkola, "Can We Survive: A Model for a Controlled Future," in *Can Life Prevail?* (Kindle Edition).
[50] Greer, John Michael. *After Progress: Reason and Religion at the End of the Industrial Age* . New Society Publishers. Kindle Edition.

grand irony of Linkola's suspension of democracy is that it would arguably bring about an even more egalitarian society than the one we currently inhabit.

Of course, any critique of democratic equality must address the elephant in the room by dealing with the problem of overpopulation. Arguably the single most polemical stance Linkola is known for espousing is the forced reduction in human population. In "Can We Survive: A Model for a Controlled Future," he openly mandated that "the present population [be] stripped of around two billion people." While such a claim may sound preposterously unreasonable to the oversocialized and those with feelings of inferiority today,[51] he noted that "the resulting figure would be roughly equivalent to that of the world population just over half a century ago, when the great ecosystems of the world began to waver and collapse." In other words, the "extremist" stance would lie precisely in arguing *against* returning to a historical norm from the fairly recent past.

It goes without saying that the only means sufficiently effective to bring about such a necessary though unpopular shift would lie in "dismantling" the myth of the "freedom of procreation," a humanistic chimera which he openly condemned as "the most senseless form of individual freedom."[52] Rather than allow the chaotic anarchy of unbridled reproduction to remain unchallenged, the Green Police would issue procreation licenses to a drastically smaller number of candidates and would do so only on the basis of merit:

> Procreation should be licensed: on average, every woman should be allowed to bear only one child [until several generations pass and the global population stabilizes.] . . . The quality of the population must in all cases be taken into account as well: procreation licences would be denied to homes deemed . . . unsuitable for the raising of children,

---

[51] Kaczynski defined the leftist as a psychological type consisting of these two traits in the 9th paragraph of the Manifesto.
[52] Pentti Linkola, "Can We Survive: A Model for a Controlled Future," in *Can Life Prevail?* (Kindle Edition).

whereas families capable of providing a stimulating environment for children would be granted several licences.[53]

Did Someone Say (Eco-)Totalitarianism?

What all of these ideas hold in common is that each demonstrates that ecological viability reliably coincides with democratic unviability. In other words, one's only hope for saving the Earth lies in circumventing the entire frustrating process of campaigning for votes, winning elections, and passing legislation through Congress and its non-American equivalents. One must simply cut to the chase and establish a strong, centralized Green Police force which will exercise strict but necessary regulations to cut population growth, economic activity, pollution, technological automation, and ecosystem disruption.

Above all, Linkola dispelled the naïve myth that one might crack the (non-existent) code to accomplish the same thing through democratic methods, a delusion often justified by pleas that one should be given just a little more time to try to deactivate a time bomb with only a handful of minutes left on the clock, even after having wasted centuries of time on repeated failures to accomplish the same task. Linkola does not mince words at all, dismissing this misplaced hope in democratic procedural solutions as a working definition of "madness" itself:

> [W]e are madly clinging to democracy and parliamentarianism, although we are all seeing that these are some of the most irrational and hopeless experiments of mankind. It is in democratic countries with a parliamentary system that world destruction, the sum of all ecocatastrophes, has reached its most advanced stage — and not by chance. The sole glimmer of hope lies in a centralised government and the tireless control of citizens.[54]

---

[53] Ibid.
[54] Pentti Linkola, "Can We Survive: A Model for a Controlled Futue," in *Can Life Prevail?* (Kindle Edition).

Precisely because the Green Police would be an unelected institution immune to democratic political pressures, it would be able to remain firm in these convictions in the face of widespread public outrage and fierce popular resistance by those who will unwittingly act against their own best interests by opposing the sole necessary measures to ensure human survival. It bears mentioning, on the other hand, that gambling on being able to outcompete rival parties who quite literally buy their way into office through selling state-sponsored benefits in exchange for votes will only guarantee that the message is either watered down to the point of meaninglessness or that the tyranny of the 51% will have free reign to guarantee ecological death for the 100%. Anyone with an interest in surviving would do well to consider whether these odds are worth it.

The media's sensationalist reaction to Linkola's willingness to propose serious solutions for ecological crises is peculiar, since the environmental problems themselves are completely uncontroversial from a standpoint of scientific objectivity. No one could possibly claim that the earth is *not* already unsustainably overpopulated, horrifically polluted, and witnessing a mass extinction as the author writes these words. Nor has this environmental devastation even succeeded in bringing about a better quality of life or greater happiness within the human population. Statistical rates of depression, anxiety, drug abuse, suicide, and other psychological woes continue to climb despite the media's frantic attempts to argue that "progress" is still occurring, much like the newscast in Orwell's *1984* which reported that the supply of everything was improving – everything, that is, except for the hunger, disease, and misery which the listener subjectively experienced to be on the rise. Even in cases where material wealth is not lacking but is arguably far too abundant, satisfaction with modern life remains tragically deficient. After receiving thirty pieces of silver in exchange for selling their natural souls to the Satan of technological gimmickry, many have found their own suburban McMansions to be just as self-destructive to them as the Field of Blood was to Judas Iscariot.[55]

Linkola has distinguished himself from the rest of the human herd primarily through his willingness to enact a leap of faith to break out of the standpoint of passive observation by crossing the seemingly impassable threshold into practical action. His proposals to enact strict regulations to forcibly curb population growth, economic activity, pollution, and ecological disruption might be understood to be the result of passing this theoretical knowledge through a mysterious filter that transforms scientific description into ethical prescription. Linkola has arguably performed the philosophical miracle of overcoming David Hume's prohibition that one can never arrive at a prescriptive command for how the world ought to be simply from a descriptive analysis of how the world is.

For Linkola, the vanishing mediator which enables the passage from science to ethics is nearly akin to a Zizekian parallax– not a dualism of two separate, coherent frames of meaning but rather a shift of perspectives with regard to the same incomplete One.[56] For Linkola, there is no need to engage in a Habermasian dialogue to intersubjectively work out a linguistic consensus regarding our collective ethical duty towards the environment, for ecologically-valid forms can simultaneously double as both scientific laws and ethical imperatives. Shifting from one to the other does not require one to exit the same single content so much as to simply refresh the page of perspectival manifestation, presenting the same object in a whole new light in the process.

In other words, Linkola's "radical extremist ideology" is simply the belief we should actually *do something* about a set of crises which are literally threatening the very possibility of complex life on Earth, problems which are already understood perfectly well on theoretical grounds but remain utterly untouchable at the level of serious practical action. If nothing else, the media's fanatical resistance to Linkola's philosophy definitively proves that breaking the stranglehold of learned helplessness in order to perform a non-

---

[55] Matthew 27:7 and Acts 1:18-19. In both accounts, Judas dies after buying the field with blood money, though the accounts slightly disagree as to whether he hanged himself on site or whether his guts burst out of his body after he arrived.
[56] Slavoj Zizek, *The Parallax View* (Cambridge: MIT University Press, 2009), p. 41.

trivial act with practical political significance is the one thing Big Brother cannot tolerate. Against all expectation, this means that establishing a strong eco-authoritarian state would not negate subjective freedom, as one might naively expect; on the contrary, it would be the single greatest act of subjective freedom which could be imagined in our current techno-dystopia.

It would be misleading to think that Linkola's proposals are simply his own inventions, as though he drafted his solutions during the kind of episode of irrational inspiration which inexplicably seizes the proverbial Kantian aesthetic genius (i.e., Mozart, Cervantes, Rembrandt) in the moment of creation of a classical work of art.[57] On the contrary, Linkola would likely consider himself to be little more than a faithful scribe writing at the dictation of the Mind of Nature itself, much like the Old Testament prophets who claimed to renounce their own creative agency in order to allow the voice of God to directly speak through their texts. In fact, one might even interpret Linkola's Green Police to be a naturalistic equivalent of what the Church Magisterium in the Vatican claims to be – an attempt to directly embody the Mind of Nature in a human institution in which the clerics suspend their own pathological wills in order to let the Mind of Nature itself speak in the public venue.

Although Linkola himself admittedly does not use the term "Mind of Nature" to refer to the set of truths which the Green Police would embody, it is notable that he explicitly warned that, if nothing else, suspending the Mind of Man would be a requirement to implement the set of necessary measures he detailed in his 1999 essay "Can We Survive? A Model for a Controlled Future":

> [The] programme [I have proposed is based on the assumption] that faith in humanity is the greatest of all follies. If man knew what was good for him, would history be full of wretchedness, war, murder, oppression, torment and misery? Would mankind have driven itself to the brink of total destruction by following millions of false beacons?

---

[57] Immanuel Kant, *Critique of Judgment* (Indianapolis: Hackett, 1987), p. 175.

In other words, it would be hopelessly naive to trust the Mind of Man to solve the very same crises it has itself created, since Man's track record for addressing much smaller crises in the past has been abysmal. If political leaders in history have often proved themselves to be incapable of overseeing a single kingdom without driving it into perfectly-preventable ruin, how could one trust the corrupt political hacks in office today with something as monumental as the fate of the Earth itself?

While Linkola has repeatedly noted that the outcome of unbridled humanistic desire is death, he has been careful to note that the Mind of Nature is not completely devoid of desire itself. In his essay "Aspects of Animal Protection" he noted that what Nature desires is simply that life should prevail, even at the cost of necessary though temporary sufferings on the part of its individual adherents:

> While nature and the whole animal kingdom are animated by an ardent desire to preserve life and freedom, nature is blind to temporary suffering [if it happens to serve these higher goals].[58]

This quote memorably demonstrates that, in addition to preserving life, the Mind of Nature desires to preserve, of all things, freedom. In contrast with the media caricature of an "ecofascist" obliteration of all human liberties under a totalitarian dictatorship by Nature, Linkola has instead noted the highly-nuanced paradox that we can only be truly free if we let Nature *make us free* first. Freedom, in other words, can only be achieved if we renounce our pathological desire for freedom and submit to the ecological constraints dictated by the Mind of Nature. In this sense, Linkola's stance is surprisingly close to Kaczynski's realization that freedom is not a humanistic escape from natural necessity, as Gadamer and other Linguistic Turn philosophers have claimed;[59] freedom, rather, can

---

[58] Pentti Linkola, "Aspects of Animal Protection," in *Can Life Prevail?* (Kindle Edition).
[59] Hans-Georg Gadamer, *Truth and Method* (New York: Continuum, 1989), p.

only exist if Nature exists, and Nature can only truly exist if it is allowed to remain outside the constraints of Modern Technology.[60] The only freedom fighters who are truly worthy of the name, in other words, are the eco-warriors who fight to preserve Nature.

The present volume shall provide the first ever English-language, book-length philosophical analysis of Pentti Linkola's ideas, especially from the 1990s onwards. While a similar book titled *The Early Philosophy of Pentti Linkola* is not to be ruled out in the long term, the present text shall focus more on his later thought than his earlier texts (although these shall also be addressed at some level) and shall emphasize, above all, his thus-far unacknowledged relation to classical philosophical thinkers such as Kant, Foucault, Husserl, Gadamer, Deleuze, Guattari, Zizek and Habermas, as well as his relation to more recent anti-technological thinkers like Ted Kaczynski, Varg Vikernes, John Michael Greer, Dmitry Orlov, Arne Naess, Michael Ruppert, and James Howard Kunstler and, of course, his obvious contrast with oversocialized leftists and liberals such as Shaun King, Ana Kasparian, Bernie Sanders, and Andrew Yang.

Drinking Away the Misery of Water Scarcity

The exact antithesis of the kind of knowledge Linkola suggested would be contained in the Mind of Nature is exemplified quite nicely by *The Doors You Mark Are Your Own*, an obscure 2015 Science Fiction novel which was supposedly authored by a fictitious Russian(?) figure named "Aleksandr Tuvin." One might describe the novel as an attempt to rewrite *Dune* while completely disregarding Ecology, an error comparable to trying to rewrite *Moby Dick* or *The Faerie Queene* without understanding Protestant Theology. Although even the one-sentence synopsis of the text emphasizes that it is set in a "a post-apocalyptic world where water is scarce," this properly ecological problem is only emphasized at a

---

445.
[60] Ted Kaczynski, "Progress Versus Wilderness," Ted Kaczynski Papers, Labadie Collection at the University of Michigan's Special Collections Library, Ann Arbor, p. 5.

few key points and is effectively invisible for the rest of the novel. It is almost as though ecological problems had the same ontological makeup as George Berkeley's empirical ideas – they only exist if there is a mind to view them and instantly vanish as soon as the subject withdraws its support.

In reality, the water shortage motif is largely just a front operation to sell a story about a pseudo-Marxist revolution which follows from an awakening where the characters realize they should move further to the left (a not so subtle infomercial to urge the readers of the novel to follow suit.) It is quite fitting, therefore, that this sort of misunderstanding of ecological crisis is rampant among the same liberal and far left political forces from which the novel apparently drew its inspiration. Liberal talking heads in the media similarly tend to think that ecological problems only exist as long as the teleprompter is displaying news of global warming and that one can stop thinking about them as soon as the discussion shifts to technological progress, strong economic growth, a universal middle class, bridging the "gender pay gap," increasing college enrolment, or opening the borders to even more illegal immigrants. All of these issues can only be espoused on the ecological assumption that more fossil fuel-based industrial activity will occur as well. Among most mainstream environmentalists, the left hand doesn't know what the right hand is doing, since promoting the same ecologically-devastating practices one has just denounced is a requirement to remain consistent with the laundry list of leftist doctrines which make little sense unless the future will be even more technologized and materially prosperous than the present. One could hardly think of a more flawed definition of Ecology.

This inconsistency is exemplified particularly memorably by the novel's opening as well, in a scene which attempts to drive home the point about water scarcity with about as much subtlety as a sledgehammer. In the scene, a medical student begs a barista to spare a cup of tea for him, despite the fact that the water shortage has become so extreme that she cannot do so without being given a very good reason. The student pleads his case to her like a dork trying to get past a bar bouncer at a posh night club by promising her that the extra efficiency the caffeine provides to his brain will help him to solve the water crisis once and for all. The water invested into that one cup of tea will therefore effectively transform itself into countless more, much like the self-multiplying talents in the Gospel of Matthew which evidence God's blessing on the good servant.[61] Although she is initially sceptical, the café worker eventually gives in and lets the student have the drink.

It is peculiar, however, that a world in which a single cup of tea cannot be dispensed unless one basically promises to "solve global thirst" as a result of receiving it is somehow absolutely awash (pun intended) with alcoholism. The novel's protagonist, for example, eventually drops out of medical school (so much for the barista's investment!) and then squanders his time living the dysfunctional lifestyle of a penniless alcoholic drinking away the misery of living through a water-scarce dystopia one cheap beer at a time. Nor is he alone in this endeavour, as he frequents local taverns to discuss "deep philosophical ideas" with his bar-hopping buddies who are somehow able to afford limitless amounts of alcohol despite being similarly impoverished.

It is outright *laughable* to imagine that the same dystopian world where one has to beg for an eight-ounce cup of tea can provide a seemingly-infinite amount of beer for basically nothing. Few people realize that the total water footprint to produce beer is enormous even by the standards of a society not currently suffering a water crisis. By some accounts, some 155 litres of water are required just to produce one litre of the stuff. Beer is quite literally the antithesis of the self-multiplying cup of tea presented in the novel's opening, since some 154 litres of water have to basically disappear down the rathole of wasted investment just to pass a single litre of finished product to a clueless, half-awake drunkard slouching on a barstool and rambling with slurred speech about how much it sucks to live in a world where water is rare (yet beer apparently flows freely for the taking). Even in the best of times, few things are quite as ecologically taxing, not to mention outright wasteful, as rampant alcoholism within a society. In fact, in Linkola's interview with the Finnish magazine *Quadrivium*, it was

---

[61] Matthew 25:14-30

asserted that in a perfect society "drugs and tobacco would be banned" and "the consumption of alcohol would be reserved for special occasions by tough pricing."[62] Ironically, *The Doors You Mark Are Your Own* opens by basically grabbing the reader by the shirt and screaming that these are *not* the best of times, especially in terms of water availability, but then proceeds to forget about that for much of the rest of the story.

There is an all too human explanation for this inconsistency in the narrative. In a Hermitix podcast appearance in 2019, John Michael Greer noted that in almost all cases, stories about the past or the future are really stories about the present time in a flashy costume from another era. For example, there is something all too "fifties" about Hollywood films about the Middle Ages produced in the 1950s; in this case, the medieval context is really a front operation to be able to think about the problems of that decade more clearly.

In some cases, writers have been driven to cloak their meditations on their own eras in disguises from another time by motivations no less pressing than avoiding capital punishment. Poets in the Roman Empire, for example, eventually learned it was much safer to write poetry about legendary heroes from extinct civilizations in the distant past than it was to speak openly about current events, since the risk of being put to death for accidentally blaspheming Classical Greek heroes like Achilles and Hercules was minimal in comparison with trying to jump through the hoops of producing acceptable discourse about the sitting emperor in Rome.[63] Similarly, the Book of Daniel used a story about the vastly-distant

---

[62] Pentti Linkola interview from *Quadrivium* #6 (2014): abridged version. Available at http://qvadrivivm.blogspot.com/2015/12/pentti-linkola-interview-from.html

[63] The context Lucan wrote in was one in which writing openly about political matters was considerably dangerous: Augustus himself banished the writers while his successors simply had them executed. Those who did write afterward chose to focus on safely distant and unrelated topics from the Greek tradition (such as Heracles) in order to avoid the risk of being charged with treason. J. B. Hainsworth, *The Idea of Epic*, (Berkeley: University of California Press, 1991), p. 123.

Babylonian Exile to really talk about the Seleucid Empire of that author's own time without fear of persecution, just as the Book of Revelation used nearly incomprehensible mystical imagery to demonize the all too earthly Roman Empire.

Likewise, it is understandable that a novel written in the United States in the mid-2010s would portray the poor drinking away their misery and gathering in shady bars to hang out because such things are accurate portrayals of how one would react to such a situation in the historical time and place in which the novel was written. It is supremely ironic, however, that the authors apparently failed to notice that such things are historical contingencies linked to a temporary situation of material abundance which is quickly fading away. Limitless alcohol availability for the poor is not at all a symptom of resource scarcity but is rather the ultimate sign of a society flooded with a temporary surplus of resources, ultimately driven by an enormous amount of fossil fuels. To write a novel which is explicitly supposed to be about resource scarcity while still employing all of the contingencies of fossil fuel abundance is the height of ecological misunderstanding.

One reviewer of the novel similarly questioned why there was no explanation for how the residents of this "nightmare scenario" deal with an issue as basic as plumbing. It is understandable that a novel which is really about a pseudo-Marxist revolution would consider little things like modern toilets to be insignificant enough to just ignore (or worse, to take for granted) but few things are quite as ecologically pressing as the enormous water footprint to flush away human waste on a universal basis (that is, with the exception of San Francisco, Portland, and Los Angeles, cities which demonstrate a troubling correlation between leftist political domination and mass open defecation.) One recent study found that some 1/3 of all water consumed by homes in the United Kingdom is dedicated simply to flushing toilets. Yet even this figure fails to capture the total cost of the endeavour, since people in the First World literally defecate into clean drinking water which was sanitized and processed at a treatment plant before arriving in the toilet in the first place. Worse still, this situation creates additional unnecessary sanitation problems in the process. Since we are the only species on Earth that intentionally mixes water with our waste, this interferes with ordinary decomposing processes and requires significant additional investment to keep under control.

It is not at all a stretch to say that the Mind of Nature would condemn using the flush toilet as an eco-crime in itself and would force its devout followers to revert to traditional humanure composting technologies, some of which are hardly more complicated than a plastic bucket and a pile of sawdust. In his 2009 classic *The Ecotechnic Future,* John Michael Greer similarly noted that human waste is actually a fairly valuable resource which would provide enormous benefit to farmers if its value were recognized and put to use; it is telling that the only technical problem we can recognize in dealing with this resource is to find the quickest and most convenient method to flush it all away. Nor is it harmful in any way, shape, or form if fully composted, since a properly-maintained "compost pile is a fiercely Darwinian place in which organisms bred in the sheltered setting of the human colon do not last long." [64] In fact, "[m]any studies have shown that faecal matter, after it has been competently composted, contains no more human pathogens than ordinary soil."[65]

Given that the only "argument" we offer against recycling it and putting it to better use in agricultural work can be summed up in the single emotive gesture of plugging one's nose, grimacing, and saying "Ewwwww!" like a four-year-old child, this example proves all too well that the Mind of Nature is simply hard-wired to have better judgment than we have. In any given ecological situation, the Mind of Nature can see the same situation much more clearly than the Mind of Man can. Where the imperfect Mind of Man only sees a disgusting pile of excrement which must be removed from sight (and smell) immediately, the Mind of Nature recognizes a vital resource which must be recycled back into the ecosystem if there is to be any hope of feeding even a modest human population after access to fossil fuels declines and we are no longer able to cheat our way to artificially large grain surpluses.

---

[64] John Michael Greer, *The Ecotechnic Future* (Gabriola Island: New Society Publishers, 2009), p. 113.
[65] Ibid.

At any rate, obsessing over the "water footprint" of a cup of tea while completely ignoring the gargantuan water costs of mass-produced vodka and universally-available flush toilets proves that the novel essentially *forgets* its own theme that water is scarce, except at a handful of moments when it wields the motif as a crude, oversized prop to advance the story by bludgeoning the reader over the head with images that scream out "By the way, this novel is kind of like *Dune*!" This is not at all to question the intentions of the novel's authors, as though they wilfully engineered these contradictions out of some malicious intention to break the Laws of Ecology while claiming to write a book founded on ecological concerns. This example proves that human finitude alone is more than sufficient to account for generating blatant ecological contradictions which will remain unnoticed unless the Mind of Nature seizes the authority to correct them. When one realizes that such an authority should be formally institutionalized into a coherent political structure in order to prevent mistakes far more consequential than writing a silly quasi-remake of *Dune*, one will have officially converted to Linkola's viewpoint.

Mirror, Mirror

One might compare this novel's failure to "see what the Mind of Nature can see" to the plot from a classic 1956 episode of *Alfred Hitchcock Presents*. "None Are So Blind" recounts the story of Seymour Johnston, a spoiled young man who refused to work because he had managed to convince himself (though, admittedly, no one else) that a far-fetched business idea he drafted up out of whole cloth would yield a large enough return on investment to excuse him from having to bother with working the sort of ordinary jobs which clearly should only be reserved for lesser mortals within the population who lack his (as yet unproven) "genius" as an entrepreneur.

Unlike most delusional daydreamers who perform the ultimate con job by tricking themselves into falling for their own get rich quick schemes, Seymour actually did possess the raw financial means to launch such a project in the real world, as he was technically the heir to a sizeable financial fortune which his father had amassed during his own lifetime before passing away. Seymour nonetheless found himself in the uniquely-frustrating position of being suspended between action and inaction due to the minor inconvenience that his father was savvy enough to realize that Seymour was too immature to be immediately entrusted with his share of the inheritance, a fortune far too valuable to be directly placed into his reckless hands before he had passed through some necessary life experiences of "growing up" to prove himself worthy of taking on the awesome responsibility of becoming steward of the estate.

  For this reason, his Aunt Muriel was tasked with acting as the sole human buffer between the fool and his (father's) money to prevent them from going separate ways as quickly as Thomas Tusser once warned they inevitably would under such circumstances. Seymour failed to recognize, however, that her Herculean efforts to prevent him from pulling the trigger on a loaded money gun which he had driven up against his own skull was the only thing preventing a figurative bullet from being lodged through his brain from a self-inflicted wound of stupidity. As he was too foolish to recognize his aunt's mediation as the blessing that it really was, he instead formulated the primary challenge of his life to be finding some way to hasten her death so that he could lay hold of the massive sum of unearned wealth as quickly as possible. Possessed by the demon of greed, he found himself willing to abandon the ethical call of conscience altogether by deciding to just cut to the chase and devise a wicked plan to kill the goose that kept the golden egg from evaporating into nothingness.

  Even from the opening scene of the episode, the audience immediately gets a strange sense that Seymour is out of touch with reality. Despite his obsessive attention to detail in the world of fantasy, he remained completely oblivious to what occurred right before his eyes if it happened to be something he would prefer not to see. His aunt, for example, eventually grew so frustrated with his incessant demands for her to release the money (a persistence to repeat despite failure which is itself a working definition of "insanity") that she lost her patience and blurted out that she was glad he lived in New York City and did not frequent her neighbourhood in Connecticut more often, since each time he did he managed to embarrass her along with himself. Seymour somehow found this analysis to be unbelievable, as he could not imagine that anyone would find his behaviour to be worthy of ridicule. His aunt struggled, however, to understand how he could *not* see that people constantly laughed at him wherever he went, but her efforts to awaken him to this pitiable state of affairs proved utterly useless. His only response was the same denial he exercised towards every other unpleasant aspect of his life: "What people? I don't see them, much less care what they think."

As though he were driven by a spontaneous desire to combine saying and showing into a single symbolic gesture by physically acting out the same selective attention to reality which he expressed linguistically in such phrases, Seymour then proceeded to shift to his favourite position of the room by posturing in front of a mirror. Despite her best judgment, his aunt tried to alert him to how his tendency to see only the fraction of reality which he found palatable extended even to his perception of himself. Predictably, her pleas fell on deaf ears. As though by instinct, he always managed to stand with a certain section of his profile blocked out from visibility:

> Seymour, do you realize that when you're in a room with another person, you not only get into a position where you can admire yourself in the mirror, but where the person you're with can only see what you call your best angle?

Even as he obsessively optimized his "best view of himself" in front of the mirror, strangely, his hand continued to rub over the section of his face which he had obscured from sight, a bizarre testament to the tendency for a troubling feature to continue to disrupt the flow of events in the real world even after being repressed symbolically. As though providing a director's commentary on his own subconscious hand-motions in real-time, he admitted, "The only way I can survive in this civilization is not to see anything unpleasant, just to pretend it doesn't exist."

If nothing else, this meeting did manage to finally convince him that any more attempts to beg her to release the money would be wasted breath. He concluded that he must instead find some way to kill her, much like the medieval heirs who had no trouble poisoning their own family in order to move up the queue to access the royal throne. As luck would have it, he even seemed to have the "perfect plan" drop down into his lap as though by divine decree from some perverse double of heaven. While casually dining in a crowded restaurant in the city, Seymour suddenly found a missing wallet left behind by some unfortunate stranger. Although it contained no money, Seymour found something which he himself proclaimed to be infinitely more valuable. A driver's license belonging to a gentleman named "Antonio Battani" gave Seymour the silver bullet to live out his most diabolical fantasies by providing him with a scapegoat to take the blame for his own crimes: "With this license anyone can become Antonio Battani. I shall create a fictitious person by [that] name who will do anything I tell him to do[, even including murder.]"

Just as Macbeth accidentally stumbled upon three witches who dictated his destiny to kill the king and seize the crown for himself, Seymour declared that "fate ha[d] placed [this] in [his] hands." In fact, fate (supposedly) gave him far more than just the identification card, as he proudly declared to his girlfriend Liza that he had instantly "been presented with a large, complex idea, complete down to the last detail" regarding the sequence of events to pull off the perfect crime. Following the logic that "it is only by an official identification that we really exist," he concluded that the physical presence of the driver's license would provide irrefutable evidence for the police to lay the blame for his aunt's murder solely upon the poor son of a gun who had lost his wallet that day. Once again, his tendency to prefer complicated symbolic abstractions over simple, inconvenient features of reality led him to think that he could fool the Big Other simply through forcing it to abide by its own legalistic games, even to the point of imprisoning an innocent man and strapping him to the electric chair to pay for the sins of another. As was usually the case, his impassioned speech failed to convince anyone except himself. For some reason, his girlfriend exploded in laughter when he revealed that he himself would take on the fraudulent identity of "Antonio Battani." Liza dismissed the entire plan as ridiculous, assuring him, "I can't think of anyone in the world who is safer than your aunt." Arguably, she had realized that a certain feature of his identity would inevitably remain unmistakable, no matter how elaborate the disguise he donned happened to be.

Contrary to his past tendency towards inaction, Seymour finally proved himself capable of getting off his ass to work, just this one time, as he obtained the proper wig, fake moustache, and distinctive clothing to recreate the mysterious figure on the identification card. He even rented a shabby apartment in New Jersey and spent some time each week living in it as "Mr. Battani" himself. Further, he went out of his way to act as rudely as possible while living "incognito" on site, driving his neighbours in New Jersey to unanimously despise this "Antonio Battani" as a uniquely monstrous being worthy of no sympathy. Of course, this was all a carefully-orchestrated farce, executed simply out of a hope that these passers-by would report these disagreeable details to the police when they later came to investigate the murder suspect.

When the time finally arrived to pull off the "perfect crime," Seymour prided himself on having left no stone unturned. He almost shed a tear recounting how clever it all was in retrospect: "There's something satisfying about finally drawing to the end of an extremely delicate and complicated operation." The only task that remained was to plant a ransom letter demanding ten thousand dollars from his aunt on threat of violence if she refused, and then sign it with Antonio Battani's name.

The only problem with his design was that when he paid his aunt one last visit to check whether she had received any suspicious mail and whether she was afraid of the threats contained in it, she somehow laughed off the question by outing him as the obvious mastermind behind the ruse. Seymour failed to see the humour in the situation and instead concluded that there was no time left to waste. He quickly committed the murder in cold blood and then immediately called the police on himself, as he had no shortage of confidence that they would be fooled by the letter that they would immediately invest all of their resources into trying to locate Battani simply on the basis of the "irrefutable evidence" of the forged signature on the note and the planted identification card in the apartment rented out in his name.

As it turned out, his aunt's community in small-town Connecticut was a bit more close-knit than the clueless city slicker had anticipated after years of living a life of urban anonymity in New York. The police officer charged with investigating his aunt's murder was, in fact, a close friend of hers and had a vested interest in bringing her killer to justice. After visiting the New Jersey apartment complex where the notorious "Antonio Battani" had resided, the detective quickly gathered as much information from the neighbours as was needed to make an arrest. In short time, he paid Seymour a visit to alert him that the case was quite close to being resolved. Seymour eagerly asked him whether he had gathered a description from Battani's disgruntled neighbours, hoping that they would simply recount that he was an angry and unapproachable ogre who was all too capable of committing the most horrendous of criminal acts at the drop of a hat. The detective responded that he had indeed received a description from them, one which would leave no room for doubt whatsoever regarding who the culprit was.

Seymour became vividly uncomfortable as the detective continued to stare at him after pronouncing these words. Particularly, the officer's eyes remained fixed on a certain section of Seymour's face which he otherwise preferred to keep out of the line of sight. When it finally became unbearable, Seymour blurted out, "Why are you staring at me?" The officer responded, "Because I can't believe it. I'm looking right at you and I can't believe it." It was all too certain that there was some gaping hole in Seymour's plan for a perfect murder, but it remained unclear what exactly it was that he had overlooked amidst his laser-focus attention to the most minute of details.

The detective continued, "Why is it that when you're talking to someone you always keep your right profile turned away." For arguably the first time in his life, Seymour found himself at a loss for words. He simply admitted, "I wasn't aware of it," as his fingers instinctively reached out to cover over the section of his face which he had spent so many years refusing to acknowledge existed. The officer refused to relent, "I remember once she told me that if anything annoyed you, you simply pretended that it wasn't there. So, you never really saw anything you didn't want to see." As he started to pull Seymour's hand from his face, he outed the criminal: "You disguised your whole self, except the part that you convinced yourself wasn't there. So, you never bothered to disguise something as conspicuous as that *birthmark of yours!*"

Seymour recoiled in horror as the grotesque stain of alterity manifested itself on his own face, like an excremental tic that was all the more foreign precisely because it was physically engrained into his own skin, the disavowed remainder which was both outside and inside the self while lacking a proper ontological designation to allow it to fit cleanly into either region. He had spent so much time constructing an elaborate symbolic edifice which required a constant subtraction of this excess out of the parameters of the equation that he failed to realize that he had left this one crucial Achilles heel exposed to enemy fire all along. Surely, the sole feature which everyone who met this dastardly "Antonio Battani" could agree on regarding his appearance was this ghastly birthmark which he alone seemed not to notice. Put briefly, he failed solely because he couldn't see the birthmark which everyone else could.

You Can't See the Birthmark

It is no exaggeration to say that *The Doors You Mark Are Your Own* is just one of countless examples of how a similarly elaborate plan to use ecological crisis as an excuse to pull off the "perfect leftist revolution" will still fail if it misses the glaring birthmark of ecological contradiction in the process. It is peculiar that a novel which contains some 700 pages of linear sprawl (arguably, a literary equivalent of suburban land management policies under Modern Technology) would be derailed by overlooking the minor birthmark of ecological absurdity. Inherent in the seemingly-bulletproof motif of a "penniless alcoholic drinking away the misery of living through water scarcity one cheap beer at a time while begging for an 8-

ounce cup of tea" lies the following birthmark: you can't produce one litre of beer without wasting some 154 litres of water in the process!

In other words, this motif is quite literally an impossible object forbidden on ecological grounds in much the same way that a five-sided rectangle is forbidden by the laws of Euclidian Geometry. The world in which this novel takes place is, quite simply, not the world you and I inhabit, as this fictitious world would have to be something like an ecological equivalent of a pseudo-geometrical grid in which one could somehow draw a square circle – an absurdity which Linkola correctly recognized could only be upheld through the abuses of language. Just as the Renaissance Spanish windmills which Don Quixote battled against are ecologically possible objects because they only require the energy inputs of wind and human and animal labour and generate negligible pollution over their entire lifetimes, the Sci-Fi future of limitless fossil fuel-burning machines which somehow never run out of fuel and never generate enough pollution to disrupt the ecosystem to the breaking point are the ecological equivalents of a two-sided triangle.

Of course, a novel which is clearly meant to be read as a work of fiction can hardly hold a candle to the ridiculousness of having the Democrat Party and its overseas equivalents waste countless pages printing legal literature promising a "green liberal utopia" (so much for saving a tree!) which is supposed to be taken far more seriously than a piece of Sci-Fi Entertainment. The "birthmarks" of ecological contradiction marring these "credible proposals for a green future" are far more horrific than anything which a self-contradictory image of an "Arrakeen alcoholic" could ever embody.

New York Times journalist Thomas Friedman's highly-overrated 2008 sensationalist tome *Hot, Flat, and Crowded* demonstrates this idiocy particularly well. Though praised by the media for its unprecedented "seriousness" towards environmental issues, even using its own title to combine concern for the Three Horsemen of climate change ("Earth as hot"), globalization ("Earth as flat"), and overpopulation ("Earth as crowded"), his solutions for these very real issues proved comically unviable. In a certain sense, Friedman is just the exact antithesis of Linkola, since the only solutions he proved willing to contemplate in this book were ones stained by a birthmark of ecological contradiction so glaringly obvious that one would have to be an entrenched media elite not to see it.

Above all, it is peculiar for Friedman to insist that the solution for these problems lies in "cutting edge technologies" which will allow the aristocracy of First World idlers to maintain their suburban comforts and elitist privileges while simultaneously saving the environment, despite the obvious fact these things are themselves the cause of our ongoing ecological crisis in the first place. The single stupidest proposal in a book filled with birthmarks of absurdity lay in his promise that someday soon corporate professionals could "save the Earth" by cutting down on the number of international flights they take by instead opting for using a promising new video calling technology which could allow them to hold crucial business meetings from their local offices or, perhaps, even from the comfort of their own suburban homes or uptown condos. In other words, Skype will save the world. What he failed to realize in his bid to "heroically cut carbon emissions" by taking one for the team by only using the modern luxury of video conferencing software on highly-sophisticated technological devices connected via the worldwide web was that commercial air travel is arguably the lesser of two evils compared to this sprawling network of artificially intelligent machines. Nor is it even a close race, as the internet has been called the single most energy-intensive infrastructure ever created by Man. Friedman completely missed the birthmark that the "eco-friendly option" will still generate more than enough carbon dioxide pollution on its own through data centres' gargantuan energy requirements to offset whatever little sacrifice some media elite "gave for the cause" by calling in to CNN from some Midwestern or Southern state via Skype rather than flying to the New York City headquarters to appear in person for a brief television segment which would be forgotten within minutes of being aired anyway. As radical as he may claim to be, Friedman somehow takes for granted that into the indefinite future, international corporate business trips will be a more or less universal obligation for "ordinary workers," despite the fact that such a thing (in its present form) was virtually unheard of just a few generations ago. The one thing he could *never* imagine is a future in which traditional peasants, fishermen, blacksmiths, and carpenters make up the population of workers once again, yet the only alternative to this modest though viable future is the far bleaker option of human extinction.

Friedman's failure to see the birthmark in his own proposals might be compared to the classic 1980s Hollywood film *They Live*, in which a blue-collar labourer migrates to Los Angeles in desperate search of employment after his factory in his home state in the Rust Belt shuts down. After securing a temporary job on a construction site, he discovers a mysterious pair of sunglasses which reveals a new side to reality that would remain inaccessible to the naked eye: the wearer of the glasses can see that some individuals within the population actually have monstrous, skeletal faces, though they remain indistinguishable from the rest of the population's when the sunglasses are removed. Under the surface of smiling everymen in business suits, a race of alien invaders silently infiltrates the ranks of the "respectable classes" in order to implement an agenda for universal human enslavement, even as the ignorant masses sleep through it all.

In addition, the glasses reveal that behind the façade of "advertisement" lies a set of sinister messages commanding the populace to "Stay Asleep!" and "Watch TV!" as the alien overlords quietly indoctrinate their sheep to accept an institutionalized passivity in order to ready them for the slaughter. Behind the façade of an infinitely variable flurry of songs, films, and TV shows pumped out by the entertainment industries lies a small set of redundant messages which all consist of so many demands to submit to the New World Order and to surrender any hope of subjective agency.

Bizarrely, this man finds that a fellow construction worker not only resists hearing about this shocking revelation on linguistic grounds – he also refuses to put on the sunglasses to see it for himself, even escalating the situation to a gruelling fight scene which drags on for minutes and embodies a level of raw violence which cannot help but strike the viewer as absurd. However, upon wearing the glasses himself, he instantly converts to join the mission and suspends his older prejudices, marching as a foot soldier in the war to save human freedom while the final moments on the clock remain.

Under this view, isn't Linkola simply the man who found the sunglasses and who can see the birthmark under the surface every time, even as the clueless masses and media intelligentsia remain naïve enough to take Friedman's proposal to "save the Earth one highly-energy-expensive Skype call at a time" seriously as a solution for the global crisis of ecological overshoot? Linkola's demand for the Green Police to push through the agenda to expose all of the diabolically-wicked eco-criminals hiding amongst the "good people" in the media, corporate, and academic aristocracies, regardless of popular opposition, is therefore simply a figurative restaging of the alley fight scene in *They Live*. In both cases, the masses will struggle vehemently against their own liberation only until the glasses are placed on their faces and the truth is plain to see. When the Will of Nature is finally allowed to speak in the public realm, these illusions will crumble as conclusively as the construction workers' flawed conceptions of reality did in the film.

The Clean Energy Hoax

The need for the sunglasses was attested equally memorably in late 2019, when Jane Fonda briefly made the headlines when she was arrested while attending a climate change protest in Washington, D.C. What was all too seldom mentioned, of course, was that she had flown in from her home state of California (basically, just to have an arrest photo-op) and had therefore participated in burning an enormous amount of fossil fuel energy in order to spend a few hours angrily demanding that the government find some way to overturn the use of those same fossil fuels. Fonda's long-distance flight was therefore basically an inverse image of the self-multiplying cup of tea featured at the beginning of *The Doors You Mark Are Your Own*: one can be granted the fuel to casually take another trip across the continent because of the promise that this one trip would surely succeed in finally bringing about the elimination of future trips of its own kind, something of a reverse-logic to the cup of tea which was given to the medical student on faith that he would solve world thirst as a result of getting a little extra caffeine to his brain.

    Nor was she alone in this endeavour, as so many celebrities and world leaders repeat the "airplane ride across the world to attend a climate change event" that it has become a humorous meme in its own right. We have quite literally reached the point where celebrities bask in their own self-righteous reflections before the mirror displaying a selectively-edited "best image" of themselves, while remaining completely oblivious to the laughter of the anonymous masses on the internet who can clearly see the glaring birthmark of ecological contradiction which they can't. In other words, the ending of Hitchcock's "None Are So Blind" has basically been universalized into a recurring online ritual.

    Although the media elites unanimously portrayed her "environmentalist suffering for the cause" as worthy of canonizing her in a secular equivalent of a medieval catholic catalogue of martyrs, she appears to have actually enjoyed the process so much that shortly afterwards, she proudly announced she was relocating to Washington, D.C. full time so she could repeat the same routine every week. During an interview with CNN's Christiane Amanpour, Fonda explained that she had decided to move to D.C. to get arrested every week largely because she felt like she had already done *everything else she possibly could* for the environment. Among the list of sacrifices for the cause she had already made, she did not include living in a hand-made cabin without electricity or running water, as Kaczynski and Linkola both had done; nor did she include hunting, gathering, or fishing with traditional methods, as both of these men had done; nor did she even include walking, bicycling, or rowing a traditional boat, as Linkola summarized his own means of travel in his essay "Half a Century of Water Fowl Surveys."[66] She cited, of all things, driving a hybrid car.

---

[66] Pentti Linkola, "Half a Century of Water Fowl Surveys," p. 57.

One could hardly imagine a more grotesque monstrosity than this machine; far from being the symbol of environmental virtue, its very existence is something of an eco-crime in itself. In fact, the birthmark of ecological contradiction inherent in marketing electric cars as somehow the "eco-friendly option" is so obvious that even an episode of *South Park* satirized it. When Kyle's father "took one for the team" by driving a hybrid car around the sprawl of South Park (an obvious surrogate for Denver's southern suburbs where the show's creators originated), he quickly found that he had increased his Environmental Virtue Index overnight so much that he had no choice but to go all the way and evolve to the next Pokémon level of "environmentally-enlightened liberals" by relocating to the San Francisco Bay Area full time.

Of course, anyone who actually lives in California will note that this place has basically turned being an ecologically-contradictory birthmark object into official state policy. This is the only state where they bully you into buying an electric car and then shut off the power for a whole week at a time when you actually need to charge it to get to work. It is peculiar that a state which has espoused the closest equivalent to "socialist resolutions of economic contradictions" has simply radicalized these contradictions even more, combining routine power outages with an extraordinarily high cost of living. San Francisco is quickly becoming the most expensive Third World slum on the planet, having paired up immorally high costs with horrifically dangerous and unsanitary conditions which could not even be dreamed up in a fantasy novel. It is patently absurd to imagine that a relatively-small condo there can be nominally valued at millions of dollars while lying directly on a filthy street strewn with more human faeces, used needles, and stagnant garbage than any African or Brazilian shantytown, places which at least have the decency to contain their raw sewage in an open trench in the road. If San Francisco has proven that the "more progressive option" is to ditch the gutter (pun intended) and just spread the filth all over the place, we might as well go all the way in admitting that the city has shown one of the classic signs of insanity, as it is literally smearing its own faeces on the walls while condemning the rest of the nation for being "backwards."

It is quite humorous to note that if one simply substituted "D.C." for the destination one was forced to move to after becoming environmentally enlightened from driving a hybrid car, one will quite literally find a piece of *South Park* satire replayed in the real world and paraded around as an example for the rest of the population to follow. The hybrid car, in other words, has basically taken on the same narratological role as the ring in Tolkien's universe: once Frodo acquired it, he could no longer remain in the Shire because he had suddenly been entrusted with an ethical duty to travel to the centre of the empire to destroy the powers of evil themselves. The irony which the "environmentally enlightened" fail to notice is that their own parodies of Frodo's quest to save (Middle) Earth would require them to *destroy* the same ring (or, in their case, hybrid car) which gave them this boost in virtue in the first place. One could hardly imagine that they can be counted on to react any better to such a test than Smeagol would when presented with the opportunity to throw the ring into the fire after having finally taken possession of it.

It is not at all funny, though, to claim that a hybrid car is "clean technology," for this is rather the height of ecological absurdity. An electric battery, one might be reminded, must still be charged with energy sources that are linked, however covertly, with fossil fuels, a process which simply sweeps the pollution under a rug in a massively hypocritical procedure which the news cameras have collectively been ordered to ignore.

The Clean Energy Hoax is arguably the ultimate example of the birthmark of ecological contradiction staining a seemingly-bulletproof plan. It is peculiar that even those on the far left who consider themselves to be "radical thinkers fighting for revolutionary change" will largely consider this "major disruption to the status quo" to consist in fighting to dump even more government funds into paying generous salaries to employ a bloated aristocracy of scientists, engineers, and administrative bureaucrats with the busy work of drafting up the "perfect crime" of finding some way to keep raping Nature indefinitely without ever having to face the consequences of doing so. Liberal elites' wet dream of a magical pollution-free machine which performs all the wonders of

Modern Technology while miraculously reversing global warming *and* growing the economy at the same time just happens to suffer from one minor defect: it could never exist.

To date, only a small handful of Orwellian thought criminals like Michael Ruppert have had the courage to note the minor inconvenience that even the most linearly-complicated clean energy projects are still marred by the birthmark of horrific pollution requirements. The following quotes from his 2009 classic *Confronting Collapse* are worth repeating in full:

> There is no method of generating energy from a source that does not produce some form of waste (pollution). Even wind and solar create waste as a result of the construction of wind turbines and solar cells.[67]

He went as far as to claim that the very term "clean energy" amounts to nothing more than a marketing campaign to raise capital for projects which are anything but that:

> The term clean coal is a marketing gimmick because the technology does not remove the poisons from either the mining or the combustion— only the exhaust gasses. It has never been implemented commercially. I repeat . . . never in the process of commercial power generation has any so-called clean coal plant produced 1 kWh of electricity.[68]

Similarly, in his fragmentary magnum opus *Anti-Tech Revolution: Why and How*, Ted Kaczynski noted that even if we could somehow implement "clean energy" infrastructure on a mass scale, the environmental consequences of doing so would quickly outpace any minor benefit they might provide. The second chapter of the text is, in fact, dedicated in its entirety to explaining why any trajectory which the industrial system follows will inevitably end in self-destruction. Among the particular examples he included to

---

[67] Ruppert, Michael C.. *Confronting Collapse*. Chelsea Green Publishing. Kindle Edition.
[68] Ibid.

explain why technological innovation is literally suicidal to the human race and the Earth itself, he included a detailed discussion of so-called "clean energy" technologies. He noted, for example, that any time one speaks about "wind turbines," one is actually employing euphemisms for the "birthmark" of radioactive waste:

> The rare earth neodymium . . . is needed in large quantities for the lightweight permanent magnets used in wind turbines. Unfortunately, most deposits of rare earths contain radioactive thorium, hence the mining of these metals generates radioactive waste.[69]

Nor is radioactive pollution the only drawback from the use of wind turbines. It is peculiar for many pacifist and animal rights hippies to espouse them when they quite literally bring about the violent deaths of countless wild animals. They might as well hold up signs bullying Congress to dump more government subsidies into "bird-mass murder machines":

> In addition, wind farms kill numerous birds which fly into the "propellers" of the turbines. Large numbers of wind-farms are planned in the U.S., China, and presumably other countries as well, and a likely result will be the extermination of many species of birds.[70]

Kaczynski went on to cite Shawn Smallwood, a renowned ecologist who warned that if wind turbines were implemented on a mass scale, they very well could bring about the total extinction of raptors.[71]

One easily-overlooked consequence of this would be an explosion in rodent numbers,[72] since one of the only ecological checks on rat populations is the raptors who are one of their few

---

[69] Ted Kaczynski, *Anti-Tech Revolution: Why and How* (Scottsdale: Fitch & Madison, 2016), p. 60.
[70] Ibid., p. 62.
[71] Ibid., pp. 62-3.
[72] Ibid., p. 63.

natural predators. One should bear in mind that rats are not only ugly to look at, as viral videos of screaming New York City subway riders who accidentally let one of them onto the train will show all too humorously. In addition, rodents act as major competitors for crops and would likely beat us at our own game if we were stupid enough to give them the ultimate advantage by killing off their predators once and for all. In 1959, bamboo flowerings in Assam, Northeast India led to an abrupt surplus of rats which quickly consumed much of the rice crop as quickly as though a supernatural plague had been summoned by Moses right out of the Book of Exodus. To this day, it continues to be known as the Flower of Famine for this reason. Yet a small surplus of bamboo flowers is child's play in comparison with the total extinction of raptors as a result of permanent technological changes which had ironically enough been pursued relentlessly by people who claimed to be *environmentalists*!

    Already in Tamil Nadu, Southern India, so much of the annual rice crop has tended to be consumed by rats that the society has traditionally tasked some low-caste men with the "job" of exterminating the rats by personally blowing smoke from simple fires through their tunnels, an activity which almost always brings about an early death from lung damage. Worse still, the job is so poorly paid that they often will simply take home the dead rats and eat them for dinner after a long day of working in the field. Although technological automation has called the future of many careers into question, the rat killer is one job which is certain to rapidly increase in demand as rodent populations inevitably grow like a cancerous tumour upon the Earth as a result of implementing the same "green solutions" which were supposed to bring about an ecological utopia. Any academic elites, Hollywood celebrities, liberal politicians, and social justice leftist college campus protesters who espouse wind turbines and the Clean Energy Hoax in general might as well volunteer themselves to take up this job as rat eaters to ensure that we all don't starve as a result of their failure to see the glaring birthmark of ecological contradiction in their seemingly perfect plans.

While he certainly does not disagree with Kaczynski and Ruppert regarding the impossibility of a "clean energy solution," Linkola slightly differs from both in that he recognizes the following inconvenient political problem: because blind spots of this kind are more or less inevitable for human subjects, the solution could never be trusted to result from allowing people to "communicate their way to a better future." Implementing Habermas's methods for "the perfect dialogue" will prove utterly pointless if both of the participants involved are equally likely to have missed the birthmark of ecological contradiction in the process, an activity as futile as allowing Hitchcock's Seymour Johnston to talk to himself about his own appearance while only viewing selectively-edited images of his face. Although it has become quite fashionable to appeal to the politically correct myth that all problems can be solved through providing the democratic institutional frameworks to free up linguistic subjects to exercise the "public use of reason" through communicative action, Linkola is one of the few thinkers with the courage to acknowledge that one must instead suspend the democratic procedure altogether and directly revert to the Mind of Nature as the ultimate authority in political action. One's only hope lies in deferring to the purified Will of Nature in order to execute its demands as faithfully as possible through a Green Police force which lacks any authority beyond its ability to overlap with the constraints of ecological law. Put briefly, the Mind of Nature must decide what is best for Man, for only the Mind of Nature can reliably be counted on to see the birthmark every time, let alone to choose to reject it.

  It bears mentioning that even if this Mind of Nature cannot be directly encountered as an empirical object within the world as such but must instead be presupposed ideally and reconstructed logically from a forensic analysis of the impersonal Laws of Ecology, this does not at all amount to a groundless superstition which would effectively gamble on entrusting the fate of the human race to the imaginary whims of some non-existent pagan god. On the contrary, the Mind of Nature embodies the ultimate standard of rationality.

Exercising the impersonal Will of Nature through the surrogate of a human institution is not at all comparable to, for example, the Medieval Catholic virtue of obeying the Church Magisterium exactly because one lacks any logical justification beyond raw submission to their authority in doing so. In Foucault's 1977 lecture series *Security, Territory, Population*, he examined extant medieval monastic literature which specifically emphasized that the monk's relation to his religious superior differed from the relation between an apprentice and master, in that the texts praised the monks for obeying demands precisely because the tasks they were summoned to perform lacked any lasting utilitarian value. Nor did they even contribute to building up the monk's personal skill set, with the hope of allowing him to someday "catch up" with the master, let alone reverse roles through surpassing him in the trade. These acts turned obedience into a purified end in itself, in that they forced the monk to embody absurdity as an ethical act as such. One could only prove that one had acted without some pathological motivation to, for example, improve oneself or produce a tangible good if one *could not* provide a rational explanation for one's own behaviour.[73]

Accusations that Linkola's plans lack rational rigour could not be further from the truth: Linkola is arguably the ultimate rationalist of our era, given that his work requires nothing short of the suspension of *all* humanistic prejudices. In his essay "Of The Evaluation Of The Book 'Into The Ecological Way Of Life [Ekologiseen Elämäntapaan]'" he responded to allegations from a figure named Vahtera who accused him of promoting "assertions which cannot withstand critical evaluation." While it is a perfectly legitimate question whether one finds Linkola's proposals unpalatable, accusations that he lacks intellectual rigour are completely unfounded, as Linkola noted himself in this essay that he only writes some one or two articles per year in order to ensure

---

[73] Michel Foucault, *Security, Territory, Population* (New York: Palgrave MacMillan, 2004), p. 176.

that each of them is "so thought out, thoroughly pondered and researched, that there is no possibility for error."[74]

In his *Quadrivium* interview, the journalists also remarked that Linkola had somehow managed to write with a beautiful poetic eloquence while speaking about issues that "are gravely real. Not realistic, not understandable, not 'basically agreeable', but real." Nor is his commitment to "real issues" a matter of happenstance, as he had consciously developed a theoretical orientation towards upholding the highest standard of empirical verification while formulating his many controversial theses:

> Linkola has boasted that his observational method is always empirical: what there is no evidence for does not exist. He has never been interested in lucks and likelihoods; he is not a gambler. This rationality gives off his modernity, his cultural background.[75]

In his 1998 "The Joy of Living Characterizes Life," for example, Linkola clarified that he opposes Darwin's conception of Nature "as the field of existence's battle" rather than as a thriving community in which life can simply take joy in its own existence. Yet his criticism of Darwin does not fall under the banner of stereotypical accusations that it should be rejected because it is excessively naturalistic or because it contradicts mystical principles of faith; on the contrary, he opposes Darwinist reductivism precisely because it "doesn't undergo observation [or] empirical research."[76] His orientation towards empirical verification is so powerful that he admitted in his 1998 "Nobility of Nature Books" that even when he reads a work of "realistic fiction" he has "a nasty habit of severely estimating the credibility of text [by asking] whether [its] facts tally."[77]

---

[74] Pentti Linkola, "Of The Evaluation Of The Book 'Into The Ecological Way Of Life [Ekologiseen Elämäntapaan],'" in *A Collection of Essays by Pentti Linkola 1993 – 2006*, p. 142.

[75] Ibid.

[76] Pentti Linkola, "Joy of Living Characterizes Life," in *A Collection of Essays by Pentti Linkola 1993 – 2006*, p. 53.

In his 1993 essay "Finland Equals Forest," Linkola provided something of a condensed "scientific method" for his own research: common sense alone is enough to dictate that a person should observe first and form judgments only afterwards. Despite their lip service to "scientific rationality," the System fails to adhere to this method because it asserts the same judgment that "more growth is needed" regardless of how abysmal the situation on the ground level becomes after they continue to execute this command *ad nauseum*. Armed with the epistemological weapons of observation and judgment, Linkola invites the reader of the essay to join him in going "through the statistics of the Department of Forest Research [to see if they are out of touch with ecological reality]."[78]

Likewise, far from reverting to blind mystical intuition, the Mind of Nature is the ultimate rational object, something of a superset in which every other rational object must be a subset in order to exist, since it merely condenses a purified system of ecological laws into a single monadic entity which can be freed from the limitations of finite human subjects. This is because it can subtract all of the pathological prejudices which would stand in the way of implementing these very same theoretical principles as ethical demands for action. Above all, the Mind of Nature differs from the Mind of Man in that it is solely oriented towards sniffing out invalid plans for the future, yet it can do so on the basis of one single criterion: the Mind of Nature can determine whether something is ecologically possible or whether it is ecologically impossible. Whereas Kaczynski employed a new Rationalist Metaphysics to demonstrate why certain objects are impossible because they are self-contradictory on logical grounds, Linkola can be understood to provide the same pathway through an Ecological Metaphysics. Linkola's ontology is roughly summed up by the principle "to be is to be ecological." Anything which fails the test of ecological viability is nothing more than a humanistic chimera, an

---

[77] Pentti Linkola, "Nobility of Nature Books," in *A Collection of Essays by Pentti Linkola 1993 – 2006*, p. 86.
[78] Pentti Linkola, "Finland Equals Forests," in *A Collection of Essays by Pentti Linkola 1993 – 2006*, p. 17.

empty label which only gestures towards nothingness and non-existence.

We will profit from briefly comparing Kaczynski's and Linkola's approaches to the same problems in greater detail. In Kaczynski's Rationalist Epistemology, for example, each of the first three chapters of his *Anti-Tech Revolution: Why and How* was largely dedicated to submitting hypothetical scenarios to the test of logical consistency in order to determine whether something which was widely posited as a credible plan for the future was actually a baseless chimera in disguise.

The first chapter demonstrated that any attempt to achieve the ideal of a self-predicting society which can steer itself into a consciously-desired future of its own choice is marred by the logical contradiction that such a society would have to have complete knowledge of itself in order to avoid the Butterfly Effect and satisfy the minimal criteria to make even one bulletproof prediction,[79] a requirement which could never be fulfilled for the same reason that Bertrand Russell's set of all sets could never be entirely disentangled from paradox.[80]

The second chapter investigated the a priori laws of self-propagating systems[81] to determine why no creature, whether human or alien, has ever refuted Fermi's Paradox,[82] despite the fact that intergalactic space travel would seem to be an inevitable result of allowing a civilization to continue with technological progress, no matter what planet they happened to inhabit. Kaczynski determined that because self-propagating systems are hard-wired to continue advancing even until they literally "advance their way into self-destruction,"[83] any civilization which might have eventually acquired the ability for intergalactic space travel would have long

---

[79] Ted Kaczynski, *Anti-Tech Revolution: Why and How* (Scottsdale: Fitch & Madison, 2016), pp. 13-4.
[80] Ibid., p. 16.
[81] Ibid., p. 43.
[82] Ibid., p. 55.
[83] See the myth of the forest clearers who destroy their own ecosystem in order to gain a temporary advantage over competing tribes. Ibid., p. 44.

since destroyed itself somewhere earlier along the same trajectory. Modern Technology is a ticking time bomb which can't *not* kill its host civilization at some point along the path. For this reason, the "technological civilization which has advanced far enough to travel across galaxies but has not yet advanced far enough to destroy itself" is an impossible object forbidden by the rationalized laws of self-propagating systems alone.

Finally, in the third chapter, Kaczynski noted that political movements are hard-wired to become corrupt after acquiring a certain amount of power.[84] Unfortunately, political movements are only capable of enacting meaningful change if they have also acquired a minimal amount of power. The political movement which is powerful enough to enact a meaningful change but not yet so powerful that corruption has become inevitable is a questionable object which at first glance would seem likely to be impossible altogether. Fortunately, he concludes that there does indeed exist a window of time during which a movement would be capable of bringing about even the most radical change of all time, the destruction of the technological system, while still lacking the corruption that would set in just a short time later. This gap between phases is, however, extremely small, so if the moment arrived one would never be able to play games with trying to bargain for saving the "good technologies" and only removing the "bad ones."[85] Much like an exotic element which can only be engineered to exist for a few nanoseconds in a laboratory before vanishing, the "political movement which can destroy the technological system" must seize the moment immediately before it disappears forever.

Kaczynski's former academic background in Pure Mathematics no doubt played a role in his interest in refuting impossible objects on rationalized grounds alone; in fact, in an unpublished letter written from prison to a young man on October 14, 1999, Kaczynski responded to a question regarding what he would major in if he could go to college all over again;

---

[84] Ibid., p. 90.
[85] In paragraph 121 of the Manifesto, Kaczynski notes that you can't separate the "good parts" and the "bad parts" of the technological system because all the parts are interconnected anyway.

interestingly, although he explicitly called formal education a "waste of time" in this letter, he still acknowledged that taking at least a few courses in Mathematics would be valuable for training a person in "clear thinking."[86]

Although Linkola has largely worked outside of the academic system, it is important to note that he did pursue botanical and zoological studies at a formal level within the university and is still considered one of Finland's most famous ornithologists. In his 2004 interview with Virpi Adammson, Linkola mentioned that at the young age of just 19 he had already edited a large book on birds and was expected by virtually everyone he knew to follow in his father's footsteps to become a great academic scientist.[87]

In his lengthy 2011 interview published in the final issue of the Finnish magazine *Quadrivium*, the magazine noted that "birds were[, in fact,] the topic of his first unpublished essays [as well]."[88] His decision to instead become a traditional fisherman continues to baffle the media and reading public. Adamsson arguably came closest to the right answer by asking whether this was an "ecological choice," or to phrase it more clearly, a choice guided by the Will of Nature.

At any rate, his theoretical background in ecology and related life sciences, while not a contradiction of Kaczynski's rationalistic approach of mathematical formalization, does provide him with a slightly different perspective for demonstrating the self-destructive nature of the industrial system. In fact, it has all too seldom been mentioned that Linkola's *Can Life Prevail?* and Kaczynski's *Anti-Tech Revolution: Why and How* are remarkably similar books, in the sense that both consist of a set of meditations

---

[86] Ted Kaczynski, Untitled and Unpublished Letter Dated October 14, 1999, Ted Kaczynski Papers, Labadie Collection at the University of Michigan's Special Collections.
[87] "Interview with Pentti Linkola 10-2-2004." Available at http://www.penttilinkola.com/pentti_linkola/ecofascism_writings/interview_10-2-2003
[88] Pentti Linkola interview from *Quadrivium* #6 (2014): abridged version. Available at http://qvadrivivm.blogspot.com/2015/12/pentti-linkola-interview-from.html

which submit hypothetical scenarios to a set of rationalized laws in order to determine whether one is speaking about some credible object or whether one is merely daydreaming about chimeras with less existence than the stuff of fairy tales.

In fact, Linkola explicitly praised Kaczynski in his notorious essay "Bull's Eye," citing the "Unabomber" as an honourable voice in the wilderness amidst a sea of vipers in the United States. In his shockingly-frank critique of the myth that the attack on the World Trade Centre on September 11, 2001 was uniquely evil among all acts of violence in the history of the world simply because its target was one of the holy sites of modern industrialism and a certain percentage of its victims were high-ranking priests and priestesses of the U.S. dollar, Linkola admitted that the ideas of *Industrial Society and Its Future* represented a promising underground movement of rebellion against the official narratives circulated by the media, academic industry, and political elites of the United States. While Linkola praised the Unabomber Manifesto for providing a courageous refutation of the insanity of unbridled technological and economic excesses which had otherwise hypnotized the masses into a suicidal march off the cliff of human extinction, he was careful to express his admiration for, above all, Kaczynski's willingness to provide a "planned and thoughtful model for an alternative society" which respected the highest standard of rationality without any need to rely on the irrational whims of human sentimentalism:

> Opposition within the United States is also strong. The case of the Unabomber springs to mind here: his planned, thoughtful model for an alternative society was presented to the Finnish public with a translation of his manifesto.[89]

Likewise, it would be incorrect to speak of the differences between Linkola's and Kaczynski's approaches as "disagreements" when each really just represents a unique perspective from which to view

---

[89] Pentti Linkola, "Bull's Eye," in *Can Life Prevail?* (Kindle Edition).

the same problems, often arriving at shockingly similar conclusions in the process.

In *Can Life Prevail?* Linkola shares Kaczynski's methodology of submitting hypothetical scenarios to the test of existential viability in order to determine whether one is pursuing something real or whether one is merely gazing into the abyss of non-existence. In his "Life Protection, Utopias, and Agriculture," for example, he explicitly warned that any talk of "utopias" under modern industrialism is "both fruitless and misleading" because this is merely a euphemism for the ecologically-impossible situation of "continuous economic growth":

> The words utopia and utopian [tend to be used to] describe reveries that are only dreamt of: things impossible, deceptive, unrealistic or which lead to ruin . . . [T]he most genuinely utopian [societies and economies] are those that have been adopted at present, as they are founded on the logical impossibility of continuous economic growth.[90]

In other words, virtually anyone who speaks about a "utopia" in modern contexts is actually just talking about an economy that never stops expanding, yet this is a purely hypothetical object which is just as impossible as a self-predicting social system or a technological society which can refute Fermi's Paradox. However, whereas Kaczynski focused on logical criteria to explain why impossible objects cannot exist, Linkola dismissed the myth of infinite economic growth as a fantasy for the simple ecological reason that such an object would require a nation to never run out of resources and never face the consequences of its own pollution and its careless decisions to disrupt the same natural cycles it depends upon for survival. Few things testify to the hubris of Modern Man quite as succinctly as the unshakeable faith that "human ingenuity" will be sufficient to overcome these ecological limitations which would be understood to affect any other animal but are somehow expected to make an exception for humans, as though a single finite

---

[90] Pentti Linkola, "Life Protection, Utopias, and Agriculture," in *Can Life Prevail?* (Kindle Edition).

cogito had become arrogant enough to challenge the Mind of Nature to a duel and believe sincerely that he or she could win.

In his 1994 essay "The Intolerable Misfortune of Technology," Linkola similarly dismissed the concept of universal automation as an ecologically-impossible scenario for the simple reason that if the process ever were fully completed, *we would all die*. Few seem to realize that the chain of possible human roles is a finite set and that the game of musical chairs is currently down to its final available slot. It is perhaps a cruel irony of Nature that our last remaining role is also our most trivial, and certainly the easiest to automate out of existence: the role of the mindless consumer:

> Through [all] these technical accomplishments and celebrated innovations, man has made himself useless. We have successfully been obliterating the roles of producer, transporter, distributor, and service man. When we also rid ourselves of the role of consumer, everything will be over except a clanking of robots for some time, then only deep silence.[91]

In his essay "Light Glimmers in the Population Explosion" he similarly refuted the myth that his own proposed reduction in birth rates would create a shortage of workers to meet vital needs, when already only about 10% of the Finnish population actually work in fields directly relevant to survival anyway. Even among the people whose jobs are praised by the System as being "absolutely crucial," most of them work in the frivolous "dream world" of entertainment, vain research projects, or, worse still, in the service of inflating speculative bubbles or in advancing the technological beast.[92] Yet even having a fraction as "large" as ten percent of the nation employed in critical areas is interpreted by the System as nothing more than a technical bug which must be eliminated through even more drastic leaps in automation. In the same essay, he speculated

---

[91] Pentti Linkola, "The Intolerable Misfortune of Technology," in *Can Life Prevail?* (Kindle Edition).
[92] Pentti Linkola, "Light Glimmers in the Population Explosion," in *A Collection of Essays by Pentti Linkola 1993 – 2006*, pp. 147-8.

that this figure will likely drop even lower to some 0.01 percent as the robots effectively gobble up the entire pool of meaningful jobs.

It is peculiar for technophiles to pretend that the final outcome of universal automation would *not* be an Earth filled with robots who will have successfully outcompeted humans in the most Darwinist sense of Natural Selection, since every leap in technological innovation simply drives more humans out of work and into a state of permanent destitution. Typically, it is claimed that this is all unproblematic because it has thus far only impacted "people whose jobs don't matter anyway," yet this is simply a reflection of the ridiculous class prejudices necessary for someone to claim that blue collar workers and skilled craftspeople "don't have real jobs" while insisting that a vastly-overpaid corporate office drone whose lazy ass never leaves a comfortable chair in an air conditioned office and who shamelessly exploits unpaid slaves even to fetch his or her coffee is the one who "really works."

It is quite humorous that modern industrialism has created an aristocracy of professional idlers who have been so thoroughly deprived of opportunities to work, even when they are "on the clock," that an entire industry has been dedicated to artificially supplementing this gap by providing gyms for them to put in a little extra time in the evening to get the same exercise they refused to do earlier that day when they were literally "at work." Few things are quite as humorous as the stereotypical image of a clueless suburbanite who drives the same distance to a fancy gym as he or she will end up walking there on an electronic treadmill, without realizing the idiocy of this exercise (pun intended).

Even more ridiculous was a proposal in early 2012 to simply cut to the chase and put the gym directly into the office by affixing work computers onto electronic treadmills in order to force corporate idlers to jog while typing. Though praised on the mainstream evening news shows as nothing short of "the wave of the future," nearly a decade later, the revolution is as far from getting off the ground as a Denver pothead's ass is from leaving a comfortable couch on which a bag of Cheetos and a funny television show are within easy reach. Above all, what the brilliant minds who designed this gimmick missed was that the entire point of becoming a corporate office drone was to avoid having to physically labor while "earning one's paycheck." Somehow, artificially inserting the medicine into the poison will not magically transform it into a super-medicine, but will rather yield an even more laughably grotesque monstrosity which only succeeds in provoking laughter from the audiences at home who could never imagine themselves being the dork behind the wheel of the bizarre snake oil which the media is trying so hard to sell to them with a straight face.

  Joking aside, in Linkola's essay eulogizing "The Finnish Body," he noted that automation has amounted to something of a death sentence in disguise, as he pronounced the grim diagnosis that "the Finnish body is [currently] degrading at a fast rate due to a lack of usage."[93] Linkola's decision to emphasize "The Finnish Body" rather than the "human body" in the essay's title arguably stemmed from his realization, corroborated in numerous other essays, that Finland had distinguished itself as one of the most automation-prone nations on the Earth. In fact, in his essay "Of The Evaluation Of The Book 'Into The Ecological Way Of Life [Ekologiseen Elämäntapaan]'" he claimed that Finland has, by a wide margin, the densest concentration of heavy-duty farming equipment in the world. At this time, Finnish agriculture had distinguished itself, therefore, as the single most highly-mechanized system in all of Europe. On the global scale, Finland had also risen to the (dishonorable) distinction of having the highest consumption and squandering of forest products in the world. The destruction of Finland's forests which Linkola had lamented in so many other essays and interviews was therefore not quite as mysterious as it might appear at first glance, since he mentioned in this piece that it is only natural that a nation which had willfully achieved such a high level of technological intermediation would simultaneously generate so much waste and environmental destruction. Yet this damage was not limited to wild habitats but extended even to the Finns themselves. In the same essay, he noted that Finland had also managed to outcompete the rest of the world to become the most

---

[93] Pentti Linkola, "The Finnish Body," in *Can Life Prevail?* (Kindle Edition).

automatized of all the world's countries, and by quite a large margin. Linkola therefore noted the paradoxical status of the Finnish body, in that excessive technological intermediation had rendered it both a "shockingly expensive" burden upon the Earth's resources and yet, at the same time, an endangered species fighting for its survival against the onslaught of artificially intelligent machines which circulated hungrily around the final remaining niches like sharks smelling blood in the water.[94]

It should hardly come as a surprise, though, that the body would basically break down due to neglect when the System is hard-wired to make people into "complete slaves to machines from a shockingly young age," as he said in his classic essay "The Finnish Body." In the same essay, he noted the tragedy that children these days don't even get to experience the joy of riding a bicycle outdoors as some combination of technological gadgets will reliably suck up all of their time like a bottom-feeding sea monster which can never be satisfied until one's entire life has passed away. Nor is it only in their leisure time that they are forced to sit indoors and stare at electronic screens. Even the school system has now normalized this monstrosity by making the use of it into a hard requirement in the classroom as well.

Nor do the children's parents even tend to recognize this tragedy for what it is, as one memorably-depressing newspaper story from the author's own locality in Southern India in 2018 mentioned that after one school removed the use of computers due to budget shortages, parents angrily demanded that the machines be brought back. It was supremely ironic that they claimed this lack of exposure to technology was a violation of their children's "basic human rights," as though computers held the same status as potable water or breathable air, when in reality, these machines are nothing more than artificial slow killers in disguise.

Linkola noted in "The Finnish Body" that even though the rest of the body's muscles are "as important as the brain," we are still letting them decline even as the educational system goes to

---

[94] Pentti Linkola, "Of The Evaluation Of The Book 'Into The Ecological Way Of Life [Ekologiseen Elämäntapaan],'" in *A Collection of Essays by Pentti Linkola 1993 – 2006*, pp. 143-4.

extreme lengths to provide the brain with unnecessary levels of artificial stimulation through giving it needless busy work while actively forbidding that the body do something as basic as *move*. He lamented that the "destruction of all physical work and exercise continues" unimpeded despite our better judgment, "paving the way for [nothing short of] eco-catastrophe" to occur as a result.

Although the spirit of learned helplessness has become so deeply-ingrained in our psyches as to make even the slightest resistance to this trend seem hopelessly out of touch with reality, Linkola is one of the few thinkers with the courage to ask whether these changes are truly "irreversible" or whether they represent only the most temporary of all fads.[95] It is even more useful in the current year of 2020 to keep in mind that less than just 20 years ago virtually *no one on Earth* had a smartphone with constant access to the internet, let alone a social media account which offered not even a moment's peace from the onslaught of notifications and trivial newsfeed updates. Our collective amnesia regarding this fact was memorably evidenced by the *Quadrivium* interviewers' amusement as they taught Linkola how to read text messages from a cell phone for the first time. The greatest shock to them was simply that "Linkola show[ed] no interest for the technique of receiving and inspecting messages," a testament to how trivial the activity which has consumed the entire world's daily life truly is.[96] Once this voyeuristic ritual was finished, the interviewers noted that Linkola instead reached for his "fishing nets and start[ed] to untangle them. His reason for doing this is that apparently his thinking always gets clearer when he's simultaneously doing physical work, a phenomenon some of us might recognise from more mundane processes like taking a shower or washing the dishes." It is perhaps only surprising that the mind's ability to think is reinforced by the body's engagement in some meaningful physical activity if one forgets that the mind can only function properly if the whole person is allowed to thrive naturally.

---

[95] Ibid.
[96] Pentti Linkola interview from *Quadrivium* #6 (2014): abridged version. Available at http://qvadrivivm.blogspot.com/2015/12/pentti-linkola-interview-from.html

Linkola warned that the outcome of this debate over the status of "The Finnish Body" is far from trivial, as what is at stake here is nothing short of the status of the human person itself. He warned that the time has come to definitively answer whether humans are ecological organisms who exist under Nature's laws or whether they are simply machines. Despite the fact that claims to a "transhumanist" evolution are currently fashionable among secularist rationalists who have not renounced their need for religious archetypes, any argument in favor of the latter viewpoint will only pave the way for the "replacement of muscle power with industrial" machinery to finish out its troubling historical trajectory. Reducing humans to robots ensures nothing except that they will be fully interchangeable with the same machines who put them out of work, and ultimately out of existence, forever.

On the contrary, Linkola has endorsed the most heroic efforts to fight against this madness in order to salvage both our ecological survival and our dignity. Among his detailed list of proposals for a better society in his essay "Can We Survive: A Model for a Controlled Future," he insisted that humans must reclaim their roles as agricultural laborers by literally killing the enemy machines, presumably, before they kill us:

> Farming will be organised in small units, while machines will be abolished and a major portion of the population will be made to practise light agricultural work.[97]

In his 2011 interview with Francisco Martinez and Larissa Vanamo, he affirmed that all of the technological inventions of the 20th Century should be "destroyed."[98] In other words, Linkola warned that a long-term peaceful coexistence between humans and machines is just another ecologically impossible situation. It really is the case that "This world ain't big enough for the two of us." If

---

[97] Pentti Linkola, "Can We Survive: A Model for a Controlled Future," in *Can Life Prevail?* (Kindle Edition).

[98] See Francisco Martinez Larissa Vanamo's 2011 interview "A Promenade with Pentti Linkola," http:// www.materialworldblog.com/ 2013/ 03/ invoking-the-apocalypse-a-promenade-with-pentti-linkola/

either of these agents hopes to continue existing, it will inevitably have to destroy the other. Uncomfortable as some might become by this inconvenient fact, it was echoed almost verbatim in the 135th paragraph of Kaczynski's Unabomber Manifesto, in which he used the allegory of the two neighbors to warn that the weaker neighbor must kill the strong neighbor if the chance ever presents itself, as the strong neighbor will certainly return the favor later on if given the opportunity:

> The only sensible alternative is for the weaker man to kill the strong man while he has the chance. In the same way if the industrial system is sick we must destroy it. If we compromise with it and let it recover from its sickness, it will eventually wipe out all of our freedom.[99]

Even regardless of the problem of classist bigotry, the aforementioned view that "automation is only a problem if it starts affecting people with good jobs" is unspeakably short-sighted, in that few things are quite as certain as a future in which the concept of a "human engineer," let alone a "human CEO," "human P.R. representative," or even a "human president" will seem as laughably oxymoronic as the idea of an "original copy," a "tragic comedy," an "exact estimate," or a "liquid gas." Few things are quite as inevitable as a future of self-engineering machines which will be perfectly confident in their own decision-making abilities to scoff at the thought of obeying any executive orders dictated by a mere flesh-and-blood mortal. These technological monstrosities will quickly find that even the most elite of their human masters are not sufficiently intelligent to be counted worthy of inclusion within the coming Kurzweilian cyber-utopia. Pushing the red button to rid the Earth of all of these lower vermin without exception would not even be inhibited by any impulses of human empathy, for that would be categorically impossible for a machine anyway.

For these reasons, in "The Intolerable Misfortune of Technology" Linkola noted the grand irony that "[f]aith in

---

[99] Ted Kaczynski, *Industrial Society and Its Future* (Scottsdale: Fitch & Madison, 2019), para. 135.

technology has absolutely nothing to do with reason."[100] It is simply an "insensible, uncritical, unquestioning religion," since anyone who thought about the matter logically would quickly realize that this runaway train could never drive itself anywhere except off the cliff of eco-catastrophe. It is supremely paradoxical that the worship of technological rationalization (in Ellul's sense of the term)[101] has provided the foundation for "the most anti-intellectual and religious culture [which] Western Civilization, or indeed the world, has ever known,"[102] insofar as exercising the freedom to think has progressively been criminalized as a thought-crime in the most literal sense of the term.

Linkola noted, however, that even the "religion" label is somewhat misleading, since there actually is an "interesting contrast" between the religion of technology and the traditional Christian church:

> The Church nowadays, whatever its faults, is gentle, understanding, and preserving. The religion of technology, on the other hand, is aggressive and destructive.[103]

However one might feel about Christianity, the values of charity for the poor, the renunciation of personal desires in order to uphold higher moral values, and the belief that humans are endowed with dignity regardless of their usefulness on economic grounds will quickly seem a little bit less worthy of demonization after the Earth is fully handed over to a Techno-Industrial System for which raw economic gain is the sole value sufficiently quantifiable and

---

[100] Pentti Linkola, "The Intolerable Misfortune of Technology," in *Can Life Prevail?* (Kindle Edition).
[101] Ellul defined Technique as the replacement of spontaneous actions with fully-rationalized and fixed forms in the early sections of his classic *The Technological Society*.
Jacques Ellul, *The Technological Society* (New York: Vintage Books, 1964), pp. 82-3.
[102] Pentti Linkola, "The Intolerable Misfortune of Technology," in *Can Life Prevail?* (Kindle Edition).
[103] Ibid.

utilitarian to pass as "real." Under this logic, humans' sole justification for existence will lie in their ability to keep the gears of the machine turning on a path which will surely end in the eventual destruction of all. In other words, if you think Jesus Christ is bad, just wait until a truly conscienceless robot is granted the authority to legislate the moral code for the entire world, a decision which likely won't find room for as modest a demand as your survival.

In fact, against secularist caricatures strictly opposing religious dogmatism and ecological awareness as incompatible forces, Linkola noted in his 1999 essay "Northern Winds Blow In Sääksmäki" that the contemporary Christian Church is actually far more compatible with Nature than any technological or industrial project is. In the essay, Linkola recounted a personal anecdote regarding a time he received a gift from nearby Sweden, consisting of an environmental manifesto drafted up by the churches in that nation. The document expressed a shockingly high level of moral consciousness regarding the Church's responsibility towards the environment, an attitude which is especially important for the Swedish churches to hold when one considers that parishes in that nation own even more forest land than those in Finland do. The document's "wish" to allow their responsibility over the whole of creation to dictate their actions is surprisingly reminiscent of Linkola's own calls for the Mind of Man to renounce its own pathological desires in favor of submission to the ecological demands of the Will of Nature, and proves that such a project can literally be elevated to the level of a religious obligation without contradiction. In the Church's manifesto, they expressed that these obligations included protecting natural diversity, minimizing chemical products, bearing responsibility for the consequences of one's own actions (rather than outsourcing them to others), and seeking out ecological methods of cultivation.[104]

Nor is Christianity the only religion which is far more compatible with the Will of Nature than the technological system ever could be. In his supremely controversial essay "Bull's Eye" he similarly warned that between the views of the jihadists who

---

[104] Pentti Linkola, "Northern Winds Blow In Sääksmäki," in *A Collection of Essays by Pentti Linkola 1993 – 2006*, p. 105.

(supposedly) carried out the September 11 attacks and the Religion of the Almighty Dollar Bill (for which the World Trade Centre was a holy site), the latter is unquestionably more dangerous and its adherents far more radically committed to carrying out unconscionable acts of violence in the name of their doctrine:

> What now remain are the Father, Son and Holy Ghost — or, rather, the Dollar, Economic Growth and Market Economy. Two Gods clashed against each other in New York: Allah and the Dollar. The servants of Allah sacrificed their own lives and the lives of a few disciples of The Dollar. The aim of the servants of market economy is to murder the whole of Creation and mankind as soon as they can. The deep ecologist and protector of life, the guardian of the continuity of life, would certainly choose Allah when things get tough.[105]

We have already seen this misanthropic "birthmark" on full display in the tendency for Silicon Valley corporations to shout the loudest about social justice and "solidarity with marginalized peoples" whenever they think this will bid up their corporate stock values, while actively driving one of the most horrific deprivations of basic human rights in the nation, as the so-called "Jungle" ranks as one of the largest, most dangerous, and most unsanitary homeless camps in the nation. This is a place in which people have allegedly been murdered at axe-point just because they were caught with some $50 in cash, barely enough money for some drug addict to get high one more time before jumping back on the endless hamster wheel of addiction which the state's "enlightened policies" regarding drug laws have actively enabled. It is peculiar to act as though "the problem" in the United States lies solely in some conveniently voiceless, sparsely-populated flyover state which such elites have never visited, even as the disavowed underclass in their own communities drops far below the minimal floor of human dignity amidst a circus of self-righteous hypocrisy, the likes of which one has virtually never witnessed before in history.

---

[105] Pentti Linkola, "Bull's Eye," in *Can Life Prevail?* (Kindle Edition).

Linkola has taken this aversion to the cult of Modern Technology seriously enough to bridge the seemingly impossible gap between theoretical contemplation and personal lifestyle practices. It is well-known that he had worked for decades as a traditional fisherman who refused to use a motorboat. He even chose to sell his fish from a horse-drawn cart and to live in a cabin near Lake Vanajavesi without running water and without electrical appliances.[106] In a lengthy interview first published in the final issue of the Finnish magazine *Quadrivium* in December 2014, Linkola's interviewers personally marvelled at the simplicity of Linkola's cabin when they arrived there to speak with him in person. Not only did they marvel that the cabin is only some forty square metres in size and consists of only three rooms, they also expressed shock that it contained an old fashioned stone oven, a typewriter, and a number of books but no television or computer. More surprising still was the observation that he had been eating from the same plastic plate for the past 30 years and washes it far less often than the average suburban germophobe might think necessary.[107]

When outdoors as well, his aversion to modern gimmicks remains firm. He noted in "The Intolerable Misfortune of Technology" that he opts for using a traditional wheel cart even when it requires a certain amount of inconvenience, such as for transporting heavy objects. In his essay "Northern Winds Blow In Sääksmäki" he emphasized that such an act should be far less shocking to the general public than it currently is, though we live in a time in which it has become regular practice even for so-called *professional laborers* to "drive a bellowing tractor" just to carry tiny loads of chipping to the rubbish heap, despite the fact these would easily fit into a wheelbarrow. This ongoing "act of sabotage" is therefore doubly tragic, since the workers deprive their bodies of

---

[106] "Interview with Pentti Linkola 10-2-2004." Available at http://www.penttilinkola.com/pentti_linkola/ecofascism_writings/interview_10-2-2003

[107] Pentti Linkola interview from *Quadrivium* #6 (2014): abridged version. Available at http://qvadrivivm.blogspot.com/2015/12/pentti-linkola-interview-from.html

exercise just as they dump unnecessary pollution into the environment.[108]

Likewise, Linkola's own decision to favor human labor and hand tools must not be read as some sort of "martyrdom for the cause" in which a life of misery is endured solely in order to "hunger strike" one's way to a major political change. On the contrary, one must not miss the deeper point that opting out of using Modern Technology simply results in a better quality of life and a higher level of personal satisfaction.

For this reason, he noted in "The Intolerable Misfortune of Technology" that most of the "seemingly rational arguments" to justify technology really just reiterate the same faulty claim that technology is good because it makes life easier. This is absolutely preposterous because ever since the invention of the stone axe we have been artificially engineering a set of far more "real problems" by actively creating more "physical meaninglessness, ruthlessness, and frustration" for ourselves, as each new round of "innovation" has simply left us with fewer and fewer meaningful things to do. Although Linkola does not explicitly adopt Kaczynski's terminology of the Power Process, there are notable similarities in their beliefs that meeting basic survival needs is not good enough if one is deprived of any opportunity to work for a goal in the process. In other words, instantly receiving the prize without having to expend any effort to obtain it will not guarantee universal happiness but, instead, depression and, eventually, insanity.[109] One of the most tragic ironies in history lay in the fact that having the System distribute instant access to food, water, and shelter to the entire population with not so much as the possibility of letting them work for these things themselves did not make us all happier than the peasants who had to toil for these same things. It only made us crazy.

Nor is each round of "innovation" even quite as reliable as the marketers claim it is when trying to push it onto the buying masses. It was almost too good a coincidence to be true that at the

---

[108] Pentti Linkola, "Northern Winds Blow In Sääksmäki," in *A Collection of Essays by Pentti Linkola 1993 – 2006*, pp. 104-5.
[109] Pentti Linkola, "The Finnish Body," in *Can Life Prevail?* (Kindle Edition).

start of his lengthy interview with *Quadrivium* magazine, the interviewers expressed annoyance that the recording equipment they had planned to use ended up failing right when they needed it. Lacking any other options, they had to fall back on using a "very secondary and recording-wise very lousy Matsui MP3 player," the quality of which was so poor that it supplied them "with very painful transcribing sessions" afterwards.[110] Yet despite this memorable confirmation that Linkola's criticisms of technology are all too well-founded, the interviewers still dismissed his "gibberish ranting about remote controllers, computers that break down all the time, digitelevisions that don't allow you to tape shows and all the unneeded gadgets advertised in Helsingin Sanomat" as unworthy of publication, assuring the reader that these comments can be passed over without a corresponding transcription: "we'll just wipe that out and move onto something more holistic." The cognitive dissonance required to maintain an ideological commitment to the goodness of technology even as it literally breaks down right in front of you is near the breaking point, certainly, but it still hovers within the realm of "as long as [I can get away with it, I'll keep using it.]"

Linkola noted in "The Intolerable Misfortune of Technology" that although this systematic elimination of opportunities to work had been progressing for some time, by the late 20th Century, man was effectively left with "no role" at all. This situation has arguably worsened considerably even since he wrote these words decades ago. Yet, somehow, it remains impossible to question this monstrosity even as its negative consequences outweigh any minor benefit it might have seemed to hold, almost all of which proved illusory anyway. He noted in the same text that when a group of candidates were asked how to solve the unemployment crisis, the only thing they could all agree on was that not a single one of them was allowed to cross the sacred boundary to utter the two blasphemous words "no machines. And yet there is no other solution, nor will there ever be."[111] A future in which

---

[110] Pentti Linkola interview from *Quadrivium* #6 (2014): abridged version. Available at http://qvadrivivm.blogspot.com/2015/12/pentti-linkola-interview-from.html
[111] Pentti Linkola, "The Interrogable Misfortune of Technology," in *Can Life*

human happiness and Modern Technology can coexist is an impossible situation for the simple ecological reason that the machines have stolen every meaningful opportunity to go through the Power Process.

In his essay "Humbug," Linkola similarly dismissed the goal of forcing the entire world's food supply to satisfy ridiculous regulations regarding temperature, timing, and chemical sanitation as impossible to implement in the long term because all of these things are merely euphemisms for an enormous amount of fossil fuel energy, technological gadgetry, and money.[112] Nor is this even a noble goal in itself, since implementing it even on a partial scale in the West has failed to bring about a better quality of life in the short term. Instead, it has only caused an enormous amount of edible food to be needlessly thrown into the garbage while damaging the environment, not to mention the immune systems of the general public as well.

There is, however, also an economic component to this tragically-miscalculated policy which is worthy of serious examination. Demanding traditional fisherman to satisfy modern hygiene standards is effectively asking them to do the impossible, since the only way to implement any of these "necessary regulations" is to force people to spend way too much money on new technologies which are simply out of reach to traditional fishermen no matter the era. Worse still, the actual purpose of these gimmicks proved to be hopelessly trivial, often amounting to so many different ways to increase the frequency of freezing, transporting, and heating operations, despite the fact that people did without all these things for millennia and lived to tell the tale.

Of course, the profit margin for a traditional fishing crew would hardly even scratch the surface of a Third World standard of living today, let alone provide the raw funds necessary to compete with mega-corporations who clearly invented these regulations out of whole cloth in a thinly-veiled attempt to pay the sanitation police to put their competition out of business for them. As a result, a sizeable number of people lost their livelihoods and were forced

---

Prevail? (Kindle Edition).
[112] Pentti Linkola, "Humbug," in *Can Life Prevail?* (Kindle Edition).

either into permanent unemployment or into the humiliating servitude of wage slavery to beg for crumbs to fall from the corporate banquet tables in a hall of debauchery paid for with blood money from both Mother Nature and one's fellow man.

Further, Linkola noted the irony that Finns were actually healthier at a time when one had never even heard the phrase "food hygiene." No fish was wasted in those days either, since virtually anything edible was considered good enough to an eye unclouded by the biases of modern corporate self-interests or the psychological pathology of biophobia. It is all the more tragic that all of the traditional shops which actually proved themselves to be just plain better at meeting people's needs while minimizing waste were needlessly "busted" by hygiene inspectors who shut them down to clear the path for a corporate monopoly that only made everyone more miserable.

In his 2016 classic *The Road to Ruin*, financial expert Jim Rickards noted that the United States legal code has become so bloated that the average citizen unwittingly commits some three felonies per day, despite his or her most sincere efforts to keep a clean balance sheet.[113] In much the same way, Linkola noted that because modern hygiene regulations are impossible to fulfil anyway, every person in the fishing industry basically has a fine waiting for him regardless of how sincerely he or she attempts to abide by the rules. In reality, this legalistic extravaganza has simply created a system of institutionalized bribery in which even the "big names" within the food industry will scoff at the prospect of actually satisfying every one of these ridiculous demands listed on the books and will simply pay the fine at the end of the day after failing their inspections. It is unavoidable that complicated legal systems become open marketplaces for corporate bribery to pass as the highest form of "modern justice."

It is supremely ironic that a technological system for which "democratic equality" is the official state ideology would directly generate so much needless suffering among the populist masses, not only through mass unemployment but even through artificially

---

[113] Jim Rickards, *The Road to Ruin: The Global Elites' Secret Plan for the Next Financial Crisis* (Hudson: Penguin, 2016).

raising food prices. Linkola notes in the essay "Humbug" that excessive reliance on regulations and technological gimmicks cannot result in anything except a drastic increase in the cost of food which has of course led a sizeable fraction of the population even in First World nations to suffer from chronic systematic hunger. The author of the present text can corroborate from personal experience that just three U.S. dollars is enough to buy enough locally-grown produce for a whole week from roadside vegetable stands in a rural village in Southern India but is hardly enough to buy two apples in the United States, let alone in even more shamefully overpriced places such as Norway or Hong Kong. By some estimates, nearly half of the food produced in the United States ends up in the trash, arguably because the hungering masses can't afford to buy it at the artificially-inflated price which the retailers demand.

Any reader who is sceptical about Linkola's dismissal of modern hygiene standards should bear in mind that this is one matter where he literally "puts his money where his mouth is," as he notes in the essay that he routinely eats jam and bread even after mould had set in. He also proudly declared that there is hardly a stream in Finland he won't drink from. Once again, in Linkola's *Quadrivium* interview, the interviewers visited his cabin in Finland and observed first-hand that he had been using the same plastic plate for thirty years for all meals and only washes it once a fortnight or whenever there is a sufficiently good reason to justify a cleaning, which apparently is not so often as the modern hygiene inspectors would imagine. [114]

Linkola emphasized himself in "Humbug" that any claim that he simply won a biological lottery by being born with a "cast-iron stomach" misses the irony that this is basically the same stomach which we were all born with! It was only the historically anomalous frenzy of over-sanitizing which leads people to fall so easily to food poisoning, as any Western tourist who has visited India and other "Third World" nations will find out from first-hand

---

[114] Pentti Linkola interview from *Quadrivium* #6 (2014): abridged version. Available at http://qvadrivivm.blogspot.com/2015/12/pentti-linkola-interview-from.html

experience.[115] The modern obsession for sheltered suburbanites to frantically fortify their McMansions against all germs whatsoever is laughably misguided, since the historical and biological norm has almost always been for children to be exposed to a variety of germs in order to build up their immunity for a lifetime. Linkola noted himself that children's tendency to lick surfaces actually does serve a vital function in their development and is only inhibited to their long-term detriment. If nothing else is certain, we can conclude that the ideal of bringing the entire world's food supply under the constraints of modern sanitation standards is, fortunately, an ecologically impossible situation which can never be fully realized due to the limits of fossil fuel availability but which will certainly continue to bring about needless suffering in the meantime.

Linkola similarly gained notoriety for his refusal to accept the logically fallacious though widely-held belief that anyone who is concerned about ecological overshoot must adopt a completely vegan diet or else be condemned as a hypocrite. He even found the refutation of this misconception to be important enough to merit a full essay of its own. In his 1999 "A Look at Vegetarianism" he concluded that universal veganism is just one more ecologically impossible situation among all the others (i.e., universal automation, a universal suburban middle class, universal sanitation, etc.).[116]

First of all, the claim that veganism is hard-wired into human nature is flatly contradicted by nothing short of human anatomy itself. He noted that from the point of view of health alone, human teeth are neither purely suited for herbivore purposes nor for purely carnivore purposes but are clearly meant to perform a combination of functions to suit an omnivore diet consisting of a wide variety of types of food. In addition, from the perspective of

---

[115] I remember getting very bad food poisoning after eating some old goat meat at a restaurant in India just a few weeks after arriving from the U.S. in September, 2018. I had suffered from frequent stomach aches in America for years before this point as a result of eating so much processed food but somehow, after getting full-blown Delhi Belly in India I have never been healthier since. There's a special place in Hell for the people who institutionally mandate poor immunity for the population in First World nations.
[116] Pentti Linkola, "A Look at Vegetarianism," in *Can Life Prevail?* (Kindle Edition).

the bowels, humans' anatomical status as omnivores is equally clear to anyone willing to see what the Mind of Nature can see.

There is, however, also a political problem with insisting that every single person on the Earth adopt the kind of vegan diets currently fashionable among woke college campus protesters in Boulder, CO or Berkeley, CA. He noted that anyone who actually has to perform strenuous physical labor on a daily basis simply cannot live on grass and salad. Few things prove vegan diets' impossibility of sustaining a population of peasants, blacksmiths, construction workers, and traditional fisherman quite as conclusively as the fact that such a diet has proven unfit even for toddlers. In 2019, the parents of a 20-month-old child in Australia were arrested after forcing their daughter to survive on a meagre diet of oatmeal, apples, tofu, and a handful of other politically correct items which ensured that "no animals were harmed in the making of this meal." One news source reported that "the child became so malnourished [as a result that] her bones fractured and her teeth fell out."[117] When I first moved to India myself, I tried living on a fully vegan diet for the first few months but soon found that even the most trivial physical tasks were utterly exhausting. It was only after I swallowed my Western biases and began eating the daily fish which make up the traditional diet in Kerala that I found the strength to perform hard labor outdoors even during the hottest and most humid months of the year.

Linkola noted in the same essay that it is all the more laughable to claim that the entire global population could be adequately fed on a 100% vegan diet when one considers that this would be forbidden on geological grounds alone. Much of the land surface of the Earth can only grow cattle fodder and is simply unfit for intensive vegetable gardening, a fact reflected to the present day in the tendency for traditional cuisines deep in Central Asia to feature heavy doses of goat, sheep, and cow meat due to the unique ecological conditions of the region. In his lengthy interview published in the final issue of the Finnish magazine *Quadrivium* in December 2014, Linkola himself noted, "there is the question of

---

[117] Andy Gregory, "Vegan Parents Sentenced for Allowing Toddler to Become so Malnourished her Bones Fractured," *Independent*, 22-08-2019.

where one lives. If you live in Finland, grain does not grow to the north of Jyväskylä. Or if it does, the crops are small. If you live in Lapland, the only options are fish and meat."[118]

Yet even if one attempted to convert all farming land whatsoever into permaculture garden spaces, one would quickly find that even plant cultivation requires inputs from animal manure to be viable on a large scale. Finally, behind the myth that vegan salads hold an intrinsically lower carbon footprint lies the rarely-acknowledged fact that much of the vegetarian diet is actually imported into cold nations such as Finland from far away. James Howard Kunstler mentioned in *Too Much Magic* that in his own Upstate New York, most apples in the grocery store originated in Chile, despite the fact that the local area was traditionally known as an apple-growing region!

Linkola noted, though, that the argument that any animal whatsoever which ends up being eaten by a human must by definition be the victim of horrific abuse also falls apart when one considers that although it is true that a factory hog will spend its entire lifetime covered in filth and will suffer mightily in the execution procedure as well,[119] a deer which is ethically hunted in the forest experiences virtually no pain at all and gets to spend an entire lifetime living freely in the wild. He emphasized that even the treatment of domesticated animals which are raised ethically at home is a far cry from industrial meat farming practices. He noted in "A Look at Vegetarianism" that cows raised on a small farm in Finland are more like family members than an exploitable industrial resource.[120] An additional irony lies in the fact that most vegan

---

[118] Pentti Linkola interview from *Quadrivium* #6 (2014): abridged version. Available at http://qvadrivivm.blogspot.com/2015/12/pentti-linkola-interview-from.html

[119] "For pigs, the situation isn't drastically different. Research done by the European Comission's Scientific Veterinary Committee has shown pigs in crates suffering from e.g. weakened bones, higher risks of leg injuries, cardiovascular problems, urinary infections and a loss of muscle mass that affects their ability to lie down."
Pentti Linkola interview from *Quadrivium* #6 (2014): abridged version. Available at http://qvadrivivm.blogspot.com/2015/12/pentti-linkola-interview-from.html

[120] Pentti Linkola, "A Look at Vegetarianism," in *Can Life Prevail?* (Kindle Edition).

"animal lovers" object to hunting wild animals on grounds that this is a dangerous intervention into Nature, while depriving their own house pets of the opportunity to live natural lives by subjecting them to conditions which flatly contradict their evolutionary conditioning.[121]

In "Joyful Chickens and Sad," he mentioned that similar contradictions underlie any attempt to grasp the situation with the Mind of Man rather than the Mind of Nature. Even as the practices of traditional farming and fishing fall under ever more frivolous legal scrutiny, the System not only tolerates true animal abuses in factory farming but even directly participates in advancing these practices by dedicating academic departments to mastering this exploitation on a purely technical level:

> It is quite striking that society not only allows animal rights to be completely ignored in factory farming and the fur business, but also supports the kind of unscrupulous research and experiments that sustains these activities, even at an academic level. In Kuopio we have a faculty of "applied zoology" where biotechnology, gene transfer and the kind of horrors futurologists dream of are being developed in the attempt to master and forge all life.[122]

Nor can one even blame the problem of global overpopulation on the consumption of meat alone, let alone on traditional fishing or responsible hunting practices. He noted in "A Look at Vegetarianism" that claims that the consumption of fish and wild game are uniquely responsible for the catastrophe of global overpopulation are also laughably disproven by the simple fact that it was historically unprecedented *grain surpluses* driven by fossil fuel use in the agricultural industry which drove the population bubble to the breaking point.[123] In fact, he noted in "Can We Survive: A Model for a Controlled Future" that a drastic reduction in grain production would be mandated by the Mind of Nature

---

[121] Ibid.
[122] Pentti Linkola, "Joyful Chickens and Sad," in *Can Life Prevail?* (Kindle Edition).
[123] Ibid.

itself.[124] The fact that we are currently growing and consuming way too much grain becomes even more apparent when one considers that a huge portion of the corn produced in the United States is wasted just to provide empty calories for the fast food, soda pop, and processed food industries. Linkola noted that we could be both better nourished and have better long-term sustainability by just "[r]eforesting a significant portion of field acreage" currently dedicated to mass-producing cereal grains and by reverting to consuming certain kinds of so-called "junk fish" which have traditionally provided sustainable and healthy sources of protein but have gone out of favour in recent times simply due to "fashion whims" and "popular prejudice."

Nor are junk fish the only food source which is neglected due to humanistic bias despite its ecological viability and nutritional value. Linkola similarly proposed that hunting certain rodents will prove sustainable even into the more or less indefinite future. Anyone who insists that this is "too much to demand" simply on grounds that rodents are "disgusting" should bear in mind that factory-"farmed" chickens rarely live longer than 42 days and spend their entire short, miserable lives covered in each other's faeces and unable to move even a few inches away from where they are trapped among countless other inmates of the most Luciferian animal prison ever devised. Anyone who has ethically raised chickens at home will know that Americans' fear that all chickens are contaminated with salmonella is actually a fairly recent historical anomaly which can be blamed virtually entirely on the horrific business practices of industrial chicken "farming." The author of the present text has personally verified that eating undercooked chickens raised on family farms in India has proven far safer than consuming anything available on the market in the United States, despite the irony that the FDA would likely bust the former as "unsanitary" while giving the green light for the worst animal abuses in history to continue unimpeded so long as some major corporation is behind the wheel of the operation.

---

[124] Pentti Linkola, "Can We Survive: A Model for a Controlled Future," in *Can Life Prevail?* (Kindle Edition).

Of course, any discussion of animal rights must acknowledge the elephant in the room that Linkola's own role as a fisherman would likely be seen as morally objectionable to those on the more extreme wings of the "animal rights" movement currently sweeping college campuses in the West, a movement, though, which all too often lacks any answers beyond the naive claim that the whole world can be saved one overpriced vegan salad at a time. Linkola personally addressed this issue in his 1999 essay "Aspects of Animal Protection" by answering the question whether his own role as both fisherman and deep ecologist is inherently hypocritical, as though one of these terms logically rules the other out.[125] Anyone who assumes that the only organisms on the Earth who "cause suffering" for fish are traditional fishermen must bear in mind that almost all fish will eventually end up being eaten not by humans but by wild predators anyway.

In fact, within the right context it does not even make sense to maintain a distinction between the two, since humans are themselves natural predators of fish as well. Recent anthropological evidence suggests that prehistoric humans tended to live very close to coastlines before the domestication of cattle, sheep, and goats, since it was only the historical anomaly of constant milk availability which allowed them to forgo the traditional protein sources which seafood had long provided before that time. In a 2004 interview with Virpi Adamsson, Linkola similarly mentioned the obvious fact that man is an "animal among animals" rather than a supernatural entity devoid of ecological context.[126] Hunting is therefore not at all a contradiction of our natural essence as predators but is rather a faithful adherence to what the Mind of Nature has permitted us to do. The grand irony, therefore, is that we can only faithfully restore human nature if we suspend humanism first.

In his 1993 essay "From Gunslingers to Environmental Disasters," Linkola clarified his stance toward hunting further by

---

[125] Pentti Linkola, "Aspects of Animal Protection," in *Can Life Prevail?* (Kindle Edition).
[126] "Interview with Pentti Linkola 10-2-2004." Available at http://www.penttilinkola.com/pentti_linkola/ecofascism_writings/interview_10-2-2003

recounting the little-known fact that when he was a "very young and fanatical conservationist," he largely viewed hunters (especially duck hunters) as the enemy, even going as far as to call them "the greatest danger" against his efforts to prop up dwindling animal populations.[127] Over time, however, he admitted that his relationship with hunters got much healthier, as both conservationists and hunters came to realize that their true enemy was not each other but rather the industrial system itself. It would do little good to debate over whether a wild bird could be ethically shot if it had already been killed by pollution from toxic chemicals or through having its habitat urbanized.[128] The true danger to birds is not an occasional bullet from a licensed hunter which only arrives at the end of an ordinary, natural life lived out in the wild; the true danger is the industrial destruction of the very possibility that such a life could be lived in the first place.

In "Aspects of Animal Protection," Linkola noted that it is intellectually dishonest at any rate to compare traditional fishing with the act of killing animals to extract furs or other unnecessary fashion items. Whereas fish provide vital sustenance for human survival, mink furs are a "useless luxury" which only serves the vanity of wealthy customers. In his lengthy *Quadrivium* interview, he noted:

> There is a great difference between fur animals and nutrition animals like chickens that lay eggs and provide flesh to be eaten. With a population of humans this big, those are indispensable nutrition while fur animals are of no use in that sense. I do follow the boycotting in that I do not order the meat of broilers anywhere, practically.[129]

---

[127] Pentti Linkola, "From Gunslingers to Environmental Disasters," in *A Collection of Essays by Pentti Linkola 1993 – 2006*, p. 37.
[128] Ibid., p. 38.
[129] Pentti Linkola interview from *Quadrivium* #6 (2014): abridged version. Available at http://qvadrivivm.blogspot.com/2015/12/pentti-linkola-interview-from.html

Be that as it may, he was careful to note in "Aspects of Animal Protection," that any fanatics who oppose all hunting whatsoever fail to realize that, on purely ecological grounds, some half of the humans on the Earth would be deprived of protein if such a ban were actually mandated on a global scale. In the absence of a modern industrial economy, there quite simply is no meat in Finland without hunting. Ted Kaczynski mentioned that in his own experience living in the wild, hunting was not a casual pastime but was carried out with life or death seriousness, since he realized that failure at it meant having to pass an entire winter without vital protein sources. The 4th section of "An Interview with Ted" is worth quoting in full:

> Another thing I learned [while living in the wild] was the importance of having purposeful work to do. I mean really purposeful work—life-and-death stuff. I didn't truly realize what life in the woods was all about until my economic situation was such that I had to hunt, gather plants, and cultivate a garden in order to eat. During part of my time in Lincoln, especially 1975 through 1978, if I didn't have success in hunting, then I didn't get any meat to eat. I didn't get any vegetables unless I gathered or grew them myself. There is nothing more satisfying than the fulfillment and self-confidence that this kind of self-reliance brings. In connection with this, one loses most of one's fear of death.[130]

Likewise, it would be preposterous to claim that hunting and fishing are intrinsically unethical acts, let alone eco-crimes forbidden by Nature itself. Anyone who argued that the Mind of Nature was categorically opposed to all hunting and fishing whatsoever would be hard-pressed to explain how the same wolves, tigers, lions, and bears they claim to be dedicated to preserving will survive if they are deprived of their sole source of sustenance by being forced to live on a diet of granola, avocado, and tofu fashionable among Berkeley hippies. In fact, the grand irony about

---

[130] Ted Kaczynski, "An Interview with Ted," in *Technological Slavery* (Port Townsend: Feral House, 2010), 405-6.

this fantasy is that if hunting and fishing were entirely removed from Nature, this would simply ensure that the ecosystem as a whole would be destroyed as a result. Ted Kaczynski noted in a letter written from prison to a figure named M. K. that attempts to preserve Nature without violence are inherently self-contradictory, since few things are quite as natural as violence. In fact, if one did somehow manage to eliminate violence from Nature this would merely provide the ecological conditions for prey species to explode in number and devour their habitats out of existence:

> [V]iolence is . . . a necessary part of nature. If predators did not kill members of prey species, then the prey species would multiply to the point where they would destroy their environment by consuming everything edible.[131]

Linkola similarly noted in "Can We Survive: A Model for a Controlled Future" that it is not only non-human animals who have a legitimate right to kill and eat prey species in the wild. Even humans can hunt and fish without devastating the food chain, provided they simply respect the ecological demands of the Mind of Nature while doing so:

> With detailed research, care will be taken to keep food chains intact and functional through both hunting and fishing: both activities will take account of the natural growth rate of species.[132]

In his 1993 "Ethics of Environmentalism" he recalled that during his youth, there was an oral tradition among fishermen consisting of a legend that at the beginning of time, the Creator had deposited a certain amount of game and fish on the Earth which was gradually being diminished by predators sneaking in to claim a share of this finite reserve of food. This legend fuelled a spirit of bitter

---

[131] Ted Kaczynski, "Letter to M. K.", in *Technological Slavery* (Port Townsend: Feral House, 2010), p. 377.
[132] Pentti Linkola, "Can We Survive: A Model for a Controlled Future," in *Can Life Prevail?* (Kindle Edition).

competition, not only among human hunters themselves but even against the wild predators which they saw as unlawful intruders upon their operations. He humorously recounted that whenever a fisherman found an empty trap in those days, he would immediately blame the gulls, ospreys, black-throated divers, and, often, other fishermen themselves, for stealing his catch.

As compelling as this urban myth might be on narratological grounds it was, however, completely unfounded scientifically. He mentioned in the same essay that ecologists eventually mapped out the natural laws to prove that, under ordinary circumstances, predators actually cannot permanently cull their prey populations without destroying themselves in the process.[133] In other words, the fantasy of a natural predator so efficient at hunting his prey that he eats the last bit of prey which God himself had placed on the Earth is something of an ecological equivalent of the old sceptic's paradox of a deity which becomes so powerful that he creates a boulder too large even for himself to lift – an absurdity which cannot ever actually come to fruition without violating a set of laws more primordial than itself. Prey are not a closed set of finite members deposited on the Earth in a single event at the beginning of time which must be preserved in the same state for all of eternity. They are, rather, an open set of constantly changing members, a living community of organisms which continually replenishes itself if allowed the ecological balance to do so. In this regard, Animal Rights extremists' attempts to spare every single organism on the face of the Earth from being killed basically just recycle the archaic legend of the "finite reserve of prey" all over again. Ironically enough, this activism will only succeed in defeating itself if it is ever implemented on a large scale, since disregarding any natural limits from predators will only ensure that the prey eat themselves out of existence by consuming the last edible plants in their habitats.

In fact, for the record, fishing is even more efficient than hunting in terms of allowing populations to naturally replenish themselves while still providing adequate nutrition for the human fishers. In this sense, Linkola's own occupation was in itself

---

[133] Pentti Linkola, "Ethics of Environmentalism," in *A Collection of Essays by Pentti Linkola 1993 – 2006*, p. 43.

something of a direct embodiment of the Mind of Nature's ethical demands for a sustainable human existence.

Finally, of course, one must acknowledge that the fantasy of a "universal democracy spanning the entire globe and billions of people" is nothing more than an ecologically impossible object forbidden by the Laws of Nature. Because this is arguably the single most important of all, a full discussion shall be deferred to the third chapter of the present text.

You Don't Know that You're Already Dead

While impossible objects are comical in the ideal realm of fiction or mathematical abstraction, they are outright deadly when converted into determinate goals to be pursued with real-world policies. Our current economic infrastructure is hard-wired to drive us off the cliff of self-destruction through chasing after ecologically impossible objects such as infinite exponential economic growth, infinitely-increasing debts with high interest rates issued to people who can't pay them back, universal automation, a global population of suburban idlers, and the transhumanist singularity. Although they seem unquestionably "real" due to mass propaganda and the pathological weakness of human finitude, any one of these terms is merely an empty linguistic label which refers to an object with as little likelihood of being brought into existence as a square circle or a five-sided triangle. Their existence would require nothing short of a suspension of the Laws of Ecology.

Tragically, although they can never be instantiated in reality, we are still able to embark on the doomed quest of sleepwalking in pursuit of them because there is a certain window of time between the decision to pursue an ecologically impossible scenario and the realization that it can never be completed, quite similar to the tendency for cartoon villains to walk off the edge of a cliff and only come to realize they have left solid ground after it is already too late. Although we can never actually realize the goals of "universal automation" or "infinitely-continuing exponential economic growth," these ideals can still function as hypothetical limits which we can approach without ever reaching, in a manner quite reminiscent of a geometrical asymptote which remains inaccessible no matter how minute the interval separating it off might appear to become.

This is one of many cases in which Linkola effectively reverses Kant's position. Kant emphasized that positive ethical ideals can never be reached by the pathological individual because no matter how much progress that person makes, he or she will always remain separated from the ideal of virtue because an abstraction can never be completely instantiated in the material world of empirical reality, especially by a human actor whose intentions will always be more or less contaminated by the pursuit of bodily pleasure.[134] Linkola, in stark contrast, emphasized that it is vice itself which represents the impossible abstraction which can never be fully reached in this life, insofar as evil is defined solely by its perversion of the Laws of Ecology. Whereas Kant argued that humans can never become perfectly good, Linkola assures us that an ecologically-contradictory situation can never succeed in becoming perfectly evil, for that would require nothing short of a complete breakdown of the Laws of Ecology. These laws will prove insurmountable even to the most diabolical of efforts by Man to overturn them in his suicidal march to "conquer Nature."

In his 2011 interview with Francisco Martinez and Larissa Vanamo, Linkola was asked whether an eco-dictatorship was really necessary if there could be any hope of just convincing people to change their lifestyles out of their own free will, presumably, through rationally explaining to them what consequences will follow from not doing so. Linkola responded that it would be preposterous to claim that we haven't already been trying to do just that for decades. There has been no shortage of intellectual "edification" regarding the current trajectory of environmental destruction; the only thing which has been lacking is any willingness to convert this theoretical comprehension into practical ethical execution. Linkola noted, in a total reversal of Kant's stance, that the reason for this inhibition is that a person will almost always react, even towards the most horrific prediction for the future, with

---

[134] Immanuel Kant, *Critique of Practical Reason* (Cambridge: Cambridge University Press, 1997), p. 30.

the same three words: "as long as." As long as First World yuppies *can* still travel to far-away nations for international vacations which consist of lying on a beach drinking beer and dozing off to a cheap thriller novel, they will. Even in their own countries, as long as the shopping malls remain open, they will still be abused for the most trivial purposes. As long as cars remain affordable, people will drive them. In other words, as long as the "absolute evil" of total catastrophe remains a little further off and maintains its status as an ideal limit which still has not actually intersected with the current state of dysfunction, the mad sleepwalk towards it will continue unchallenged, simply because "pure evil" has not yet been actualized within the world, any more than "pure good" could be within Kant's ethical universe. Linkola explicitly noted, however, that each day that this madness continues simply uses up more natural resources and dumps more pollution into the biosphere.[135] Fixating on the abstraction of "absolute evil" only distracts one from the little evils which pile up with each day in which funding for the incomplete project goes on leaking out into the real world.

For another example of this incomplete journey to embody evil within the world, one might consider how James Howard Kunstler's Cassandra-like warnings that the construction of American suburbs was the single greatest misinvestment of resources in human history continue to fall on deaf ears, as politicians favour policies to promote even more suburban sprawl and investors trip over one another in their attempts to reap profits from ever-laxer regulations over irresponsible land development.[136] The only problem with this unbridled enthusiasm for forcing the entire global population to "upgrade" to suburban living is the minor inconvenience that it would require the Laws of Ecology to be overturned, since it is already so wasteful and so costly that only a minority of humans actually get to do so even today. To date, the only "refutation" of Kunstler's warnings consists of claims that

---

[135] See Francisco Martinez Larissa Vanamo's 2011 interview "A Promenade with Pentti Linkola," http:// www.materialworldblog.com/ 2013/ 03/ invoking-the-apocalypse-a-promenade-with-pentti-linkola/

[136] James Howard Kunstler, *Too Much Magic: Wishful Thinking, Technology, and the Fate of the Nation* (New York: Grove Press, 2012).

suburban sprawl is simply the way which every "normal person" *should* live, despite the fact that absolutely no one on Earth lived this way until a few decades ago, not to mention the irony that even among those who currently do, no one actually enjoys the institutionalized boredom and alienation which follows from doing just that! This appeal to psychological normality is doubly humorous, since claiming that anyone who can recognize ecological absurdity is "mentally ill" merely serves as an excuse to continue pursuing policies of collective madness unchallenged.

Linkola himself was crystal-clear in "Can We Survive? A Model for a Controlled Future" that the Mind of Nature forbids long commutes and suburban sprawl as inherently unethical:

> Once methods of transport become limited, the population will have to disperse in order to live closer to raw materials and sources of sustenance [and will have to return to traditional methods of] farming, fishing and gathering.[137]

In fact, in the same essay he went as far as to channel the Mind of Nature's demand that the only just way to deal with suburbs is to physically purge them from the face of the Earth. Just as he argued that power plants cannot be left intact to serve as historical remnants of the current age of madness but must be demolished lest they be put back to use again at some point in the future, we can safely conclude that suburbs and power plants are quite literally to be treated as weapons of mass destruction, for which even the slightest risk of having them end up in the hands of a mad dictator is enough to disqualify them from existing. Put briefly, *the (buildings in the) suburbs must be destroyed immediately!*

> Most buildings in the suburbs will be demolished, along with construction sites, parking lots and streets, which will all be forested.[138]

---

[137] Pentti Linkola, "Can We Survive? A Model for a Controlled Future", in *Can Life Prevail?* (Kindle Edition).
[138] Ibid.

Unfortunately, every day that the mandated insanity of suburban sprawl continues to function adds cumulatively to the total bill of destruction which will come due quite shortly. In real world terms, these doomed projects still eat up gargantuan amounts of crucial resources during the window of time before it is recognized explicitly that the entire project was a tragic waste of effort because the goal was a mirage in the desert all along. We shall find ourselves in the same unfortunate position as the runaway slave who gobbled up mouthfuls of sand in the delusion that a banquet feast had magically appeared in the middle of the Arabian Desert near the end of the classic Malayalam novel *Goat Days*.[139] Any attempt to convert abstractions of this kind into a reality is simply a euphemism for the self-destruction both of the human race and of the Earth. Democracy is quite literally institutionalized collective ecological suicide.

It is important, though, to avoid Zizekian metaphors of a "gap of the Real" to describe the proverbial birthmark in these plans, whether we understand the Real to be the inaccessible gap which eludes symbolization or the distortion inherent to the symbolic which thwarts the attempt to access the missing Thing in the first place. Zizek's later, mature view on this paradox of the Real, an antinomy which can arguably be captured only through parallax, is synopsized memorably in his short 2012 book *The Year of Dreaming Dangerously* with the following quote:

> The Real is simultaneously the Thing to which direct access is not possible *and* the obstacle that prevents this direct access; the Thing that eludes our grasp *and* the distorting screen that makes us miss the Thing.[140]

---

[139] Although little known outside Southern India, *Goat Days* is a truly exceptional novel which provides an account of the true story of a Malayali's journey to Saudi Arabia as a migrant worker, including the many horrors of being trapped in an illegal goat herding job in the middle of the desert. As fate would have it, the path to escape proved even more dangerous.
Koyippally Benyamin, *Goat Days* (New Delhi: Penguin India, 2012).
[140] Slavoj Zizek, *The Year of Dreaming Dangerously* (London: Verso, 2012), p. 25.

Contrary to expectation, these motifs are precisely *not* how Linkola would describe the birthmark of ecological impossibility, insofar as these would lead one to describe the birthmark as an empty hole in a symbolic system which can only be described negatively or, worse still, praised for its dialectical dissolution of fixed structures.

Zizek concludes *The Year of Dreaming Dangerously*, in fact, by describing ecological crisis in exactly these terms, even seeming to invest hope into its potential to shake the foundations of the global capitalist order, insofar as an unprecedented environmental catastrophe would seem to provide the ultimate opportunity to submit the System to the terror of abstract negation. Under Zizek's Hegelian viewpoint, this dissolution of the status quo would not be entirely problematic, since one could place one's trust in the guarantee that it would unexpectedly birth some new post-capitalist order like a Phoenix from the ashes of the flames of determinate negation.

While this short book was almost entirely devoted to harshly critiquing global capitalism through meditations on the then-current debates over Occupy Wall Street, the Arab Spring, the London Riots, and the monetary crisis in Greece, Zizek finished the work by actively excusing himself and Marxists in general from the duty of providing a detailed image for what the post-capitalist future might look like. He argued that there is no need for him as an individual to pull back the game show curtain to reveal what the coming improvements might be, since the negation of the current order is sufficient in itself to dialectically birth some new way of doing things. It is not a problem, therefore, to work from a negative approach, for this is the only pathway to respect the "openness" of our future to radical change. If one opted out of focusing on negation, one would close off the current order into a solidified totality in which true change would be precluded forever:

> [W]e should return from Marx to Hegel, to Hegel's "tragic" vision of the social process where no hidden teleology is guiding us, to where every intervention is a jump into the unknown, where the result always thwarts our expectations. All we can be certain of is that the existing system cannot

reproduce itself indefinitely: whatever will come after will not be "our future."[141]

It is deeply troubling that Zizek cites none other than an "extraordinary environmental catastrophe" as one possible unexpected shift that will "swiftly change the basic coordinates of our predicament." Rather than resist this through careful planning, he warns that "[w]e should fully accept this openness, guiding ourselves on nothing more than ambiguous signs from the future."[142]

Under this view, it very well might seem that "ecological impossibility" is simply one more type of negation among all others, insofar as the birthmark would seem to actively "negate" the Earth through killing it with a set of far-fetched projects which burn a path of destruction through the natural world with each step of "progress" they make. Under this negation-centric view, one should not make an effort to stop the runaway train of, say, universal suburbanization before it blows up the Earth through forcibly punishing the eco-criminals who pursue it, since the potential for a new status quo resides precisely in allowing this procedure of abstract negation to run its course on the pathway to a higher Notional form. Linkola's calls for the Green Police to forcefully halt this madness by restoring the proper order embodied in the Mind of Nature would seem to be just one more naïve positivist Metaphysics among all the others.

This analysis of the situation proves itself to be unsatisfactory for the simple fact that the birthmark in our plans is not merely a negative gap of emptiness but is rather a precise form which just happens to contradict the laws of ecological validity. This is arguably similar to how the second black cat in Edgar Allen Poe's classic short story of the same name bore a white birthmark which initially appeared to be an indeterminate blob with no meaning but was eventually properly identified as a symbol for the gallows pole, a haunting reminder to its owner of the fact that he had hanged his first black cat in cold blood.[143]

---

[141] Ibid., pp. 134-5.
[142] Ibid., p 135.
[143] Edgar Allen Poe, "The Black Cat" (Kindle Edition).

Likewise, the problem with the birthmark is not that it is nothing whatsoever, but precisely that it is symbolically determinate while still containing only the message of death. By the time one finishes unscrambling the inscription as though it were one of the incomprehensible images which slowly materializes into a set of legible alphabetical letters through Robert Langdon's detective work as the "world's top symbologist" in one of Dan Brown's novels,[144] one will find that the only reward awaiting the reader at the other end of this scavenger's hunt is one's own death. It is no coincidence that Poe's narrator in "The Black Cat" recognized the symbol of the gallows in the cat's birthmark just in time for his own demise to arrive as well.

In other words, the negative judgment that something is *not* possible is not the same as the infinite judgment that something is *im*possible, as even Kant's 18th Century table of judgments clearly distinguished these as ultimately residing in distinct transcendental categories of thought.[145] Linkola implicitly goes beyond Kant, however, by suggesting that an ecologically impossible situation is comparable to a five-sided triangle, an object which is not simply negative without any further qualification because it still does include a set of instructions for how one *would* draw such a figure. The five-sided triangle is impossible for the very specific reason that any attempt to execute this set of instructions will fail because it would require a suspension of the more general Laws of Geometry to be carried out. The figure is forbidden not only through its own self-contradiction, but by its inability to overcome the limitations of the geometrical grid in which it would have to be instantiated.

We can therefore extrapolate that Linkola slightly differs from Spinoza, in that Spinoza argued that impossible objects were sufficiently refuted simply through their own self-contradiction: the "reason for the non-existence of a square circle is indicated in its nature . . . because it would involve a contradiction." [146] On the

---

[144] Dan Brown, *The Da Vinci Code* (London: Transworld Publishers, 2004).
[145] Immanuel Kant, *Critique of Pure Reason* (London: Penguin, 2007), p. 99.
[146] Baruch Spinoza, *Ethics* in *The Rationalists* (New York: Anchor Books, 1974), p. 179.

other hand, Spinoza claimed that it is only positive objects which would require an appeal to the more general Laws of Geometry and other rational fields, since the affirmation of a real object is a more logically-taxing operation than the negative refutation of a false one: the "reason for the existence of a triangle or a circle does not follow from the nature of these figures but from the order of universal nature in extension." Spinoza's revolution lay in overturning the traditional idea that Reason might be limited to refuting impossible objects on the basis of some logical self-contradiction, by showing that a rationalized grasp of universal nature in extension could hold the key to unlock the positive affirmation of possible objects as well.

For Linkola, however, the image of the "penniless alcoholic drinking away the misery of living through a water-scarce dystopia one cheap beer at a time while begging for a small cup of tea" is not only forbidden by its own self-contradiction but by the way that the entire *world* embedded within that novel is forbidden from existence through its contradiction of the system of ecological law itself.

Ecologically impossible situations are therefore not empty gaps of nonexistence but are more like bundles of viral code which reliably kill the host whenever they are integrated into some broader whole. From this perspective, suburban sprawl is quite literally a deadly virus that is killing the Earth through hijacking its infrastructure and inducing it to continue replicating the "algorithm of death" until it loses the ability to function altogether.

Arguably, Dostoyevsky was the first modern thinker to realize something close to this idea, as the true point of his massive novel *Demons* was that a flawed ideology is sufficiently powerful to possess a group of nihilistic Russian intellectuals as though they were a herd of swine from the Gospel of Luke[147] and then drive them off the cliff to their deaths, despite the fact that the ideology in question was specifically built around utopian plans to overturn the current corrupt social order and replace it with an ideal society which happened to suffer from the minor inconvenience that it

---

[147] Luke 8:32-6. This is also the passage which Dostoyevsky himself quoted at the opening of the novel *Demons*.

could never exist. In other words, before Dostoyevsky and Linkola, one might have assumed that something would have to satisfy the existential requirement of Being before it could accomplish a higher order action such as killing its host; after Dostoyevsky and Linkola, we realize that you are more likely to be destroyed by that which does not and cannot exist (interestingly, Francisco Martinez and Larissa Vanamo noted in their 2011 interview with Linkola that he does travel "into civilization" to attend academic seminars on Dostoyevsky who is, apparently, one of his favourite authors.)[148] For both Linkola and Dostoevsky, the impossible is that which is truly deadly.

Linkola's Mind of Nature is the ultimate "geometrical grid" of ecological validity, the condensed set of *a priori* conditions which must be satisfied in order for a hypothetical situation to pass the test of existential viability. Far from regressing from "communicative rationality" back to the primitive barbarism of pre-modern tyranny, Linkola's ethical code provides the theoretical foundation for the single most highly-rationalized political system in history.

It's not just a Crime – It's an Eco-*Crime!*

One might argue that the single biggest religious shock in recent history lay in having the Vatican appoint a pope who considered the most important theological issue of his era to consist in formally legislating the extent to which the Mind of Nature and the Mind of God overlap. Pope Francis's encyclical *Laudato Si* was an attempt to utilize the ultimate megaphone of religious authority in order to forcefully awaken the global Catholic population to accept the obvious fact that ecological crimes are in fact moral crimes as well. In other words, God cares about the Earth too.

Although his intention was to prove that sins against God and misdeeds against Nature are not separated by a dualistic gap but are rather formally identical to one another, all too many of the

---

[148]See Francisco Martinez Larissa Vanamo's 2011 interview "A Promenade with Pentti Linkola," http:// www.materialworldblog.com/ 2013/ 03/ invoking-the-apocalypse-a-promenade-with-pentti-linkola/

catholic laity have missed the point completely by effectively treating the papal decree as so much magic dust which the "vicar of Christ" is free to sprinkle at will on any actions he happens to fancy in order to abruptly transform them into "sins." It is all too understandable that this would seem to be the case, as such a view is more or less consistent with the Vatican's tendency to change its mind regarding the "official list of mortal sins" in the past. It is peculiar to think that someone who ate meat on Friday in past centuries could still be serving time in Hell for it today while someone who does so in our era gets a "Get Out of Hell Free" card for exactly the same activity. Under this view, the Vatican effectively "removed the dust" from these actions for no reason except that it felt like doing so.

From a Linkolan perspective, though, it is deeply troubling to realize that for the Mind of Man, blatant ecological contradictions cannot stand on their own but instead require a supplement of "papal authority" in order to be recognized as such. In other words, almost no one is able to recognize eco-crimes as problematic on the basis of their formal contradictions alone.

Nor is this shortcoming unique to the explicitly-religious framework of the Vatican, as even the secularist liberal media has effectively treated "hate" as a new codeword for "sin," a mysterious supplement which transforms an ordinary misdeed into a supernatural offense. One *South Park* episode, for example, asked why exactly it was that killing a man was a crime but killing a black man was a "hate crime." This double designation would seem to be entirely unnecessary and redundant, since any violent crime against another person is by definition already hateful. Controversial as it might be to state the obvious truth, designating something a "hate crime" is arguably just a code word to signal that its victim can claim the status of *not* being a "white heterosexual Christian male," since negating even one of these categories is sufficient to lay claim to some form of intersectional oppression. "Hate" is therefore a mysterious object which would seem to be completely empty of meaning in itself, insofar as it merely indicates some performative act on the part of the justice system to add a little extra weight to a crime simply on the basis of an arbitrary decision rooted in a political power which is far more contingent than any of the aristocracy today would like to admit. Hate is something of a higher order super-content which cannot stand on its own but must be combined with a lower-level object in the same way that a vampire can only be animated through sucking the blood of another creature.

It has been truly depressing to observe how even Pope Francis's official stamp of supernatural "sin" over the crimes of pollution, climate change, and resource depletion has not been sufficiently powerful to change many minds on the issue. All too often, the same people who angrily defended the Church hierarchy amidst its mishandling of its numerous child molestation scandals on grounds that its authority was "infallible" have suddenly begun to whisper amongst themselves the possibility that Francis might be the first illegitimate pope and that the banner of "papal infallibility" might not be applicable to him after all, simply because he believes ecological limitation is real. It is chilling to realize that many of these "devoutly religious" people quite literally found it easier to defend clerics' sexual abuse of innocent children than to accept even the most modest demand that they consider the ecological consequences of their own privileged lifestyles. It will be one of the great ironies of history if the straw that finally breaks the Catholic laity's faith in "papal infallibility" is just the "completely unreasonable demand" that clueless First World suburbanites slightly cut down on their economic consumption.

With these cases in mind, one might legitimately wonder whether the term "eco" holds the same status as "sin" or "hate," an empty super-content which holds no meaning beyond its role in reinforcing the authority of some bureaucracy that happened to dictate it. Under this view, there are no eco-crimes as such, only crimes which have been retroactively stamped with this prefix through an arbitrary decision by the Mind of Nature or the Green Police which lacks any justification beyond itself. This view is, of course, entirely mistaken for the simple reason that the birthmark is not a mysterious gap of negativity without any further qualification but is rather a precise form which is invalidated simply because it contradicts the broader laws of ecology. For this reason, Linkola is never satisfied to designate any violation of the Mind of Nature as an eco-crime without providing a bulletproof justification which is always founded on exposing the ecological impossibility of the situation in question.

In his essay "Humbug," for example, he noted that the "professional hygiene inspectors" tasked with ensuring the nation's food safety have only succeeded in forcing people to throw an unconscionably-enormous amount of perfectly good food into the garbage for no reason except that it did not satisfy ridiculous requirements to remain at exactly the right temperature for exactly the right amount of time in facilities sanitized with exactly the right blend of artificial chemicals. All of this is, of course, simply a euphemism for the luxuries of fossil fuel energy, Modern Technology, and an enormous amount of money. It is strange to act as though things could never possibly be any other way, since even in Linkola's early lifetime the traditional fishermen who kept Finland adequately fed managed to do so while violating every rule in the book.

It bears mentioning that all of this regulation has actually defeated its own purpose, since far from improving the general health of the public, the ridiculous levels of over-sanitation currently mandated by clueless bureaucrats have actually just made everyone much sicker. The mysterious rise of auto-immune disorders is largely just the result of inhibiting the body's immune system from doing its job by forcing it to exist in artificially-sterile environments for no reason except that "germs are scary!" It is all the more laughable, therefore, that the most common marketing slogan stamped on labels for hand sanitizers in India includes references to the product's "immunity boosting" powers. Ted Kaczynski concisely summarized the damaging effects of modern sanitation in a letter written from prison and dated to November 23, 2004:

> It's worth mentioning, by the way, that improved sanitation too seems to have had unanticipated negative consequences. [There is] evidence that modern sanitation has brought about a sharp increase in autoimmune disorders such as allergies, inflammatory bowel disease, and type 1 diabetes.

Furthermore, while the poliomyelitis virus has probably been around since time immemorial, paralytic polio was relatively rare prior to the Industrial Revolution. Only after industrialization were there epidemics of paralytic polio that left large numbers of people disabled for life, and it is hypothesized that these epidemics were a result of improved sanitation.[149]

Even as recently as Freud's era, the patient who constantly washed his or her hands was believed to be a person who suffered from delusions which were supposedly displaced symptoms born out of a frustration with a purely sexual origin.[150] In our era, something which even *Freud* recognized as weird behaviour has simply been universalized as an ethical mandate from the Hygiene Police. Put briefly, it is precisely the *health* inspectors who have destroyed our health. One could hardly imagine a more chilling testament to the consequences of allowing bureaucratic arrogance to challenge the Mind of Nature in an act of idiocy always guaranteed to fail. It is only too tragic that they had to bring the rest of the population down to an outcome of unnecessary destruction along with them.

In addition to being just plain stupid, the health inspector's meddling which, at least in the United States causes nearly half of all food produced to end up in the trash, cannot honestly be described as anything except a heinous eco-crime worthy of the most serious of all punishments. Linkola explicitly favoured dumping these technicians of waste into the same landfills which

---

[149] Ted Kaczynski, "Letter to David Skrbina, November 23, 2004," *in Technological Slavery* (Scottsdale: Fitch & Madison, 2019), p. 173.

[150] "Other forms of neurosis, characterized by intensive worry, are the expression of an exaggerated sexualization of acts that are ordinarily only preparatory to sexual satisfactions; such are the desires to see, to touch, to investigate. Here is thus explained the great importance of the fear of contact and also of the compulsion to wash."
See the 20th lecture ("General Theory of the Neuroses") in his *General Introduction to Psychoanalysis*.
Freud, Sigmund. Delphi Collected Works of Sigmund Freud (Delphi Series Eight Book 9) . Delphi Classics. Kindle Edition.

they needlessly filled with so much edible food, a fitting penalty for this anti-green police force of institutionalized idiocy who squandered so many hours of hard work invested by the agricultural workforce as well:

> If only I had power to match my will, I would deport all the hygiene inspectors to the landfills where they have disposed of so much good food that was produced with the nation's hard work.[151]

In his essay "Sales Season," Linkola similarly invokes the term "criminal act" to describe the senselessness of having an entire industry dedicated to loading idle retired folks onto oversized luxury yachts (better known as "cruise ships"), knowing full well that the sheer boredom of being stuck at sea for so long will drive them to get drunk just to forget how dull it was to take this trip in the first place:

> [C]an there be a more worthless and criminal act than to waste the remaining natural resources to build luxury cruisers so that the rotting carcasses of humanity might sail around the Caribbean in their whiskey haze?[152]

Once again, it is not enough to call out the cruise ship industry for its stupidity without emphasizing the specific ecological reasons why what they are doing is wrong. Linkola was careful to note that the criminal act itself lies in "wasting [so much of] the remaining natural resources" in order to intentionally engineer a situation in which one literally has to drink away the misery of being incarcerated on the same floating prison one paid an exorbitant price for the ticket to board.

Linkola mentioned in "The Finnish Body," though, that one doesn't have to board a cruise ship to step foot onto a physical embodiment of ecological contradiction. Even as people willingly abandon traditional outdoor pastimes such as bicycling despite the

---

[151] Pentti Linkola, "Humbug," in *Can Life Prevail?* (Kindle Edition).
[152] Pentti Linkola, "Sales Season", in *Can Life Prevail?* (Kindle Edition).

fact that these activities are both healthy and cheap, they have gone to absolutely ridiculous lengths to construct giant recreational facilities such as enormous gyms, ice rinks which function in summer, and indoor football stadiums capable of hosting games in the winter. One could only imagine that these monstrosities function as indulgences which are meant to pay off the debt for all the simple exercises one refused to do earlier by paying them off with a gigantic "return of the repressed" later.

Worse still is the perversion of "motorsports," something he cited as "environmental crimes which must be banned" as soon as possible. Yet in addition to being reprehensible on ecological grounds, they are ridiculous on conceptual grounds alone, in that these are built on the inherently self-contradictory idea of a sport which doesn't use the body at all. One could only imagine that the post-petroleum future will condemn the abandoned Nascar tracks in North Carolina and New Hampshire every bit as vehemently as Medieval Christians demonized the Roman Coliseum, since wasting energy to drive circles around the same track for hours on end will be recognized as the eco-crime that it truly is. For these reasons, Linkola closed the essay by arguing that physical exercise is something of an act of war against the System in itself, since anyone who bicycles or walks is defending against the onslaught of machines.

Linkola has gained notoriety for his willingness to not mince words when describing the need to punish eco-criminals in the most literal sense possible. In his "Life Protection, Utopias, and Agriculture," for example, he avoids clichés regarding "forgiving those who know not what they do." He spares not even a moment's hesitation in condemning those who engage in "agribusiness farming" as "not deserv[ing] the slightest sympathy":

> Then there are the tough guys of the agricultural world [who will] invest, mechanise, increase, buy half of the village's lands with no concern for the debts and charges they are incurring in trying to satisfy the EU wishes by acquiring tremendous numbers of cattle, pigs or chickens and hectares upon hectares of crops. These walking environmental

catastrophes, with their agribusiness farming, do not deserve the slightest sympathy.[153]

Once again, it is for specific ecological reasons that he charges these "walking environmental catastrophes" with the crime of recklessly overloading the land with ill-treated livestock to provide cheap, subpar-quality meat for industrial consumers. The *Quadrivium* interviewers provided a laundry list of horrors committed against chickens on a daily basis by the factory farming industry, many of which are almost too grotesque to repeat, including "filthy rooms, drugs, deformities, eye damage, blindness, bacterial infections of bones, slipped vertebrae, paralysis, internal bleeding, anemia, slipped tendons, twisted lower legs and necks, respiratory diseases and weakened immune-systems."[154] The grand irony, of course, is that so much of this food will end up in the trash anyway due to needless meddling by "health inspectors" that the long-term damage to the land and the unnecessary suffering by the overcrowded animals were doubly wasted. In Linkola's 1997 "Preservation of Traditional Landscape and Nature," he lamented: "the historical period when man enriched nature is over: modern field cultivation is a form of economy that [only] heavily impoverishes nature."[155]

He arguably went a step further in his essay "Against Highway Crime," in which he responded to a series of news articles portraying people sabotaging a highway project as dangerous thugs while completely missing the point that the makers of the highway were themselves the real criminals. Nor is this merely metaphorical, as he explicitly asserted that "building a motorway is undoubtedly a criminal activity, classifiable among major crimes."[156] For this

---

[153] Pentti Linkola, "Life Protection, Utopias, and Agriculture," in *Can Life Prevail?* (Kindle Edition).
[154] Pentti Linkola interview from *Quadrivium* #6 (2014): abridged version. Available at http://qvadrivivm.blogspot.com/2015/12/pentti-linkola-interview-from.html
[155] Pentti Linkola, "Preservation of Traditional Landscape and Nature," in *A Collection of Essays by Pentti Linkola 1993 – 2006*, p. 52.
[156] Pentti Linkola, "Against Highway Crime," in *Can Life Prevail?* (Kindle Edition).

reason, Linkola proposed with complete seriousness that any officials involved with the construction of highways must be tried and convicted in court.[157]

Nor is this harsh judgment limited only to highways, as Linkola noted that converting green space into parking lots is also a "criminal act" for the role it plays in worsening "a situation where humanity is on the verge of destruction and ecocatastrophes are looming large."[158] One could only begin to imagine how many eco-criminals might be tried for this offense, as the United States has literally devolved into one giant parking lot lined with countless identical strip malls, gas stations, and fast food restaurants. A century ago, one could hardly have imagined that there would come a day when even *churches* would be located in strip malls. There was a time when the community church required a certain amount of architectural sanctity to reinforce the feeling that one was entering "the house of God," but in our era it can be squeezed into a tight space in between a tanning salon and a payday loans office and just a few doors down from a sleazy liquor store on the edge of a gigantic parking lot with two or three tacky fast food joints squeezed in for good measure. It is no exaggeration to say that the most common sight a person will see in his or her entire lifetime is asphalt.

Linkola's ability to suspend human prejudices in order to recognize the Will of Nature without bias has led him to realize the fairly obvious though unspeakable fact that it is not only the politicians, bureaucrats, and engineers who created the highways who are guilty of a grave eco-crime. Anyone who even *uses* a highway has Mother Nature's blood on his or her hands and is perfectly liable to be tried as well: "All actions that encourage, increase, ease or speed up traffic are criminal activities."[159] One of the most pressing tasks for the Green Police will be to outlaw suburbanites' three-hour daily commutes by openly acknowledging these acts as the diabolically-wicked crimes that they really are. It is far too easy to demonize a small handful of elites; it is much more

---

[157] Ibid.
[158] Ibid.
[159] Ibid.

difficult to call out the "ordinary people" for their own wrongdoings. Nature, of course, tends not to discriminate on the basis of class.

Once again, the "eco" prefix is not an arbitrary stamp which lacks any content in itself, as Linkola is perfectly specific about which horrific ecological consequences highways bring about to justify his harsh judgment:

> Among ecocatastrophes is climate change which . . . will [eventually] blight a large share of the globe's harvests through drought and make northern regions (like Finland) unsuitable [for human settlement.][160]

It is no exaggeration at all to say that politicians who campaign on the promise of investing tax dollars into building new highways or lowering the price of fuel to facilitate driving on them (two proposals which have proven so safe that they are truly bi-partisan) should instead rephrase these slogans as promises to wilfully engineer mass famine through guaranteeing catastrophic droughts which will devastate Finland and many other nations to the point of uninhabitability. Highway crimes are eco-crimes because "[t]he upsetting of the gaseous balance of the atmosphere, to which traffic crucially contributes, is one of the major causes of climate change."[161]

It's also quite peculiar to act as though critics of highways are "violent radicals" simply for holding the wrong thoughts in their heads, while one outright ignores the mass violent extermination of "[t]rillions or quintillions of animals and plants [which] are [continuously] being wiped out on motorways."[162] Nor is this destruction an easily-reversible error. The consequences are likely to be permanent even if human extinction does manage to occur as a result of precisely this clueless ritual of happy motoring. Linkola himself noted:

---

[160] Ibid.
[161] Ibid.
[162] Ibid.

> The road across Lake Vanajavesi in Konho, for instance, has wiped out a large colony of birds, spoiling the river's habitat forever. Hardly a greater sin could have been committed on the face of the Earth.[163]

In his 2012 essay "Visualize Gasoline," Peak Oil activist Richard Heinberg similarly noted that even though we spend countless hours driving on highways, we still fail to recognize them for what they really are: rivers of gasoline which have blotted out whatever natural ecosystem had to be paved into oblivion to allow this technological Sherman's March to burn a pathway of pure destruction through Nature:

> If you do this visualization exercise, you might find yourself seeing rivulets, streams, and – in the case of big freeways – *rivers* of gasoline coursing across the land. For the United States as a whole, four hundred million gallons of gasoline enter and leave the flow every day, But, since we routinely carry more gasoline with us than we intend to use immediately, the total amount in car gas tanks at any given moment is roughly seven times larger, so that America's gasoline rivers slosh with 2.8 billion gallons on any given day.[164]

Highways, in other words, are literally rivers of billions of gallons of gasoline, but they are peculiar rivers, in that rather than provide an ecosystem which can host a thriving community of life forms, they are more like dead zones which only guarantee that any animal "foolhardy" enough to enter the stream will face a premature transformation into roadkill. Heinberg goes as far as to call them "rivers of death":

> Gasoline rivers are no place for nonhuman life forms: only the most daring of weeds and foolhardy of animals venture

---

[163] Ibid.
[164] Richard Heinberg, "Visualize Gasoline," in *Afterburn: Society Beyond Fossil Fuels* (Gabriola Island: New Society, 2015), p. 33.

there, with the latter often ending up as roadkill. Indeed, highways could be thought of as rivers of death.[165]

While it is politically fashionable to pay lip service to condemning war for its mass destruction of life and of landscapes, Linkola is one of the few thinkers sufficiently capable of "seeing the birthmark" to state the objective fact that highways, for example, are actually even *more destructive* than any war in history. He openly states that "no war has ever led to such wastelands."[166] In his essay "The Green Lie," he explicitly warns in the most literal sense possible that roads are *slaughtering* the forests they invade:

> Now a network of gravel roads extends for hundreds of thousands of kilometres, dividing the woods into small sections and slaughtering the Finnish forest. This road network has had a further devastating impact on woodland ponds, which are now filled with an array of fibreglass boats, and surrounded by booths and buses.[167]

"Natural Porn Killer"?

This collective willingness to ignore the mass violence against animals inflicted by highways and the countless vehicles of mass destruction it enables is peculiar, because violence is arguably the only remaining "sin" which has not been de-canonized from the catalogue of supernatural offenses. Even the secularist, post-religious culture of moral relativism has reserved this one exception to its otherwise-universal ban on talk of immorality.

Under the modern worldview, for example, one might consider pollution or resource depletion to be bad ideas on pragmatic or technical grounds, but only violence still holds the status of a sin designated by the (non-existent) gods themselves as a sacrilegious offense. Most people would consider even the worst environmental catastrophes like Chernobyl, the Aral Sea disaster, or

---

[165] Ibid., p. 34.
[166] Ibid.
[167] Pentti Linkola, "The Green Lie," in *Can Life Prevail?* (Kindle Edition).

the BP Oil Spill to be unfortunate accidents resulting from stupidity, without bringing themselves to openly designate them as immoral. Condemnations of acts of violence, on the other hand, are almost always guaranteed to coalesce into a truly bipartisan consensus of self-righteous denunciation. Only violence still retains the mystical aura of *evil*.

One of the most memorable reminders of this disparity between our treatment of violence and the rest of the categories of the ethical code was found in the media's reaction to serial murderer and rapist Ted Bundy's final interview before his execution in 1989. The confessions captured in this final dialogue proved so compelling that they birthed an urban legend and spawned an oral tradition among pastors, priests, and youth group leaders within the Christian community which continues unimpeded even to the present day.

Bundy's status as the most notorious serial rapist of all time presented something of an enigma, as investigators struggled to crack the mystery regarding what could have possibly motivated a charismatic, handsome, and intelligent law student with a promising future to commit the most heinous crimes of sexual violence against anonymous strangers, often against women whom he had met in public venues such as grocery stores. Even after he was captured and incarcerated, he refused for years to acknowledge that he had committed the crimes at all, let alone provide the missing link within his personal biography to explain why.

The final night before his execution in prison, Bundy rejected countless interview requests from "respectable journalists" and shocked the media by agreeing to speak only with Dr. James Dobson, an evangelical activist known today primarily for heading the Focus on the Family organization. In the interview, Bundy broke the silence by admitting that it was none other than his exposure to hard core pornography at a young age which had planted the seed which eventually drove him to commit the most abhorrible crimes against women. Bundy explained that porn, like any other drug, suffered from the problem of diminishing returns. The more times one uses it, the stronger the dose needs to become in order for one to capture the same high. At the beginning of his addiction, he was satisfied with the relatively tame material found in dirty magazines that had been thrown out in his neighbourhood alleyways, but this quickly lost its shock value and he found himself seeking out ever more potent forms of the drug. Eventually, even consuming the most deranged material proved dull if it was not supplemented by some element of reality which could only be obtained through finding a living victim to offer human blood for the ritual of evil. What the demon inside him required, he claimed, was human sacrifice. A string of dozens of brutal rapes and murders followed, culminating in the abduction of a 12-year-old girl and his eventual arrest.

It has been truly disturbing to watch the media trip over themselves with "debunking" efforts to prove that Bundy's own explanation for his behaviour could not possibly be correct. One documentary featured interviews with porn industry insiders and "criminal justice experts" who suggested that the consumption of even the most degrading forms of modern pornography is not only perfectly harmless in its effects but is even an indicator that a person is "normal," as though anyone who *doesn't* spend every evening isolated in front of a laptop screen with his hand down his pants watching a brutal 25-man gang rape should be seized by the "mental health police" and carried away to an insane asylum to be monitored for signs of dangerous behaviour, an analysis so backwards in its reasoning that one would suspect that only massive corporate funding by entities with a financial interest in keeping the population addicted to their product despite its harmful effects (including extreme erectile dysfunction which prevents one from sexual functionality in the real world) could buy it. It is peculiar for these "scientific rationalists" to act as though Bundy's claims lack empirical confirmation, since it is a well-known fact among professional sex addiction therapists that level-six porn addicts *routinely* end up in prison as a result of having to take their addiction to a level beyond any legal limit after having consumed everything the market has to offer, often turning to criminal acts of violence because their erectile dysfunction had gotten so bad that they literally could not get aroused without seeing gore.

It is similarly comical that the media has turned to filling the void of explanation for Bundy's crimes by arguing that the "dangerous material" he found while riding his bicycle through the back alleys of his neighbourhood was none other than detective comic books. Because these graphic novels depicted fictional acts of murder which were required to provide the impetus for the whodunnit narrative to unfold, these cartoon images supposedly provided the true psychological distortion which led an otherwise normal boy to act out depraved fantasies with real victims (under this view, one could only wonder how many more Ted Bundies might materialize as a result of shoot-'em-up video games such as *Call of Duty* and *Gears of War*.) The not-so-subtle conclusion, of course, is that murder mystery books should be banned by the government, but even the most disgustingly sadistic forms of pornography should be freely distributed to all, simply because affirming the latter builds up one's "sex positive" index.

One should bear in mind that the human suffering required to produce the kind of hard core pornography required to temporarily satisfy today's addicts' demand for taboo situations and violent shock value is far from trivial, as one industry veteran alleged that one of her fellow female performers endured physical abuse so extreme that a piece of the muscle in her anus literally fell out on the set while filming a brutal anal scene, proof of the blatant hypocrisy inherent in the System's demand to simultaneously condemn violence and espouse unrestricted "sex positive" excesses so long as they boost the net worth of a handful of corporations. In addition, the story of another female performer's death in Southern California in the early 2000s, which allegedly occurred while filming "a bondage scene gone wrong," suggests that escalation to the point of cold-blooded murder might not be unheard of within an industry which created its own hard-wired requirements to demand ever more extreme forms of novelty.

One could hardly imagine a more chillingly-conclusive piece of evidence that violence is the only remaining sin, in that one could literally argue that cartoon images of cheap remakes of Sherlock Holmes are more dangerous than videos of real violence in porn simply because the latter are cloaked in the humanistic chimera of "sexual liberation" and the negation of "Victorian moralism." One should bear in mind that Modern Technology inherently contradicts hundreds of thousands of years of human evolution, no matter what its content might be, and that the negative effects on one's physical and psychological functioning are undeniable. Whatever pornography might have meant in an earlier century, it cannot mean anything except one of the most extreme forms of technological domination today.

Who's Anti-Fascister Than Thou?

Arguably, even more conclusive proof that violence is the only remaining sin lies in the media's fanatical demands that the populace should acknowledge no value whatsoever in Ted Kaczynski's monumental body of theoretical work, simply on grounds that he is a "convicted murderer." This self-righteous trumpeting by the media had proven so pervasive that Kaczynski found himself summoned to defend nothing short of the concept of violence itself in order to break the spell of oversocialization among his critics. Ted Kaczynski has repeatedly noted, for example, that this categorical aversion to all violence whatsoever is actually a fairly recent phenomenon. In past centuries, violence was not only tolerated; under the right circumstances, it was even admired.[168] It is no coincidence that the nobles of Medieval Europe were the warrior caste who were respected precisely because they were summoned to engage in the most graphic acts of real-world violence in order to fight for one's honour, family, and people. Nor can this aversion to violence be blamed on Christianity, for the most religious centuries of Western History were also the most heavily-characterized by warfare.

Kaczynski has noted that condemning all violence whatsoever is simply a technical requirement for the System to function smoothly, as Modern Technology has a hard-wired need for human subjects to maximize their docility under its constraints. Aversion to all violence is therefore nothing more than a

---

[168] Ted Kaczynski, "Morality and Revolution," in *Technological Slavery* (Port Townsend: Feral House, 2010), pp. 242-3.

euphemism for greater technological domination, as the only context in which such a claim could possibly make sense is one in which the System has expanded to the point of being able to regulate every single movement among the populace.

It is all the more ironic that the sole reliable exception to this universal prohibition against violence is in the idea of a "just war," a privilege which is almost exclusively granted to the single most destructive war in history. Kaczynski is one of the few thinkers with the courage to openly acknowledge the fact that although World War II was a horrific example of human warfare, there was no fundamental difference between it and the countless other examples of human warfare that had occurred before. Kaczynski had the courage to acknowledge this near the end of "Morality and Revolution":

> [The Axis Powers in World War II] merely tried to repeat on a larger scale the kinds of atrocities that have occurred again and again throughout the history of civilization. What modern technology threatens is absolutely without precedent. Today we have to ask ourselves whether nuclear war, biological disaster, or ecological collapse will produce casualties many times greater than World War II [and] whether the human race will continue to exist or whether it will be replaced by intelligent machines or genetically-engineered freaks.[169]

The System's claim that the Axis Powers represent the sole universally-valid exception to the ban on violence has ironically led many intellectual elites to openly endorse the most grotesque forms of violence simply in order to prove how "anti-fascist" they are. This has of course provided the green light for the media to act as though a group of violent thugs who bust in old men's skulls with crude caveman clubs for no reason except that they had gathered to attend an event featuring a conservative speaker are "the good guys" simply because they dressed in black and paid lip service to

---

[169] Ted Kaczynski, "Morality and Revolution", in *Technological Slavery* (Port Townsend: Feral House, 2010), p. 244.

social justice while violently terrorizing the local population in an act of self-righteous hypocrisy which would make the Reformation-era papacy blush.

The race to become "anti-fascister than thou" has become something of an Olympic sport which has driven the oversocialized to embody the most embarrassing forms of absurdity to beat each other out for the trophy for "who can defend the sole acceptable act of violence in history in order to condemn all other instances of violence." It is deeply disturbing that Italian director Pier Paolo Pasolini's final film *Salò o le 120 giornate di Sodoma*, a cinematic remake of the Marquis de Sade's *120 Days of Sodom*, continues to be praised by academic industry elites for its supposed "aesthetic value" despite the fact that it was long banned for portraying the most horrific acts of torture, paedophilia, and the forced consumption of human faeces in the guise of a "deeply intellectual work of art." Honest reviewers of the film have expressed deep regret after watching it at all, even admitting it caused them to have trouble sleeping for weeks afterwards, a fact which the author of the present text can corroborate himself despite the fact that he only managed to stomach some one third of the film before feeling forced to shut it off. The only justification which the "professional intellectuals" offer for the extreme acts of, quite literally, *Sade*istic violence within the film is that these fulfil the political function of "capturing the evil of Mussolini's fascists" in order to reinforce the belief that World War II was the only acceptable example of violence in the history of the Earth.

We have quite literally reached the point where the System demands that detective novels be burned in an act of mass censorship while simultaneously heaping critical acclaim upon the most disgusting cinematic trash simply because it serves a technical function for the System by reinforcing the idea that the only acceptable example of violent force has already come and gone and will never return. In other words, it has become our ethical duty to throw the tamest whodunnit crime novels into the fire while simultaneously giving ourselves over to be strapped into a theatre chair to watch the "Italian pseudo-art film" equivalent of a snuff flick just because it reinforces the idea that "Mussolini was definitely worse than Mao and Stalin," despite the fact that the latter collectively killed some 70 million people in the name of "class struggle." Our goodness under Modern Technology is arguably to be measured by our willingness to let our eyes be forced open to let the cinematic equivalent of a lobotomy be performed on our brains by allowing traumatic images which can't be unseen to be burned into our memories forever.

It is strange, in fact, that fascism has come to stand as the sole symbol for pure political evil, since Mussolini's government only performed some 2,000 political executions in its entire lifetime. Compared to the 45 million deaths under Mao alone, it is hard to imagine why Mussolini is routinely portrayed as one of the evillest men to have ever existed but Communism is still largely considered a viable solution to the problems of modern industrialism. This is not at all, of course, to downplay Mussolini's many flaws, but it is flatly intellectually dishonest to pretend that Modern Technology does not pose an incalculably graver danger to human existence than he ever could have.

This tendency to withhold the universal ban on violence for this single exception is therefore inherently self-contradictory, insofar as to say that violence is justified to win one war of many but is not justified to prevent the end of human existence itself is the kind of illogic which Kaczynski thought had to be overturned, if nothing else, to retain some logical consistency in one's beliefs. Yet Kaczynski warned at the end of "The Coming Revolution" that even to say that the current System and the totalitarian states of the 20th Century are equally destructive is a gross exaggeration. The current System is far worse:

> [I advocate p]unishment for those responsible for the present situation. The scientists, engineers, corporation executives, politicians and so forth who consciously and intentionally promote technological progress and economic growth are criminals of the worst kind. They are worse than Stalin or Hitler, who never even dreamed of anything approaching what today's technophiles are doing.[170]

Blotting out the cognitive dissonance of reserving World War II as the single exception worthy of being designated "the ethical use of violence" while arguing that all of Kaczynski's writings be removed from public circulation requires an impressive level of mental gymnastics for the additional reason that this war entailed an unspeakably vaster toll of destruction than any lone wolf working from a remote cabin in the woods could ever dream of accomplishing.

Kaczynski's belief that an ideal court of justice in a hypothetical future would find it fitting to punish engineers, corporate executives, and politicians might seem "completely unreasonable" to the oversocialized today, simply on the flawed belief that these people were "completely harmless" to anyone except, of course, Mother Nature herself, the destruction of which was the sole purpose of their work. In a classic unpublished essay titled "When Non-Violence is Suicide," Kaczynski exposed the illusion that the corporate aristocracy is categorically incapable of violence by noting that this is merely the case today because the System already handles all the dirty work for them.[171] In the absence of a functioning technological system to pump wealth into their bank accounts at everyone else's expense and provide a heavily-armed police force to defend their interests at gunpoint, he warns that these people will almost certainly prove themselves to be far more dangerous than the worst highwaymen and gangs in this post-collapse world. It would be unspeakably naïve to imagine that they *couldn't* be capable of resorting to extremely sadistic forms of violence to restore their privileged lifestyles once again, simply because they lack any need to do so now.

Linkola has similarly demonstrated an unusual willingness to acknowledge the possibility that, in the coming era of the Green Police, the Mind of Nature might legislate harsh prison sentences for any engineer, scientist, sanitation inspector, or regulatory bureaucrat caught implementing industrial practices fashionable

---

[170] Ted Kaczynski, "The Coming Revolution," in *Technological Slavery* (Port Townsend: Feral House, 2010), p. 216.
[171] Ted Kaczynski, "When Non-Violence is Suicide" (unpublished manuscript).

today. Linkola's willingness to not grant a uniquely privileged status to white collar professionals simply because they work prestigious jobs within the System extended even to his refusal to join in the media frenzy of proclaiming September 11 as uniquely tragic among all other losses of life in World History. The consequences for refusing to play along with the media's biased narratives are not to be underestimated, as Ward Churchill was fired from his job as professor at the University of Colorado at Boulder (the author of the present text's own alma mater and supposedly one of the most "radical leftist" of all universities in the United States) for suggesting that the World Trade Centre was a legitimate military target because of its role in facilitating "the technical functioning of empire" and its direct contribution to widespread suffering around the world.

Linkola arguably went a step further even than Churchill by arguing in his 2001 essay "Bull's Eye" that it would be misplaced even to think that the media claimed that the loss of life in this attack easily outweighed 100 million deaths under communists in the 20th Century only because its victims were Americans rather than anonymous thought criminals in China, Russia, or Southeast Asia. Although the media would not openly say it, the tragedy of 9-11 did not extend to all the janitors, food service workers, and security guards who lost their lives that day. Rather, it was only the high-ranking corporate aristocrats who merited a nonstop virtual funeral as martyrs for the Religion of the Dollar Bill:

> Those who died in the attack were not simply humans: they were Americans; and not ordinary Americans, either, but the priests and priestesses of the supreme God of this age: the Dollar. The passengers of the domestic flights are not a valid sample of humanity either, but a wealthy, busy, environmentally damaging and world-devouring portion of mankind.[172]

---

[172] Pentti Linkola, "Bull's Eye," in *Can Life Prevail?* (Kindle Edition).

In other words, Linkola is one of the few thinkers sufficiently immune to the pressures of political correctness to acknowledge the obvious fact that the media has effectively created a new caste system in which humans' "intrinsic worth" is measured not only by how much money they have but literally by how much ecological damage they cause. In typical Orwellian fashion, all lives are equal but some lives are more equal than others if they happen to belong to the "wealthy, busy, environmentally damaging and world-devouring portion of mankind." The irony, of course, is that these people cannot honestly be described as anything except eco-criminals in disguise but are paraded around by the media as the "model citizens" who define the minimal standard for a "normal existence," a standard from which even the slightest deviation supposedly amounts to a total failure at life or a suspected case of "mental illness."

Linkola did not mince words regarding the standard of evil to which the United States has fallen, affirming during his interview with *Quadrivium* that there is no other "country on Earth as crooked as the United States," a nation which has only succeeded in claiming the trophy as the most "corrupted, swollen, paralysing and suffocating political entity" on Earth and whose highest priorities on the global stage include "financing and arming all sorts of harmful governments and guerilla troops all over the world" simply in order to keep its own bloated aristocracy of suburban idlers stocked with petroleum for their SUVs and fast food for their bellies.

Linkola found the United States to be a sufficiently wicked target to justify an entire essay of harsh critique. In his "The United States – The Enemy of the World," he admitted that although there is a minority of ecologically admirable figures within the United States (he cites the Amish in particular), the nation has still come to represent a level of evil virtually unequalled even among the cast of wretchedly bad actors on the global stage today.[173] Nor can this be blamed uniquely upon a kleptocracy of elites who had stolen democratic representation from the masses; on the contrary, it is

---

[173] Pentti Linkola, "The United States – The Enemy of the World," in *A Collection of Essays by Pentti Linkola 1993 – 2006*, p. 172.

precisely the *majority* in America who have chosen technological gimmickry and suburban comfort over their own traditional ways of life. The sad truth is that small town America was not driven into destitution at gunpoint – no, people willingly sold out their local shopkeepers and craftspeople and abandoned their own traditional skills just to get cheap plastic hair dryers and coffee makers imported from China at slightly lower prices, and for the opportunity to wander within a sprawling plaza which initially felt like a Disneyland of low prices but quickly lost its marketing glow after the paint dried on the newly-constructed walls and they realized they had no other options left.

Yet it is not only corporate monopolies which the democratic majority has willingly voted into power, as they overwhelmingly agree each election to grant another term to the same corrupt political establishment which maintains power equally comfortably regardless of whether a Republican or Democrat figurehead sits on the ornamental throne of the White House. In this essay, Linkola openly asked why exactly it was that these same bloodthirsty oligarchs suddenly decided to inspect Iraq for weapons of mass destruction, when they were the only ones in history who had ever used nuclear weapons on civilians and who continue to make credible threats of violence with their massive nuclear arsenal. He ended the essay by expressing hope that history might repeat itself again in the form of allowing the United States to follow the same fate of decline as other arrogant militaristic states which bit off more than they could chew by invading one too many nation at the same time, a prophecy which will eventually prove sound.[174]

In his provocative 1999 essay "War, Man and Kosovo" he similarly noted the hypocrisy that the same Western nations which bombed hundreds of thousands of people in Germany during World War II could escape the arbitrary designation of "war criminals" simply because these acts were carried out by the winners of the war who stocked the academic departments with historians sufficiently biased to write favourably about the events for future generations of readers; worse still, these same nations could

---

[174] Ibid., p. 174.

somehow seize the moral high ground to condemn the comparatively small conflict in the Balkans as barbaric, yet found that bombing them in turn was the only means to "fight for peace" (a blatant example of Orwellian doublethink in itself.)[175]

Nor was the World Trade Centre worthy of sympathy when one considered that its sole purpose was ecological destruction through keeping the gears of the global industrial system moving. Far from lamenting its destruction as the "single most tragic event in World History," Linkola was reputed to have marvelled that "It was a magnificent, splendid choice" just two weeks after the attacks, as his *Quadrivium* interviewers explained:

> The Towers were the best target anyone could have picked out of amongst all the buildings of the world. The surveillance and police control and decrease in foreign trade and air traffic caused by the attacks were all welcome effects to him.[176]

In an ideal future, however, it is precisely these eco-crimes which will be punished rather than celebrated.

Kill the Cats?

Nor is Linkola satisfied with extending harsh legal punishments to human malefactors. He has gained widespread notoriety for his willingness to punish eco-criminals even if they are animals, despite the fact that extreme forms of "animal rights activism" are becoming trendy among college students, as though the humanistic chimera of democratic equality had been extended to include every animal on the face of the Earth in order to prohibit that even a single one of them might be killed for any reason whatsoever. This belief that animals must be included in the democratic mass is peculiar,

---

[175] Pentti Linkola, "War, Man and Kosovo," in *A Collection of Essays by Pentti Linkola 1993 – 2006*, p. 163.
[176] Pentti Linkola interview from *Quadrivium* #6 (2014): abridged version. Available at http://qvadrivivm.blogspot.com/2015/12/pentti-linkola-interview-from.html

since the term "demos" is explicitly the Greek term for people, yet this only confirms that the Mind of Nature has been disregarded to the point where even distinct species are all lumped together into a single monstrously-indeterminate mass which will only hasten the destruction of all species. Few things are quite as "democratic," precisely in this perverse sense, than the coming mass extinction.

It is all the more ironic that this grotesque perversion of the concept of ecology is the official ideology espoused by those who claim to be "radical environmentalists." This madness is exemplified quite memorably by the way that the city of Los Angeles is currently generating a homeless population so gargantuan (one might be reminded, through espousing some of the "most progressive policies" in the nation) that the city's sprawling internal slums have provided the raw ecological conditions for medieval diseases such as typhus and even the bubonic plague to silently make a comeback within the exploding rat population which found the mountains of stagnant garbage lining the streets to be a perfect breeding ground for disease. Yet even in the face of a series of plagues which will kill many of the very poorest residents of the city, the animal rights movement has driven the oversocialized within the city to seek legal action to ban the use of rodenticides. It is all too easy to imagine that the same "oversocialized college students with feelings of inferiority" who shout the loudest about publicly loving the animals may someday find that the same epidemics they assumed would only affect poor people living in tents on Skid Row might find a pathway onto their own college campuses, much like Edgar Allen Poe's Prince Prospero found out the hard way that holing himself up with his fellow elites behind the palace walls still failed to provide sufficient protection to keep the Red Death safely on the outside where it could only kill everyone else.[177] The social justice movement is not far from becoming a death cult in which we will be required to detonate the suicide bomb of ideological purity, despite the fact that any benefit from such public acts of virtue signalling will not do a person any good after he or she dies from doing so. The universal

---

[177] See Poe's classic short story "The Masque of the Red Death."

ban on violence, extending even to a population of plague-carrying rats which exploded to an artificially high number only as a result of human negligence and industrial interferences in the local ecosystem, is simply the cyanide-laced Kool Aid which the brainwashed are forced to guzzle to their own demise.

Against the politically correct image of a ban on violence which is so universal that one cannot harm a single animal for any reason whatsoever, Linkola has affirmed the necessary though unpopular truth that not every organism within an ecosystem is created equal. From a strictly ecological perspective, some animals represent an "invasive species" whose presence within the broader whole will eventually prove disruptive enough to destroy it altogether. In his 1993 "Ethics of Environmentalism," he exposed the truth that any animal which survives through freeloading off of Man's interventions into the ecosystem cannot be treated as though it held the same status as one of a member of a species indigenous to that region which survives solely through its own efforts in accord with Nature. While efforts must indeed be invested into preserving the native populations, the invaders must be recognized as "harmful" animals which cannot be granted the same rights as the natives or, in some cases, any rights at all. [178]

Interestingly, Linkola clarifies his stance in this essay by claiming that it would be something of a mistake to think of the latter as being a part of Nature at all: they are, instead, simply a smaller part of "the death sowed by Man," effectively holding the status of living and breathing contaminants in an environment, or perhaps technological monstrosities which actively contradict the natural order of the place into which they were ejected. He goes as far as to argue that any little birds' eggs or fledglings eaten up by these creatures at springtime might as well be included in the total amount of food which Man himself had consumed, since it was only through his meddling in the ecosystem that they were enabled to do so in the first place.

For this reason, Man must not adopt a spirit of learned helplessness towards these ongoing eco-crimes perpetrated by these

---

[178] Pentti Linkola, "Ethics of Environmentalism," in *A Collection of Essays by Pentti Linkola 1993 – 2006*, p. 44.

animals, as though their activities were simply an impersonal "act of God" akin to a tsunami, hurricane, or flood. Rather, he asserts that because it was simply Man's own recklessness that allowed this to occur, Man must seize the responsibility to "prevent" them in the future and to stop these criminal acts dead in their tracks now as well. In other words, there is a categorical difference between a natural disaster and a technological one: while the Mind of Nature would force us to allow the former to unfold, it actively mandates that we prevent the latter, even by drastic means which cannot help but be interpreted as "animal cruelty."

Many would be shocked to find that one such invasive predator very well might be living in their own homes. In his essay "The Suppressed Nightmare of Conservation," for example, Linkola went as far as to openly designate the house cat as one of "the worst" animals in Finland because of its devastating effects on local bird populations.[179] It is an objective fact that any time and effort invested into propping up collapsing bird populations in Finland will easily be negated by unrestricted hunting by cats. It requires a certain amount of cognitive dissonance, in fact, to *not* see that cats do not fit into the broader set of puzzle pieces within the Finnish ecosystem for the simple fact that they are not native to that region at all, as they are Egyptian predators which were only introduced into Finland through the artificial meddling of human agents who disregarded the Mind of Nature in favour of their personal preference to ignore the birthmark when it served a self-interested utilitarian purpose.

Linkola explicitly contrasts ecological objectivity and human preference by noting that behind the humanistic chimera of a "cute" house pet lies the inconvenient fact that cats are hard-wired to embody the instinct to hunt and will continue acting out on it even after being brought into people's homes. In fact, he notes that this was exactly why cats were domesticated in the first place, as their human captors found their natural tendency to control rodent populations to be a sufficiently-valuable trade-off to justify the costs to keep them on site all the time.

---

[179] Pentti Linkola, "The Suppressed Nightmare of Conservation," in *Can Life Prevail?* (Kindle Edition).

Linkola has distinguished himself as one of the few adherents to the Mind of Nature objective enough to acknowledge that even the claim that cats should be allowed to remain in people's homes on grounds that they only hunt the "bad animals" like mice is inexcusable because even though they are loathed by humans as pests, mice are still an integral part of their ecosystems. Their total elimination from existence would indeed prove devastating to the broader whole. Whereas the Mind of Man only sees a disgusting and inconvenient pest, the Mind of Nature recognizes that mice fulfil a legitimate role within an ecological whole which has thoroughly adapted to their presence. For this reason, mice have as much right to life as any other animal in that system. Arguably, a definition of Deep Ecology is precisely the ability to suspend personal biases in order to respect objective truth, even when it requires one to affirm the right for the most detested of vermin to continue existing.

Nonetheless, Linkola noted in this essay that one sign that the Mind of Man has become completely disconnected from the Mind of Nature lies in the insanity that killing any cat whatsoever has literally been made illegal through a recent law punishing anyone who drowns a cat with jail time. It bears mentioning that drowning cats was a perfectly legitimate and humane activity which had been done for countless generations whenever a situation meriting it arose, yet we have reached the point where the Mind of Man effectively legislates that cat populations explode beyond any natural limit, an inevitable result which will follow from the fact that cats have no natural predators in Finland. Contrary to the widespread media caricature that Linkola is uniquely concerned about curbing overpopulation when it applies to humans, he has openly acknowledged that overpopulation is equally problematic when it applies to cats and other invasive predators. This turn of events, in fact, may very well provide the raw technical foundation for cats to cover the entire world within due time, perhaps even outliving their human masters in the process.

Linkola concludes the essay by suggesting that, at minimum, regulations should be imposed to require any cat which wanders outdoors to be on a leash. For any cat caught killing a bird, the owner should be prosecuted. Of course, he acknowledges that any attempt to preserve nature that conflicts with people's desires can never be implemented except through a forceful reversion to the Mind of Nature and the Green Police.

In Linkola's lengthy *Quadrivium* interview, he went much further than suggesting that cats be held on leashes: he affirmed that cats pose so great a threat to the native population of wild animals that they must be "eradicated absolutely." [180] In fact, of all the foreign beasts living in Finland, he awarded them the title of the single "worst" one. Controversial as such claims might be to those indoctrinated into the humanistic chimeras of modernity, one would have to wilfully supress the facts to deny, as he says himself, that a single cat will easily kill as many Finnish birds as all the hunters in the country put together, given that the latter are restricted by the requirements of their hunting licenses but cats are sanctioned by the government itself in their unregulated pillaging of the landscape.

Yet the house cat is far from the only example of a foreign predator which had been artificially introduced into Finland to the detriment of the local ecosystems. In his essay "The Animal Protector as an Apostle of Doom," he exposes the absolute madness behind proposals that there should be a conservation program for minks! This gets the problem exactly backwards, since Linkola noted in his "Half a Century of Water Fowl Surveys" that the most prominent reason for the ruin of Tavastia's water bird populations lay in the introduction of the wild mink into their habitats; this was a fairly recent anomaly which only began as recently as the end of the 1960s.[181] In his 1993 "Ethics of Environmentalism" he recounted that this devastation remains ignored by office bureaucrats and suburban couch potatoes glued to electronic screens but is easily observed by anyone who ventures into the wild to observe native bird populations first-hand; in his own experience following bird nests in the summertime in Finland, he found that it

---

[180] Pentti Linkola interview from *Quadrivium* #6 (2014): abridged version. Available at http://qvadrivivm.blogspot.com/2015/12/pentti-linkola-interview-from.html

[181] Pentti Linkola, "Half Century of Water Fowl Surveys," in *A Collection of Essays by Pentti Linkola 1993 – 2006*, p. 59.

is quite rare to see any one of these birds survive through the whole season.[182]

From an ecological standpoint, therefore, nothing could be more absurd than fighting to protect these invaders, because minks are arguably the Finnish equivalent of the dingoes which had infiltrated Australia. It is not at all controversial to acknowledge that the only ethical stance for dealing with dingoes is forceful, violent extermination because they are vividly terrifying animals, but because minks and cats are intrinsically "cuter" such a statement would seem unthinkable, even to the environmentalists who claim to take ecological issues seriously. In his "Ethics of Environmentalism" he similarly noted that one lady who wrote into a newspaper proposed an extermination program to rid the earth of viper snakes (arguably, just because they are "scary"), yet Linkola argued that one should instead extend that gesture to minks even though they seem on the surface to be less intimidating.[183] In "Animal Protector as the Apostle of Doom," Linkola does not mince words on the issue: "This vermin mink raccoon should be vanquished down to the last."[184] According to him, the only ecologically-justified response is that *you have to kill them*!

It is peculiar that such a statement will prove offensive in a time in which the cult of "universal human rights" has obtained the status of religious law in an era which simultaneously mandates secularism, despite the fact that minks are not even human! In his discussion of animal rights in "Human and Animal Nature," he went as far as to argue that minks and other invasive predators which were artificially introduced into an ecosystem to the detriment of the native animals there have no rights at all. In his "Ethics of Environmentalism," he asserted that "unscrupulously stern rules must be applied to foreign predators, both imported and immigrated." While he admits that any foreign plant or animal which does not harm the native population can more or less be

---

[182] Pentti Linkola, "Ethics of Environmentalism," in *A Collection of Essays by Pentti Linkola 1993 – 2006*, p. 45.
[183] Ibid., p. 46.
[184] Pentti Linkola, "The Animal Protector as an Apostle of Doom," in *Can Life Prevail?* (Kindle Edition).

tolerated, if the intruder's presence proves harmful to the natives (he cites minks by name as an example of such a predator) then "the verdict of the environmentalist is absolute": one must adopt a stance of all-out-war against them.[185] This stance will only seem extreme if one ignores the ecological fact, as he mentioned in his "Joy of Living Characterizes Life," that any efforts to grant minks a set of "basic human rights" will eventually drop the number of their prey all the way down to zero.[186]

Nor is this blatant unwillingness to punish eco-crimes limited to the realm of cats and minks. Far more troubling is the System's tendency to abuse the very concept of justice by actively rigging the System to reward and protect the very worst eco-criminals while punishing whistle-blowers who attempt to get too close to the truth. Linkola alleged in his 2000 essay "Is the WWF Favouring Crime?" that the WWF (not the wrestling organization, by the way) tends to obscure the fact that any reference whatsoever to forestry is a euphemism for cutting down trees; likewise, this organization is *a priori* incompatible with any efforts towards natural conservation. Linkola concludes that the WWF is just a part of the racket of the logging business rather than one of its regulators and is therefore an organ of "a criminal industry" rather than a police force with any serious intention to keep it under control.[187]

Even as early as Linkola's 1989 *Johdatus 1990-luvun ajatteluun* (*Introduction to the Thinking of the Nineteen Nineties*), he cut the crap by simply pleading guilty to the media's charges of being hateful: regarding the builders of the Sääksmäki bridge, he admitted, of course "I hate, I hate and I hate, as recklessly as a man can ever hate anything or anybody" the "rapists, murderers and destroyers of all" who carry out this madness simply in order to pick up a paycheck for themselves.[188] Yet this corruption is not

---

[185] Pentti Linkola, "Ethics of Environmentalism," in *A Collection of Essays by Pentti Linkola 1993 – 2006*, pp. 45-6.
[186] Pentti Linkola, "Joy of Living Characterizes Life," in *A Collection of Essays by Pentti Linkola 1993 – 2006*, p. 55.
[187] Pentti Linkola, "Is the WWF Favouring Crime?," in *Can Life Prevail?* (Kindle Edition).
[188] Pentti Linkola interview from *Quadrivium* #6 (2014): abridged version.

limited to the laborers who sell their souls out for a little extra money, as even the regulators themselves are the greatest of all the villains. In "Against Highway Crime," Linkola noted the irony that the current Police of Progress (the perverse double of the Green Police) are simply tasked with protecting eco-criminals whose policies are hard-wired to bring about death, while the Green Police would act solely with the interest of protecting life:

> The role of the police should also be re-evaluated: is it to protect criminals, or could it be to protect life instead?[189]

In fact, in his 1995 "A Letter to Hannu Hautala" he went as far as to condemn Finnish law as the "arch enemy" which "environmental conservationists are fighting against," in that this set of laws is merely an instrument in the service of inflating the bubbles of economic growth through the "raping of nature" and even the "ruining of coming human generations." There is no question of compromise with the current set of mandates it upholds: "it must be re-written" altogether if one has any hope of surviving.[190]

It is not difficult to follow this reasoning to its logical conclusion: our current political framework is rigged to ensure that life *will not* prevail by protecting the same eco-criminals who are wilfully orchestrating this catastrophe. It is peculiar that the oversocialized inmates of the System who will recoil with melodramatic theatricality at the slightest mention of violence are wilfully participating in bringing about the single most catastrophic and wide-reaching act of violence in the Earth's history.

The Objective Factor?

In Linkola's 2004 interview with Virpi Adamsson, he further shocked audiences by claiming that although the media obsesses

---

Available at http://qvadrivivm.blogspot.com/2015/12/pentti-linkola-interview-from.html
[189] Pentti Linkola, "Against Highway Crime," in *Can Life Prevail?* (Kindle Edition).
[190] Pentti Linkola, "Letter to Hannu Hautala," in *A Collection of Essays by Pentti Linkola 1993 – 2006*, p. 21.

over war and terrorism as the worst evils on the Earth, these are merely "second class problems" compared to the true ongoing catastrophe of overpopulation and materialism.[191]

Yet even the media's moralistic condemnation of war is more apparent than real, as Linkola had the guts to mention in his "War, Man and Kosovo" that the global audience reacts to war breaking out anywhere within the world with the same voyeuristic gaze and raving cheers as a group of kids swarming in to watch a pair of schoolboys fighting during the middle of recess.[192] Nor are they even consistent regarding the tragedy of the loss of life, as any man between the ages of 18 and 40 is considered a legitimate target while the same man suddenly becomes a "civilian casualty" after exiting that age interval. Similarly, any woman is categorically considered to lie "outside" the fight, despite the fact that women have always formed a critical "backbone" of any war.

He noted in this essay, however, that even these gender biases pale in comparison with the media's failure to grasp the true significance of the (then recent) struggles in the Balkans: behind the façade of "ethnic conflict" lay the reality that "[t]he disgusting tragedy of overpopulation is strongly behind the wars of Yugoslavia."[193] In fact, he noted at the end of the same essay that while the naïve viewer estimated the damage of the conflict solely in terms of lives lost, the "guardian of the biosphere, who estimates the state of the world from the viewpoint of the population explosion and consumption of matter and energy" will realize that the energy and resource cost to reconstruct all the damaged buildings would continue to wage a silent war in the background, even as the media and world leaders applauded a successful peace treaty.[194]

---

[191] "Interview with Pentti Linkola 10-2-2004." Available at http://www.penttilinkola.com/pentti_linkola/ecofascism_writings/interview_10-2-2003

[192] Pentti Linkola, "War, Man and Kosovo," in *A Collection of Essays by Pentti Linkola 1993 – 2006*, p. 160.

[193] Ibid., p. 162.

[194] Ibid., p. 163.

In Linkola's 2011 interview with Francisco Martinez and Larissa Vanamo, he went even further by claiming that "the only problem" is overpopulation and that "all other problems are a consequence" of this single underlying issue. In this interview, he refused even to contemplate the interviewers' suggestion that the present enormous population could be sustained if lifestyles were only engineered to be more sustainable.[195] Nor was he willing to take any globalist response to the crisis seriously if it did not immediately begin with addressing overpopulation. In the same interview, he dismissed all U.N. meetings and all international conferences as "complete junk" if they do not satisfy this demand because, in Linkola's own words, overpopulation is the "only thing." When the interviewers expressed shock that he could insist that it could be the only issue among so many other seemingly-important ones, he clarified that all other issues (i.e., climate change, mass extinction etc.) were dependent upon this one. Linkola's view is therefore remarkably close to Kaczynski's own terminology of an objective factor to which all other factors of a situation are dependent. Yet whereas Kaczynski claimed this "principal factor" was technology, Linkola continues to insist that it is overpopulation.[196]

In his essay "Light Glimmers In The Population Explosion," he called overpopulation the "foremost" of all questions, since nothing short of the fate of the globe's life is determined by this one issue. The "definitive problem" and, ultimately, the "only integrally important problem on this planet" is simply how many bodies inhabit the Earth.[197] Similarly, in his 1993 "The Core Question of Life" he called "population explosion" the "problem of problems" and the "foundational difficulty of our existence" to which all other decisions (regarding secondary problems) must be proportioned if

---

[195] See Francisco Martinez Larissa Vanamo's 2011 interview "A Promenade with Pentti Linkola," http:// www.materialworldblog.com/ 2013/ 03/ invoking-the-apocalypse-a-promenade-with-pentti-linkola/

[196] See the first chapter of my book *The Philosophy of Ted Kaczynski* for a fuller discussion of the objective factor.

[197] Pentti Linkola, "Light Glimmers in the Population Explosion," in *A Collection of Essays by Pentti Linkola 1993 – 2006*, p. 147.

they are to be taken seriously. In this essay, he shot back against accusations that he himself overemphasizes this one issue while ignoring other equally-important ones by insisting that it's not even possible to think about it "too much." In fact, even thinking about it from one's first thought in the morning to one's final thought at night will not be enough, for the problem has grown to a size which is literally beyond the grasp of the human intellect to conceptualize.[198]

In his lengthy 2011 interview with the Finnish magazine *Quadrivium*, his interviewers similarly synopsized Linkola's entire philosophy as an extended meditation on this one issue:

> The big fat T-bone of each Linkola interview can be reduced to one word: overpopulation . . Nothing strains the planet as severely as the amount of human flesh and the level of production, manufacture and consumption dictated by this flesh, which is mirrored in the huge environmental disruptions of erosion, deforestation, emissions, ozone depletion, water, earth and air pollution and garbage disposal we face today.[199]

In the same interview, Linkola himself noted that focusing on overpopulation actually (to risk offending Finland's best ornithologist) kills two birds with one stone: isolating this one topic is both far more exhaustive and far simpler as an elucidation for the world's problems than the pseudo-explanations currently fashionable even among the bureaucracies tasked with diagnosing the origins of our current social and environmental woes. To use his own example, in response to critical water shortages around the Earth, the professional bureaucrats within the U.N. and other organizations go to ridiculous lengths to construct elaborately-overcomplicated euphemisms regarding the "misuse" or mismanagement of water resources, sometimes even falling back on

---

[198] Pentti Linkola, "The Core Question of Life," in *A Collection of Essays by Pentti Linkola 1993 – 2006*, p. 126.
[199] Pentti Linkola interview from *Quadrivium* #6 (2014): abridged version. Available at http://qvadrivivm.blogspot.com/2015/12/pentti-linkola-interview-from.html

far-fetched conspiracy theories to shift the blame elsewhere. Yet this is all unnecessary, because simply stating the obvious fact that there are too many people using a finite supply of water is forbidden by the laws of democratic equality and the cult of the unique, irreplaceable individual. Somehow, the longer explanation covers far less territory while the single word capturing the objective factor as such spans the entire global issue with a single word.

Because of his adherence to the concept of an "objective factor" rather than a plethora of disconnected explanations, Linkola's *Quadrivium* interviewers called attention to a feature of his writings which any perceptive reader will have noticed: unlike so many of his contemporaries, Linkola virtually never speaks of "capitalism," preferring the term "market economy" instead. What is all too easy to miss is that his refusal to allow his theories to be sucked up into the established system of Marxist dogma simply stemmed from his realization that Marx got the objective factor wrong: even if one theoretically could overcome capitalism, this would prove useless on ecological grounds if one left the problem of overpopulation intact or, worse still, provided the economic conditions for it to explode even further.

In the same interview, Linkola shocked the audience by asserting that if one truly succeeded in isolating the objective factor of overpopulation, one would realize that many acts which are virtually unanimously regarded as being indisputably moral are, in fact, grotesque violations of ecological law. He cited, for example, a hypothetical scenario in which a nation somewhere on the Earth overstepped its own ecological limits by completely exhausting its potable water reserves or abusing its own farmland's ability to produce food, even to the point of causing a nation-wide famine or water shortage. Controversial as it might be, he argued that the only ethical response is to allow such a nation to face the consequences of its own recklessness and short-sightedness. Of course, whenever such an event occurs today, the response is instead to perform Herculean leaps to cross the globe delivering water and food from afar, no matter how absurd the energy cost to do so might be. He claimed that understanding overpopulation to be the objective factor would allow one to realize that if a major earthquake or tsunami happens across the world, Finns *should not* invest any of their own resources and effort into sending aid, because this would only interfere with a natural procedure which humans would have no trouble allowing to run its course if it had affected, say, a group of field mice which had accidentally eaten their way through all of their natural food sources and were then left to face the natural consequences for doing so. Linkola argued that Nature's way of controlling overpopulation should be respected, no matter which species it happens to affect.

It is peculiar, then, that even though overpopulation is the greatest "war" of all time, though waged silently and imperceptibly in the background, it continues to be praised as a perverse "reign of peace." This distortion of the ultimate war into a *Pax Americana* of modernity can only be explained through our religious adherence to the dogma of materialism, something which is itself favoured only because it promises every man, woman, and child on the Earth a lifetime of mall-shopping, fast food-munching, soda pop-guzzling, and celebrity tabloid-chasing bliss. In fact, the two problems of materialism and overpopulation cited in his 2004 interview are arguably two sides of the same coin, since the only reason why so many humans are brought into the world anymore is to be given the opportunity to be consumers, as this is the sole "basic human right" which all can agree they are entitled to have. This mass destruction hard-wired into materialism/overpopulation goes on being endorsed even by those who claim to be pacifists, simply because they cannot see the birthmark which the Mind of Nature can see.

Chapter Two
Nature Does Exist:
Linkola's Metaphysics

Shrooming with Demons

In early 2019, Alex Jones shocked the world with an abrupt, glorious return to the Internet after being banned from all the major technological platforms the previous year. It was difficult not to shed a tear to see an old friend hobble back into the cyber-town after an extended absence, with many remarking that, regardless of whether one agrees with any of his conspiracy theories, the Internet never was quite the same since "Uncle Alex" disappeared.

Jones' lengthy extravaganza on *Joe Rogan Experience #1255* did not disappoint. Whereas it was traditionally supposed that "legendary events" required generations of time to elapse before being canonized as such, Jones' four hours and 40 minutes of magic on the podcast instantly obtained mythic-level fame, literally within minutes of being uploaded.

Arguably the single most bizarre moment of the entire rambling discussion lay in Jones' claim that the latest trend sweeping Silicon Valley elites was to ritually consume certain hallucinogenic drugs which were known to open a pathway of communication to mysterious disembodied voices which might occasionally speak profound truths. Even David Icke, the single most bizarre intellectual of our era, has repeatedly attributed much of his own idiosyncratic philosophy to a divine message that "Only love exists, everything else is illusion" which was narrated directly into his mind by a spirit with an Australian woman's accent as he lay in a daze for hours in the Brazilian rainforest after ingesting one such drug.

Although bizarre on the surface, Jones's claim that it is not only pariah Reptilian conspiracy theorists but the most powerful billionaires in the world who have found inspiration in this venue is not so bizarre as it might seem. This proposition, in fact, fits all too

141

well with the culture of an area in which people have reportedly turned to drinking unfiltered stream water in a desperate attempt to get the tiniest competitive advantage over one another. One *Fortune* article lamented that the trend was putting public health at risk in the name of pseudo-science and conspiracy theories:

> After his widely-maligned startup Juicero shut down in September, founder Doug Evans immediately hopped on a much more obscure health trend. While at Burning Man, he went on a 10-day cleanse drinking only "raw" water – that is, water that is unfiltered and untreated in any way. Now, the company that supplied Evans' water, Live Water, is among those attracting attention and investment from Silicon Valley's health-conscious elite. Enthusiasm for "raw water" is also, health experts say, spreading dangerous misinformation and discredited conspiracy theories that could put public health at risk.[200]

Another *Medium* article, aptly-titled "Why is Silicon Valley So Damn Sad (and Suicidal)?", noted that drinking stream water was simply one more item on a lengthy bucket list of bizarre stunts which might hold the key to leading a person to "figure it out," whatever "it" might be. Somehow, though, the one thing not included on this list was the one thing that matters most: maintaining one's mental health:

> People here — in The Valley — are drinking untreated stream water, the same ones that tout sane sciences and daily mindfulness habits, because they both may provide the keys to "figuring it out," whatever out may be. But why are so many self-pillaging? It's simple, really . . . Everyone seems hellbent on building the next YouTube, or Facebook, or Instagram, or Lyft, or have been hired on by those who yearn to, working their staff down to the proverbial bone — bone marrow, that is. It's a culture of scarcity; a community

---

[200] David Morris, "Silicon Valley's Next Big Idea: Untreated Drinking Water," *Fortune*, 01-01-2018.

where there's never enough success, money, time, not of anything. So, therefore, acquiring a fuck-ton of said something is of the utmost importance. Above all. But at what cost, what's the price tag for those lofty salary earnings, social capital gains, and satiated scarcities? Well, frankly, it appears to be their mental health.[201]

Within the global industry, high-profile names have similarly turned to mining tricks from the seemingly pre-rational Occult Tradition by submitting their own bodies to an ascetic mortification of the flesh in order to beseech the figurative gods of greed with the chance to hit a worldly jackpot by scoring the idea for "the next big thing." In 2018, it was reported that Pavel Durov, widely referred to as the "Mark Zuckerberg of Russia" after founding *VK*, allegedly embarked on an extended abstinence from *all food* in order to find the golden thread in the labyrinth to an original idea which apparently had not yet materialized from following any other less extreme pathway:

> The founder of Telegram has given up eating food in the hope of coming up with new ideas . . . He is known for his dietary restraint, having given up caffeine, meat, drugs, alcohol and fast food over 15 years ago. Last month he revealed he was limiting the food he eats to fish and seafood, but on Thursday he announced he had given up food altogether. "This month I'm trying something more radical, with consuming no food at all," he wrote on his Telegram channel. "I've been on a water fast for the last six days and am feeling great so far. Since zero food consumption improves clarity of thought, I also got many things done."[202]

---

[201] Matt Charnock, "Why is Silicon Valley So Damn Sad (and Suicidal?)," *Medium*, 20-07-2018.
[202] Anthony Cuthbertson, "Telegram Founder Gives Up Eating to Come up with Great Ideas," *Independent*, 06-06-2019.

The same article provided a disclaimer explicitly warning readers "do not try this at home":

> Such an extreme fast like the one Mr Durov is undertaking is not recommended by medical professionals and there is little evidence to suggest it could increase creativity. The NHS warns that even intermittent fasting comes with numerous health risks, such as heartburn, and can also trigger eating disorders.[203]

In other words, rationalist-materialist billionaires within the technological industry today are literally fasting like Medieval Catholic nuns with the hope of being granted a mystical vision from the Beyond in return, basically hoping that their game-changing idea will materialize out of nowhere like a secular equivalent of Catherine of Sienna's *Dialogo* with God himself![204] Nor is this sort of spiritual exercise unique to Christianity, as the Hindu Tradition contains numerous stories about devotees being granted bizarre favours from the gods simply because they completed extreme ascetic exercises in the deities' honour, despite the fact that these people were themselves evil and their requests were nothing short of ridiculous.[205] Even in our era of postmodernist scepticism, Dan Brown's *Lost Symbol* portrayed the novel's villain as enduring an extended fast as part of his final initiation into the highest levels of Black Magic and the Global Illuminati.[206]

By these standards, it is perhaps not so weird after all to think that the world's wealthiest and most powerful CEO's have turned to tripping on hallucinogens in order to ring the spiritual telephone number to consult freaking *demons* for advice on how to become even richer. Whereas the story of Faust selling his soul to Satan in exchange for worldly success represented the ultimate

---

[203] Ibid.
[204] Caterina da Siena, *Libro della divina dottrina: Dialogo della divina provvidenza* (Kindle Edition).
[205] Murty, Sudha, "Brahma's Folly" in *The Man from the Egg* (Haryana: Puffin, 2017).
[206] Dan Brown, *The Lost Symbol* (London: Corgi, 2009).

moral scandal in the Renaissance and Late Middle Ages, today ringing up evil spirits in order to score a massive financial fortune for oneself has simply become one more gimmick on a bucket list to be pursued with the casual attitude of "don't knock it 'til you try it."

From Linkola's perspective, however, one must ask whether this is not just a purified attempt to directly consult the Mind of Progress itself, reduced to a disembodied voice dictating the direction society must proceed by spoon-feeding detailed instructions to a group of billionaires who are more than financially capable of executing these commands in the real world, however far-fetched or harmful they might be. The greatest irony about democracy, in other words, is that it is no longer the case even that the elites are able to make their own decisions out of self-interest while pretending to let the democratic masses "speak for themselves." The helm of the ship has effectively fallen out of any human person's hands and has been handed over to voices which belong to no person at all and can only be summoned by dropping out of Earthly reality and abusing highly-potent drugs to enter the Twilight Zone.

In fact, the Mind of Progress's domination of the procedure is so extreme that it has recursively dictated the a priori conditions for how the ritual must be performed even before saying a single word as such within this forum. One must bear in mind how bizarre it is that even communicating with demons can no longer just occur by visiting a human psychic located in a weird office in a shady neighbourhood within the city, as had traditionally been done. No, now it must be performed on purely materialistic grounds, by consuming a physical substance which stimulates certain regions of the brain to release the same types of chemicals emitted while dreaming, as Joe Rogan alleged during his podcast talk with Jones. Only this way can one remain in good standing with the Mind of Progress's demands to respect the ideology of materialism even while re-enacting the most absurd of spiritual rituals.

Golden State Nightmare

Under Linkola's view, the ultimate form of madness is the delusion of trying to coerce ecological reality to fit a linguistic chimera retrieved from the Mind of Progress. Doing so inevitably leads to insanity because a constant state of cognitive dissonance is required to pretend to *not* see that any attempt to do so ends in failure. In this sense, the Mind of Progress is not only to be opposed to the Mind of Nature, but even to the perfect cogito embodied in Descartes's God. Whereas the Cartesian God is infinitely more rational than the human cogito (i.e., the human cogito is imperfect and fallible but God's cogito is perfect and infallible), the Mind of Progress is *even more ecologically irrational* than its most deranged adherents, which is not a small accomplishment at all!

One must openly ask whether California's progressive political machine is simply the antithetical inverse-mirror image of Linkola's Green Police, an institution whose sole rationale lies in suspending human biases in order to directly embody the Mind of Progress in its purity regardless of the personal whims of the humans who are forced to live under its mandates. In other words, Linkola's proposal to suspend democratic compromise in favour of "absolute ideals" is something which has quite literally been implemented already within "liberal utopias" like California, only with the Mind of Progress rather than the Mind of Nature at the helm of the experiment. If we have already suspended real democratic input from the masses in order to force through a dogmatic set of (pseudo-)ethical laws whose origin very well might lie in voices rambling during hallucinogenic tripping episodes, how could one possibly object to doing ostensibly the same thing in order to save the Earth through obeying the mandates of Ecology, the ultimate rational science?

One must bear in mind that whereas the Mind of Nature is exclusively dominated by non-linguistic ecological laws, the Mind of Progress is solely populated by linguistified, humanistic chimeras whose virtue is precisely that they are impossible. Catchwords such as universal automation, sex positivity, open borders, bloated bureaucracies, extreme government regulation, never-ending real estate bubbles, and the decriminalization of property and drug offenses might as well be a set of pseudo-Platonic Ideas mined directly from the Mind of Progress and valued solely for their complete lack of ecological viability. With its fanatical commitment to forcing through every one of these policies with no regard for the protest of ordinary voters within the state, the progressive machine of California has enacted a direct short circuit between societal organization and the Mind of Progress by executing these mandates without any regard for the minor inconvenience that virtually everyone's living conditions radically deteriorate as a result of doing so.

It is supremely ironic that a state which was once associated with stereotypical images of "radical environmentalism" (such as in David Klass's aptly-titled 1994 novel *California Blue*) has actually become a purified microcosm for environmental counter-sense. It is peculiar for the self-righteous there to pat themselves on the back for banning plastic straws from coffee shops or installing solar panels on their corporate headquarters' roofs while simultaneously being responsible in one form or another for some 10% of global electricity consumption through propping up the beast of the world wide web which John Michael Greer once called the single most energy-intensive piece of infrastructure ever constructed by humans.[207] Even more humorous is the claim that living conditions within San Francisco, Los Angeles, and even the smaller cities within the state live up to the ideal of "ecological utopias" just because one might occasionally find a complicated array of recycling bins where one would normally expect trash cans. Zizek noted in his 2014 *Absolute Recoil* that these bins come with instructions and lists of exceptions so detailed that it can take a person half an hour of reading and serious thinking just to throw away one's garbage,[208] yet one can only suspect that all of this complication merely serves as a way to distract residents and visitors from noticing that the massive homeless camps which the cities' own real estate bubbles had created were providing the conditions for rat populations to explode in size, even to the point where the bubonic plague and other medieval diseases are making a

---

[207] John Michael Greer, "The Death of the Internet: A Pre-Mortem", in *Archdruid Report*, Vol. 9 (Chicago: Founders House, 2018), p. 129.
[208] Slavoj Zizek, *Absolute Recoil* (London: Verso, 2014), p. 364.

comeback within the state as the author writes these words. One must resist the urge to openly laugh at the tragedy that this is a place where one can act like getting rid of trash cans and plastic straws in exchange for the Black Death and extreme carbon dioxide pollution from data centres is a good trade-off, let alone an example for the rest of the world for what "green living" should ideally look like. More and more people have begun to notice the birthmark, though few have the courage to admit it.

Even on an economic level, the state embodies ecological counter-sense as a matter of official policy. Once again, extreme real estate inflation has created the single most shameful homelessness crisis in the world, driving people to float on makeshift rafts outside the city as though images from the dystopian Sci-Fi film *Water World* were being fulfilled like Nostradamus's prophecies. Unfortunately, this was all entirely unnecessary, as this housing crisis was driven by the presence of a set of Silicon Valley corporations which have driven countless families within their own communities to live on the street but have never made an honest profit themselves due to extremely-high energy costs and a business model which largely offers services for free in exchange for establishing a lifelong addiction among the entire global population. Worse yet, these financial losers continue to nominally "grow" at unsustainable rates, simply as a result of receiving massive investment inputs from a handful of very big fish among the highest ranks of the financial elite, as well as through hopelessly unrealistic stock value appraisals and enormous loans from the usury industry. A corporation which steals ordinary workers' right to housing and three meals a day yet never makes a single dime of profit for itself cannot be honestly described as anything except ecological impossibility.

In early 2009, Fox News's Glenn Beck aired a notorious special titled *The War Room* as part of a broader meditation on the possibilities for just how bad the future might become under the combination of the incipient Great Recession and Obama's mishandling of the situation through espousing "socialist" reforms which Beck promised would only bankrupt a nation which was already trillions of dollars in debt. Without question, the most controversial segment featured Gerald Celente of the *Trends Journal* (a frequent guest on the Alex Jones Show as well) who claimed that rising poverty and economic instability would eventually drive America's major cities to resemble the Third World slums found in Mexico City and Calcutta (to use his own examples), in which anyone with wealth would be forced to live behind high walls and hire private body guards to escort him or her safely among the impoverished masses in order to ward off would-be kidnappers, robbers, and ransom agents who would swarm after the scent of gold like sharks smelling blood in the water.

Although the segment was widely ridiculed, even inspiring Colbert to run his own *Armageddon Room* special encouraging viewers to stock up on soybeans on grounds that this would replace the dollar as economic currency after a coming financial collapse, a short ten years later none other than Fox News itself began airing reports that living conditions in San Francisco had deteriorated to the point where wealthy citizens had turned to hiring private cops to protect neighbourhoods which the police had more or less abandoned to criminals to plunder at will. Even the tabloid gossip-cast *Inside Edition*, hardly anyone's idea of a conservative media outlet, decided to openly test how quickly a car loaded with goods visible to pedestrians on the street would be broken into and stolen within San Francisco. Within no time, the opportunists arrived and exercised their newfound privilege to take other people's stuff at will, with no regard for the fact that the misdeed was being recorded by the television cameras for international audiences.

Celente's only error lay in assuming that this nightmare scenario which sounded laughable just one short decade earlier would organically materialize as a matter of inevitable historical forces of Western decline. It is all the more depressing that this sorry state of affairs was, in fact, consciously legislated into existence by a set of bureaucrats who prided themselves on being "more enlightened than thou." It was precisely through figuratively granting "The Mind of Shaun King"[209] a blank check to dictate the

---

[209] Shaun King is in one sense simply the most faithful adherent to renouncing his own will for the sake of embodying whatever truths the Mind of Progress holds. I am not literally claiming, of course, that Shaun King legislated these policies

city's policies on grounds of perfect conformity with the currently-trending code of social justice that such rampant social *injustice* was institutionalized.

For example, Shaun King's fantasy of a state where politicians clamp down not on criminals but rather on "police brutality" itself has basically been realized as a matter of official state policy in San Francisco, as the city has removed their own cops' ability to crack down on any burglary under $950 on grounds that "punishing petty theft is the true injustice." The shopkeepers forced to foot the bill for constant shoplifting are expected to take one for the team by paying a financial tithe from out of their own pockets to keep the Religion of Progress rolling along, despite the fact that they themselves gain absolutely no benefit whatsoever from sending their money to the Mind of Progress, a religious scammer who has put even the very worst prosperity gospel televangelists and Dark Age popes to shame.

King's justification for this suspension of any meaningful action on the part of cops is, bizarrely, justified on grounds that they cannot be trusted to do the right thing because their minds just might contain the wrong thoughts. In fact, King literally claimed that cops' true crimes lay not in performing questionable actions but, rather, in having flawed imaginations. In a 2016 article titled "It Must Become Illegal for Police to Act Violently Using Only Their Inaccurate Imaginations," King insisted that "[p]olice are being taught not to act on the reality of a situation, but on the imagined possibility of a threat." Inevitably, the "imagined threat" which King claimed was buried deep on the inside of their skulls was racial in nature. By claiming that the problem is ultimately that cops just might be thinking the wrong thoughts about people on the basis of race at any moment of the day, King has literally argued that a new Orwellian thought police force should be instituted to monitor the lower-order cops from one level up, "regularly screening police for racial biases" in order to ensure that only cops with clean imaginations will be allowed to roam the streets.[210] We can only

---

himself.

[210] Shaun King, "It must become illegal for police to act violently using only their inaccurate imaginations," *New York Daily News*, 23-08-2016.

suspect, though, that these "imagination cops" will soon require their own regulators to screen out whether they themselves are racist too. Eventually, the screener of the screener of the screener of the screener of the screener of the cop will become a coveted, highly-paid "job" within the bloated bureaucracy of self-righteous wokeness, even as the ground level of the city becomes filthier, more crime-ridden, and more dangerous than ever before.

In another 2016 article titled "Changing the Culture of Police Brutality Needs to Happen on the State and Local Level," King went as far as to suggest that "wokeness" should be made into a job requirement for the police:

> Righteous, fair, woke, informed men and women from all races, ethnicities, religions and nationalities must become police officers and prosecutors all over this country. I understand why we don't want to be a part of the system, but until we do, we will always be fighting the system from the outside in.[211]

In other words, the solution is to only allow card-carrying social justice warriors to become police officers, though one cannot help suspecting that this might just be a desperate call for unemployed recent graduates with PhDs in Postcolonial Intersectional Queer Feminist Critical Race Studies to find jobs *somewhere*, if only as the same cops they spent their graduate school days viciously protesting against. The city of San Francisco has proven, however, that this calibration of individual minds is actually unnecessary, since the bureaucratic machine of the city has already mandated "wokeness" at an impersonal institutional level through directly embodying the Mind of Progress in a short circuit between abstract ideal and political machine.

In a 2018 *Intercept* article titled "Despite Liberalizing Marijuana Laws, the War on Drugs Still Targets People of Color," Shaun King similarly dismissed the entire war on drugs as nothing more than an excuse "to let cops be racist" in disguise, with the

---

[211] Shaun King, "Changing the culture of police brutality needs to happen on the state and local level," *New York Daily News*, 07-09-2016.

implication that if you don't want junkies shooting up heroin in front of your kids as they walk to school over filthy and dangerous pathways, you must just dislike people with a different skin tone from yours (even if these junkies are the same "race" which you happen to be):

> THE HUGE FAILURE we know as the "war on drugs" is back in full force under the Trump administration, thanks in no small part to Attorney General Jeff Sessions's retrograde tough-on-crime approach to drugs. It's not hard to understand why someone like Sessions, with a history of racism, would love the war on drugs: In reality, it was always a war on a very particular set of people — and you can probably guess who those people are.[212]

It is peculiar for King to act as though drug laws have never been tougher, though, since his fantasy of "ending the war on drugs" has already been fully realized within San Francisco. Yet this has only made dangerous narcotics dealers into a new caste of "untouchables" who exist above the law in a bizarre reversal of the traditional Indian meaning of that term, as their immunity to the slightest action from the police has effectively elevated them to a uniquely privileged status within the society. The old adage that "crime doesn't pay" has been fully reversed: here, one gains special privileges over law-abiding citizens precisely through shamelessly breaking the law, even to the point of committing widespread manslaughter by driving junkies to die by overdose just to raise one's own personal fortune.

Although Shaun King's humanistic abstractions of "social justice," "racial wokeness," and "the end to police brutality" reliably catch fire on Twitter among his countless devoted followers who prove their unceasing commitment to doing the "hard work of radical political activism" by tapping their thumbs on their smartphone screens a few times per day to retweet him, the transition from the social media realm of technological

---

[212] Shaun King, "Despite Liberalizing Marijuana Laws, the War on Drugs Still Targets People of Color," *The Intercept*, 26-01-2018.

linguistification to the material world of ecological reality only generated a dystopia in which armed robbery and massive open drug markets were forced down the citizens' throats, despite the minor inconvenience that the democratic masses were submitted to *even more suffering* as a result. It is peculiar that the same secularist rationalists who scoff at the Traditionalist Roman Catholic concept of offering up one's sufferings to God in order to grow spiritually through ascetic purification would effectively demand the same thing of their citizens, since suffering for the Mind of Progress has literally become a religious obligation in these places.

Although few have the courage to openly challenge the Mind of Progress with words, far more people have voiced their opposition simply through voting with their feet. The ongoing mass exodus from the state proves that leftists are already dogmatically clinging to the Mind of Progress even in the face of widespread misery. For a resident of the city, walking in other people's faeces, dodging heroin needles on the sidewalk, enduring daily car break-ins, and living on makeshift boats to avoid paying extravagantly-overpriced rents are all just necessary sacrifices for the cause. For those with a sane mind, these are collective expressions of insanity which are doubly tragic for the simple fact that ecological conditions have actually been worsened precisely through all the eco-crimes committed in this Mecca of Intersectional Wokeness.

Unfortunately, the secular prophets of virtue have not remained content to ruin only their own state but have turned to exporting their misery to the rest of the nation and, in fact, to the rest of the globe. It is peculiar that the centre committed to the task of automating other people's jobs out of existence forever can claim to be uniquely committed to social justice while submitting millions of voiceless, anonymous Others in distant flyover states and Third World nations to the ultimate injustice by depriving them of their very ability to work, as well as their access to food, potable water, and shelter.

Nor is the loss of income and meaningful work the only disease of modernity which they have exported across state lines in order to financially benefit themselves. Traditionally, California was only one of two states in the nation (along with New

Hampshire, of all places) in which the production of hard-core pornography had been legalized. It is no exaggeration to say that what they have really been exporting to the rest of the world is just so much artificially-induced erectile dysfunction, an embarrassing form of physical suffering which must simply be accepted through a "heroic ascetic mortification of the flesh" because the ideology of sex positive wokeness has been willed by the Mind of Progress itself.

California has also exported social media addiction to the rest of the world despite the fact that it has been repeatedly proven to cause depression and anxiety, in addition to simply wasting an enormous amount of time. It is tragic to think that millennials who have already passed away unexpectedly had probably wasted their entire lives scrolling down a newsfeed looking for something shocking or funny which could be shared just to get a bucket of likes from people they don't even know. Many hold the ambition to stop using social media someday in order to start "really living life," only to find that the end of one's life often arrives sooner than the end of one's addiction.

It is all the more laughable to claim that this pseudo-democratic state of affairs has realized the ideal of giving unbridled freedom of choice to the people while simply mandating this institutionalized suffering solely on grounds of conformity with the Mind of Progress. The Mind of Progress actually makes us less free while celebrating license, and causes us more pain while worshipping pleasure.

Universal Basic Dignity

Despite the fact that he has already dropped out of the presidential race by the time the author writes these words,[213] Andrew Yang's failed campaign has still provided a useful opportunity to respond to the negative consequences of following the commands of the Mind of Progress (especially those exported from his own Silicon Valley to the rest of the world) which are otherwise accepted

---

[213] February 29, 2020.

unquestioningly by the media and academic intelligentsia. We will profit from briefly examining his proposal for Universal Basic Income in order to question whether this is a dogma from the Mind of Progress or an ecologically-valid truth from the Mind of Nature.

Yang distinguished himself from the other 2020 Democrat Party hopefuls through an unusual willingness to speak plainly about the central issue of our era by recognizing that it was unemployment caused by technological automation (especially within the Rust Belt states), rather than "racism," "xenophobia," or a Russian conspiracy which drove Donald Trump's unprecedented victory in 2016. In fact, Yang's primary criticism of Trump is that his response to this problematic trend has not been nearly radical enough. Bypassing euphemisms about China or the southern border, Yang simply cut to the chase by warning the masses that the robots have stolen their jobs and are currently creeping up on stealing what few ones remain. Although the automation of millions of truck driver, radiology, call centre, retail, and low-level legal jobs supposedly nears the point of completion as the author writes these words, Yang warns the voters that it would be useless to try to resist this "inevitable" historical trend. In fact, opposing it outright is doubly unnecessary for the simple fact that it holds nearly-utopian potential to make a better future, provided the right person figures out how to break into the gold mine to claim the prize waiting for us on the inside.

Yang noted, though, that this positive outcome can never be unlocked by the industry itself because capitalist market forces are intrinsically hard-wired to pursue their own financial self-interest regardless of the social or ecological consequences of doing so. The only viable option is to seize executive control of the political realm in order to provide responsible oversight for this new type of economy which is materializing for the first time ever. Only if this is accomplished can one hope to ensure that the masses are not left behind in the forward march of technological progress. The solution is therefore like a treasure buried inside a vault which can only be accessed by an extrinsic agent. Pandora's Box can never open itself, since only a coordinated political program executed by the president himself can place humanistic ethical values over raw numerical profit considerations.

For Yang, this can only mean one thing: taxing the enormous industrial productivity of the technological industries in order to distribute shares of this wealth in the form of a Universal Basic Income check mailed out to each adult citizen of the United States every month. Yet he was careful to note that the purpose of doing so would not only be to ensure that basic survival needs such as access to food, housing, and potable water are met. Universal Basic Income would also provide the masses with a financial subsidy to allow them to pursue their own personal interests. During his viral appearance on *Joe Rogan Experience #1245*, Yang himself provided the example that a hypothetical family in a small town in the Midwest would be able to play around with launching a bakery if they received their UBI check each month; in the absence of that financial security, they would remain unable to gamble on such an idea.

A perceptive reader may have realized that we should simply cut the euphemisms and acknowledge that what Yang is really proposing is that each citizen be guaranteed the basic human right to go through the Power Process, even if it is only through the most trivial of surrogate activities. There is, in fact, nothing in Andrew Yang's proposal which was not already predicted by Kaczynski decades ago in the so-called Unabomber Manifesto. In paragraphs 173 and 174, he warned that continued technological development would eventually make all human labour superfluous. Deprived of the ability even to work, humans would find themselves unable to justify their existence on grounds of their productivity or talents, since competition with the machines in either category would have long since become impossible. While it is certain that continued "technological innovation" will eventually make human work impossible to preserve, it is much less clear what will be done with these useless masses whose survival needs will quickly acquire the status of a financial burden upon the System. If the elites are ruthless, they will simply exterminate the masses in order to save the resources which would have gone to feeding and housing them for "more worthy causes." If, however, the elites are "soft-hearted liberals" they will at least ensure that people are given surrogate activities to pass the time even though the ability to do any truly meaningful work relevant to survival would have long since disappeared. Although the inmates of this situation might get to experience pleasure in some base and stupid sense of the word, they could never be free, as they'd drop down to the status of domesticated animals. The 174th paragraph is worth quoting in full:

> On the other hand it is possible that human control over the machines may be retained. In that case the average man may have control over certain private machines of his own, such as his car or his personal computer, but control over large systems of machines will be in the hands of a tiny elite—just as it is today, but with two differences. Due to improved techniques the elite will have greater control over the masses; and because human work will no longer be necessary the masses will be superfluous, a useless burden on the system. If the elite is ruthless they may simply decide to exterminate the mass of humanity. If they are humane they may use propaganda or other psychological or biological techniques to reduce the birth rate until the mass of humanity becomes extinct, leaving the world to the elite. Or, if the elite consists of soft- hearted liberals, they may decide to play the role of good shepherds to the rest of the human race. They will see to it that everyone's physical needs are satisfied, that all children are raised under psychologically hygienic conditions, that everyone has a wholesome hobby to keep him busy, and that anyone who may become dissatisfied undergoes "treatment" to cure his "problem." Of course, life will be so purposeless that people will have to be biologically or psychologically engineered either to remove their need for the power process or to make them "sublimate" their drive for power into some harmless hobby. These engineered human beings may be happy in such a society, but they most certainly will not be free. They will have been reduced to the status of domestic animals.[214]

In other words, distributing shares of Universal Basic Income is simply a means to an end to ensure that everyone retains the right to Universal Basic *Dignity*, as Yang is perceptive enough to know that the true crime of unregulated automation would be to deprive humans of any opportunity to go through the Power Process. In this sense, Yang is simply the "soft-hearted liberal" among the technological elites which Kaczynski warned about decades ago, someone who ran a presidential campaign on the promise that surrendering any right to labour on serious tasks will be compensated for just because we'd get to keep our surrogate activities.

Universal Basic Income for the Rich

Although it is somewhat admirable that Yang has called for people to maintain a minimal share of Universal Basic Dignity, it is quite troubling that he has assumed that fighting for the right to work is useless because the technological trend towards automation is "inevitable." Anyone who scratches the surface of the problem will quickly find that the disappearance of work is only "selectively inevitable" and overwhelmingly targets people on the basis of class. In a 2019 appearance on the Hermitix podcast, John Michael Greer noted the irony that although it would be quite easy to automate investment banker and stockbroker jobs out of existence, enormous effort is instead dumped into cracking the mystery to engineer self-driving trucks which don't kill too many innocent people on the way to saving corporations a little more money. Needless to say, even the best efforts to do so will inevitably result in a heap of corpses reminiscent of the mass graves of the Black Death. As the body count from self-driving cars has already begun to tick up,[215] we can only imagine how many more human lives must be needlessly sacrificed to the Mind of Progress to answer its demand

---

[214] Ted Kaczynski, *Industrial Society and Its Future* (Scottsdale: Fitch & Madison, 2019), para. 174.
[215] Daisuke Wakabayashi, "Self-Driving Uber Car Kills Pedestrian in Arizona, Where Robots Roam," *New York Times*, 3-19-2019

to automate away only working-class people's jobs, no matter how preposterous or dysfunctional the effort might be. It is peculiar that the same secularist elites who scoff at the medieval hagiographies of Catholic martyrs who died in the name of religion would find no trouble demanding that a certain percentage of their fellow humans take one for the team by letting the suicide bomb of self-driving trucks carry them away to an early funeral as "martyrs for the Religion of Progress," a demand for self-sacrifice in which both you and I very well might find ourselves involuntarily included someday soon.

Few have the guts to mention the inconvenient fact, however, that the privileged within corporate and financial aristocracies have already been granted a universal basic income check even after their jobs had been automated away, yet they have also gotten to keep their nominal jobs simply in order to maintain their dignity as "functional, hard-working contributors to the good of society." Wall Street veteran and best-selling financial author Jim Rickards has provided one of the more memorable examples to demonstrate that real work has already basically disappeared from the daily routines of those who hold prestigious jobs within the present-day economy. As recently as a 2019 interview with Silver Bullion TV, Rickards claimed that at this point almost all of the trading on the New York Stock Exchange is carried out by electronic brains running on autopilot.[216] In his 2014 bestseller *The Death of Money: The Coming Collapse of the International Monetary System,* he recounted that during his days working at Long Term Capital Management, a trendy New York hedge fund, "showing up to work" largely just meant that the employees would amuse themselves and each other with playing golf while the company A.I. handled the trading for them. At least at the beginning, the machine was so much better at generating profits that it would have been pointless for the humans to interfere with its apparently-flawless execution. Worse still, the machine's obvious superiority to fallible human minds created a perverse incentive for

---

[216] See Jim Rickards interview on his new book *Aftermath,* "James Rickards Exclusive - Prepare Now to Survive the Aftermath of the Next Global Financial Crisis", available at https://www.youtube.com/watch?v=ojuNdko_Bw4

passivity to literally become one's ethical duty. One's "job" was to pass the time away in hitting a tiny white ball around a golf course because interfering with the A.I. would have ruined the entire operation. Far from "rewarding those who work hard," the System progressively makes human labour into a new sin which must be repressed with mindless surrogate activities.

In other words, automation has already obviated the need for human agency even within the vast majority of "meaningful, fulfilling careers" which are precisely the jobs which supposedly require creative thinking rather than mindless repetition. Kaczynski noted in the 40th paragraph of the Manifesto, for example, that holding down a "respectable middle-class job" does not require a person to exert himself or herself in any serious physical or even intellectual sense, since at this point virtually all the real work is handled by machines. All that is truly required is the modest effort to show up to work on time and, above all, submit oneself completely to obedience to the System's rules:

> In modern industrial society only minimal effort is necessary to satisfy one's physical needs. It is enough to go through a training program to acquire some petty technical skill, then come to work on time and exert the very modest effort needed to hold a job. The only requirements are a moderate amount of intelligence and, most of all, simple OBEDIENCE. If one has those, society takes care of one from cradle to grave.[217]

According to Rickards, the final outcome of allowing this runaway train to drive itself with no human engineer at the helm was that it nearly crashed the American Economy in 1998. He notes that Long Term Capital Management required receiving a major bailout from the rest of Wall Street to prevent a domino effect from claiming still more carnage among New York hedge funds.[218]

---

[217] Ted Kaczynski, *Industrial Society and Its Future*, in *Technological Slavery* (Scottsdale: Fitch & Madison, 2019), para. 40.
[218] Jim Rickards, *The Road to Ruin: The Global Elites' Secret Plan for the Next Financial Crisis* (Hudson: Penguin, 2016).

Although this strategy worked in the short term, crisis merely resurfaced ten years later in the more widely-known 2008 financial crash which launched the Great Recession. By this point, however, the problem had exploded in size far beyond the scope witnessed in 1998. Rickards claims that this event contradicted expectation among the highest ranks of the financial elite because they presumed that outdated equilibrium models were sufficient to predict the behaviour of the market; on the contrary, Rickards breaks with the conventional wisdom by arguing that the resources of Complexity Theory are required to explain why the size of the problem increased exponentially rather than linearly relative to increases in the size of the system itself. Whereas in 1998 one hedge fund required a bailout from Wall Street to prevent a full-scale economic crash, in 2008 it was Wall Street itself which required a bailout to prevent an even ghastlier outcome. In this case, the Fed stepped in to provide the bailout which was so massive that effectively no other agent could shoulder the burden for it. Rickards has gained notoriety in recent years for warning that this cycle will repeat once again sometime around the year 2018. This time, however, it will be the Fed itself which will require a bailout; at this point, seeking out a "bigger fish" to provide the funds may very well prove futile.

Regardless of the truth value of Rickards' predictions regarding a coming financial crash, one thing which is certain is that his experience at Long Term Capital Management provides a chilling testament to how renouncing human agency in favour of technical efficiency has led to unpredictable effects, many of which would have been dismissed as flatly impossible at the time their origins were unwittingly set in place by the human pseudo-agents who have been entrusted a task far above their pay grade. Yet even more simply, Rickards provides just one of countless examples of the glaring double standard inherent in forbidding working class labourers from the slightest protest against letting their jobs disappear, while artificially rigging the System to ensure that high-ranking corporate office workers get to keep their jobs simply in order to allow them the dignity of going to work each day, even if the latter literally means playing golf on the company's dime.

Jim Rickards' example has basically proven that Andrew Yang's call for universal basic income as a safety measure to allow humans to keep going through the Power Process even after their jobs had been "inevitably" automated out of existence has basically already been granted for salaried employees within the usury industry, figures for whom the surrogate activity of showing up to work just to hit a tiny white ball around a golf course all day literally became their "job" even after their line of work was automated away by A.I. Although no one has had the guts to admit it, these people were allowed to keep their jobs afterwards simply because it was recognized that forcing them to sit around all day with nothing to do would amount to a crime against their humanity. The greatest natural sin, as Bronze Age Pervert realized, is to deprive an organism of its ability to clear enough space to develop its abilities or, in Kaczynski's terms, to deprive someone of the ability to go through the Power Process.

It is deeply troubling to realize that this sympathy has not been extended to working class labourers, since it was presumed either that they had no feelings at all or that they gained no personal dignity from doing "lowly jobs" anyway. The only solution the media would entertain on the rare occasions the topic was discussed at all was that anyone laid off at a factory should simply "suck it up," borrow six figures of student loan money to go to a university, and rise up to a "real job" which would consist of sitting on one's ass in some air-conditioned corporate office setting. What they failed to mention, of course, was that this far-fetched attempt to leap across class lines into the corporate aristocracy would only be remotely possible if that person first abandoned all of his or her customs in exchange for the values and social code of the wealthy. In other words, the media has quite literally mandated a class-based genocide in which lower-class labourers would be forced out of existence, either through losing their livelihoods and dying early deaths due to a lack of financial resources or through magically transforming into wealthy people through harshly repudiating everything that made them who they were before. Though virtually no one has the guts to admit it, the universities' degradation into social justice indoctrination camps has simply institutionalized this mandate for lower-class college students to prove their renunciation of their own customs through outdoing one another in theatrical displays of public hatred against their own backgrounds. It is quite sad to think that one's "ethical duty" on a college campus today is to harshly condemn every rural American as a racist, misogynist, homophobe bigot whose very existence is the cause of all the problems in the world, simply out of the hope of being granted a high-paying job among the elites in exchange for throwing one's own family, neighbours, and friends under the bus.

This definitively proves that democracy is simply one more ecologically impossible chimera among all others. We never actually achieved the mandate for "all lives to be the same" because this abstract claim to equality clearly only extends to salaried employees of corporate, academic, or government bureaucracies. Linkola's call to suspend democracy is not so radical as it might seem, since democracy has already failed to be what it was supposed to be.

In this sense, we might argue that Andrew Yang ran his campaign on an "ontological argument," insofar as he was the candidate who wanted to preserve Being by allowing people to maintain a minimally-functional ecological horizon of agency and dignity. Ultimately, what Yang argued for was simply to allow humans to retain a minimal share of dignity by allowing them to keep going through the Power Process even after the last remaining forms of work had vanished. At some level this actually does fit into Linkola's belief that work is a fundamental part of the ecological essence of Man. A human who cannot work is no human at all, since its essence will have been negated on properly ecological grounds. We are literally fighting for our right to *be!*

Selectively Inevitable

Linkola's primary disagreement with Yang lies in his skepticism towards any claims of "inevitable technological changes." In his great defense of human labor in the essay "The Finnish Body," he couldn't help asking whether what appear to be irreversible changes are actually just temporary fads in disguise.[219] One of the more memorable instances which proved that the System's own definition of "inevitability" is far more fluid than is ordinarily admitted lay in an idiotic 2019 *New York Times* article titled "The Making of a YouTube Radical." The article was at least nominally supposed to be a courageous act of journalistic integrity which took up the hard work of doxing "racist far right vloggers" who had not only been hosted by the platform, but had even been boosted to international fame by the algorithm's tendency to promote videos on the basis of numerical considerations rather than ideological ones. The article warned that the inevitable result of allowing the ignorant masses to choose which videos they want to watch by "liking" controversial videos that were suggested to them by the algorithm is that "reprehensible racists" will abuse the lax moderations and the lack of conscious oversight on the platform to radicalize sizeable audiences of disillusioned youth while the cyber-gatekeepers sleep through it all. We are told that they will then go on quietly submitting impressionable "young white men from remote flyover states like West Virginia" to frequent, prolonged sessions of cyber-brainwashing which will quietly transform an entire generation of young gamers into accidental racists. Reinstating the human talent judge over the rigid algorithm must be forcibly pushed through in order to prevent this "frightening outcome" from materializing, even if it means pushing back against the trends which the impersonal forces of technological progress seemed to have chosen for themselves as though by divine decree.

    It is supremely ironic that the same mainstream media which is otherwise completely indifferent to the prospect of American workers losing their jobs to automation, offshoring, and illegal immigration and typically assumes a stance of complete powerlessness in the face of "inevitable technological changes" would basically insist on making one notable exception to both by calling for the job of the Hollywood talent agent to be forcibly brought back through consciously de-automating it back into existence. This is almost like a liberal version of Pentti Linkola's call for the Green Police to enforce conscious executive action to

---

[219] Pentti Linkola, "The Finnish Body," in *Can Life Prevail?* (Kindle Edition).

reverse the automation of jobs out of existence and return them to their rightful human owners. Even the politically correct corporate media talking heads who would harshly condemn Linkola's calls to suspend democratic procedures and market forces to consciously halt technological overshoot as "eco-fascism" would arguably reserve one single exception for the case of restoring the human role of "talent judge" who chooses celebrities based on corporate marketing trends and political ideology rather than let the ignorant masses exercise their own will as consumers.

Behind the façade of a theatrical display of offense against the "racism" supposedly hosted on the site lay the reality that what the media really found troubling was that so many people *who don't look like celebrities* somehow managed to become famous. This unspoken requirement that one must first "look like a famous person" in order to become one is quite paradoxical, since it is not merely a supplement which pushes a person over the top to international recognition after he or she already has the sufficient talent to sing (i.e., Maria Callas),[220] act (i.e., Gina Lollobrigida),[221] or play sports (i.e., Ana Ivanovic).[222] Rather, there is a certain *je ne sais quoi* inherent in the appearance of a celebrity which functions perfectly well even if it only ever remains on a purely symbolic level. Even after years of living in India, I have never seen a single Kareena Kapoor film but her overwhelmingly frequent appearances on billboards, tabloid news articles, and advertisements signal that she's someone who *should* be a movie star, even if the films as such need not be located. Quora users continue to debate the question "How is Katrina Kaif still surviving in the [Bollywood film] industry without acting skills?" yet this completely misses the point, since she already looked like someone who should be a famous actress before she had starred in a single movie. In a certain sense, she was given a set of films in order to nominally fill in a pre-existent void of fame with some concrete material, rather than earning the fame as a prize at the end of the tunnel only *after* having done the hard work of making a set of brilliant works of art.

---

[220] Greek opera singer.
[221] Italian actress.
[222] Serbian tennis player.

In other words, the celebrity industry is the exact opposite of a meritocracy, since one is effectively given the rewards for one's accomplishments before actually performing the labour to earn them. On the other hand, cases in which an Average Joe spontaneously creates mystifying works and is only retroactively recognized as someone who should fit the role as its creator are so aberrant that they generate media attention simply because of their unusualness. One 2013 article presented Zizek as the "Enigma of the Celebrity Philosopher" by publicly wondering how such a strange figure managed to climb his way to international stardom despite not looking anything like a celebrity. Although much has been made of their differences, one thing which Slavoj Zizek and Jordan Peterson both have in common was the unexpected nature of their rise to intellectual rock star status, since neither one of them quite "looked the part" of a public intellectual as the media would have defined it. In other words, actually *working* one's way to the top is not the norm at all but is a catastrophic anomaly which the System actively works to screen out.

The media's realization that this signtive gesture towards fame will continue to work even if one never actually arrives at the accomplishment which made that person into a celebrity led them to simply reduplicate this condition back into itself. Whereas Brittney Spears looked like someone who should be a pop star even though she couldn't sing but still had to produce all those terrible albums anyway just to have a nominal accomplishment to fall back on, Kim and Kourtney Kardashian bypassed the frustrating procedure of going through the motions to establish an album, film, or sporting event as an excuse for why the media would be talking about them on a nonstop basis: they simply became famous for being famous. The media found that they could keep borrowing from the future by deferring the explanation indefinitely, since the financial reward for focusing on the present moment trumped all demands for ethical journalism. The Kardashians simply looked like they should be famous for something, even if that something never was determined.

Although the media will never admit it openly, what really bothered them about the rise of "amateur vloggers" and renegade talk radio hosts such as Stefan Molyneux, Alex Jones, Paul Joseph Watson, Steven Anderson, J.F.G., and Styxhexenhammer666 was that they lacked this fetishized attribute of fame, since most of them pretty much just looked like "ordinary guys." One might argue that Styxhexenhammer666 and Steven Anderson are the exact opposite of Kim and Kourtney Kardashian, since they got famous on the basis of nothing except talent, even to the exclusion of any mystical aura of "fame" and despite numerous coordinated attempts to halt their progress. It was precisely this democratization of fame which the media misidentified as a bug within the algorithm which must be fixed as soon as possible, without realizing the irony that it was exactly because the technology had succeeded all too well on purely technical grounds that this unexpected scenario unfolded.

The grand irony about our supposedly post-metaphysical democracy, in other words, is that its highest social ranks are still defined by the same sort of archaic publicity Habermas claimed was restricted to the Medieval Era.[223] Just as the King need not produce any works or perform any deeds as such to prove his greatness because he could simply publicly represent some fetishized inborn power which he *is*, the cult of celebrities effectively treats films, albums, and sporting events as public representations of celebrities' mysterious inborn power rather than as works of art or competitive ventures which are meant to inductively build up an ordinary person's right to earn a spot at the table through having to actually work for it.

It must be emphasized that it would be misplaced to confuse this mysterious *je ne sais quoi* with *any* positivistic attribute, even including "beauty," since it is not terribly difficult to find obscure Iranian travel vloggers on YouTube who are more physically attractive than the highest-paid actresses in Hollywood yet still lack the unnameable pseudo-quality which endows the latter with the right to walk as goddesses among mere mortals. This is the ultimate elitism, since it reverts to the ancient pagan mythologies of gods who retain their status as gods even after having lost at worldly competitions against mortals, such as in the scene in *The Iliad* when

---

[223] Jürgen Habermas, *The Structural Transformation of the Public Sphere* (Cambridge: MIT Press, 1991), p. 7.

Diomed physically defeated several of the deities fighting for the Trojans but was still warned that his status as a mortal could never be overcome:

> When [Diomed] was coming on for the fourth time, as though he were a god, Apollo shouted to him with an awful voice and said, 'Take heed . . . and draw off: think not to match yourself against gods, for men that walk the earth cannot hold their own against immortals.'[224]

The greatest irony, in other words, is that the media sounded the alarm simply because their own liberal ideals of democracy, meritocracy, and technology intersected too well for their own good. Because non-human technology cannot scan for this pseudo-attribute of godly power, its blindness to the human factor of "charisma" led it to promote ordinary vloggers on purely meritocratic grounds, above all, through their superior ability to engage with real human audiences through generating likes, shares, and comments among "the ignorant masses." In other words, it was precisely because the technologically-driven democratic meritocracy which the System pretends to want actually did arrive that they freaked out and tried to reverse it forcibly, even to the point of restoring human talent judges and pushing back against "inevitable technological changes."

Of course, far more serious than allowing a controversial right-wing vlogger to get millions of followers on social media was the ultimate example of a nouveau riche pariah sneaking past the gatekeepers of the System on purely democratic grounds enabled by Modern Technology. The 2016 United States election proved that the System actually has a very conservative view on who should be granted access to the highest positions within the political establishment, since it was precisely when the ignorant masses exercised their democratic right to vote and when an outsider bypassed traditional media by directly tweeting to his millions of followers and investing his own hard labour to hold rallies across

---

[224] Homer, *The Iliad* (New Delhi: Fingerprint! Classics, 2017), p. 68.

the nation to spend the evening with thousands of "ordinary folks" that the System sounded the alarm that a catastrophe had inexplicably occurred, without realizing that the ultimate nightmare was simply that their dream of democratic meritocracy intersecting with technological change had come true all too well.

Linkola and Spengler: Flush the Toilets Down the Drain!

Linkola has distinguished himself from virtually any mainstream thinker through his refusal to surrender to the learned helplessness of bowing down before *any* change which is supposed to be "inevitable." In his 1993 "Finland Equals Forests," for example, he noted that it is peculiar for people to treat the deforestation of Finland as though it were an "inevitable" natural disaster like a tsunami or an earthquake, when it is only through a set of decisions legislated by human bureaucrats and corporate executives and executed by machines and paid labourers that this madness goes on. In other words, it is entirely logically fallacious to lump technological disaster and natural disaster together into the same amorphous category of inevitable historical occurrences which were simply "destined to happen" and against which any attempt at human agency is useless.[225] Even claims that economic pressures mandate this state of affairs are ill-founded when one realizes that some ninety percent of the wood harvested from the forest goes to unnecessary luxury items rather than to meeting basic survival needs.[226]

Linkola's refusal to renounce any attempt to overturn "inevitable changes" was largely driven by his realization that these claims to inevitability are often selectively applied to arrangements which just happen to benefit some powerful person on a financial or political level. In his essay "Human Nature and History," he noted the irony that the only changes which the media will acknowledge as "inevitable" are the ones which happen to benefit a small minority of elites:

---

[225] Pentti Linkola, "Finland Equals Forests," in *A Collection of Essays by Pentti Linkola 1993 – 2006*, p. 19.
[226] Ibid., pp. 19-20.

> It would be intellectually absurd for anyone to argue that the prevailing culture and way of life in his era, the direction life has taken in his age, has been unavoidable. [To say that] competition and information technology are the sole options in this epoch and for this country, is foolish. These options have nothing to do with historical inevitability: they are arbitrary choices made by a small group of individuals — small, yet amazingly powerful and influential in its folly.[227]

In fact, claims that "things could never possibly be done any other way" are laughably contradicted by the wealth of diverse ways of life which had existed even into the recent past:

> Even a brief glance at history brings forth a vast spectrum of alternatives. The human species has developed a huge variety of cultures and ways of life.[228]

In addition, appeals to "human nature" simply amount to attempts to smuggle naturalistic inevitability back into the human person himself or herself by casting the explanation for the tragedy of industrialism back into the cavern of one's own unconscious desires. Linkola, however, has called out the Freudian hypothesis regarding "drives and instincts" as simply one more form of learned helplessness, this time locating inevitability within one's own self while still feeling powerless to change it:

> Again and again, "human nature" is fatalistically invoked as one of the reasons for the impending collapse of the world. The deeds of mankind are [supposedly] determined by "drives and instincts"; as such, they are inevitable and irreparable . . . This [appeal to human nature], however, does not make all [such] deeds unavoidable.[229]

---

[227] Pentti Linkola, "Human Nature and History," in *Can Life Prevail?* (Helsinki: Tammi, 2008).
[228] Ibid.
[229] Ibid.

Claiming that "inevitable historical changes" follow from human nature is supremely ironic, for human nature properly understood simply is the life force required to be free enough to resist the suicidal march of technological and economic overshoot, not to mention all of the tacky marketing gimmicks which currently pass as "culture." In his 2004 interview with Virpi Adamsson, Linkola noted that even though wild Nature is constantly being divided into smaller and smaller pieces like the weaker neighbour's land in Kaczynski's Manifesto,[230] even clinging to a tiny piece that remains can provide a source for one to regain access to a minimal share of one's own lifeforce.[231] In other words, there is no freedom without Nature, and no Nature without freedom. For this reason, Linkola noted in his 2004 author's preface to *Can Life Prevail?* that the ultimate political goal of his own proposals is simply the preservation of this life force and therefore of human freedom: "What matters for me is the preservation of life on Earth until a distant future."[232]

The greatest irony Linkola observed was that this life force can only be affirmed through suspending democratic debate. His disagreement with Habermas is not over how the dialogue should be conducted but, rather, whether it should be attempted at all. For example, in his essay "Life Protection, Utopias, and Agriculture," Linkola shocked readers by denouncing the demand to respect the cultural normativity of our current situation (one of Habermas's central rules of communicative action) by warning that any requirement for thinkers to be connected to the present historical context is thoroughly counter-productive and actually *inhibits* the realization of any truly bold ambitions for utopia. In an era in which the academic clichés of "respecting cultural context" and insisting that "nothing happens in an historical vacuum" have been repeated

---

[230] Ted Kaczynski, *Industrial Society and Its Future*, in *Technological Slavery* (Scottsdale: Fitch & Madison, 2019), para. 135.
[231] "Interview with Pentti Linkola 10-2-2004." Available at http://www.penttilinkola.com/pentti_linkola/ecofascism_writings/interview_10-2-2003
[232] Pentti Linkola, "Preface by the Author," in *Can Life Prevail?* (Kindle Edition).

to the point of meaninglessness, Linkola has shown an unusual willingness to go against the grain by denouncing any demand for us to be "grounded in the present system" as worse than useless. It bears mentioning that this would only seem to be requirement if one were engaging in Habermasian dialogue with a human Other situated within a cultural context. This is, of course, entirely irrelevant to our situation because our dialogue is simply with the Mind of Nature itself, something which has not the tiniest bit of care for anyone's cultural biases. One might go as far as to argue that a dialogue with the Mind of Nature can only be possible if we actively *suspend* all cultural biases, especially our own. Against Habermas's politically correct academic sensibilities, Linkola warned that any failure to do so would only paralyze the very process of working towards a solution: "Any binding to a given societal model paralyses the whole thinking process."[233]

Because of his scepticism towards the usefulness of communicative action as Habermas understood the term, Linkola has explicitly called for us to collectively hit the "reset button" on our society in order to wipe the slate clean and start all over again. Just as Ted Kaczynski declared in the 179th paragraph of the Unabomber Manifesto that "[i]t would be better to dump the whole stinking system and take the consequences,"[234] Linkola has accepted the unthinkable conclusion that because everything within the current social order has been engineered to pursue economic growth and ecological collapse, "Nothing in these systems is worth improving." What we need right now is precisely to flush all of this "historical-cultural context" down the commode of history (recursively flushing the very concept of a modern toilet down along with it):

> The worst mistake that anyone thinking about society can make is to envisage the prevailing system as the starting

---

[233] Pentti Linkola, "Life Protection, Utopias, and Agriculture," in *Can Life Prevail?* (Kindle Edition).
[234] Ted Kaczynski, *Industrial Society and Its Future* (Scottsdale: Fitch & Madison, 2019), para. 179.

point: to begin from a tabula rasa, a clean slate, is an absolute must in order to develop any sort of programme.[235]

Similarly, in "A Refresher Course on the State of the World," he concluded that because the current mass extinction is unfolding at a rate and scale which is unprecedented not only within human history but within the history of any species on Earth, we have no choice except to categorically "abandon the whole western . . . way of life" without exception.[236]

Contrary to expectation, Linkola's reasoning behind these shocking demands was based on the realization that our system is just one among many others, both which have existed in the past and which will exist in the future, provided human extinction doesn't arrive first. Far from embodying any stereotypical bias of "Western ethnocentrism," Linkola reached this controversial conclusion simply by radicalizing his acceptance of the same "cultural relativism" which the intelligentsia claim to believe in as well:

> Human history across the world offers a wide range of societal models: the model that happens to be the prevailing one in our own society does not represent any intrinsically superior point of reference.[237]

In this sense, Linkola holds far more common ground with Oswald Spengler than has thus far been acknowledged. Spengler's monumental philosophy of history in *Der Untergang des Abendlandes* was built on the realization that any attempt to understand the history of other cultures required a suspension of one's deepest cultural biases in order to discover which ones underlay those of some foreign way of thinking. Spengler noted that

---

[235] Pentti Linkola, "Life Protection, Utopias, and Agriculture," in *Can Life Prevail?* (Kindle Edition).
[236] Pentti Linkola, "A Refresher Course on the State of the World," in *Can Life Prevail?* (Kindle Edition).
[237] Pentti Linkola, "Life Protection, Utopias, and Agriculture," in *Can Life Prevail?* (Kindle Edition).

any attempt to understand the Ancient Egyptians or Classical Greeks, for example, can only proceed if one realizes that these cultures not only had different surface-level artefacts than we have; they also had a different underlying logic to their civilizational accomplishments. In other words, it is not only the surface-level symbols which are different in other cultures, for any of these is itself intelligible only if one possesses the underlying "prime symbol" which effectively serves as the key to unlock what will remain a profound mystery without this translational schema.

In the fifth chapter of that work, Spengler expanded on this argument by observing that the key to understanding the broader set of cultural symbols, of which even mathematical symbols were just a subset, lay in identifying what he called "the prime symbol" of a culture. He believed that the prime symbol was a basic presupposition unique to a particular culture's worldview, which in turn provided an underlying condition for its other symbols to make sense. For example, he noted that for the Ancient Greeks, the prime symbol was the "[compressed] material and individual body." For the Western Europeans, the prime symbol continues to be "pure infinite space." For the Arabians, the prime symbol remains the enclosed "cavern." Spengler claimed that one could reliably identify the prime symbol's influence over cultural artefacts as diverse as architecture, music, and sculpture. For example, the Western European fixation on "pure infinite space" provides the cultural rationale behind Gothic Cathedrals' tendency to have raised ceilings, even if these do not serve any utilitarian purpose as such. Similarly, the Arabian prime symbol of the cavern provides the rationale behind the construction of mosques even to the present day. The Classical Greek prime symbol of a compressed body provided the rationale for their tendency to believe that absolute perfection should be embodied in the medium of temple statues, for in these statues the gods' and goddesses' bodies could defy logic by being both eternal and yet more youthful than any mere mortal who stands in their presence.

Interestingly, Spengler did not believe that the prime symbol was simply a word, for he held the prime symbol to be something more originary than any linguistic construct. Although a culture had

countless linguistic symbols, these were all merely derivative relative
to the prime symbol which provided their condition of intelligibility in the first place: "the prime symbol . . . is not presentable by words, for language and words are themselves derived symbols."

Spengler believed that Mathematics, like language, would be impossible to actualize within a specific culture outside the influence of a particular prime symbol. Despite our tendency to claim that Mathematics is the purified form of scientific objectivity, Spengler realized that the prime symbol would subtly influence even one's best intentions toward mathematical rigour by coercing the results to reflect a certain cultural worldview which was anything but objective. There is not even any such thing as an unbiased, non-cultural answer to the question over the fundamental definition of numbers. Whereas the Greeks insisted that the number "3" must be positive because their prime symbol was a compressed somatic body, the Indians were freed up to contemplate a "3" which was neither positive nor negative in itself, for the latter were merely secondary qualifications over something which was originally not a "something" at all. It is no coincidence that the numerical concept of zero arose in the same culture in which the spiritual concept of nirvana was understood to be neither life nor death and neither a waking nor sleeping state.

Because each culture had a unique prime symbol, Spengler noted that "[e]ach Culture has its own new possibilities of self-expression which arise, ripen, decay, and never return." Civilizations are not static objects which can exist in the same condition forever but are rather bound by a finite life cycle of morphological development which reliably ends in decline and death. For this reason, Spengler found it useful to speak of "the drama of a number of mighty Cultures, each springing with primitive strength from the soil of a mother region to which it remains firmly bound throughout its whole life cycle; each stamping its material, its mankind, in its own image." He found that each has "an allotted span of life" and a relativity to other cultures because each is "a self-contained phenomenon embodying and expressing [its own] soul." A culture is something which one must place "beside. . . the Egyptian, the Indian, the Babylonian, the Chinese, and the Western" as equally legitimate worldviews in a universe uniquely beholden to no one prime symbol above any other.

In other words, Spengler's radicalism lay in his decision not only to critique higher-level cultural artefacts, but the cultural presuppositions which underlay them; not only the symbols, of a culture, but the *prime symbol* as well. In fact, Spengler went as far as to realize that this cultural relativism applied not only to the Ancient Greeks, Egyptians, and Indians, but even to his own Western European Faustian culture: "So also will the Western world be incomprehensible to the men of Cultures yet unborn."[238] Linkola has similarly distinguished himself through his willingness to call into question not only the surface-level ideologies and rituals of our era, but the deepest presuppositions as well, by proposing that democracy, technology, economic growth, and progress themselves be suspended rather than utilized as non-negotiable starting points to solve the same problems which they themselves created in the first place.

Acceleration and Deceleration

It is therefore a perfectly legitimate question to ask where Linkola's own philosophy is to be situated on the continuum from Accelerationist to Decelerationist tendencies. On one hand, Linkola has explicitly called for "slowing down" the pace of technological progress in order to scale back to pre-modern and traditional ways of life. This is not merely a cultural problem for humans but is necessary to save even Nature itself. As he noted in his 1998 "Panic or Peace in Nature?" there is no shortage of empirical evidence from Nature that the pace of recent changes to the environment is far too rapid for the Earth to adjust to, easily outpacing organism's hard-wired abilities to adapt in real-time. Nor will they be able to close this gap by being given a few more chances; they will instead respond with an "avalanche of extinctions."[239]

---

[238] Oswald Spengler, *Decline of the West: Volumes 1 and 2* (Kindle Edition).
[239] Pentti Linkola, "Panic or Peace in Nature?," in *A Collection of Essays by Pentti*

Yet even on the level of human culture, he has called for humans to decelerate to a more modest pace of life. In "The Objection Raised by the Deep Ecologist" section of "The ABC of the Deep Ecologist – Part One" he noted that "qualities of humility and abstinence" will be necessary to stop the runaway train of progress before it destroys us along with itself. Fortunately, these virtues are not entirely absent today, as "[t]hese qualities [continue to] manifest themselves in some populations through [traditional] customs, ways of life, ideas and worldviews."[240] One might argue that it was only the historical anomaly of modern technological progress which briefly suspended the traditional wisdom that such qualities would be necessary to preserve human life into a future which could not cheat its way to success with machines, fossil fuels, and fraudulent money. For this reason, he affirmed that "[t]he protector of life will try to strengthen [these traditional ideals] so that the progress leading to utter devastation might stop, or at least slow down."

In addition, in his 2004 interview with Virpi Adamsson, Linkola was asked whether any cultures remained on the Earth which had preserved their traditional ways of life against the pressures towards globalism which had caused his fellow Finns to abandon their own traditions in favour of a mindless life of American-style consumerism. He responded that among the Bushmen and some other African tribal cultures, there are indeed pockets here and there which continue to resist progress and mechanization by clinging to "slower cultures" which espouse a pace of life more reminiscent of the pre-industrial past.[241]

However, it would be somewhat misleading to imply that Linkola would favour slowing down to more traditional cultural forms because he valued these as an absolute good in themselves. Rather, for him these are largely just a means to an end to revert to

---

Linkola 1993 – 2006, pp. 52-3.
[240] Pentti Linkola, "The ABC of the Deep Ecologist – Part One," in *Can Life Prevail?* (Kindle Edition).
[241] "Interview with Pentti Linkola 10-2-2004." Available at http://www.penttilinkola.com/pentti_linkola/ecofascism_writings/interview_10-2-2003

Nature itself, yet Nature is indigenous to no one human culture and is beholden to none of them.

In this sense, quite surprisingly, Nick Land's demand to accelerate capital not because we like capitalism but precisely because we want to push it to the point of a Singularity where its own laws are suspended is not necessarily incompatible with Linkola's own preference to wipe the cultural slate clean through pushing the modern worldview into a cultural Singularity of sorts, much like the one which Zizek described in his 2014 *Absolute Recoil:*

> Singularity refers to a point or region in space-time in which gravitational forces cause matter to have an infinite density, so that the laws of physics are suspended. This suspension of laws as the key feature of a singularity allows us to use the term in other contexts – Ray Kurzweil, for example, defined the Technological Singularity as a "future period during which the pace of technological change will be so rapid, its impact so deep, that human life will be irreversibly transformed.[242]

Nick Land's view of accelerating to the point of Singularity is not necessarily incompatible with Linkola's call to push the humanistic chimeras of the Mind of Progress to explode themselves into the nothingness which they had always already been by wiping the slate clean and suspending all cultural presuppositions as equally arbitrary. Crucially, however, Linkola's motivation is precisely *not* to reach a negative void without any further qualification, but rather to clear sufficient space for the Mind of Nature to reaffirm Being, much like how fundamentalist Christians believe that Christ can speak in the Second Coming only if apocalyptic chaos first dismantles the last remaining traces of cultural normativity and economic stability. On an ontological level, Linkola would favour this Singularity not as a destruction of Being in favour of nothingness, but rather, as the only hope to allow Being to be

---

[242] Slavoj Zizek, *Absolute Recoil* (London: Verso, 2014), p. 389.

salvaged in the form of ecological conformity with the Mind of Nature. It is precisely in leaving the dysfunctional System of technological and economic excess untouched that nothingness would squeeze out the possibility of Being.

In his "Can We Survive: A Model for a Controlled Future" he admitted that although he does not know exactly how the Natural Magisterium will rise to power within the real world, the only thing which is certain is that it won't be through winning democratic elections:

> I will leave open the question of how those few wise individuals might rise to power and how the programme for the preservation of life might be implemented: I simply do not know the answer.[243]

Linkola's 2004 interview with Virpi Adamsson closed with Adamsson's question whether life *can* prevail, in reference to the title of his recently-released book of the same name. Linkola's only response was that although the text presented all of the necessary conditions one by one for how this could happen (effectively presenting an ecological equivalent of Euclid's *Elements*, a rationalized geometry for how Nature *could* thrive), he still admitted that on grounds of raw probability alone the most likely outcome is that, abandoned to the world's current trajectory, this life will not be able to survive.

Given the impossibility of life prevailing within this context of democratic and technologized globalism, he admitted in "Can We Survive: A Model for a Controlled Future" that apocalyptic conditions are the most plausible scenario for the rise of the Mind of Nature to take control of the political system. In other words, short of destructive chaos and extreme desperation, it is almost impossible to imagine that this shift could occur at all:

> Will salvation come at the last moment, after massive catastrophes? . . . Or will this happen suddenly, without

---

[243] Pentti Linkola, "Can We Survive: A Model for a Controlled Future," in *Can Life Prevail?* (Kindle Edition).

notice, through some collective flash, like the utterly unpredictable collapse of socialist systems?[244]

Although Linkola's references to violence remain more or less ambiguous, he has categorically insisted that it could hold a legitimate use within the coming Green Police State and, arguably, in the transition process as well. In his 2011 interview with Francisco Martinez and Larissa Vanamo, when asked whether he hypothetically supported the idea that violence might have a legitimate role in bringing about the end of democracy and the establishment of a green dictatorship, he noted the irony that it is *only* if one used violence to establish this ideal state that life could be "saved."[245]

Although Linkola expressed some amount of regret in the same interview that his own writings have sped up the destruction precisely by warning people that it will come, there is reason to argue that his negative references to "speeding up" the catastrophe are not necessarily the same as Land's concept of "acceleration." On one hand, he admitted that human desire is so perverse that it will double down on consuming right now precisely because it knows that shortly afterwards the catastrophe will arrive. People turn to "partying like there's no tomorrow" precisely when they find out that there won't be one. This is because whereas speeding up the madness of democracy and consumerism only hastens the arrival of non-being and nothingness, acceleration to the point of Singularity where the chimera is suspended would be the only viable path to usher in the restoration of Being itself.[246]

One need not extrapolate beyond Linkola's own words to find confirmation for this principle, as in his lengthy *Quadrivium* interview he explicitly condemned "the world of computers" as a "space of elated nothingness" completely devoid of real Being.[247]

---

[244] Ibid.
[245] See Francisco Martinez Larissa Vanamo's 2011 interview "A Promenade with Pentti Linkola," http:// www.materialworldblog.com/ 2013/ 03/ invoking-the-apocalypse-a-promenade-with-pentti-linkola/
[246] Ibid.
[247] Pentti Linkola interview from *Quadrivium* #6 (2014): abridged version.

As a remedy, he prescribed for Finns to be relocated to "lingonberry and blueberry forests or the pea farms in Kokemäki" in order to be immersed in Being through reclaiming the realm of ecological validity over the pseudo-forms of technological artifice.

Likewise, the interviewers were fair enough to push back against popular caricatures which portray Linkola as a "nihilist" convinced that the world has been driven into the pure negativity of "meaninglessness." What these caricatures miss is precisely the fact that "Linkola has explicitly stated on many occasions that nihilism is not an answer to him" since the entire point of his work is to affirm life and to uphold Being against the onslaught of technological nothingness.[248]

In his *Quadrivium* interview, Linkola was explicitly asked to clarify his stance regarding the need for a "blank slate" in "Life Protection, Utopias, and Agriculture." He responded that any reversion to a new "tabula rasa" will not be an end in itself but will be useful only if it is immediately paired with its apparent opposite – a "terribly strong leader to keep the people in control." Far from disintegrating the current order to open the floodgates for unbridled anarchy, the entire purpose of this suspension would be to provide an even more rigid set of controls over human nature lest it drive itself to extinction:

> Man is an impossible creature if it's not tied to anything. It squanders, consumes, produces, squanders, consumes, which is not conceivable at all in the long run. You need a strong and responsible lead, be that one person, an oligarch, or a board of several strong persons.[249]

One might argue that if it were granted the political power it rightfully deserves, the Mind of Nature's prescriptive mandate for

---

Available at http://qvadrivivm.blogspot.com/2015/12/pentti-linkola-interview-from.html

[248] Pentti Linkola interview from *Quadrivium* #6 (2014): abridged version. Available at http://qvadrivivm.blogspot.com/2015/12/pentti-linkola-interview-from.html

[249] Ibid.

how human life must be reformed after this point is reached could be condensed in a single concise formula: "the natural form is the true form." It is precisely the ecologically valid forms of Nature which we must directly embody in the political institution itself. Yet far from renouncing the joys of life through begrudgingly accepting irrational ascetic renunciation, Linkola closed his set of controversial proposals in "Can We Survive: A Model for a Controlled Future" by noting the irony that you'd actually get a higher standard of living this way:

> Besides guaranteeing its main goal, the preservation of life, the suggested model of society would also secure an incomparably better standard of living. What are the sweet, cherished traits of the modern world that man would lose? Record suicide rates, exhausting competition, unemployment, stress, job insecurity, alienation, desperation, the need for psychological medication, bodily decay, individual arrogance, quarrel, corruption, crime...[250]

In other words, Man can't be trusted to legislate a "genuine life" for himself, since only the Mind of Nature can dictate how to properly achieve it, above all, through "protect[ing] the people from itself!" Left to its own devices, the Mind of Man cannot give himself anything except catastrophe:

> Why, then, is a strict central government needed? [A look back at the] shameful history of mankind [shall demonstrate that if the democratic] masses, are given the chance to choose, like magpies they will again and again go for the shiny things, leaping like butterflies into the flames. A government led by a few wise individuals is necessary to protect the people from itself . . . All other actions are nothing but a way of playing with fire, waiting to get burned.[251]

---

[250] Ibid.
[251] Ibid.

Ironically, the Mind of Man misses the point regarding the correct path of action *despite the fact* that ethical prescription and scientific description are not antithetical forces but are rather two sides of the same coin. It is precisely through "searching for an explanation for the world" on a rationalistic level that one can unearth the proper social forms necessary to preserve it:

> I find some worth even in mere [theoretical] speculation . . . Ultimately, I am resigned to simply searching for an explanation for the world, with no reformist aim in mind – at least for the time being.[252]

On the other hand, the secular liturgy "that is constantly hummed around us: the liturgy of the prophets of economic growth, of competition, efficiency and 'competence'" are flawed simply because they fail to accurately describe the state of the world, insofar as each of these requires an outright disregard for ecological law in order to pass as sane. Madness for Linkola is simply the affirmation of a humanistic chimera and the abandonment of ecological law. Language, abandoned to its own devices, is simply a collective form of insanity.

Zizek vs. Linkola:
(The Mind of) Nature Doesn't Exist?

Because Linkola's ontology is summed up by the phrase "to be is to be ecological," he essentially argues that an object only exists if it is a subset from the Mind of Nature which does not violate its rationalized laws; otherwise, it is nothing. A perceptive reader will likely realize that this is something of an inverse image of Zizek's own idiosyncratic understanding of Being, one which is so unusual as to drive Zizek to claim that "Nature doesn't exist." For Linkola, of course, this is the ultimate absurdity, insofar as Linkola basically revises David Icke's thesis regarding love into the claim "Only Nature exists, all else is humanistic illusion."

---

[252] Ibid.

Furthermore, Zizek's correlate to the disappearance of Nature lies in a call to understand the Cartesian subject as equally devoid of content. Yet this empty subject is simply one more embodiment of democratic modernity in disguise. Zizek's substanceless cogito satisfies the same demand to suspend ecological context as Kant's requirement for the ethical subject to be purified of naturalistic pathology and Habermas's call for the communicative subject to be reduced to an abstract participant with no lingering "Metaphysical" qualifications regarding social status. These three figures, therefore, make up Linkola's collective antithesis on the levels of ethics (Kant), politics (Habermas), and ontology (Zizek). Although Linkola's contrast with each shall be discussed thoroughly in the present text, we shall begin by examining Zizek's ontology in direct opposition with Linkola's.

Although Zizek has repeatedly elaborated on his bold claim that "Nature doesn't exist" over the course of his nearly innumerable writings and conference talks, the final chapter of his 2008 book *In Defense of Lost Causes* was dedicated in its entirety to providing the full theoretical explanation for why what Linkola would consider to be the ultimate absurdity could somehow appear to pass as sane even to, admittedly, one of the greatest philosophers of our era. Zizek included an extended discussion of ecological crisis within this book in particular because it fit into his broader theme of trying to redeem the totalitarian spirit of "big changes" in an era when this had become unfashionable even among the self-proclaimed "radical" thinkers." He did so by seeking to address the problem of ecological crisis through its relation to global capitalism, post-humanism, and revolutionary terror (in the French Revolution sense of the term). Zizek warned the reader from the start that maintaining aversion to totalitarian terror has merely made us all into Fukuyamans in disguise. The Social Justice Movement, for example, has basically accepted that capitalism and western democracy are here to stay, so the only task that remains is to make them "more tolerant," which is itself just a euphemism for calls to make them more inclusive on commercial grounds alone by extending the range of corporate marketing patents to even more new niches within the global population.[253]

It is quite telling that many of the far leftist calls for open borders often presuppose that this "ethical mandate" simply consists of the moral duty to allow people from Third World nations easier access to become First World consumers. Even while claiming to champion the causes of Syrian refugees and illegal immigrants from El Salvador on humanitarian grounds alone, it is simply taken for granted the true "horror" they are fleeing from is not Middle Eastern warfare or drug cartel violence so much as the Hell of lacking access to a First World standard of living. Recent claims that banning flights from Wuhan, China after the coronavirus epidemic began was inherently "racist" provide chilling evidence that even Edgard Allen Poe's Red Death would have to be granted a visa to enter our neighbourhoods today lest we be accused of discriminating against it on the basis of colour, even if the price for doing so is literally our own deaths.

It is quite telling, at any rate, that leftists only fight for open borders in wealthy Western nations with a very high level of technologization and remain completely indifferent to the fact that a poor Middle Eastern nation like Yemen, for example, is virtually impossible to enter by legal means. One extreme travel vlogger, for example, had to leap through ridiculous hoops to arrange a car to drive him over the border from Oman, crossing past numerous terrorist-controlled checkpoints just to get a few more views on YouTube. Not coincidentally, one of his next videos documented suffering an extreme case of traveller's diarrhea after consuming local food from a war-torn nation with woefully inadequate infrastructure and sanitation standards. Somehow, leftists are not terribly interested in opening the floodgates for anyone to cross *this* border without permission, yet the reason is simply that it does not offer one the "basic human right" of being an irresponsible, wasteful, and mindless First World consumer. Behind the façade of "ethical concern over race" lies the supremely ethnocentric view that First World nations are so superior to any other on economic grounds alone that residents of other nations basically have a moral

---

[253] Slavoj Zizek, *In Defense of Lost Causes* (London: Verso, 2008), p. 421.

obligation to themselves and their families to seize their share of the pie there, even by illegal means.

In a 2012 interview with *RockTribune*, Norwegian Black Metal musician and ecophilosopher Varg Vikernes similarly noted that the only reason there is an "ethical mandate" for open borders in Western nations but nowhere else is because of their relative economic wealth compared to the Third World. In this interview, he claimed that:

> The industrialization of Europe has been a disaster to us. Our wealth has attracted all the most destructive and dangerous parasites on this planet, and they are destroying Europe from within, in all ways imaginable. I truly wish Africa and all of Asia had been filthy rich, so that all the parasites would leave us alone and go there instead.[254]

Although Vikernes's response to this issue is indeed strongly-worded and will be unpalatable to many a reader, one should still seriously consider his claim that it is not only the Western nations which have been given a "moral obligation" to let anyone and everyone be First World consumers within their borders; it is also the global population itself which is given the demand to migrate into wealthier nations for no reason except those based on the crassest standard of economic materialism, despite the fact that their own traditional cultural values often disintegrate as a result. The motif of an Indian family relocating to America simply to make more money which then ends up losing their values in the process has become a recurring theme in Malayalam cinema, no doubt because it has been empirically confirmed all too many times. It is ironic that the same Western intellectuals who claim to fight tirelessly to preserve indigenous cultures against the onslaught of global capitalism would favour the strategy of guaranteeing their collapse through mandating mass migrations to occur for no reason except sheer greed.

---

[254] "Interview with Varg Vikernes RockTribune (April 2012), by Maarten Van Leest and Morbid Geert," available at
https://www.burzum.org/eng/library/2012_interview_rocktribune.shtml

In Linkola's lengthy interview published in the final issue of the Finnish magazine *Quadrivium* in December 2014, the interviews referenced a quote Linkola had made during the seventies that the average person native to Asia or Africa who was suddenly provided a Western standard of living would likely increase his or her consumption ten or one hundred times what it originally was in his or her native country.[255] Though it will surely offend the politically correct sensibilities of First World liberals, as far as the Mind of Nature sees it, unbridled immigration into the First World cannot mean anything except a massive social rehabilitation program which trains people to needlessly multiply their resource waste, often without even increasing their happiness in the process!

In addition to increasing resource waste and fossil fuel consumption, Linkola mentioned in his essay "Light Glimmers in the Population Explosion" that immigration cannot honestly be evaluated except as a catalyst for even more overpopulation within nations which have already exceeded their ecological capacity. The Mind of Nature is sufficiently immune to social justice bullying to acknowledge the unavoidable ecological fact that the enormous problem of overpopulation in First World nations such as Finland is only made even worse by the flood of immigrants which leftists demand be let in for no reason except to become better consumers. Even if one did somehow manage to reduce the number of newborn infants in such a nation, these efforts will all prove useless if these blank spaces are immediately filled by migrants arriving by the tens or hundreds of thousands from other nations. Likewise, the Mind of Nature could not possibly mandate anything except that one "tighten the immigration politics" considerably in order to prevent the nation from tipping over into ecological overshoot.[256]

Nor is this simply a matter of "keeping out Third World Others," as the leftist stereotype would hold. Linkola noted in the

---

[255] Pentti Linkola interview from *Quadrivium* #6 (2014): abridged version. Available at http://qvadrivivm.blogspot.com/2015/12/pentti-linkola-interview-from.html

[256] Pentti Linkola, "Light Glimmers in the Population Explosion,'" in *A Collection of Essays by Pentti Linkola 1993 – 2006*, p. 148.

same essay that it has somehow become a requirement even for natives of First World nations to move around to different countries, apparently, just for the hell of it. Although living abroad for no reason has become a fashionable way to boost one's cosmopolitan index, Linkola asked why exactly it has suddenly become an ethical requirement that "all Belgians move to France or Holland, or that all Dutchmen move to Germany or Belgium." Why is it that these days "[n]obody lives in the country they were born in. Is that the principal thought of the Green League? That is a question that should still be posed. What is the terrible glory of living somewhere you were not born or raised?"[257]

In his 2011 interview with Francisco Martinez and Larissa Vanoma, however, Linkola contradicted popular stereotypes against him by arguing that, in fact, all immigration is *not* necessarily bad. To clarify, he provided his own example of a Finn willingly opting out of living in his or her own First World nation to relocate to a clay cabin in Africa and accept a lower standard of living. He considered this to be a perfectly legitimate form of immigration because it actually slows down the process of environmental destruction. Of course, this is the exact opposite of what the System demands, in that the unwritten rule of immigration activism today is that it is *only* considered legitimate if a Third World citizen crosses into a First World nation in order to gain access to a share of a larger pie of fossil fuel energy and technology. Behind euphemisms of tolerance and compassion, the truth is that anyone who does so will only be doing one thing: speeding up the depletion of natural resources and, in turn, dumping more pollution into the biosphere.[258]

Similarly, when I made the international news for (legally!) fleeing to India to escape student loan slavery (among other reasons), I was amused to find angry, rambling messages from people I didn't even know end up in my social media inboxes before I discontinued these accounts. These people seemed to believe that I didn't have a choice to "downgrade" to a less energy

---

[257] Ibid.
[258] See Francisco Martinez Larissa Vanamo's 2011 interview "A Promenade with Pentti Linkola," http:// www.materialworldblog.com/ 2013/ 03/ invoking-the-apocalypse-a-promenade-with-pentti-linkola/

intensive lifestyle in a Third World country, even though this was precisely what I wanted to do with my own life and is even, in fact, accepted by Linkola as a perfectly ethical form of immigration.[259] In our era, you don't have the right to use less energy, even if you ironically get a higher standard of living in the process, since the universal demand for "inclusion" in the First World industrialist mode of life is a hostage situation from which you are not allowed to escape. One *South Park* episode portrayed the characters being trapped in a room with a group of aggressive salesmen who would not take "no" for an answer while trying to sell them a condo in Aspen, Colorado which they couldn't afford and which they didn't even want. Yet even calling the cops to bail them out proved useless, since they too were part of the organized racket to make money by forcing people to buy a product against their will. It is no exaggeration to say the Police of Progress in our era have similarly turned to forcing people to be more wasteful than they want to be, simply by making every other traditional lifestyle illegal by abusing bogus "health codes" to concentrate power in a handful of corporations which ironically do a much worse job at meeting the same needs.

  It is even more ironic, therefore, that unbridled illegal immigration actually directly contributes to *lowering* the wealth and standard of living for the working classes in the First World and, ultimately, for the migrants themselves. When I was growing up, the agricultural counties in Colorado were known to be places in which migrant labourers would rent out backyards in order to pitch tents there over the growing season months because they were unable to afford an apartment with the mere three dollars per hour they were being paid illegally. Needless to say, there was no question of hiring a citizen to do the same job (i.e., "Legal Workers Need Not Apply!") because the cost would simply be too high for businesses which had abused leftists' obsession with "racial wokeness" as a technical strategy to maximize their own profits. Likewise, the motif of a nation which adopts "open borders" yet still maintains prosperity for its population is just another

---

[259] Ibid.

ecologically impossible object, a situation motivated by greed which somehow ends up making its adherents even poorer as a result.

Given his aversion to playing games with "making global capitalism more inclusive," Zizek begins his argument against Deep Ecology in *In Defense of Lost Causes* by claiming that ecological crises can only be understood if it is treated as one of the antagonisms of global capitalism rather than as some independent problem, let alone as a substantial entity in itself. To clarify this admittedly obscure point, he argues that ecological crisis holds roughly the same status as Third World slums, insofar as each is just another one of the excesses generated by the "substantial base" of the global capitalist system.[260] However, ecological threats also force us to re-evaluate the old standard clichés about how waiting around for the System to self-destruct through its own contradictions and flaws will be "good enough." On the contrary, for the first time in history, we are living in an era where one subjective intervention has the potential to "directly intervene in the historical substance" through a single catastrophic disturbance. For example, it is not impossible for some bio-warfare agent to escape a laboratory and bring about human extinction as a result of just one subjective error (similar to how conspiracy theorists speculated that the 2020 coronavirus pandemic was the result of a top-secret biowarfare experiment gone wrong, though it remains uncertain what the truth value of this theory might be.)

Far from being a postmodernist era which has gone beyond subjectivity, the old Hegelian phrase "not only as substance but also as subject" is more relevant now than ever before.[261] Although ecological thinkers stereotypically tend to recycle Adorno and Horkheimer's Frankfurt School-style calls for renouncing human "instrumental reason" in favour of Mimesis or some other mystical stance of reverence for the Other, Zizek argues that this actually gets the problem completely backwards: what we need right now is precisely to seize subjective agency. He cites the case of Chavez in Venezuela, who succeeded in rebellion precisely by "going legit"

---

[260] Ibid., p. 420.
[261] Ibid., p. 421.

within the state system rather than remaining an outsider (though, of course, this quote has not aged particularly well in recent years, as Venezuela eventually devolved into one of the most dysfunctional nations on Earth precisely as a result of Chavez's socialist interventions).[262]

Zizek argues that this logic of reclaiming subjectivity in order to seize the state actually fits the empirical facts on the ground quite well, since it is precisely the big industrial polluters and CEO's today who continue to "resist the state" by circumventing its regulations, especially ones related to the environment. We must instead grab power by the state if we hope to achieve a meaningful change.[263] Even in light of this realization, however, Zizek still held some reservations about how to do ecology properly. No ecological stance can be legitimate, for example, if it disregards the class struggle criteria of a Marxist rebellion against capitalism; or, in Linkolan terminology, any deep ecologist who cites fidelity to the Mind of Nature to legitimize the oppression of the "polluting poor" will have to be disqualified.

Interestingly, Zizek seems to identify ecology as a smaller part of the broader critique of global capitalism, rather than the "objective factor" of the situation, to borrow Ted Kaczynski's terminology from his prison-era letters. For this reason, we can consider Zizek's stance in direct contrast with Linkola's since Linkola is exactly the thinker for whom ecology is the fundamental issue and for whom capitalism could never be "deeper" than ecology in any hierarchy of concerns. This is because capitalism is itself merely a humanistic chimera which can never be fully realized within the world due to its inherent unnaturalness but can still gobble up gargantuan chunks of resources in its mad quest to literally *be* the impossible. Because of his reversal of these priorities, Linkola would see no reason to show any favour in giving Third World slum dwellers a "free pass" on their admittedly enormous contribution to pollution, as the majority of plastic in oceans originated from a small set of rivers in Africa and Asia. This is because the economic and political issues are simply a means to

---

[262] Ibid., p. 427.
[263] Ibid.

an end to enforce the same ecological restrictions regardless of personal bias.

Zizek, on the other hand, would claim that ecology cannot be the main issue since it is only one of four areas confronting us even within its own secondary position relative to global capitalism (along with intellectual property rights, new scientific developments, and new forms of apartheid/walls.) Any attempt to address ecology without respecting this broader context of capitalistic self-contradiction is bound for failure. This warning is not merely hypothetical, as Zizek notes that without the proper context, ecology devolves into the engineering problem of how to maintain "sustainable development" through drafting up a green form of capitalism. We need not wait for decades to see this materialize, as he claims that Whole Foods and Starbucks have already done just that – they have merged consumption and political activism into a single act by promising, for example, that there is "No need to feel bad about spending $5 on a cup of coffee, since a fraction goes towards building schools in some currently-fashionable Third World nation."

Ecology is a problem of an antagonism, stemming from a context much broader than itself, rather than a static object in itself. For this reason, it is impossible to actually address it *without* a certain amount of terror being involved, since the very ontological character of a dialectical antagonism defies the naïve metaphysics of ordinary objectivity. Interestingly, Zizek argues that the classic Kierkegaardian distinction between attitudes of "fear" and the willingness to confront the "trembling" of terror provides the true standard to determine how authentic one's response to all of these problems will be. Whereas fear attempts to maintain stability against threats, only terror openly confronts the "shattering experience of negativity" necessary for any real change.[264] More precisely, fear shies away from the abstract negation of dialectical change, while trembling is the position necessary to fully accept the implications of a Hegelian dissolution of reality, the reduction of our current order to one more contingency among any other on a

---

[264] Ibid., p. 433.

complicated dialectical pathway which can be trusted to birth a new form from out of nowhere quite soon.

Zizek claims that most deep ecologists are actually stuck in the naïve, pre-Hegelian mode of fear, since for them preventing disturbances and clinging to some semblance of order and stability is the main goal which motivates their strategy for confronting ecological dangers.[265] Deep ecology is therefore just one more means of distrusting big changes, yet this only reinforces the hegemonic ideology all the more by reifying it into a precious object which must be safeguarded against collapse, no matter the cost. It's no coincidence, then, that most environmental activists actively resist totalitarian "big picture thinking," often by favouring small changes within the local community over any attempt to change the whole world all at once.[266] Richard Heinberg, for example, has repeatedly emphasized the return to local production and local trading as a necessary measure to smoothen the transition to the coming post-petroleum era. Above all, he has praised this "little revolution" for its limited scope and personal feasibility, as shopping at farmers' markets and gardening at home are simple lifestyle changes which can and should be adopted by individuals and families as soon as possible in order to provide a parachute to slow down the fall from the burning airplane of industrialism before it crashes to the ground on its own.[267]

Zizek claims, however, that there is something far more radical at work in this attitude than just a desperate attempt to "not rock the boat too much." He notes, for example, that our current trajectory is more or less powerless to save Nature in its integrity, since it is actively just paving the way for Nature to disappear. Yet ironically this goal is advanced precisely by encroaching upon depriving Man of his status as a natural entity.[268] Cracking the biological codes to unearth how organisms function transforms them from naturalistic mysteries into fully replicable and

---

[265] Ibid., pp. 438-40.
[266] Ibid., p. 440.
[267] Richard Heinberg, *Afterburn: Society Beyond Fossil Fuels* (Gabriola Island: New Society, 2015).
[268] Slavoj Zizek, *In Defense of Lost Causes* (London: Verso, 2008), p. 435.

manipulable electronic appliances, even ones which corporations are free to patent the "intellectual property rights" on. Paradoxically, it is precisely when Nature vanishes as an impenetrable mystery that Man himself ceases to exist as one as well.

We can find this disappearance of Nature in the way that John Zerzan's critique of "Man's domination over the Earth" is actually somewhat out of date.[269] Far from merely seeking to control Nature or clone it faithfully, contemporary scientific projects are actually oriented towards producing something radically new.[270] A.I. for example is not about replicating the human brain, but about generating something altogether different and unquestionably superior. Even Ted Kaczynski's obscure, unpublished 1971 essay "Progress Versus Liberty" warned decades ago that metaphors of reproducing the human brain are inherently misleading, since whereas human brains are intrinsically limited in size to a few pounds, supercomputers are limited in size only in hard electrical engineering requirements which the industry is constantly making leaps to overcome. In addition, whereas brains are inherently democratic, since every person only has one of them, supercomputers are so expensive and so energy-intensive that only a handful of mega-corporations and world governments can own them and will no doubt utilize them solely to promote their own interests.[271]

Yet it is not only lifeless electronic machines which risk breaking our expectations regarding what can and cannot happen within reality, as fantasies of a new biological monster that can infinitely reproduce itself asexually bring the psychoanalytic motif of the "undead life" one step closer to becoming a literal empirical object in the world.[272] Zizek warns, however, that the practical response from mainstream ecologists who realize these things on a theoretical level is misguided, since all too often they retreat into

---

[269] John Zerzan, "Number: Its Origin and Evolution," in *Elements of Refusal* (Kindle Edition).
[270] Slavoj Zizek, *In Defense of Lost Causes* (London: Verso, 2008), p. 436.
[271] Ted Kaczynski, "Progress versus Liberty" (unpublished essay).
[272] Slavoj Zizek, *In Defense of Lost Causes* (London: Verso, 2008), p. 437.

the escapism of turning Deep Ecology into a new religion, positing Nature as an "unquestionable authority which" is free to impose limits on human subjects to curb their dangerous activity.[273]

This criticism is not entirely unfounded, as Linkola himself has mentioned the paradox that Nature cannot be grasped through a strictly materialistic viewpoint, or even through utilizing the resources of logic and human reasoning alone; it can only be appreciated as such if one maintains a reverence for the sacred while contemplating it. In his "Refresher Course on the State of the World" he lamented that the universal secularization which materialism mandates has deprived even Nature of any trace of holiness it once enjoyed:

> The guardian of life, however, does not derive all of his power and assuredness from reasoning and logic. The basic principle of life protection, the conservation of the Earth's life as a lush and diverse whole, is also perceived as being sacred: as something incomparably holier than anything man might regard as such (not that in this age of cynical despair much holiness is left!).[274]

Similarly, in Linkola's 1999 essay "The Tragedy Of Kuhmalahti" he lamented that roadsides in Finland had progressively come to be cleared of all natural vegetation whatsoever under the euphemism of "cleaning the village road[s]." Yet it would be misplaced even to cite any utilitarian purpose behind this nonsense, as this eco-crime occurred simply in order to satisfy suburban idlers' aesthetic biases regarding what developed land should look like. Through this mindless mass-slaughtering of living plants, these eco-criminals had wilfully transformed forest into "desert." Yet in addition to degrading the land materially, they had also robbed it of its original character as a "spiritual landscape." Linkola openly wondered whether it would ever be possible to travel this place again as it had traditionally been, or whether it had

---

[273] Ibid., p. 439.
[274] Pentti Linkola, "A Refresher Course on the State of the World," in *Can Life Prevail?* (Kindle Edition).

been irreparably converted into so much more industrial waste devoid of any spiritual value. While a clueless happy motorer who speeds down the motorway at 75 miles per hour will likely be completely indifferent as to whether it is devoid of living plants, Linkola noted that the experience for the hiker and cyclist are quite different in this regard. Lacking an artificial shelter from the natural world which a bloated SUV would provide, hikers and cyclists traveling in open air down a pathway will constantly absorb the sights and impressions on the side of the road and will surely feel the disappearance of life from this place, even as the clueless gas guzzler will remain oblivious to this tragedy as he or she blasts down the highway blaring Eminem while texting and driving.[275]

Linkola realized, in other words, that Nature can somehow only appear as Nature if it is disclosed within a horizon of meaning that retains its spiritual value. The total materialization of Nature does not free it up to be what it always really was; it destroys it. Nor is this an original invention on Linkola's part, since Julius Evola also noted in his *Revolt Against the Modern World* that within the world of Tradition, Nature could only be grasped as Nature if it was disclosed within a spiritual mode of sanctity rather than as so much brute material stuff.[276] To understand Evola's distinction between the spirit of Tradition and that of modern civilization, we must first examine the doctrine of the two natures. Under this traditional view, one must contrast a physical order with a metaphysical order; mortal nature with immortal nature; the inferior realm of becoming with the superior realm of Being; and the visible, tangible dimension with the invisible, intangible dimension.[277] Because the notion of reality accessible in the world of Tradition provided the intellectual resources to accommodate both sides within these pairs of terms, it was much broader than the truncated fragment which we consider today to be all that is worthy of consideration from a crass materialistic viewpoint. In fact, even Nature itself did not refer to

---

[275] Pentti Linkola, "The Tragedy Of Kuhmalahti," in *A Collection of Essays by Pentti Linkola 1993 – 2006*, p. 103.
[276] Julius Evola, *Revolt Against the Modern World* (Rochester: Inner Traditions, 1995), p. 4.
[277] Ibid., p. 3.

the world of natural science known today, but corresponded to an invisible spiritual reality instead.[278]

"Space," the 19th chapter of the text, explored the problem of Nature in much greater detail. Evola noted that our conception of space today is basically that of an indifferent container filled with bodies and motions;[279] this modern conception of space is so empty, in fact, that Kant went as far as to literally call the World just a regulative Idea, a product of the subject's own synthetic activity. In the traditional view, however, space was understood to be alive and to be saturated with qualities and intensities. Each region was endowed with its own virtues and was understood to participate in the powers residing there.[280] Rather than be substitutable for one another with total indifference, every direction corresponded to unique spiritual influences.

Given this understanding of space, Nature was not simply the indifferent material of physical science but was instead seen as the symbol of transcendent realities. Evola was very careful to note, however, that this "experience of Nature," while obviously not the secularized naturalistic "stuff" familiar to the modern scientist, was also something quite different from the Romantic experience of the Sublime familiar to the modern poet. It was, instead, the real rather than figurative sensation of the unique supernatural powers that were understood to permeate particular places.[281] This presupposed, of course, that the borders between the I and the Not I were fluid and, in some cases, were partially removed.[282] Nor has this been overcome today, as Evola warned that Man is not free from the spiritual dangers even as he openly mocks them, for the complexes of collective unconscious, emotive and irrational currents, and collective influences are far more harmful under such a stance.[283]

In "The northern Atlantic Cycle," the 25th chapter of the text, Evola began an explanation for why the cult worship of

---

[278] Ibid., p. 4.
[279] Ibid., p. 148.
[280] Ibid., p. 149.
[281] Ibid., p. 150.
[282] Ibid., p. 152.
[283] Ibid.

Mother Earth is not a faithful embodiment of this attitude but is itself a perversion of Tradition and a degradation of its original viewpoint. This must not, however, be misinterpreted as a critique of the idea of viewing Nature as a source of spiritual power; rather, it is precisely because it accomplishes this pneumatic hermeneutics towards Nature in a superior manner that the Golden Age ranks higher than the lower cults of Mother Earth. If anything, the cult of Mother Nature represented an early stage of decline only because it gestured in the direction of the sort of physical materialism which later came to dominate the Western psyche under the Scientific Revolution.

Interestingly, in this chapter Evola cites a climate change as a factor that ended the Golden Age and set into motion a new Atlantic Cycle. As the polar region shifted to freezing weather and long night times,[284] a great migration began for the "Northern primordial race."[285] Evola claims that this movement to new lands resulted in a series of struggles with the indigenous races which tended to worship lower demons and embody characteristics of animal nature. The result was the establishment of a caste hierarchy, one largely organized on the basis of spiritual sophistication. In fact, the true point about the worship of lower animalistic forces was that they ranked closer to the modern norm of materialism.

In the "North and South," the 26th chapter, he noted that with the Atlantic Cycle, we see a shift from the symbolism of the previous Hyperborean civilization.[286] We can observe this shift even with regard to the representation of the same referent. Whereas the later Helios represents the sun through a pattern of ascents and descent over the horizon, the earlier Apollo portrays the sun as a dominating and unchanging source of light. At this point, we get the new symbol of the winter solstice, the disappearance and rebirth.[287]

---

[284] Ibid., p. 189.
[285] These can actually be grouped under two headings, one moving from North to South, another moving from West to East. Another migration to the Americas may have reached a now lost island in the Atlantic which very well may be Plato's Atlantis.
Ibid., p. 195.
[286] Ibid., p. 203.

This entails a shift to the Mother, the Earth, the generating waters. This new cycle is the Silver Age.

Evola argues that there are certain signs of decadence observable in this shift. Whereas the purest civilization embodied the symbolism of fixed stars, the newer symbols are instead those of transient waters. In addition, the shift from the immobile sun to the moon represents a decline in spiritual sophistication.[288] Interestingly, Evola argues that all of the various symbols of lunar spirituality ranging from the Far East to pre-colonial Mexico can only be understood properly if they are "dematerialized" and "regarded as universal references to" the same sort of "lunar spirituality."[289] Whereas the North was associated with the spiritual symbols of the sun and fire, the South was associated with Mother Earth and feminine, lunar spiritualities of Nature.[290] The South is therefore associated with fertility, but fertility of a naturalistic kind. The danger in this situation therefore lies in the temptation to get lost in Nature and lose any interest in the higher calling to strive for transcendence.

In "Civilization of the Mother," the 27th chapter, he noted that with this feminine civilization, we can observe a type of decadence relative to the past age. If the woman is posited as the principle of generation from which every other life emerges, this necessarily devalues each of these lower beings as something "conditioned, subordinated, lacking life in itself, and ephemeral."[291] In Crete, in fact, even the gods were understood to be mortal since the Earth was their mother as well. This shift in emphasis from fixed spiritual essences to natural generation leads to a worldview populated by ever more fragmentary, materialized, and distorted echoes of the past meanings which were better understood in the Golden Age.[292] This is because the overemphasis on the Earth leads

---

[287] Ibid., p. 204.
[288] Ibid., p. 205.
[289] Ibid., p. 207.
[290] Ibid., p. 209.
[291] Ibid., p. 211.
[292] Ibid., p. 213.

one to renounce rising higher to heaven in order to return to one's subterranean origins.²⁹³

The lunar symbolism of this era is similarly a deviation away from the Golden Age in that it portrays the moon as a purified Earth begotten of a woman.²⁹⁴ The tendency to focus on the familial generation from the Mother leads to collectivism in the social body, characterized by fantasies of a perfect community and a world which can be rid of social conflicts by returning to Nature.²⁹⁵ The Lunar spirit is therefore one of mystical unity and brotherhood.²⁹⁶ In other words, the problem with the cult of Mother Nature is not that it is too spiritual and not materialistic enough – it is precisely that it is far too materialistic and not nearly spiritual enough!

In Chapter 30, "The Heroic-Uranian Western Cycle," he noted that regardless of some incidental cases where elements of Tradition were preserved in it, Christianity is fundamentally anti-traditional and is itself an even more degraded manifestation of these same troubling tendencies towards collectivism and materialism. Christianity basically embodies many of the same anti-traditional features of Democracy, much to secular humanists' surprise.²⁹⁷ For example, by making all souls immortal rather than reserving this for the heroic in Valhalla or by emphasizing guilt and the negative fear of Hell over more positive motivations for spiritual ascetic acts they deviated from the norms of Tradition and promoted views that are actually far closer to the dominant ideology of modernity than one could realize without an understanding of the Golden Age.²⁹⁸ This virus of democracy and anti-tradition has led to some features we simply take for granted today, such as the need to view Nature in purely physical terms, or to reduce knowledge of the gods to linguistified myths and nothing more, temptations to which even the greatest Western philosophers such as Socrates and Kant were accused by Evola of falling prey.²⁹⁹ The same trends towards

---

²⁹³ Ibid., p. 214.
²⁹⁴ Ibid., p. 215.
²⁹⁵ Ibid., p. 216.
²⁹⁶ Ibid., p. 217.
²⁹⁷ Ibid., p. 258.
²⁹⁸ Ibid., pp. 258-9.

democracy, linguistification, and materialism which supposedly define the "progress" of modernity are, in reality, nothing more than symptoms of decadence which could be discerned, albeit on less advanced levels, even in the first signs of decline from the Golden Age of Tradition.

In his 1994 prison manifesto *Vargsmål*, Varg Vikernes similarly argued that Nature can only be understood properly if it is disclosed within a horizon of spiritual meaning rather than a materialistic reduction to indifferent physical stuff. Norse Mythology, for example, is simultaneously a window into spiritual truth and natural truth, yet he was careful to insist that one dimension is not reducible to the other.[300] That is to say, although the mythological account does not contradict the scientific explanation, contemporary science has not at all rendered the archaic mythologies worthless. In fact, no matter how much progress the scientists might make in their understanding of Nature, Vikernes claims that the wealth of knowledge contained in the Old Norse myths will always remain a "bottomless well" in comparison. For example, in the opening section of the text he claims that one has only really understood the mythological motif of the giant if one has understood that it is a personification of an uncontrollable force of nature, a force which only comes under control through the godly strength of Odin and his brothers. The world itself was created through such an act of divine battle, in which they transformed the unruly giant Ylmir into the natural order of the world as we know it. When Odin and his two brothers killed Ylmir, the giant's skull became the heavens, his blood became the oceans, his flesh became the earth, his hair became the trees, and so on. It is important to note, however, that this myth does not at all reduce the Earth to a dead lump of matter which lost its spiritual significance sometime in the vastly distant past; it is not just another example of John Zerzan's "will to dominate Nature." A principle of giant's life remains discernible within natural phenomena even to the present day, provided one still has the mythological resources to grasp it.

---

[299] Ibid., p. 262.
[300] Varg Vikernes, *Vargsmål* (unpublished, unofficial 1997 English translation from Norwegian manuscript).

For example, Norse Mythology tells us that the wind emerges when the giant Hrsvaelgr, clad in an eagle's skin, beats his wings. The waves of the ocean similarly result from the giant Egir's activity. One only retains this ability to "see the giants" behind the natural forces, however, if one retains the mythological framework of the traditional worldview. Opting for the crass materialist reductivism of contemporary scientism will never allow the natural phenomena to appear in quite the same way; at best, one will be left with an empty shell which is somehow untrue without being incorrect. Removing the pneuma leaves only linguistification.

Similarly, during an interview after being captured by the System, Ted Kaczynski was asked to describe an ordinary day from his pre-arrest life in the Montana wilderness. One of his fondest memories lay in reflecting on the times he spent hunting rabbits in the snow, a crucial source of protein to get through the harsh winters near the Canadian border in the absence of artificial inputs from the agro-industrial system. Interestingly, he emphasized that although he obviously had to kill these rabbits for his own survival, he always made sure to perform a spiritual ritual of thanking the demi-god "Grandfather Rabbit," as he had personally named it, after performing the act.[301] Nor was this the only spirit with whom he communicated while living in the wild. In a letter to "M. K." he recounted that he decided to start a revolution against the System after personally promising the spirit of a spring in Montana that he would take revenge for the irreversible damage which technology and humans were inflicting against it as more and more of the forest was sacrificed to urban development:

> I stopped and said a kind of prayer to the spirit of the spring. It was a prayer in which I swore that I would take revenge for what was being done to the forest . . . and then I returned home as quickly as I could because – I have something to do! You can guess what it was.[302]

---

[301] Ted Kaczynski, "An Interview with Ted," in *Technological Slavery* (Port Townsend: Feral House, 2010), p. 400.
[302] Ted Kaczynski, "Letter to M.K.", in *Technological Slavery* (Port Townsend: Feral House, 2010), p. 375

These references to "the spirits of Nature" might perplex a reader with even a cursory familiarity with Kaczynski's biography, in that he has repeatedly explicitly identified himself as a materialist. He noted in a letter to David Skrbina from April 5, 2005:

> I do think it's highly probable that the machines will eventually surpass the human brain in intelligence. I'm enough of a materialist to believe that the human brain functions solely according to the laws of physics and chemistry. In other words, it is in a sense a machine, so it should be possible to duplicate it artificially.[303]

An unpublished letter from prison dated to October 12, 1998 echoed this belief without any ambiguity whatsoever. In response to an explicit question on the matter, he responded that he was a materialist, plain and simple, and that all human behaviour can in principle be explained through the Laws of Physics.[304]

Nonetheless, as early as his unpublished 1971 essay "Progress Versus Wilderness" he lamented that although the physical suffering caused by Modern Technology is undeniable, it is not the only damage which humans have had to endure under this historical anomaly of modernity. In addition, he claimed that people's need for wilderness could be grouped among "other spiritual needs" which technology inhibited them from realizing. In fact, he claimed that the "benefit of the whole man" was held back under these conditions, though this passage is admittedly quite obscure and terse.[305] Nonetheless, even a self-proclaimed materialist recognized that Nature can only appear as Nature if it is disclosed

---

[303] Ted Kaczynski, "Letter to David Skrbina, April 5, 2005," in *Technological Slavery* (Port Townsend: Feral House, 2010), p. 329.
[304] Ted Kaczynski, Unpublished and Untitled Letter Dated October 12, 1998, Ted Kaczynski Papers, Labadie Collection at the University of Michigan's Special Collections.
[305] Ted Kaczynski, "Progress Versus Wilderness," Ted Kaczynski Papers, Labadie Collection at the University of Michigan's Special Collections.

through a hermeneutical horizon in which its spiritual value is recognized; the complete, systematic removal of this dimension is precisely what Modern Technology has pursued at ever finer grades of sophistication. The result has not been a perfect view of Nature but rather the disappearance of any possibility of seeing it for what it really is. Zizek's claim that materialist rationalism causes Nature to vanish as a substantial entity is therefore correct, but only insofar as he misses the deeper point that this is only ever a secondary perversion, one which was recognized even millennia ago as a hermeneutical *failure* rather than a purified grasp of the truth.

Given his materialistic biases, therefore, Zizek finds this conversion to Deep Ecology as a "Religion of Nature" (i.e., Linkola, Vikernes, Kaczynski, and, to a lesser extent, Evola etc.) to be the greatest delusion of all, since he claims that this merely negates the Cartesian dimension of radically negative subjectivity by elevating Nature to a new Sacred mystery which must never be unlocked, only bowed down to in pious reverence. He says himself, "[W]e are not Cartesian subjects extracted from reality [in this context], we are [instead reduced to the status of] finite beings embedded in a biosphere which vastly transcends our horizon."[306] For this reason, he argues that Deep Ecology is just one more call for the renunciation of Cartesian subjective agency in favour of some reified organic whole which has simply restored the cosmos to its archaic status as the ultimate pre-given substance.

Zizek claims therefore to hold the solution to unlock the mystery for why, despite all of their calls for people to "radically change their behaviour" to prevent collapse, the big changes never actually arrive. This is no coincidence, since this Deep Ecology is actually all about shying away from revolutionary disruptions in order to maintain some semblance of a functioning status quo.[307]

Although environmentalism is often associated with the political Left, Zizek finds that it is actually an inherently conservative movement, since the attitude prevalent there is that "any change can only be a change for the worse."[308] This resistance

---

[306] Slavoj Zizek, *In Defense of Lost Causes* (London: Verso, 2008), p. 439.
[307] Ibid., pp. 439-40.
[308] Ibid., p. 441.

to change is, however, precisely a *misunderstanding* of how Nature works, since Nature cannot be understood except through the motif of change. It is even more ironic to cite Darwin as a secular prophet for this attitude, since Darwin's real point was that Nature is not a static whole which must be maintained; Nature constantly improves![309]

In other conference talks etc. Zizek has mentioned that it's peculiar to try to defend Nature against catastrophe, because Nature actually is itself already the catastrophe. The fact that some 90% of human DNA is "junk" is evidence that evolution did not occur through some perfectly-engineered plan which was "figured out" in advance. It was in itself something of a catastrophe, accident, and contradiction.[310] Zizek repeats his famous quote that "Nature doesn't exist" in order to reinforce his controversial view that human activity is not some extrinsic obstacle which must be eliminated to allow Nature to function properly. At this point, there is quite literally no such thing as "Nature without human activity." If we disappeared tomorrow, Nature itself would collapse because it has fully adapted itself to all of our intrusions.[311] Contrary to expectation, this realization that Nature doesn't exist is not the madness of solipsistic idealism; it is the only stance possible for someone who has successfully acquired the mindset of a materialist. The true materialist accepts that "Nature in itself" is an idealist fiction because even Nature cannot be the type of Whole which would have to be posited within the naïve Metaphysics of yesteryear.[312] This drives Zizek to openly promote the seemingly-contradictory stance of an "ecology without Nature" as the only viable path forward, because the irony is that the very obstacle to ecological progress is our belief that Nature exists as a whole.[313] Deep ecology calls for humans to abandon their delusions of grandeur and incorporate themselves back into the lifeworld miss the point entirely, since it is precisely the horizon of the common

---

[309] Ibid.
[310] Ibid., p. 442.
[311] Ibid.
[312] Ibid., p. 444.
[313] Ibid., p. 445.

sense lifeworld that inhibits us from actually taking ecological threats seriously. If one gazes at the sky in its immediacy, for example, one *won't* see the hole in the ozone layer, only a clear blue sky. This escapist retreat into natural beauty is exactly the problem. In other words, the Deep Ecologist misses the object precisely by trying to preserve it in all of its beauty and integrity.

Paradoxically, taking the plunge into materialism does not erase the Cartesian cogito by swallowing up the magical agency of subjectivity into the black hole of lifeless matter. Rather, the more materialized the objective body becomes, the more empty the cogito is revealed to be. Yet this void of empty subjectivity is exactly the confrontation with radical negativity which totalitarian "big picture" revolutions entail.[314]

Zizek revisits Heidegger's stance on technology by showing that for Heidegger, the biggest danger is not that some unexpected catastrophe will occur which will reveal all the hopes of unbridled technologization to be false; on the contrary, the real danger is that the catastrophe *won't* arrive, and that the machine will function smoothly until the very horizon of hermeneutical openness is silently closed off forever.[315] Zizek warns that even Deep Ecology has fallen prey to this smooth incorporation. After all, isn't recycling simply a technological project to maximize the usefulness of resources and prevent waste?[316] In other words, isn't the program to recycle simply an example of a coordinated social *technology* oriented towards maximizing efficiency?

Zizek also condemns the dismissal of the coming post-human universe as inherently "meaningless." This is actually a very conservative way to view it, since it ignores the real point that post-humanism is all about the possibility of a multitude of possible meanings.[317] In fact, any aversion to post-humanism which promotes withdrawal back into the natural life-world will fail to solve the problem of Modern Technology. It is only through seizing the radical abyss of negativity that we can find that post-humanism

---

[314] Ibid., pp. 446-7.
[315] Ibid., pp. 447-8.
[316] Ibid., p. 448.
[317] Ibid., p. 449.

provides an unexpected outlet to liberate us *precisely as empty subjects*. Rather than remain stuck at the level of being "symbolic plants" rooted in a certain ecological milieu, technology actually allows us to embrace the subjective position of radical negativity, the true meaning of the Cartesian cogito.[318] He closes the book with the following cryptic quote: "Against the background of this acceptance, we should mobilize ourselves to perform the act which will change destiny itself and thereby insert a new possibility into the past".[319]

Even as early as Zizek's first English-language book, his 1989 classic *The Sublime Object of Ideology,* he broke out of obscurity to obtain international recognition largely through his decision to push back against misconceptions circulated among the half-educated within academia which erroneously grouped Lacan as "just another post-structuralist." This tendency to treat Lacan as just another Derrida or Lyotard completely missed the point of his work, which was that there is indeed one exception to such frenzied attempts to submit everything whatsoever to linguistic deconstruction: the psychoanalytic patient's symptom is the only substance in the early Zizekian universe. If it is deconstructed, the subject will only find his or her entire world dissolve as the knot which held it all together fell to pieces. Yet even the attempt to disintegrate it is more illusory than real, as the symptom is precisely that excess which returns with a vengeance despite one's attempts to exorcise it from one's world:

> It is precisely the symptom which is conceived as such a Real kernel of enjoyment, which persists as a surplus and returns through all attempts to domesticate it, to gentrify it . . ., to dissolve it by means of explication, of putting-into-words its meaning.[320]

Contrary to expectation, Zizek's unusual decision to equate symptom with substance was simply the logical conclusion of his

---

[318] Ibid., p. 452.
[319] Ibid., p. 460.
[320] Slavoj Zizek, *The Sublime Object of Ideology* (London: Verso, 1989), p. 69.

commitment to the doctrine of materialism, a topic which he attempted to combine with an idiosyncratic treatment of Quantum Physics in his sprawling thousand-page book from 2012, *Less Than Nothing*. Paradoxically, contemporary science can only lead one to affirm a materialism without matter, in which the very illusion that matter is a set of solid, mechanistic building blocks lacking change or agency gives way to a materialism in which the Ancient Greek binary between "something and nothing" is superseded by the supremely bizarre category of something which is "less than nothing":

> [S]ubstance is not only always already lost, it only comes to be through its loss, as a secondary return-to-itself—which means that substance is always already subjectivized.[321]

In this materialist universe which somehow comes to fruition only if matter is de-substantialized, Zizek argues that Deep Ecology misses the point entirely by remaining committed to the Metaphysical illusion that Nature is a fixed substance which must be faithfully preserved in its essence and defended against Man's exterior interventions. This misses the point that both substance and subject must "lose their identity" in this configuration:

> Take the case of ecology: radical emancipatory politics should aim neither at complete mastery over nature nor at humanity's humble acceptance of the predominance of Mother Earth. Rather, nature should be exposed in all its catastrophic contingency and indeterminacy, and the unpredictable consequences of human agency fully assumed.[322]

Zizek's insistence that "Nature doesn't exist" is, of course, for Linkola, the ultimate absurdity: Nature is the only substance, yet by this Linkola does not mean the naïve view of Nature qua a materialistic object which must be opposed to the fluidity and openness of human subjectivity; rather, Linkola's insistence on

---

[321] Zizek, Slavoj. *Less Than Nothing* (London: Verso, 2012), p. 259.
[322] Ibid.

Nature's precedence over all other types of objects lies in his commitment to the Mind of Nature as a rationalized system of laws dictated by the demands of ecological validity. This makes up the ultimate superset in which any valid configuration must be a subset in order to exist. The dissolution of this Mind of Nature would indeed collapse the world (much like the Lacanian symptom in the early Zizek's universe), yet not merely on the level of psychoanalytic individuality but on the level of ecological collectivity as well.

Nature is not a Materialist

Clever as his argument might be on theoretical grounds, Linkola would argue that Zizek missed the irony that even the Mind of Nature is not a materialist. In fact, few things contradict the Mind of Nature quite as thoroughly as this ideology. In his essay "Sales Season" he mentioned the utter absurdity of consumerism by recounting that some non-alcoholic wine he ordered at a restaurant while traveling was the single most expensive food item he had ever purchased. The idiocy inherent in luxury food item prices is itself, however, just one symptom of the general madness of materialism which had engulfed modernity.[323] Although taken for granted as obvious truth accessible on the basis of common sense alone, he noted that this "extremely material zeitgeist" we live under is a historical anomaly which is contradicted by eras even as recent as the one he lived through in his childhood. It was not so long ago that overcoming mere materialism for the sake of rising up to higher principles was valued as the ideal norm. This was not completely unfounded either, for past generations were perceptive enough to realize the nasty consequences of wilfully disconnecting themselves from these higher orders of meaning. Linkola notes that, without question, the worst form of materialism in world history is the Reign of Money which currently exercises unrestricted dominion over the Earth:

---

[323] Pentti Linkola, "Sales Season," in *Can Life Prevail?* (Kindle Edition).

> These ever-present giant-letter signs displaying sums of money are [all just an] expression of the extremely material Zeitgeist we are living in. [Past generations] bemoaned and disapproved of materialism, always attempting to get rid of it for the sake of "higher goals" (let us simply say in the name of ideology, philosophy, science and art). Now, [however,] we have entered the time of the most manifest and absolute materialism ever known to the world: the reign of money.[324]

Linkola notes in the same essay that even when he was a child, it was generally understood to be impolite to discuss the topic of money. Now, however, one's dollar-value is literally one's only value:

> Consideration and good manners were of utmost importance to these people [of the past], who followed one basic rule: never to discuss money, even if occasionally one might have pondered upon his own financial situation.[325]

In his "Thoughts And Memories About The Old Educated Class - A View Into The Century's Ideological History" he recounted that it was not so long ago that realizing that money was the one topic which one was never allowed to discuss was precisely the "mark of education."[326] Classiness was not at all the modern pseudo-category denominated solely in dollars; it was, rather, defined as a striving for a "deeply spiritual life" and an active resistance to any temptation to drop down to the lowest common denominator of materialistic greed. Even if one did happen to come by a considerable surplus of money, it was understood that one had a duty to the community to divert this to "supporting culture and charity" rather than to inflating one's own net worth even further. In

---

[324] Ibid.
[325] Ibid.
[326] Pentti Linkola, "Thoughts And Memories About The Old Educated Class - A View Into The Century's Ideological History," in *A Collection of Essays by Pentti Linkola 1993 – 2006*, pp. 110-1.

fact, even among the educated classes one's level of material consumption was still quite modest without dropping them down to stereotypes of a joyless "monastery" of ascetic renunciation.[327]

These days, of course, all of this will likely sound as farfetched as the fairy tales compiled by the Grimms. In his "Sales Season," he lamented that gone are the days when one could even smile at one's neighbours, let alone chat with the mailman or the shopkeeper down the road in order to maintain the local community. Civility is long dead, as behind the façade of a democratically levelled society in which all lives are equal lies the reality of a new caste system in which one's value as a human being is only measured in the crassest of numerical terms. A person quite literally has a price on his or her head to determine whether he or she is worthy of the most basic of human rights: recognition:

> [C]lass and its values are almost dead: they have been completely stamped out. Some old geezer or grandma may still be living in their own minority culture, greeting all neighbours, stopping to talk to the janitor, radiating a puzzling smile of friendship to a nation of windbreakers [but most everyone else has lost this ability].[328]

This tragedy has become so widespread that few even among the older generation can recall that it was not so long ago that even the intelligentsia itself was far more tolerable. In his "Thoughts And Memories About The Old Educated Class - A View Into The Century's Ideological History," Linkola explained that the modern expectation associating the educated class with elitist snobbery and environmentalist hypocrisy are actually a fairly recent innovation which was more or less unknown even in his own childhood. At that time, for example, he recalled that the university's janitor at his father's workplace would attempt to reduce resource waste by "cutting the [ink] with water," yet this was precisely because he had "learned the values of education so deeply" through exposure to the educated class.[329] This is of course

---

[327] Ibid., p. 110.
[328] Pentti Linkola, "Sales Season," in *Can Life Prevail?* (Kindle Edition).

a far cry from the degradation of the "educated class" exhibited in recent years, in which an ever-shrinking minority of super-elite academics erect ever more complicated barriers to keep the ignorant masses on the outside of their own ivory tower "sanctuaries" in order to ensure that the purity of the priesthood of progress is safeguarded against the contamination which even a doctorate degree-holding adjunct would bring in if he or she were allowed to sit in the presence of the mighty intelligentsia and interrupt their "serious intellectual work," which largely consists of constructing ever more elaborate pseudo-explanations for why all the problems in the world stem from the crime of having gender-specific bathrooms assigned within a false binary of male and female categories which ignore the recent findings of "experts" that some 68 gender categories, in fact, really exist. If only every gas station in America had 68 different bathrooms on site, the world might be rid of war, disease, famine, and ecological crisis.

The rapid decline of the educated class is, however, only one smaller part of a degradation of society as a whole which has coincided almost perfectly with the rise of Modern Technology. Linkola noted in his 2004 interview with Virpi Adamsson that Finland was far more pleasant precisely before industrialization had accelerated (i.e., in the 1950s and earlier), since this was a time when things which would seem "primitive" to later generations such as horses and ploughmen were still common sights to see but, overall, people were far more cheerful, no doubt, because these traditional chores kept them occupied with meaningful work to do.[330] The ultimate reason why this era was so much better was, of course, that Nature was allowed far more room to thrive. In his lengthy interview with *Quadrivium*, he recalled:

---

[329] Pentti Linkola, "Thoughts And Memories About The Old Educated Class - A View Into The Century's Ideological History," in *A Collection of Essays by Pentti Linkola 1993 – 2006*, pp. 110-1.

[330] "Interview with Pentti Linkola 10-2-2004." Available at http://www.penttilinkola.com/pentti_linkola/ecofascism_writings/interview_10-2-2003

> In the past, you couldn't even imagine that there would be no workhorses in Finland. I was already an old man when there were four hundred thousand workhorses here in the sixties. Then they started to get fewer but I always assumed there would be enough for those who truly needed them. In the last two or three years we've gotten into a situation where even if I won the lottery and promised one million euros for a workhorse, I wouldn't be able to get one because none exist. This is what we're left with.

In his 1993 "From Gunslingers To Environmental Disasters," he concluded that Finland has succeeded in turning completely upside-down in the short timespan of just less than fifty years.[331]

Similarly, in his 1993 "Finland Equals Forests" he admitted that selling out their forests to the Satan of industrial greed had indeed brought Finns a larger quantity of material luxuries (i.e., millions of cars, electronic entertainment devices, unnecessary buildings, cruise ship vacations etc.). However, "foremost, because of this wealth people are more frustrated, unemployed, unhappier, more suicidal, immobile, worthless and without purpose than ever before in history. A downright miserable exchange."[332] Somehow, the cure turned out to be the poison, yet people continue to demand "higher pay" as the only solution for the same problems caused by too much money.

In an exceptionally cringeworthy online posting which was later deleted from the site that hosted it, one professional software engineer could not help asking the Internet why exactly it was that women he tried to hit on would still rather hook up with a meat-headed bartender rather than a six figure salary corporate professional, despite the obvious fact that the latter has "a better job" and a lot more money. Or to phrase it without any polite euphemisms, why do women still obey their own natural instincts dictating how they respond to "outdated" factors like physical

---

[331] Pentti Linkola, "From Gunslingers To Environmental Disasters" in *A Collection of Essays by Pentti Linkola 1993 – 2006*, p. 37.
[332] Pentti Linkola, "Finland Equals Forest," in *A Collection of Essays by Pentti Linkola 1993 – 2006*, p. 20.

attractiveness and social charisma when they should just shut up and let the money speak for itself? This fellow appears to have expressed dismay that the "democratic rationalization of society" still lingered behind its ideal, since these hard-wired social instincts were getting in the way of a perfect world in which, apparently, even the most intolerable, boring, graceless, and physically unattractive brute could just buy his way to get any woman he happens to desire with cold hard cash. One also cannot help but suspect that what really bothered him about the guy across the counter pouring beer and whiskey for a living was simply the fact that some working-class Average Joe could compete with someone from a higher social class and win, even on the basis of his own personal talents. In a perfectly-modernized society, in other words, the distribution of money alone would fix outcomes in advance to privilege those who happen to have more of the stuff, however questionable the means by which they obtained it; after all, it is an open secret that the technological industry does not actually make an honest profit but instead skates by on fraudulently-high stock prices and through massive loans from the usury industry, yet its adherents still claim to have succeeded on "purely meritocratic grounds." This case proves that, apparently, behind the politically correct façade of egalitarianism lies the fantasy of a society which is *completely* rigged to favour the rich, even to the point of forcing women to date or marry men they do not find attractive on any level, simply because these guys happen to have more money than they do. It is peculiar that the same liberal figures who condemn forced marriages within tribal societies as hopelessly primitive remnants of the patriarchal past would essentially argue for the same thing in their own societies by promoting arranged marriages determined not even by tribal elders with at least some level of human judgment but rather by the impersonal pseudo-agency of the dollar bill itself, something which may eventually be granted license to place a figurative gun to a beautiful woman's head and force her to share the bed of an unattractive man against her will simply because he happened to have corporate connections and a high salary. In other words, the same modern liberals who would condemn Achilles' and Agamemnon's fight in Book 1 of *The Iliad* over which "brave warrior" had earned the right to carry off Briseis to his own tent along the Trojan coast would find no problem substituting money for war as the abstract mediator which determines how defenceless and voiceless women are distributed to the victors of fossil fuel-based technological imperialism.

In the process of this ongoing reduction to materialistic abstraction in which financial pseudo-values overwhelm any other criteria, organic communities have crumbled into ever more isolated, intolerable, and entitled suburban humanoids who somehow find that the more money they get, the less pleasant their lives become, yet argue that the solution lies in angrily demanding even more money. It is comical that the supposedly "radical political thinkers" of our era such as Ana Kasparian of the Young Turks argue that "higher pay for the middle class" is the supreme ethical call of our time, without realizing that the average American suburbanite already has a higher standard of living than any Ancient or Medieval emperor. Her 2016 article "The Real Reason We're Not Having Kids" proves that few problems in our era ever demand solutions which are not denominated solely in cold hard cash, in that her article ostensibly demands that each suburbanite be granted some $300,000 to cover the "absolute bare minimum costs to raise one child":

> If the federal government is so concerned with why people are deciding against having kids, maybe they should consider how little support and protection the middle class gets when it comes to being parents. Paid leave would be a good start and increasing wages would also help.[333]

During the 2020 Democrat Primary debacle, leaked documents revealed some Bernie Bros had threatened that "Milwaukee would burn" if their candidate was not given the nomination, yet one cannot interpret this credible threat for violence as anything except evidence that the supreme ethical mandate of our era is just the demand to give a group of clueless First World idlers even more

---

[333] Ana Kasparian, "The real reasons we're not having kids", RawStory, https://www.rawstory.com/ 2016/ 08/ the-real-reason-were-not-having-kids/

free stuff than the fossil fuel miracle has already dropped into their laps through flooding the government feeding troughs with more taxpayer-funded free junk. It is no exaggeration to say that crass materialistic greed has been elevated to the status of a secular crusader's call, opening the floodgates to pillage and burn cities as the "only ethical option" in a Holy War fought for the "higher cause" of raw financial self-interest.

Like Linkola, Dmitry Orlov has noted, however, that Americans' expectation that people's value is solely to be measured by their yearly income is not even normal by Soviet standards, since it had to be artificially engineered through a system in which costs, regulations, and inflation had been wilfully driven to criminally high levels.[334] Yet even the financial shenanigans of the usury industry are not sufficient in themselves to account for this tragedy.

Instead, Linkola shocked readers in his essay "Sales Season" by pulling the mask from the culprit's face to reveal none other than *journalists* as the main source lying behind this change to a materialistic "zeitgeist," dismissing them as "an unbelievably irresponsible, vile, and harmful category of men" as a result.[335] Linkola's insistence that journalists are to blame for this crisis suggests that, paradoxically, even materialism is not a naturalistic purification of humanistic bias but is, rather, the ultimate humanistic chimera, since it requires linguistic abuse from the talking heads within the media to be implemented on a mass scale, as the following chapter shall examine in much greater detail.

In this essay, Linkola dismisses the myth that the media serve the role as "professional intellectuals," since anyone with a functioning hermeneutical horizon can see the obvious fact that they are just so many "monkeys running after the latest trend" who lack even the ability to invent an original thought of their own, simply "emulating each other like sheep" in order to follow the direction in which the rest of the lemmings are running. Few people realize, in fact, that the term "pundit" was originally derived from the Sanskrit term "pandita," a word for an extremely learned person – an expert,

---

[334] Dmitry Orlov, *Reinventing Collapse: The Soviet Experience and American Prospects* (Gabriola Island: New Society Publishers, 2011)
[335] Pentti Linkola, "Sales Season," in *Can Life Prevail?* (Kindle Edition).

if you will. Few terms have declined in their meaning quite as much as a word virtually synonymous today with "blathering asshole" or "professional bullshitter." This is arguably the single most memorable case to prove that Heidegger's lamentation that "language [no longer] speaks in the word" is well-founded.[336]

It is peculiar that these professional bullshitters pride themselves on taking up the hard work of interpreting the news for the rest of the human population by implicitly justifying this outsourcing of a faculty as basic as *thinking* itself on grounds that the ignorant masses are "too stupid to do so for themselves." It is frightening to imagine that they have seized control of our thinking when they have proven themselves to be unfit even to direct their own. Recently, two MSNBC talking heads claimed on air that Michael Bloomberg spent 500 million dollars on ads but could have instead given every American one million dollars; they insisted that even if Bloomberg had done so, he would have still had money left over afterwards to spend on other stuff, definitive proof that "there is way too much money in politics." Unfortunately, anyone with a fifth-grade education could see that this is a mathematical error nearly akin to mistaking the number one for the number one million.

Linkola is one of the few thinkers with the guts to acknowledge that behind the façade of being "professional thinkers," their function is no different from that of a sales sign plastered over a shop window: it is simply to fill peoples consciousness with senseless rubbish in order to erect walls around serious issues like overpopulation, pollution, and extinction by barring any real problems from entering the public discussion. He concludes that what we really need right now is "a new Jesus to drive the merchants out of the temple," a movement he admits he himself "would immediately join as a disciple."[337]

---

[336] See Heidegger's later collection of talks *On the Way to Language* for his view that language is not a set of labels to be stuck onto objects but is rather something which speaks in the word. This speaking has declined in modernity. For example, the Ancient Greek term for an "atom" speaks of that which cannot be cut further. The modern technical term, however, blots out this speaking and instead serves as an arbitrary label.

In addition to harshly critiquing journalists, in his 1993 essay "Armoured Idiot" Linkola openly wondered why sociopsychological theory has still failed to provide an explanation for why stupidity and intelligence are distributed within the population "not nearly in accordance with the statistical probabilities." Rather than occur equally across all strata of society, "there are some fields of study and some professions to which stupidity specifically accumulates, makes a nest, as it's said." Idiocy has become something of a job requirement for professional "sociologists, meteorologists," and, of course, "economists." One could make a strong case for adding academic philosophers to this list, though Linkola does not do so himself.[338]

Saving Nature?

It is peculiar for leftists, even including Zizek himself, to cite the philosophy of materialism as the saviour of Nature, since Linkola noted in his essay "It is Dark in the Woods" that it is precisely because the ideology of materialism has squeezed out any higher standard of value that the logging industry, for example, can't approach the forest from any perspective *except* one denominated solely by raw financial gain. In the aftermath of the flight of the traditional gods, the only one which remains is the dollar bill and its overseas equivalents. Contrary to expectation, it is not spiritual superstitions which drive the mindless plunder of the Earth; rather, it is precisely because its spiritual dimension has vanished that the Earth is reduced to a purely materialistic lump of goods to be mined for money, even though the latter can only be wasted on the most trivial of consumer goods anyway:

> [W]ith regard to morals, . . . the industry's only gods are the bank and the market: the industry would readily sell its own grandmother.[339]

---

[337] Ibid.
[338] Pentti Linkola, "Armored Idiot," in *A Collection of Essays by Pentti Linkola 1993 – 2006*, p. 7.
[339] Pentti Linkola, "It is Dark in the Woods," in *Can Life Prevail?* (Kindle Edition).

Contrary to expectation, therefore, modernistic materialism does not provide one with a "better understanding" of Nature as it is in itself, but instead results in a complete lack of understanding of anything which falls outside of this one specific money-making goal. Yet one could be even more specific and note, as Linkola does, that this reduction is simply the process of technologization in disguise:

> A merchant's plans for profit do not extend beyond the horizon. To produce an advantageous forest statistic is the most profitable of businesses. It is worth investing in, budgeting great sums of money for, preparing with care and cleverly disguising [the truth].[340]

Generating figures that look like surpluses even if they don't happen to really exist is therefore nothing more than a technical solution to the economic problem of maximizing profit, a stance which logically follows from espousing the ideology of materialism:

> Can anyone picture the forest industry publishing a statistic that points to a decrease in timber reserves or, worse still, a catastrophic decline? . . . [Insiders] will [continue to claim] that timber reserves are increasing even when the last currant bushes are being torn from peoples' yards and sent to the pulp mills.[341]

In other words, materialism is not the pathway to grasp Nature without archaic superstitions – it is, rather, just another form of technology, another apparatus to dominate Nature by distorting its essence to a lifeless reserve of industrial matter.

Not coincidentally, Linkola explicitly cited this materialist destruction of "piety" towards Nature as the final and worst phase in a long process of decline. His 2004 "A Refresher Course About

---

[340] Ibid.
[341] Ibid.

Forest" ends with the grim depiction of a sacred forest which had been left "untouched until the very last moments, mainly out of piety" but was suddenly opened for business to exploiters as soon as those two magic words "clearance sale" had been pronounced over it by the czars of greed. Now, the "final solution is under way" and "all restrictions have become void" as the "death dealers and officials of the apocalypse" move in for the kill and any final traces of that "archaic sense of honour" are drowned out by the roar of industrial machinery pillaging the land, all for a tiny financial return which will be squandered immediately by the fools who stole it from Nature anyway: "Finis Finlandiae."[342] Materialism is simply the technological linguistification of Nature.

Linkola vs. Husserl: Suspending the Unnatural Attitude

Given his fundamental suspicions against linguistification and his affirmation of ecological forms, one might go as far as to consider Linkola's philosophy to be something like a Phenomenology founded on Natural Reason rather than Transcendental Reason. In fact, despite this fundamental disagreement, Linkola's warnings regarding language are actually far closer to Husserl's than has been previously noted, with the exception of the following distinction: whereas Husserl warned that a statement could pass the grammatical rules of natural language syntax but still fail to pass the test of transcendental validity, Linkola implies that a linguistic statement is useless if it fails the test of ecological validity.

In Edmund Husserl's fourth logical investigation, he warned that linguistic nonsense and logical nonsense are quite different things which are often confused for one another simply because people lack more explicit terms to separate them. While nonsense (*Unsinn*) merely contains grammatical errors on the level of natural language, the more forceful term "counter sense" (*Widersinn*) refers to statements which contain no grammatical error as such but still offend against logic, typically through generating labels which refer to impossible objects. This is not merely a problem of speaking of

---

[342] Pentti Linkola, "A Refresher Course about Forest," in *A Collection of Essays by Pentti Linkola 1993 – 2006*, p. 33.

strange naturalistic life forms such as unicorns or jackelopes which certainly *could* exist, even though they don't; it is a problem of offending against the laws of reason itself by abusing the lax rules of linguistic grammar to formulate statements about objects which would require a suspension of the *a priori* laws of logic in order to exist, such as a square circle or a rectangular shape with five 90 degree angles.

One might argue that detecting counter sense requires a far more sophisticated type of mind than catching linguistic nonsense would. Even a fairly primitive computer would easily detect the latter on the basis of testing statements against the backdrop of a small set of grammatical rules, but only a transcendental subject capable of gaining real insight into the rationalized structures of its own consciousness itself could deduce whether an object is possible or impossible on transcendental grounds alone. Husserl's methodology for discovering whether an object *could* exist on transcendental grounds required a very strange intermediary position between the mechanistic abstraction of computeristic formalism and the biological vitality of embodied personhood, since neither would be able to recognize these types of structures on their own. Neither a machine nor a mere animal could see what the transcendental subject could find within itself.

Interestingly, he insisted that obtaining the proper mindset required an active suspension of nothing short of the *Natural* Attitude itself. By this, Husserl meant that one could only make progress in unearthing the purified structures of transcendental consciousness if one avoided the trap of getting stuck in one's ordinary standpoint towards experience, in which one would understand oneself to be an embodied person situated within a physical world extended in space and enduring over time. This attitude would only lead one to interpret the contents of experience as so many naturalistic objects spread out within that world and would inevitably cause one to waste precious time in endless debates over the metaphysical status of those objects. This is precisely the methodological roadblock which would distract one from recognizing the purified forms which had already been revealed to consciousness itself with no need to be artificially reconstructed on symbolic grounds alone, much like the Purloined Letter in Edgar Allen Poe's short story of the same name: it is impossible for the detectives to find it precisely because it was placed out in the open. As the investigators proceeded to check every spot in which it might be hidden, effectively disassembling the entire apartment in the process, it was sitting quietly in the spot reserved for letters all along, exactly where it was supposed to be.

It is supremely ironic that whereas Husserl emphasized that one can only arrive at a purified view of transcendental possibility and impossibility through suspending the Natural Attitude, Linkola argues for precisely the opposite view: one can only gain a purified view of Being (or more precisely, of ecological possibility and impossibility) through instead *radicalizing* the Natural Attitude.[343] One must suspend the Mind of Man in order to acquire the Mind of Nature itself, however imperfectly.

One of the benefits of reverting to the Mind of Nature is that ecological counter sense can be exposed without any regard for the kind of rhetorical nonsense which would otherwise cloud one's judgment by tricking one into wasting time entering into linguistic debate with a chimera which does not exist in the least. For example, although virtually no one has the guts to admit it, the cause of most of the economic suffering in the world today is financial inflation driven by usury. Even Linkola's own personal biography has been scarred by this injustice, as his *Quadrivium* interviewers recounted that Kaarlo Linkola, his father, "died from a blood-clot related complication after undergoing prostate surgery when his son was nine years of age . . . He left behind a large life insurance, which, according to his son, was devoured by wartime inflation."

Usury's financial distortion of natural forms is not an accidental bug to the system but is rather the true underlying purpose at work from the moment a new-born baby is thrown to the wolves of life under Modern Industrialism. The ugly truth about the liberal fantasy of "universal college attendance," for example, is

---

[343] Obviously, Linkola did not mean this in exactly the same way that Husserl used the term natural attitude. However, it is still an irony and play on words worthy of using.

that this turned out to be nothing more than a politically correct dog whistle to force an entire generation of people into state-mandated student loan slavery. While the results were financially devastating on an individual level, it is rarely acknowledged that student loan usury has made our situation far worse than it needed to be on ecological grounds as well.

One might consider, for example, the utter insanity represented by the fact that even though a fairly large number of people in the West would prefer to live simpler lifestyles akin even to those of Ted Kaczynski or Pentti Linkola himself, they simply are not able to because the road to self-sufficiency is blocked by financial chimeras with less existence than the goblins and trolls of fairy tales.

Although they would seem laughably unrealistic today, traditional occupations such as living as a fur trapper or a goat herder were relatively common less than two centuries ago. Today, however, they are ruled out not due to a lack of interest among the public, but rather because they simply don't generate enough raw cash each month to cover expenses which are only so high because the usurers have flooded the system with so much fake money. Worse still, even after one finishes college and finds that the door to the corporate aristocracy has been locked from inside and the debt collectors are quickly moving in for the kill, one finds that one still cannot opt for a simple lifestyle living off the land, simply because it does not generate enough cash each month to cover exploding student loan payments.

Even the value of the "college experience" itself has been almost entirely drained of real Being, as "education" has become just one more linguistic chimera among all the others. It is quite troubling to realize that a college acceptance letter has devolved into little more than a cleverly-marketed ticket of admission to attend a five-year-party on a landed cruise ship. In exchange for attending the state-sponsored sin-fest where five years of binging on the basest material excesses, including abundantly-available illegal drugs which administrators realize are a valuable marketing asset rather than a "problem" to be stamped out, one can count on spending the remainder of one's life in a financial Hell paying one's bill for these indulgences by handing over one four-figure monthly payment at a time.

Yet in our era, even someone with no personal debt (a specimen which is almost as difficult to track down as Bigfoot) who sincerely desired to go off the grid and survive in a log cabin without electricity or running water would be prohibited by grotesquely-overinflated real estate prices which are sustained only through the humanistic chimeras of "quantitative easing" and a financial aristocracy grown rich through charging interest on money that doesn't exist. It is bizarre that one would have to effectively become a millionaire just to attempt to a live a medieval peasant's lifestyle, since it would require something like a seven-figure mortgage with high interest rates just to become a simple subsistence farmer with enough land to feed one's family on a meagre diet of home-grown crops and the occasional meat from on-site livestock.

In 2014, it was reported in the news that Jason Brown, a former St. Louis Ram who was at one point the highest-paid center in the NFL, had quit professional football in order to become a sweet potato farmer in rural North Carolina.[344] Undeterred by his lack of formal experience in agriculture, he embarked on an independent training course through watching YouTube videos for free and through trial and error on his own land. When the time arrived for his first harvest, he proudly declared to the news camera that he had never felt more successful in his life, despite his considerable athletic and financial accomplishments in the past. Interviewers were, however, enormously shocked to find that he lacked any interest in making a profit off of all of his hard labour and instead gave away his entire harvest to feed the poor, citing the Bible verse John 21:17 ("feed my sheep") as the properly religious inspiration which motivated his unusual decision to return to the land in the first place. While Brown's story is no doubt worthy of the highest level of admiration, it still demonstrates something quite troubling about the historical era in which we live, in that this story proves that someone would basically have to be a professional

---

[344] Tony Manfred, "Ex-NFL Player Who Made $25 Million Quit Football At Age 29 To Become A Farmer," *Business Insider*, 20-11-2014.

athlete with a multi-million dollar fortune just to buy a farm in the countryside and live a traditional peasant lifestyle. In other words, the irony about our era is that a man can only hear the spiritual call to turn his back on Mammon and serve Christ instead if he had already been "blessed" by the god of greed first.[345] It is quite chilling that one can't even take the leap of faith to obey Jesus' command to feed the poor unless one somehow has access to enough financial capital to pay a seven-figure bribe to the gatekeepers of the usury industry just to pursue a lifestyle which the very poorest peasants in the Medieval Era were free to live out without any further barriers than being born into the profession. There are undoubtedly countless people stuck in "dead end jobs" who would love to quit the life they are bound to and go back to living off the land but find that this is not even an option unless they somehow win the lottery first.

     Similarly, it is truly bizarre that universal suburbanization gobbled up the entire nation of the United States in order to provide a technical solution to remove "outdated" modes of social organization which predated the historical anomaly in which every single adult had his or her own private car and the price of petroleum was low enough to make commuting 150 miles per day seem normal and (even more laughably) indefinitely economically feasible. Somehow, though, the solution became its own problem, since "keeping up with the Joneses" simply meant being trapped in a dreadful non-place in which one had to endure the frustration of spending four hours every day idling on stagnant freeways choked with six lanes of traffic going each way, as well as the boredom of being isolated in a cardboard McMansion in a pseudo-community filled with the same boring cookie-cutter strip malls, fast food restaurants, retail centres, and gas stations as any other location in the United States would have. Paradoxically, historic neighbourhoods constructed before the invention of the automobile suddenly became an exotic fascination in themselves, as countless disgruntled suburbanites fled in a mass exodus from anonymous locations all across the heartland with the dream of getting to live in

---

[345] Matthew 6:24

New York City, Washington, D.C., or Boston, simply in order to dwell in a neighbourhood filled with old-fashioned architecture, walkable streets, and unique shops and restaurants which could not be found anywhere else in the world. The ensuing real estate bubbles in such locations made living there into a highly-coveted prize which could motivate one to sell one's soul out to the System, even though a tacky apartment infested with rats and cockroaches in New York could still be valued at well over one million dollars simply as a matter of supply and demand.

What virtually no one stopped to realize, though, was that this experience of living in a densely-populated, walkable neighbourhood filled with old-fashioned architecture and unique restaurants and shops is something which can be found even in rural villages and poor urban neighbourhoods in India, yet for a price so low as to be virtually free by American standards. I myself get to experience something far more fascinating than any East Coast American city while paying just 50 dollars per month to rent a whole house in India, in a rural village so obscure as to not even have a Wikipedia page, no less! In other words, I get the real thing virtually for free while someone in the First World would have to pay millions of dollars just for a cheap imitation of it, even in the "most happening" spots in America. Just as Jason Brown's story proved you basically have to be an NFL star just to return back to the land as a peasant, an American effectively needs to be a millionaire just to live like a Third World slum dweller or like an urban citizen did during the 19th Century. Somehow, the archaic object which was removed from circulation precisely because it was deemed fit only for pre-modern peasants and manual labourers somehow morphed into a luxury item which the highest-ranking elites had to fight for, as Zachary Levi (star of the NBC show *Chuck*) told Jay Leno on his show in 2011 that after achieving international celebrity status he had finally gotten to live out his lifelong dream of having a flat in Manhattan and getting to walk around New York and ride the subway; in other words, you have to be a Hollywood star just to have the opportunity to *walk!* Don Lemon of CNN similarly praised New York City as a Mecca of excitement since it had so many unique shops and restaurants which his own native flyover state of Louisiana did not, without realizing that every rural town in the American South had a thriving local economy not so long ago and that these were wilfully dismantled and its participants driven out of business solely in order to promote corporate greed in the name of "technological progress."

In addition to directly generating economic inequality and social unrest, usury has also forced the entire population to commit eco-crimes against their will. Because a universally-indebted population ends up needing far more cash than it otherwise would have needed, even the poor are forced to be major polluters. A minimum wage labourer begging for a handful of crumbs to fall from the elites' banquet tables by clocking in twenty hours per week at three different part-time gigs will still have to drive an extraordinarily high number of miles every week in order to travel from one poorly-paid job to another among the suburban sprawl of his or her metropolitan area. Worse still, such a person would still be unable to afford a luxury as basic as a roof over his or her head even after committing tragically irreversible pollution against the environment. Usury is arguably the worst of all eco-crimes, the ultimate sin forbidden by the Mind of Nature, since it is not a single crime in itself so much as it is a virus which replicates itself over countless nodes within the population into which it had been released in an act of financial fraud akin to the bio-terroristic poisoning of a water supply. One could speculate that the Green Police would immediately be summoned to remove this cancer from the Earth before proceeding to any other duties. It is not unreasonable to argue that the Mind of Nature would conclude that it had no choice but to destroy usury before usury destroyed the Earth. It is too early to determine whether the Mind of Nature would propose capital punishment for anyone caught scamming the masses with this crime, but this would hardly be historically unprecedented; publicly hanging such criminals was, in fact, the historical norm which was only discontinued quite recently and will arguably prove to be a perfectly reasonable response in the far future as well.

Usury is a peculiar humanistic chimera, in that its scandalous character was easily recognized for centuries and only came to be obfuscated into public acceptance in recent years. It is strange to think that something once considered a damnable offense worthy of capital punishment has now come to be seen not only as a necessary evil to be able to live a normal life but has even come to be seen as a good in itself. One should bear in mind that all of the work to keep a good credit score simply facilitates one's ability to maintain the "privilege" of being exploited by usurers by being issued even more debt. Yet whatever the validity of traditional religious condemnations of usury might be, it is a fact that financial inflation driven by usury is ecological counter sense which utterly fails the ontological test of Being. It is impossible to extract an infinite amount of real wealth out of a finite planet, yet this is precisely what the usurer demands by universally issuing massive loans with no regard for the borrower's ability to pay back and no concern for the inherent value of a product.

Linkola and the Creationists

Linkola differs from Husserl for the additional reason that whereas Husserl largely considered truth to be the result of the transcendental subject's self-investigation of its own mind, Linkola is far closer to Plato or to Thomas Aquinas, for whom truth was found precisely in leaving behind the fallen, corporeal Mind of Man in order to become acquainted with the eternal truths of the World of Ideas (Plato) or the Mind of God (Aquinas), respectively.

One difference between medieval and modern views on Christianity lies in the following strange reversal which is virtually never noticed. Modern Christian evangelists and apologists largely consider their jobs to consist of finding some way to make the Bible's divine revelations catch up with secular standards of human rationalism by piecing together complicated arguments to reveal unexpected connections between bits of scientific evidence and passages from scripture in order to prove that one does not contradict the other.

Although Ken Ham, the Australian fundamentalist who founded the Creation Science Museum and Ark Encounter in Kentucky, has become something of a condensed symbol of "antiscientific ignorance" among secularist and atheist circles, this stereotype completely misses the point that he has arguably taken this requirement to find some way for divine revelation to catch up with contemporary science more seriously than anyone else before him. For example, few people realize that he has staffed his Creation Science Museum with academic professionals holding PhD's in the hard sciences from secular R1 universities. This is an enormous change from just a single generation ago, when creationist Kent Hovind drew flak from secularists for calling himself "Dr. Dino" (even insisting on having his local phonebook in Florida list his official name as "Dr. Kent Hovind," something which virtually no one with a PhD even from a "top-rated university" would request) despite the fact that his doctorate degree was in (the "pseudo-science" of) biblical ministry and was allegedly purchased for a few hundred dollars from an unaccredited online school called Patriot Bible University, an alma mater which was widely mocked in online memes for supposedly being located in a private house in the obscure mountain town of Del Norte, CO. As a Colorado native myself, I actually do remember driving through Del Norte some years back while crossing the Rocky Mountains and was intrigued to find that it was surrounded by miles of potato farms and consisted of little more than a handful of houses, a gas station, and perhaps a few other public buildings such as a post office and a neighbourhood market. As someone with a rural background myself, I am not mocking this town but I do hope to emphasize that just one generation later, Ham realized this standard was completely unacceptable and instead sought out professionals from "respectable" universities, even including Ivy League schools such as Harvard and Brown, and from scientific fields as such. In other words, Ham realized it wasn't good enough to just defend the faith from within the closed circle of fundamentalist true believers; he had to go out into the world to find labourers for the harvest who could beat the academic scientists at their own game precisely because they were academic scientists themselves. Before Ham, it was enough to be a creationist; in the present moment, however, one must be a creation *scientist* if one hopes to have any credibility even within the same evangelical circles which are so often accused of categorically rejecting scientific rationalism.

I remember in 2006, my own high school in southern Colorado was swept up by the fundamentalist wave that had consumed nearby Colorado Springs as the "evangelical Vatican," even to the extent that my school was eventually sued for violating the separation of church and state and even received court orders to desist from inviting pastors on campus and from blasting Christian rock songs during school assemblies. Yet one of the most memorable religious events hosted at my school lay in their decision to invite a creationist with a PhD in Microbiology to defend the biblical account of the origins of life. It is quite telling that dual citizenship in both worlds had suddenly become a requirement just to defend the religious half of the equation; it was not nearly enough to be an expert in the scriptures, since bridging the gap with the hard sciences was their only hope in remaining relevant in a world defined by materialistic rationalism.

During his infamous debate with Bill Nye, Ham also memorably tried to prove his adherence to this principle of scientific rigor by admitting that the research papers posted on his own creationist website were so technical that even *he* couldn't synopsize them on stage; instead, he simply redirected the audience to visit the website on their own time and look up the articles themselves. Yet far from "proving his intellectual ineptitude," this episode demonstrates that Ham realized that this surrender to scientific specialization, which progressively shrinks down to tinier and tinier ghettos of experts who are only able to talk to each other, is precisely the definition of modern rationality rather than a negation of it.

In fact, Ham's debate against Nye was simply an attempt to stage the same archetypal myth which had been circulating in the creationist collective consciousness for years before. One memorably notorious Chick Tract portrayed the urban myth of a college student who interrupts class and marches to the front of a crowded lecture hall in order to debate his own biology professor on the theory that "we came from monkeys" and beats him simply by having better empirical data at his disposal. In the urban legend, the student's victory proves so conclusive that he draws enthusiastic, nearly unanimous applause from hundreds of peers in the auditorium, driving the professor to storm out of the room and admit his humiliation at having been publicly exposed as a fraud.[346] Ken Ham, however, found he had to "think bigger" than even this version of the story, as he tried to live out this fantasy for himself with the world as his audience and YouTube as his virtual venue, instead of the much more modest demands of a battle within a single college classroom.

It is a little-known fact that medieval thinkers such as Thomas Aquinas understood this controversy to hold the exact opposite orientation: the problem was not how to make divine revelation catch up with human reason, but to find some way to make Man's own limited intellectual abilities catch up with the infinitely-superior revelations from the Mind of God. In Aquinas's sprawling, multi-volume *Summa Theologica* (one of the longest works of philosophy ever written), he defended sacred doctrine's status as a legitimate science on grounds that the "science of God and the blessed" provided a foundation for sacred doctrine in just the same way that arithmetic provided a foundation for the study of music and geometry provided a foundation for the study of perspective. In other words, the fact that the science of God could not be deduced solely with the limited resources of Man's own intellect was not at all a drawback but was instead definitive proof of its superiority to any merely human science:

> I answer that, Sacred doctrine is a science . . . because it proceeds from principles established by the light of a higher science, namely, the science of God and the blessed. Hence, just as the musician accepts on authority the principles taught him by the mathematician, so sacred science is established on principles [directly] revealed by God [himself]. [347]

---

[346] See the Chick Tract *Big Daddy?*, available online at https://www.chick.com/products/tract?stk=55
[347] Thomas Aquinas, *Summa Theologica I,* in *Introduction to St. Thomas Aquinas* (New York: Modern Library, 1948), pp. 5-6.

Even though the media has realized that Arizona pastor Steven Anderson is the single most controversial pastor alive today, they have largely missed the true reason *why*. His stance towards religion is incomparably more radical than Ken Ham's and other mainstream evangelical thinkers for the simple reason that Anderson has proven himself to be completely indifferent to supplementing the Bible with any extrinsic source, even from the archives of Natural Science. Though unthinkable today even among his fellow creationists, this is more or less the same attitude which Thomas Aquinas exhibited nearly a millennium ago regarding the unquestionable superiority of divine revelation over the empirical findings of Man. It is quite telling that adopting a stance more or less consistent with all Christians in the Middle Ages has proven sufficient to have one banned from numerous countries and labelled one of the most notorious thought criminals of our era.

Although Linkola's interests are ecological rather than religious, he similarly understands that the problem is not at all to find some way to help the Will of Nature "catch up" with the fashions and whims of the Mind of Man. Rather, the problem is to find a way to suspend all humanistic biases by positing the Mind of Nature not as the perfected double of the Mind of Man, but rather as an absolute standard of truth and rationality with no need for any of our accomplishments to validate it.

In other words, the stereotype that evangelical creationists like Ken Ham are the last few remnants of pre-modernity, the final bitter clingers who have not received the memo that they have to upgrade to scientific rationalism, could not be further from the truth; the Creation Science Museum is definitive proof that we are living in an era in which humanism has become so absolute that even the Mind of God can no longer stand on his own authority. It is quite literally the case that the same people who claim to believe in an omniscient and omnipotent deity would feel that this same God now requires help from humans to take up the hard work of carrying him on the stilts of scientific rationalism by supplementing his own lack with the power and knowledge which must be mined from out of academic sources alone. In other words, Linkola's scepticism towards the Mind of Man is actually far more radical than virtually any religious fundamentalist's today, including those who fight to prove that the Earth is 6,000 years old and that Noah staffed the Ark with two of each kind. Even these widely-mocked Biblical literalisms are less controversial than the blasphemy of saying "no democracy," let alone "no machines."

Double Vision: Linkola and Kant

Linkola is therefore far more radical than Husserl as well, in that the extraction of a purified ecological form is not merely a theoretical activity of intellectual speculation; the ecological form is always already, in itself, an ethical demand for action as well. One can never simply contemplate the Mind of Nature without executing the Will of Nature, for one has only truly understood the former if one is willing to implement the latter.

Because ethics can only ever be fully understood if it is explicitly treated as a matter of philosophy, our understanding of Linkola's stances will always remain incomplete unless these are submitted to a rigorous philosophical analysis which makes explicit how exactly it is that an ethical system based on desire must be subordinated to an ethical system based on necessity. In particular, Linkola's unusual claim to have identified a relation between pathological desire and linguistic rationality can only be exhaustively treated through contrasting him with Kant, who effectively argued for the exact opposite view of ethics. For this reason, the present chapter shall close with a serious examination of these two thinkers' similarities and differences.

Kant opened *The Critique of Practical Reason* by explaining that his own treatise on ethics would differ from other philosophers' failed attempts to deal with the topic because he recognized that the problem of morality could never be solved through an empiricist approach. Empiricism proved itself to be unfit for the task primarily because any treatise on ethics must deal with the problem of freedom (i.e., an act is ethical only if it was done freely in accord with the subject's will), yet Kant noted from the beginning of the text that freedom is a problematic notion. He did not mean this in a figurative but rather in a strictly technical sense. Freedom is given in a problematic categorical mode – neither with the apodictic necessity of mathematical truth nor through a simple assertion which affirms its presence, but rather as something for which it is perfectly possible to think about it at great length without any guarantee that it actually exists.[348]

Because of the problematic mode in which freedom is given, it is fundamentally misguided for people to assume that freedom can be treated as an empirical problem which can be solved by one of the natural sciences, for this approach would presume that freedom was a physical object of some sort. In order to remain consistent with their own logic, the proponents of this view are almost always forced to equate the concept of human freedom with the object inside one's skull, effectively asking whether the brain as a psychological lump of flesh is a free thing or not. Even centuries after Kant wrote these words, the media continues to miss his point by publishing "breaking news" articles every few years reporting that some obscure discovery from the Physics, Biology, or Chemistry department on campus has definitively proven that the human body is not free because all of its actions are determined through some sort of naturalistic necessity. Yet this is entirely irrelevant to the kind of freedom Kant was interested in, which could only be freedom in the transcendental sense.[349]

Since I launched my first YouTube channel in 2011, I have received thousands of messages from students, teachers, and general enthusiasts of philosophy all over the world. One particularly memorable correspondent was a PhD candidate at a top-ranked philosophy department in the West who notified me that one of his or her professors had received an enormous grant[350] to solve the problem of human freedom once and for all, presumably by digging through the archives of cutting-edge Physics research to piece

---

[348] Immanuel Kant, *Critique of Practical Reason* (Cambridge: Cambridge University Press, 1997), p. 3.
[349] The Moral Law is something which we can know, and freedom is the condition of it
Ibid., pp. 4-6.
[350] If I recall correctly, in the millions of dollars.

together some ad hoc argument to prove that the brain is not smart enough to see that its own movements are fully determined by some impersonal naturalistic force, with the exception, of course, of a handful of Nobel Prize-winning "geniuses" who had kindly filled in that gap of explanation for the rest of us.

Far from celebrating this discovery as the "victory of reason over superstition," this professor was insightful enough to realize that the social consequences of this announcement were not likely to be good. Deeply troubled by the implications of his work, he apparently began losing sleep imagining how the human race would react after he broke the news to them that they had always already been unfree and would remain so forever. He imagined that, deprived of any hope for transcendent meaning, the raving masses would likely turn to rioting, looting stores, and setting businesses and homes on fire as the very possibility for ethics vanished along with the human freedom which would be required to make it possible. While the Dostoyevskyan warning "If God doesn't exist, anything is morally permissible" describes a decline in organized religion which did indeed arrive without shaking the Earth too much, apparently the true danger lies in this professor's warning that "If *we* don't exist, then anything is morally permissible." Needless to say, in the years since I received this message it seems that the riots never did arrive. One can only imagine that this professor's "monumental announcement" probably consisted in its entirety of pumping out a little-read academic monograph which continues to collect dust on a handful of university library shelves, as well as a speaking tour through a dozen or so campuses in which audiences of half-interested graduate students showed up just to get some free coffee.

Hum(e-)our aside, Kant noted that empiricists will inevitably fail to address both freedom and morality because one can only do so on rational grounds.[351] The shortcomings of trying to understand these issues empirically were best demonstrated by Kant's predecessor David Hume, who was eventually driven to dismiss the ethical question altogether after concluding that there is

---

[351] Ibid., p. 7.

no way to deduce how the world should be simply from scientifically observing how the world actually is. In part, this conclusion followed after Hume noticed a certain logical problem in the very concept of an ethical law. A moral code can lay claim to the status of "law" only if it holds necessity at some level, yet Hume warned the reader that any perception of necessity within the contingencies of human morality was actually an elaborate illusion. What appears to be necessity within the flux of empirical reality is, in fact, just custom because what appears to be a cause-effect relation within a chain of events is simply coincidence.[352] The famous example of a baseball player who scratches his nose before hitting home runs provides only the most comical example of the absurdity inherent in arguing that *any* one event causes another. What appears to be determination is really just adjacency, the coincidence of having two events situated next to one another on a line of disconnected acts.[353]

While Kant accepted that necessity cannot be found within the Thing in Itself, he castigated Hume for missing the point that causality is a categorical rather than empirical concern.[354] Cause and effect may not "really exist" at the level of material objectivity, but their role in providing a transcendental basis for experience to be meaningful cannot be dismissed without fundamentally misunderstanding the structure of human subjectivity. In fact, Kant warned that in the absence of a transcendental system to provide the proper framework for categorical features of experience such as cause and effect, the inevitable result would be an unbridled scepticism.[355] If appearances are reduced to being *nothing more than appearances* by depriving them of any deeper foundation beyond themselves, one will lose the ability for any type of certainty.

Kant found this regrettable outcome to be entirely unnecessary for the simple reason that it was based upon a very subtle equivocation with regard to the word "necessity." While the

---

[352] Ibid., p. 10.
[353] Ibid., p. 45.
[354] Ibid., p. 46.
[355] Ibid., p. 47.

empiricist presumed that necessity must be something one can feel, the rationalist instead recognized necessity as something which one could see. The empiricist, in other words, presupposed the existence of some biological body in which the event of some material discharge could take place concomitantly with "the feeling of necessity." The rationalist, however, had no such commitment to the existence of a human body, or of *any* material object for that matter. The necessity of the Pythagorean Theorem, for example, does not depend on any subjective feeling in order to be true, for it would remain equally valid whether it was registered by a robot who lacked biological components (i.e., the Kurzweil fantasy machine) or by a gnostic spirit who lacked a physical body of any kind (i.e., the Platonic soul).

For this reason, Kant realized that only a rationalistic approach could provide a bulletproof foundation for ethics, in that the moral code would have to apply equally to any subject whatsoever regardless of its unique personal circumstances. On the other hand, he warned that universalizing the stance of empiricism would leave one with nothing except the most extreme form of scepticism, as the ceaseless flux of material becoming would squeeze out any other dimension of meaning and would inevitably destroy the very possibility of ethics. [356]

Kant introduced the text by noting that the need to respect this preference for rationalism over empiricism caused him to essentially reverse the order of operations he used in *The Critique of Pure Reason*. Whereas the first critique began with an analysis of the senses, proceeded to concepts of the understanding, and finished with rational principles, the second critique had to instead begin with rational principles, proceed to concepts, and finish with the senses. Kant's justification for this reversal lay in his realization that freedom could never be accounted for within a chain of other events bound by the laws of "empirically conditioned causality." If one opted for this approach, one would inevitably get stuck in a paradox of infinite regression which would effectively make freedom impossible. Because every empirical cause is conditioned

---

[356] Ibid., p. 11.

by a preceding cause and so forth, one would never actually arrive at a position where the will could act freely.[357]

The will can only be free if it is an empirically *un*conditioned causality, a causality which somehow exercises an autonomous decision within the real world *without* being bound to any position within the empirical chain of causes and effects. Zizek memorably synopsized the problem of transcendental freedom as the problem of a "hole in the texture of phenomenal reality" in his 2014 book *Absolute Recoil*:

> Kant's notion of freedom implies a discontinuity in the texture of natural causes, that is, a free act is an act which is ultimately grounded in itself and, as such, cannot be accounted for as an effect of the preceding causal network – in this sense, a free act *does* imply a kind of hole in the texture of phenomenal reality.[358]

On an ontological level, freedom can only exist if it lacks any proper place within the world. On an epistemological level, freedom is by definition something which one *cannot* provide a fully transparent explanation for, especially not as one more natural phenomenon among the set of all others. Zizek explained that if one ever did manage to complete the project of "[f]ull scientific . . . naturalization," this would logically rule out the very possibility of designating any subjective act as free: "if we could fully account for our moral acts in terms of natural causes, in what sense would we experience ourselves as free?"[359]

Kant began Book One by mentioning that there is also a logical problem with trying to derive universal laws from unique empirical situations. Whereas most people confuse maxims which hold for only one will with laws which hold for the will of every rational being, Kant emphasized that only the latter could provide a proper foundation for a universal ethical code.[360] Above all,

---

[357] Ibid., p. 13.
[358] Slavoj Zizek, *Absolute Recoil* (London: Verso, 2014), p. 20.
[359] Ibid.
[360] Immanuel Kant, *Critique of Practical Reason* (Cambridge: Cambridge

individual situations are inadequate because of their tendency to pathologically affect the will, or contaminate it with motivations founded on impure desires. Typically, this takes the form of acting in order to obtain pleasure for oneself rather than for the sake of the ethical law's intrinsic rightness. Kant's most famous example of a pathologically-motivated decision which does not pass the ethical test was actually quite subtle, in that working hard and saving money so that one could safely retire after a certain number of years is generally accepted as "the right thing to do" but still fails as an ethical law in the proper sense of the term because it is conditioned by a desire for an empirical object – the bodily sensation of pleasure resulting from living out one's final years comfortably.

On a technical level, Kant realized that the pathologically affected will demonstrates a certain conflict between the individual maxim and the universal practical law and can therefore never provide the conditions for a properly ethical act.[361] Norwegian deep ecologist Arne Naess went as far as to describe Kant's philosophy as one in which the ultimate ethical act is the one which a person actually *hates* performing.[362] There is an inverse relation, in other words, between pleasure and morality. Only the act which is carried out despite the fact that one will not derive the tiniest bit of pleasure from doing so can truly be called ethical.

Kant concluded that, in order to be pure, Reason's lawgiving must presuppose only itself. A rule can be objectively, universally valid only if it holds without any reference to subjective conditions, which would by definition be unique to one contingent situation.[363] Theorem I of the text stated that if one were to take the path of presupposing some desired object while acting, this would

---

University Press, 1997), p. 17.
[361] Ibid.
[362] "[T]he supreme test of our success in performing a pure, moral act is that we do it completely against our inclination, that we, so to say, hate to do it but are compelled by our respect for the moral law."
Arne Naess, "Self-Realization," in *Ecology of Wisdom* (London: Penguin, 2008), pp. 92-3.
[363] Immanuel Kant, *Critique of Practical Reason* (Cambridge: Cambridge University Press, 1997), p. 17.

inevitably mix empirical contents into one's motivations and would fail to furnish any practical law.[364] Because any concern for matter implies a representation of some object and a desire to make it "really exist" on an empirical level, this is by definition pathological.

The shortcomings of such a stance are not merely hypothetical, as David Hume's philosophy had more than conclusively confirmed that the possibility for a non-pathological act eventually vanishes altogether as one travels deeper into the rabbit hole of a fanatical commitment to empiricism. Hume was eventually led to surrender to the illusion that we cannot be anything *except* slaves to the passions, as an ethical act free of pathological motivations was basically ruled out as an a priori impossibility in a universe where only matter "really exists." Yet despite Kant's detailed refutations, Hume's viewpoint merely foreshadowed the troubling trajectory of postmodernism and its suspension of all transcendent standards of meaning from the 20th Century to the present day. The Linguistic Turn's reduction of all existence to a single immanent discharge of desiring-production as the driving force behind a set of linguistic games driven by the pathological motivation to advance one's own self-interests was an all too predictable outcome of allowing the runaway train of postmodernity to drive itself off the cliff of insanity. This topic shall be revisited in much greater depth in the discussion of Linkola in relation to Habermas, Deleuze, and Guattari in the third chapter of the present work.

Kant's second theorem in the text stated that all material practical principles come under the same principle of self-love or the pursuit of one's own happiness.[365] On a technical level, motivations founded on self-love must be ruled out because the pleasure arising from the representation of some hypothetical thing belongs to the senses rather than to the understanding.[366] Pleasure, in other words, is felt on a bodily level rather than understood on an intellectual level.

---

[364] Ibid., p. 19.
[365] Ibid.
[366] Ibid.

Another major problem lies in the asymmetry separating these two spheres from one another; while feelings are always subjective, concepts are by definition objective.[367] Because of their material and subjective nature, the only questions one asks with regard to experiences of pleasure include "How much pleasure are we talking?" and "How long will it endure for?" In fact, Kant compared pleasure to gold (in his era, the ultimate material good) since in either case, no one really cares where it came from because possessing it will feel roughly the same regardless of whether its origin is good or not.[368] Today, we might as well say the same thing of petroleum – it will fuel one's car just as well whether it was obtained through morally-reprehensible resource wars in Iraq or through permanently environmentally-damaging fracking practices in West Texas. To the clueless suburbanite filling up the ole' SUV at the gas pump, any one gallon of the stuff smells about the same as any other.

Fortunately, Kant noted that there is a way to determine the will which bypasses the sense-path altogether. Because Reason lies outside the chain of empirical causes and effects, it can determine itself immediately without any need to pause and provide a representation of a desired feeling or object which would cause it to deviate into the impure realm of pathological material sensations. This elimination of material contaminants alone would qualify Reason as law-giving.[369] Theorem III of the text made this rule explicit by noting that if one subtracts everything material from a law, all that remains is the form.[370] This "mere form of the law" is, therefore, a peculiar type of thing because even though it is not an

---

[367] Ibid., p. 20.

[368] Ibid., p. 21.

[369] While Kant admitted that it does make sense to speak of Reason as also dealing with desire, this desire refers to a higher faculty and is not to be mistaken for the lower, pathologically determined kind.
Ibid., p. 22.

[370] Desire for happiness is therefore especially deceptive insofar as in one sense it might seem to be universal in the sense that everyone has it (i.e., everyone wants to be happy) but even if a huge majority accord, any exception will undo its universality.
Ibid., p. 25.

object of the senses and does not belong among the appearances, it can still be represented, but only by Reason itself.[371]

In other words, practical reason can determine the will by the mere form of a practical rule without presupposing any feeling, or even any other empirical condition whatsoever.[372] If a law is truly objective, we can trust that it will hold the same determining ground of the will in all cases and for all rational beings regardless of the unique empirical features of any given context.[373] For this exact reason, no law can follow from the pathological desire for happiness because that is based *solely* on material rather than formal criteria. The purified will, though, is precisely one which is independent of empirical conditions and determined by the mere form of the law and nothing more.[374]

With Theorem IV (any practical precept which brings with it a material or empirical condition must never be reckoned a practical law), Kant emphasized that general rules and universal rules are not the same thing, despite widespread confusion over these terms.[375] Kant mentioned the important distinction that although you can get general rules from the principle of, say, seeking happiness, you can never get a properly universal rule from it.[376] This is because whereas a general rule can provide advice, only a universal rule can issue a command in the proper sense.

There is also a difference in clarity. Duty, as purified form, is crystal clear while the concept of "advantage" is inherently obscure due to its contamination by empirical contents. At any rate, an ethical law must have objective necessity and must be cognizable a priori by reason alone without any need for supplementary help from experience. In other words, empirical universality is not good enough.[377]

---

[371] Ibid., p. 26.
[372] Ibid.
[373] Ibid., p. 23
[374] Ibid., p. 28.
[375] Ibid., p. 31.
[376] Ibid., p. 33.
[377] Ibid., p. 24.

In addition, even if one does obtain universality rather than generality, one must be careful to distinguish theoretical from practical universality. Although one can discover universal rules of skill, these are theoretical universals rather than practical universals. Kant's own memorable example of the rule "If you want to eat bread, you must construct a mill" does not mandate constructing mills as an ethical demand in the proper sense of the term.

Kant's analytic in the second critique proved that pure reason can be practical (that is, it can determine the will independently of any empirical content) only because it is autonomous.[378] In other words, it is inherently contradictory to even speak of practical reason in the context of a chain of causes and effects of a merely material nature. Interestingly, Kant explained this through explicitly contrasting a free being truly endowed with willpower (i.e., a human subject) with a machine which only appeared to be (i.e., artificial intelligence). Somehow, even the traditional religious explanation of morality which situates Man within a complicated system of rewards and punishments wielded as machinery at the hands of God himself is ultimately just a very subtle form of materialism in disguise, for subordinating Man to a chain of positive and negative stimulants reduces him to a mechanistic robot whose movements are fully determined by extrinsic factors. To be an autonomous human which is capable of an ethical act requires something different and, from the standpoint of scientific naturalization, something completely inexplicable: transcendental freedom.[379]

Kant contrasted the first critique's formula that "there is no knowledge without intuition" with the approach in the second critique which favoured exploring a "pure world of understanding," the native territory in which the moral law was situated as a purified form devoid of all naturalistic elements.[380] He insisted as forcefully as possible that the second critique must begin with pure practical laws "and their reality" instead of with the intuition of worldly things.[381] In other words, there is no bridge connecting naturalistic

---

[378] Ibid., p. 37.
[379] Ibid., p. 35.
[380] Ibid., p. 38.

description to ethical prescription. The channel linking knowing to doing is a Fountain of Youth which can never be located for the simple fact that it does not exist. [382]

Kant's realization that ethics required something of a suspension of the natural world in favour of the formal world of rational abstraction led him to what has all too seldom been recognized as one of the most important debates in the entire text and certainly one of the most crucial to understanding his opposition to Linkola. He examined whether a law of practical reason might ever be found to "hold as a universal law of nature".[383]

From Kant's perspective, one important distinction between an ethical law and a natural law is the following: if the will were understood as a naturalistic object, it would be subject to the Laws of Nature. In true freedom, however, it is Nature itself which is subject to the human will.[384] Whereas private inclinations can indeed be understood in accord with pathological laws of natural matter, ethics in the proper sense of the term cannot, for that deals with the purified practical laws of Reason itself.

Another justification for Kant's approach is that freedom qua absolute spontaneity is an analytic principle of pure speculative reason, in that it must be both unconditioned and self-determining causality.[385] Likewise freedom cannot be exemplified empirically among the set of appearances, since nowhere among them can you find an absolutely unconditioned x.[386] A moral principle is a law of causality, therefore, only if it locates the determining ground *above* all conditions of the sensible world.[387]

---

[381] Ibid., p. 40.
[382] He admits that although consciousness of moral laws is indeed consciousness of freedom, we still cannot quite explain how such consciousness might be possible, but this is okay.
Ibid., p. 41.
[383] Ibid., p. 39.
[384] Ibid.
[385] Ibid., p. 42.
[386] Ibid., p. 43.
[387] Ibid., p. 44.

In addition, the meaning of the term "object" changes if one is dealing with it on practical rather than theoretical grounds. Somehow, it is not self-contradictory to speak of an object which is independent of the requirements of physical possibility but is an object of Reason nonetheless.[388] Insofar as practical reason has objects, they are only the good and the evil (i.e., the good is the necessary object of desire, while the evil is the necessary object of the faculty of aversion.) Because good and evil are not physical substances which occur within Nature, an understanding of them cannot be based on empirical factors such as pleasure because there is no *a priori* connection between feelings and the representation of an object.[389] The empirical flux of matter, in other words, is precisely what must be subtracted in order to obtain a rationalized grasp of these terms. Ultimately, you can only grasp the good if you squeeze Nature out of your understanding of it.

Kant noted that there is another problem with thinking of the good in empirical terms. If the good were merely synonymous with the (physically) agreeable, it would never be good in itself, since it would only be good instrumentally; it would only ever be a means to an end to obtain the feeling of pleasure.[390] Yet such a view misses the point that good and evil are not feelings at all but are, rather, actions.[391] The good is an object of desire for any subject and evil is the object of aversion for any subject whatsoever because this abstraction beyond individual contexts is the requirement to rise up to grasp these non-physical things as such.[392] In fact, Reason is precisely what raises Man above the lower status of mere animality to place him in a position to be able to desire the good in itself, something which a lower animal would be incapable of grasping due to its enslavement to its hard-wired instincts and to its ecological context. Though Gadamer and Zizek phrased this same idea in the terminology of the Linguistic Turn rather than of Kant's transcendental rationality, this is a requirement of modernity which

---

[388] Ibid., p. 50.
[389] Ibid., p. 51.
[390] Ibid.
[391] Ibid., p. 52.
[392] Ibid., p. 53.

they both later reinforced through their own distinctions between the lower ecological context of animals and the higher linguistic agency of Man.[393]

Under this view, Reason cannot be just another mode which Nature has equipped for man to serve the same ends as those to which animals are also directed; it can only be directed towards the highest end, one uniquely visible to higher rational beings.[394] This, in turn, can only be understood through finding the connection between pure will and pure reason: "Only a formal law which prescribes to reason nothing more than the form of its universal lawgiving as the supreme condition of maxims can be a priori determining ground of reason."[395]

Kant emphasized that what we are dealing with here is *not* a law of nature but, rather, a law of freedom. This contrast lay in his recognition that the underlying structures at work in each case are fundamentally incompatible with one another. Whereas the categories of Nature (i.e., the theoretical concepts) designate indeterminate (physical) objects in general for possible intuition, the categories of freedom are directed to the determination of a free choice, for which no corresponding intuition could be given.[396]

Compelling as Kant's stance might be on theoretical grounds, Linkola finds the concept of "an ethical suspension of Nature" to be the ultimate absurdity, for it is only through ecological law itself that one can directly generate the corresponding ethical imperatives. Kant got the problem exactly backwards, in that the pathological temptation to act unethically does not emerge from a naturalistic contamination of a universal rationalized ideal, as Kant more or less argued. Instead, Linkola realized that the pathological temptation to act immorally arises precisely from humanistic rationality's contamination of the natural form, insofar as this intrusion of linguistification into a strict

---

[393] See chapter two of my fourth book *The Hermeneutics of Ecological Limitation: Ecophilosophy Beyond Environmentalism* for a fuller discussion of this.
[394] Ibid., p. 54.
[395] Ibid., p. 56.
[396] Ibid., pp. 56-7.

ecological configuration cannot mean anything except a violation of the true laws of ecology in favour of the pseudo-laws of language.

Humanistic ideals such as progress, technological innovation, absolute equality, consumerism, and democracy continually seduce Man to sin against the environment, despite the fact that all of these things lack any existence beyond the realm of language and actively induce Man to suspend his own ecological context and his individual contingencies in order to become another anonymous subject akin to any other within the democratic mass. Kant's demand for one to drop down to the status of an ethical agent and nothing more than an ethical agent is therefore simply a subtle call for one to join in with the democratic mass by blending in amongst an amorphous chain of empty, contentless redundancies.

Likewise, the problem is not that these humanistic evils have not been sufficiently purified of naturalistic contingency, as Kant might argue; the problem is that they lack Nature altogether. As was mentioned in the first chapter of the present text, the birthmark is simply an ecologically impossible situation which can never be fully realized within the world but can only go on gobbling up resources on the dead-end path to try to reach an abstract limit which will always lie out of reach, no matter how close one appears to be towards reaching it. Subtracting Nature does not yield pure good but only pure evil.

Whereas Kant argued that the ethical law can be grasped only if it is purified of Nature, Linkola implied that the ethical law itself simply *is* Nature purified of all humanistic chimeras. Humanistic chimeras such as democracy, technological innovation, and progress are precisely the pseudo-rational forms purified of natural content which Kant unwittingly gestured towards, yet ironically these only succeed in yielding an anti-ethical code of pure evil. On the other hand, Linkola's proposals for an ideal society in which private electricity, artificial intelligence, machines, and fossil fuels cease to be used and human bodies are instead restored to their role as labourers are simply so many ecologically-rationalized forms purged of all humanistic bias.

The irony is that while for Kant the pathological temptation is bodily sensation (which merely demonstrates the flux of empirical contingency), for Linkola, the pathological temptation instead drives one to fall for the seduction of humanistic chimeras despite the fact that these are abstractions with no existence beyond a linguistic form. An evil act is simply to believe that these are ontologically superior to the laws of ecology.

This is not at all to suggest that Linkola disregards formal criteria altogether when considering ethical problems. His critique of Kantian form was simply based on his realization that the linguistic forms of human rationality are not the only kind of abstract structure which could serve as a basis for a purified moral law. Far superior are the ecological forms of the Mind of Nature itself, a set of laws which are not transcendentally discovered through allowing the subject to examine itself, but are rather derived through suspending the subject's own mind in order to allow the Will of Nature to speak directly. Kant's error ultimately lay, therefore, in favouring the formal validity of the Mind of Man's rational thought process over the formal validity of the Mind of Nature's system of ecological law. Somehow, only the latter can yield an ethical code of virtue, while the former will only lead one to embody evil. The following chapter shall be dedicated in its entirety to examining Linkola's distinction between language and ecology.

Natural Form is True Form

In his "Life Protection, Utopias, and Agriculture," Linkola argued that most of the suffering today is caused simply by the abandonment of natural forms. In this essay, for example, he lamented that one reason why Man feels lost and directionless is because his traditional occupation as farmer had been removed. Yet this was entirely unnecessary, since it required an enormous artificial intervention on the part of the industry to force through this historical anomaly: "the complete end of agriculture and absolute triumph of industrial farming are shaping [the] market economy [into an unnatural state of affairs]."[397] Worse still, even

---

[397] Pentti Linkola, "Life Protection, Utopias, and Agriculture," *Can Life Prevail?* (Kindle Edition).

the few remaining people who are farmers almost always retire early to become idlers. Yet this is also tragically unnecessary since they often do so on the basis of "expert forecasts regarding the future which just happen to suffer from the minor flaw that they outright contradict the yields the farmers are already making on their own farms:

> There are tens of thousands of farmers . . . who, as humbly as they slaughter cattle, are handing over their estates and houses, closing their business and retiring even if only middle-aged, to become forty or fifty year-old idlers. The saddest thing is that the reason why these farmers are leaving is that they are scared by all the talk about the decline of the farming business, even if the money they are making from milk, meat and grain is still enough to support them.[398]

Likewise, the natural form is not only epistemologically correct (i.e., true); it is also ethically correct (i.e., moral). Returning to traditional farming is not a revolutionary project or a hopeless delusion; it is simply the restoration of the same natural form we have embodied for millennia, one driven by ecological limitation as much as by psychological essence: "What of course will never change is the fact that we will always derive our sustenance from agriculture."[399] In his essay "The Misery of the Countryside," he noted that the historical anomaly of moving the vast majority of the population *out of* agriculture to meaningless service jobs or unemployment was not a natural disaster with no explanation; it was the result of "political decision making" which reflected the financial interests of a set of all too human actors. In the attempt to maximize their own profits, they "snuff[ed] out the countryside" by rigging the game to make it virtually impossible even for the tiny minority of family farmers to stay in business without frantically buying up more land and equipment in order to somehow make a

---

[398] Ibid.
[399] Pentti Linkola, ""Life Protection, Utopias, and Agriculture," in *Can Life Prevail?* (Kindle Edition).

profit against artificially-lowered prices and stiff competition from a technological apparatus wielded by a handful of "big fish."[400] One's only option after losing despite these Herculean efforts is, of course, to drop out of the game entirely.

The culprit which disrupted this norm is not at all difficult to find, for even the most malicious human would have been powerless to accomplish so profound a shift without the aid of Modern Technology. In "The Green Lie" he revealed that any talk of using machines to "save labour" misses the point that it is far closer to the truth to speak of them "stealing labour" from us:

> That clearing in the forest was made with two-man saws. Much labour was available back then, as it still is today, even if it were to cut down trees with knives. Machines, however, were already looming upon us and were soon destined to strike at the heart of the wilderness . . . depriving man of all he deserved: mighty labour, effort and struggle.[401]

Although the naïve view might be deceived into misinterpreting this loss of labour as a blessing which might free Man up to pursue more worthy goals, the truth is that this merely deprived us of our ability to embody natural forms on a physical level, abandoning the human body to languish in the formlessness of endless idling before electronic screens. This ecological truth, however, also doubles as ethical truth, since being robbed of these forms represented a moral evil as well.

Yet it is not only our own bodies that suffered as a result of this catastrophic intrusion. Entire ecosystems were distorted beyond recognition as a result of unprecedented scales of damage which these weapons of mass destruction enabled. Linkola recounted, "The first chainsaw I heard . . . signalled an horrendous break in my life," [402] as the introduction of moral evil coincided perfectly symmetrically with the violation of natural order:

---

[400] Pentti Linkola, "The Misery of the Countryside," in *A Collection of Essays by Pentti Linkola 1993 – 2006*, p. 107.
[401] Pentti Linkola, "The Green Lie," in *Can Life Prevail?* (Kindle Edition)
[402] Ibid.

> [After the introduction of chainsaws, the trees] vanished before my eyes, melting away like snow. Ancient pinewoods disappeared along with dense spruce forests; bushes of nurseries replaced them — when, that is, they were replaced at all. Every birch thicker than a leg disappeared. Aspen groves were methodically driven to extinction.[403]

Once again, the theoretical violation of an ecological form is simultaneously the ethical violation of a moral law.

Even the solution to the ongoing global plastic crisis is not so mysterious as it might seem, as restoring the natural form of human labour over the technological imposters would simultaneously squeeze out the technical foundation for this issue to exist in the first place. It is a fact that no matter how talented you might be as a blacksmith or woodworker, you simply can't produce the sort of junk pumped out by the modern technological System with hand tools. There's no way to regulate plastic except to not make it exist in the first place.

In his 1999 essay "To Car and Motor-Column," Linkola responded to a news story regarding an unfortunate car accident in which a few elk tried to quickly cross a highway in Finland while a rush-hour traffic jam created a brief window of time for them to attempt the leap of faith. Even these majestic creatures proved incapable of surviving the feat, however, as an impatient commuter collided with them while trying to get a tiny advantage in the rat race. While many mainstream environmentalists proposed converting the highway into a tunnel in order to prevent future accidents with wildlife, Linkola insisted that this half-serious proposal missed the point that this fatal accident had occurred even *after* the authorities had already mandated reduced speeds as a safety measure. In other words, the compromise had already been implemented without saving human or animal lives. Just as Kaczynski warned that playing games with trying to keep the good technologies while only removing the bad technologies will prove a

---

[403] Ibid.

waste of time because there is no such distinction, Linkola affirmed in this essay that the fantasy of a rationally-planned highway which does not kill any humans or animals is an ecologically impossible object which will remain inaccessible no matter how many technical fixes are implemented to improve the currently-existing infrastructure. On an ethical level, because the chimera intrinsically violates the structural form of ecological viability, it had already committed an ethical transgression even before any elks or humans had died on it. The contradiction of natural form is always already the introduction of evil into the world.

Whereas the problems of plastic and highways are often understood to be problems of human nature being too smart for its own good, even to the point of inventing monstrosities so disruptive even it cannot control them, this actually gets the problem exactly backwards. It was precisely the *violation* of human nature and the introduction of artificial machines which brought about this mess. Since human nature is included in the broader superset of Nature, and ultimately, the Mind of Nature itself, even man himself is just one more natural essence which must be maintained. Linkola's sole ethical mandate is just to let people *be* by allowing them to embody the proper ecological form which the Mind of Nature had already delineated. Far from retreating into mystical obscurantism, Linkola's understanding of how humans *should* act is immediately derived from his understanding of how humans are, outside the meddling of technological distortions.

In his 2004 interview with Virpi Adamsson, for example, he noted that the "will to life" is not synonymous with technological domination, as the early Frankfurt School argued; rather, the will to life actually grows stronger when humans are allowed to preserve Nature rather than dominate it.[404] Likewise, following the Will of Nature is not a masochistic "mortification of the flesh" which would justify mindless suffering in the present on the gamble of a reward in the afterlife. On the contrary, Linkola noted in his 1998 "Panic or Peace in Nature" that anyone who has observed Nature on a deeply

---

[404] "Interview with Pentti Linkola 10-2-2004." Available at
http://www.penttilinkola.com/pentti_linkola/ecofascism_writings/interview_10-2-2003

personal level will realize that it is precisely in Nature that one finds the purest expressions of joy in the world. In his extended observations of birds in the wild, for example, Linkola found that they are simply far happier than suburban humanoids trapped in their cardboard prison cells and office cubicles.[405] Nor are birds so much happier than humans only when they are consumed in tasks such as obtaining food. Even when they appear to have "nothing to do" they are content. In stark contrast, one of the strangest features of modernity is that boredom has become so serious a problem for humans that it has generated an entire industry dedicated to producing enough senseless noise to block out any opportunity for a person to sit in silence long enough to start thinking about how meaningless industrial life is. Linkola notes himself that, given this comparison, "One enviously wonders at how there is so much rest, pleasantry and 'beautiful idleness' in the lives of birds."[406] One cannot avoid the conclusion that it is only through maintaining Nature that one can find joy; Modern Technology and true happiness are logically incompatible objects which can never be joined together.

Even decades before *Can Life Prevail?* first saw print, Linkola attempted to provide impressively-detailed speculations for what the coming "natural society" might look like, the arrangement in which humans directly execute ecologically valid forms as their ethical duty within the real world. As early as his 1979 *Toisinajattelijan päiväkirjasta* (*From the Journal of a Dissent*), he argued that if one upheld the Will of Nature, one would renounce the pathological temptations for high pay and cheap products (two unquestionable dogmas of modernity) and instead realize that the workforce must remain cheap to maximize employment and raw materials should remain expensive in order to limit consumption. In addition, resource waste should literally be treated as a crime on par with murder, or perhaps even higher. Excessive interconnection among distant nations must cease, as one turns one's attention inward to one's own close circle of family members and to

---

[405] Pentti Linkola, "Panic or Peace in Nature?," in *A Collection of Essays by Pentti Linkola 1993 – 2006*, p. 53.
[406] Ibid.

immediately-neighbouring tribes and allows "the dead to bury their own dead" half the world away.

Controversial as such a stance might be in an era in which technological globalization seems to have shrunk the Earth to a single amorphous pseudo-community, Linkola reinforced this attitude when interviewed on Finnish television. In a YouTube clip from an undisclosed date, Linkola was asked whether Finns have a moral obligation to open the borders for refugees fleeing starvation in Africa. When Linkola dismissed other nations' crises as irrelevant to Finns' concerns, the interviewer misinterpreted this as a demand that Finns should simply watch the crisis unfold on television while refusing to act ethically in response, yet Linkola pointed out that even the hours spent idling in front of a television set were already a violation of the ethical code in themselves. Far from providing the ultimate medium for "moralistic engagement with the real world," wasting those hours staring at flickering pixels on the TV had already broken the moral code of Nature. [407]

In his more recent "Can We Survive? A Model for a Controlled Future," Linkola provided an even more detailed prescription for how an ideal society might successfully build a bridge to connect theoretically viable configurations with their corresponding ethical acts of execution. As one might expect, this would require a radical shift in how children are educated in their earliest years. For example, the Will of Nature would mandate that emphasis on foreign language and mathematics be decreased within the institutions. Instead, children would be given an "all-round education" in the natural sciences, world history, and their native language of Finnish. Equally importantly, they would be allowed to develop their physical abilities with sports and through establishing camp schools in the wilderness.[408] Rather than emphasize the brain alone while neglecting every other part of the body, these schools would mandate that citizens learn how to use tools and to minimize food waste.

---

[407] See "Pentti Linkola Interview in English,"
https://www.youtube.com/watch?v=CCd6qisIFKo
[408] Pentti Linkola, "Can We Survive? A Model for a Controlled Future," in *Can Life Prevail?* (Kindle Edition).

In addition to teaching children how to be better as individuals, the school would mend the social fabric through building a stronger community from the earliest ages. Above all, this would be accomplished through stopping the teaching of competition, as this will only lead to industrial excesses for the remainder of one's life. The underlying philosophy of materialism, the secular dogma of our age, will be phased out and its corresponding "commercial sciences" will be discontinued.

In a shocking reversal of the contemporary cult of "smart classrooms," the educational system of the future will recognize the need to literally teach kids to reject technology by showing them that it could only ever be the master and never the slave of Man. Further, any rhetorical appeal to "innovations" are merely euphemisms for destruction in disguise:

> The school system, like the whole of society, will be extremely prejudiced against technology. Suicidal Society has taught us that every new phase of technological advancement is more destructive than the previous one. It has also taught us that technology is never a servant, but always a master. Tested solutions will be kept for decades, preferably centuries. Discoveries unrelated to the repair or preservation of technology will not be allowed.

A general ban on information technology will ensure that humans move from delusion to reality, and from virtual abstraction to the realm of material and concrete experience.

In general, disciplinary punishments will grow harsher, with an emphasis on drastically increasing the penalties for crimes against the environment which are not even recognized by the current legal code. However, Linkola has suggested that sending some eco-criminals away on religious retreats and rehabilitation programs in the mountains to purify their minds might also prove sufficient in many cases:

> The people most responsible for the present economic growth and competition will be transferred to the mountains

and highlands to be re-educated. To be employed for this purpose will mostly be ex-sanatoriums with a healthy climate located on pine ridges.

In turn, wasting paper on trashy novels, tabloid newspapers, and pulp publications will be banned, as producing junk literature will be formally recognized as the eco-crime which it has always already been. Even the newspapers which are allowed to remain will be significantly trimmed down in size by forbidding the use of advertisement and the printing of redundancies. This aversion to waste naturally leads to a general ban on drugs, one of the great destroyers of human productivity:

> From an economic perspective, society would not be able to endure the health damage and disruptions wreaked by drugs. Hence, society will forbid the consumption of drugs, including tobacco. Through pricing, the consumption of alcohol will be limited to only the largest festivities. With the population adequately under control, no home distilling will take place. Borders will be closed to prevent smuggling.

Similarly, rather than allow people to consume any junk they happen to desire simply because it "tastes good," food rationing by the state guarantees nutrition while preventing obesity:

> Most commodities will be rationed: rationed foodstuffs will be allotted according to the age, body build and profession of each citizen. In such a way, even the bulkiest performers of heavy work will be guaranteed sufficient nutrition; but then again, obesity will be unknown.

Under this plan, he promises that "Not a crust of bread will be wasted," an unspeakably vast improvement over the current situation in which some 40% of all the food in the United States ends up in the garbage.

Of course, the worst waste of all can only be eliminated through killing its root cause: one must ban all financial artifice:

> Monetary transactions not aimed at immediate material acquisition will come to an end. Stock markets will be shut down; investments will stop.

It is no exaggeration to say that the destruction of usury is the only way to ensure a truly serious plan to address the fear of extinction. In other words, the delusion that one can make money from money will literally destroy life on the planet if left untouched:

> The programme I have outlined is truly born of agony: agony and fear of collective death, the dread of extinction. This fear, however, does not result in dark humour, but in an absolutely serious plan.

The remainder of the present text shall examine Linkola's rejection of linguistification, as well as its political correlate democracy, in much greater depth in order to demonstrate why it is only through negating nothingness (humanism) that we can restore Being (ecology.)

Part II
The Green Police

"A reporter asked the candidates how the problem of unemployment might be solved: that bewildered band of believers, those embodiments of all human mistakes, just gave a blank stare. No one was capable of crossing the sacred boundaries to blaspheme God by uttering two simple words: no machines. Yet, there is no other solution nor will there ever be." – Pentti Linkola, "The Intolerable Misfortune of Technology"

Chapter Three
Did Somebody Say Ecofascism?
Language and the Failure of Democracy

Competing with the Kardashians:
The Media's Silence on Impending Ecological Crises

For all of the reasons detailed in the previous chapters, Linkola emphasized the need to entrust political decisions to the Mind of Nature over democratically-elected politicians, an irrefutable conclusion following from the fact that ecological blind spots in which the figurative "birthmark" can't be seen are more or less unavoidable to finite human subjects. On one hand, it is true that a lack of education from a scientific standpoint alone will account for many errors in ecological understanding. One might imagine that the Middle East and North Africa might have profited from farmers in the Ancient World being better educated about the tendency for ploughs to create deserts if overused. The Easter Island Disaster arguably exemplifies this problem even more conclusively. It is believed that natives there completely exhausted the island's supply of trees in a short-sighted attempt to build enough fishing boats to feed a population which had grown fatally dependent upon seafood for its survival but had miscalculated the wood-costs to maintain such an arrangement in the long term. It is hard to imagine what rational justification the person who consciously decided to chop down the final tree on that remote island could have provided, even to himself, as he used up the last of a crucial resource with no plan for what to do afterwards. Arguably, we are all collectively reliving this fatal act on a daily basis as we squander the final economically-viable reserves of non-renewable fossil fuels with only the vaguest appeals to "a coming algae economy" as the justification to keep maintaining an unsustainable living arrangement founded on suburban sprawl, three-hour daily commutes, global trade networks, and nearly limitless armies of energy-hungry machines.

Far more troubling, however, are cases where one actually does know on an intellectual level what one should do but finds that one simply lacks the motivation to do it. Even as early as Paul's epistles, Christians have wondered why they somehow end up committing the same sins over and over again, even after they explicitly decide that they want to stop doing so: "For I do not do the good I want to do, but the evil I do not want to do – this I keep on doing."[409] In a 2004 interview with Virpi Adamsson, Linkola mentioned himself that the problem is not solely that so few people can "see" the birthmark sufficiently to see where we have come from, where we are, and where we are heading; the problem is preventing these few people from succumbing to the despair of suicide or of suffering a psychotic breakdown following from the depression of realizing on theoretical grounds how hopeless the situation seems; instead, he affirms that these people should accomplish a leap of faith from theoretical comprehension to ethical execution, seizing the moment on practical grounds regardless of how bleak the facts are.[410]

Similarly In his lengthy interview published in the final issue of the Finnish magazine *Quadrivium* in December 2014, he admitted, "The thought often seems to be that if you don't commit suicide, you're not logical." Of course, he does not endorse this at all, since "if the aware ones commit suicide, we're left with the ones that do not even recognise these things. In that respect, the idea of suicide does not hold," since the only solution will lie in having those who have found the sunglasses seize the moment for concrete ethical action.[411]

John Michael Greer similarly mentioned that after he had launched his *Archdruid Report* blog, he started frequently receiving fully-rationalized plans to transition to a post-petroleum society.

---

[409] Romans 7:19.
[410] "Interview with Pentti Linkola 10-2-2004." Available at http://www.penttilinkola.com/pentti_linkola/ecofascism_writings/interview_10-2-2003
[411] Pentti Linkola interview from *Quadrivium* #6 (2014): abridged version. Available at http://qvadrivivm.blogspot.com/2015/12/pentti-linkola-interview-from.html

Often, these proposals were drafted up by professional engineers who demonstrated the most flawless commitments to technical viability. Despite having bulletproof consistency at a purely logical level, to date, not a single one of them has ever been put into action. Greer's interest in the occult led him to acknowledge the unspeakable truth that you can never bridge the gap between gnostic rationality and spiritual motivation simply through developing a more linearly complicated model. No number can leap across the boundary separating the world of reason from the world of spirit simply by becoming fancier on numerical grounds. [412]

In "A Refresher Course on the State of the World," Linkola himself noted that Finns are actually pretty well educated on ecological issues from a scientific standpoint yet they still end up directly supporting the very same policies which violate all of these laws.[413] As he notes himself, the following are all "generally accepted scientific facts": the seas are polluted with oil; food chains are fundamentally disrupted; deforestation is rampant; entire ecosystems are poisoned; and we are somehow wilfully converting productive, renewable green spaces into the most unproductive, not to mention just plain ugly, monstrosity of all by turning them into parking lots! There is no debate whether these points might be challenged on the level of scientific factuality. If disputes do occur, they are usually restricted to adjusting specific figures, yet the underlying ecological problem remains the same regardless of any numerical variations. No one could possibly claim that there is any doubt whether these crises are scientifically validated. The real issue is instead something much more uncomfortable to contemplate, since the true question is only whether learning this data will play any role in affecting individuals' actions. Linkola notes that there is so little difference in personal behaviour between the "unenlightened" and the "enlightened" that we can effectively conclude that exposure to scientific data will never be enough to bring about a change in one's lifestyle. In fact, he claims that the

---

[412] John Michael Greer, "The Failure of Reason" in *The Archdruid Report*, Vol. 1 (Chicago: Founders House, 2017), p. 156.
[413] Pentti Linkola, "A Refresher Course in the State of the World", in *Can Life Prevail?* (Helsinki: Tammi, 2008).

only notable difference between the two groups is that among the enlightened there is "more chattering to be heard" over the issues (or in the present day, there is "more tweeting to be read" among the enlightened). In its worst form, this chattering devolves into an ongoing "rustling of papers" within the First World bureaucracies where so-called "experts" are paid generous salaries in order to go through the motions of drafting up solutions to precisely the same ecological crises which their own agencies bring about.

Needless to say, the only solutions the experts will pursue will be ones which do not threaten their own standard of living, let alone harm economic growth for the nation at large, as that is the sole bi-partisan point of universal consensus. Habermas's faith that all problems can be solved through communicative consensus suffers from precisely this "birthmark." The only consensus which can be counted upon to reliably result, even from a meeting between seemingly-opposed conservative and liberal discussants, is that economic growth must be preserved no matter the consequences. Both Democrat and Republican candidates, in other words, can at least agree that the Earth should be destroyed for a few more years of middle-class privilege among their voter bases.

In his essay "Can We Survive? A Model for a Controlled Future" Linkola revisited the issue by explicitly concluding that the problem is not our failure to process the data. It's simply our failure to react to it. In other words, the passage from knowing to doing is inhibited by some mysterious obstacle which can never be obviated through linearly amassing more bits of scientific data. One can never perform the leap of faith from knowing to doing simply through becoming better at knowing: "[N]either mankind nor the nation [of Finland] are reacting to this [scientific] information [regarding impending ecological catastrophes] in any way at all."[414]

Linkola was careful to note that this is not merely a problem for laymen, but even for professionals who staff the bureaucracies which are explicitly entrusted with the task of applying this data to find real world solutions. In other words, these are the people for whom transitioning from knowing to doing is quite literally their

---

[414] Ibid.

job! In his 1993 essay "It is Dark in the Woods" he noted that he had once asked a forester to explain how the "mafia" of the forestry trade functions, since this is an institution in which there is no rational excuse for their complete lack of motivation to rectify "the most disgusting and twisted policies implemented in the field." These continue to be exercised despite the oversight of people who are at least nominally supposed to be "professionals" at the job of correlating scientific data with practical solutions. Linkola could not help asking, "Why is almost all criticism coming from outside the profession?"[415] In other words, why does criticism only emerge from people who are *not* on the payroll of the mafia?

When Linkola asked who compiled the data on the forest, he found that the trail of evidence led to a group of people who are a far cry from disinterested scientists. Their direct involvement in selling timber represents a grotesque conflict of interest which requires them to claim that surpluses of timber reserves are increasing no matter how much the forests shrink. This profit motive cannot coexist with any effort towards conservation.

These cases demonstrate all too clearly that even after learning that a catastrophe is certain to occur, we somehow cannot actually incorporate this into our plans for the future. Real ecological collapse is basically impossible to transform into a projected event which can be anticipated with any level of seriousness, as it cannot be coerced to fit into any position within the coordinates of our historical destiny, not because it is an empty gap of non-existence but rather because it actively exceeds any space which might be provided for it. Ecological catastrophe is nearly akin to death in Martin Heidegger's *Being and Time*: it is the non-event which only happens insofar as it doesn't happen.[416] One cannot disclose it as an ordinary occurrence, for when it finally does arrive a subjective blackout will extinguish the clearing in which it would have to take place.

This failure to transform theoretical comprehension into practical engagement, founded on an inability to take the futurity of

---

[415] Pentti Linkola, "It is Dark in the Woods," in *Can Life Prevail?* (Kindle Edition).
[416] Martin Heidegger, *Being and Time* (Albany: State University of New York Press, 1996), p. 234.

the catastrophe seriously, is exemplified particularly memorably by the utter absurdity inherent in the way that "news about the impending end of the world" has to compete with the most trivial tabloid gossip about celebrities, and almost always loses the battle for airtime. Linkola himself noted:

> In the media, news about the impending end of the world is drowned amid thousands of other news items. Even though news concerning the gradual suppression of life is really the only significant news, which all other human aspirations are subordinate to, it never really makes the headlines. The most striking titles and the most enormous amount of space is reserved for unbelievably uninteresting nonsense: Diana, Clinton etc.[417]

This quote has aged particularly well, even by Linkolan standards. It is quite humorous to note that in the present year of 2020, news of another presidential impeachment and another royal family diva are continuing the same reality show with new faces. One could simply substitute "Trump" for "Clinton" and "Meghan Markle" for "Princess Diana" and yield the same results. Some twenty years after Linkola wrote these words, we find ourselves to have been stalling in the mud with our foot on the pedal for decades, with no end in sight for this institutionalized passivity. The ecological crisis, however, has not rested over these years; it has quickly outpaced us like a tortoise running laps on a sleeping hare.

Linkola does not mince words regarding the dangers of succumbing to laziness and inaction, as his essay "Of The Evaluation Of The Book 'Into The Ecological Way Of Life [Ekologiseen Elämäntapaan]'" condemned patience as "a quite terrifying attitude when we are [in the] midst [of] a massive wave of [the] biosphere's extinctions and the death and end of everything in our sight." For every day we choose to sleep as Rome burns, the "prospects of erosions, ozone, carbon balance, vanishing of forests and dissolving of green acreage" will remain "unyielding."[418]

---

[417] Pentti Linkola, ""Can We Survive? A Model for a Controlled Future", in *Can Life Prevail?* (Kindle Edition).

Not coincidentally, Ulysses and his Greek comrades also waited until night fell and the Trojan warriors were passed out drunk in the streets to strike them dead after they had willingly brought them through the city gates. Media praise for technological innovation is the Trojan Horse of our era, convincing the masses to bring killer robots into every home and even persuading parents to allow them into toddlers' bedrooms with no regard for how unconscionably dangerous they are. The proverbial Trojan wine which has lulled us into this sleepwalk into the abyss is ironically an excess of stimulation provided by smartphone screens which literally follow us out of the house anywhere we go and hardly allow us a moment of rest even while we are sleeping.

In 2012, the makers of a short YouTube documentary interviewed a group of marines who had returned to the United States after an extended deployment in Afghanistan. While overseas fighting in a war zone, they imagined their daily struggles being broadcast on the evening news back home, as concerned citizens around the nation followed the drama from their living rooms. They assumed, after all, that the general public would recognize that a war which had already claimed countless lives was the most pressing series of events unfolding at that time in history. Upon returning to their native country, however, they were shocked to find that mention of the war was almost completely non-existent and that hourly updates on the Kardashians were actively drowning out any less-fashionable news from appearing on the television screen. One must take this a step further, though, and ask why news of nothing short of the "destruction" of the Earth, which Linkola claimed in a 2004 interview with Virpi Adamsson is "happening all the time," can never manage to find airtime in between segments reporting what outfit Kareena Kapoor was wearing during her latest public appearance.[419] In Linkola's 1995 "Vuotos and Suomen

---

[418] Pentti Linkola, "Of The Evaluation Of The Book 'Into The Ecological Way Of Life [Ekologiseen Elämäntapaan],'" in *A Collection of Essays by Pentti Linkola 1993 – 2006*, p. 146.

[419] "Interview with Pentti Linkola 10-2-2004." Available at http://www.penttilinkola.com/pentti_linkola/ecofascism_writings/interview_10-2-2003

Kuvalehti" he asserted that not only Finland but the world itself has "only one problem, one emergency, one crisis: the collapse of the environment, nature, natural systems"[420]

But it is not only the cult of celebrity worship which is actively blocking out any chance for humans to realize the catastrophe they are wilfully creating. In addition, Linkola argued in his 1994 essay "Sales Season" that the blare of media noise is unavoidable even if one does not own a television, since it is literally plastered all over the physical locations one is forced to frequent in a modern city. Giant advertisements on shop windows prevent more than just sunlight from entering buildings; a wall of sales stickers will block out your thinking, the light of Reason itself, from shining through a mass of jumbled "half off" banners which basically hold your brain hostage and force it to just give in to buying the latest slightly-reduced item on the "for sale" rack:

> It has been a while since sun or moon have shone their rays in any grocery store: shop windows have now been plastered full of moronic price announcements all ending in 95 . . . The other sad consequence of having all these signs up is that people's thoughts are burdened: their thinking is constantly being drawn towards trivial nonsense. Every day people are forced to wade through hundreds or thousands of price tags just to figure out where to buy the cheapest tomatoes or mackerel.[421]

In his essay "A Logging Story," Linkola noted that this manufactured blare of noise has drowned out even the human voice, an endangered species which is quickly becoming as difficult to locate on the other end of a phone call as Bigfoot within the forest. In this essay, he illustrated this trend through recounting the story of how a Finnish village had no phone lines working due to an unexpected weather event. Several weeks later, he found out the hard way that even when one attempted to call a hotline for help at a

---

[420] Pentti Linkola, "Vuotos and Suomen Kuvalehti," in *A Collection of Essays by Pentti Linkola 1993 – 2006*, p. 97.
[421] Pentti Linkola, "Sales Season", in *Can Life Prevail?* (Kindle Edition).

time of crisis from a friend's phone, this digital S.O.S. would inevitably be met with the jingle of elevator music and, after some time, a robotic voice with an automated menu of pseudo-communicative pathways, all of which basically led to the same dead end of throwing the phone against the wall with frustration (so much for the expert's knowledge on "maximizing customer satisfaction!") From a properly Linkolan perspective, the supreme irony is that even in an era defined by grotesque overpopulation, it has become harder than ever before to find a human person when you actually need one. For this reason, Linkola argued that, unthinkable as it might seem in the 1990s when he wrote this essay, let alone to today's smartphone zombies, you can indeed live without a phone; the only adjustment required is to change how human lives are organized.[422]

Arguably, telephones seem necessary in direct correlation with how unnatural this "organization of human lives" is allowed to become. A telephone is not at all necessary for a person situated in a natural living arrangement such as dwelling within a hunter gatherer band of less than a hundred members or even within a medieval-style village, in which peasants seldom travelled further than a few miles away from the place where they were born. "Needing a cell phone" is simply a euphemism for the historically anomalous situation of being an inmate within the open-air prison of suburbia, the single most unnatural living arrangement ever devised. Not coincidentally, it is the least psychologically satisfying and the most expensive in history as well, another example of how violating the Mind of Nature doesn't even succeed in bringing about a better quality of life in exchange for inflicting irreversible environmental damage upon the Earth.

To return to his "Sales Season," it is peculiar that the same "progressive" societies which constantly praise the idea of "going green" so long as it merely remains a hypothetical plan for the future (a new year's resolution which is always bumped up to the next year whenever January 1 arrives again) would ignore the enormous material cost to keep the advertisements flowing like

---

[422] Pentti Linkola, "A Logging Story," in *Can Life Prevail?* (Kindle Edition).

there's no tomorrow. In the essay, he acknowledged the sheer environmental cost of producing a non-stop blare of noise which pedestrians don't even enjoy having to see:

> And where does all our pious talk about the saving of paper and energy go when new posters are affixed everyday, myriads of supermarket catalogues are shoved into every mailbox, magazines devote dozens of pages to food advertising and hundreds of thousands of cars travel from one discount store to another seeking [the latest slight reduction in prices?][423]

In 2011, it was reported that the United States Postal Service was struggling to cover costs as the Great Recession worsened and the economy continued to falter with no end in sight. There was even talk that the institution might declare bankruptcy, after which it might be forced to privatize. Though absolutely unthinkable in previous decades, such a thing was not unheard of at that time; in fact, something like it had already occurred in some other Western nations. One news agency caught wind of the story and was determined to warn citizens that the nightmare scenario looked frighteningly likely. A reporter travelled to a sleepy bedroom community in New Jersey and proceeded to knock on doors, sounding the alarm like a modern-day Paul Revere with the hopes of capturing their reactions to the ultimate shock live on camera.

    People's responses did indeed prove to be newsworthy, but for all the wrong reasons. Many of the residents of the neighbourhood noted that they had already stopped receiving mail, but that was because they had gone out of their way to pay a fee to willingly opt out of the system. In an age where any desired communication arrived by email or social media anyway, their mailboxes had devolved into nothing more than spam receptacles for local businesses to dump their paper trash. There was once a time when checking the mail was among the most exciting moments of the day; by 2011, it had simply become a drudging task to clear

---

[423] Ibid.

the pizza delivery coupons and department store mini-catalogues out and then throw them straight into the nearest trash can, a chore which was about as much fun as cleaning out a space where animals relieve themselves when the call of Nature sounds. Estimates varied, but the total amount of wasted material to produce advertisements that almost always made a beeline into the wastepaper basket (a term even more fitting than before) was well into the tons. If nothing else, this news story proved that in the years since Linkola wrote "Sales Season," the advertisement industry has become so dysfunctional that people were willing to pay a fine just to shut them up, much like a street musician who is so bad that the only dollars he receives is from pedestrians asking him to stop singing.

Yet it is not only the paper on which the advertisements are printed that represent an enormous waste of natural resources. Linkola noted in his "The Doctrine of Survival and Doctor Ethics" that the black magic of marketing blinds us to the obvious fact that it is precisely the last reserves of our "finite natural resources" which are thoughtlessly piled into the shopping carts during the "clearance sale" frenzy.[424] Few things are quite as tragic as processing an irreplaceable miracle of Nature into a cookie cutter product which is indistinguishable from millions of other identical copies of the same model which are only to be pumped out of the factory assembly line, loaded onto a semi-truck, hauled to a for sale rack, driven home, and then dumped into a pile of other junk in an already cluttered house before being thrown into a storage unit in which one will pay a monthly fee just to get it out of one's sight for the rest of one's life.

Linkola has distinguished himself as one of the few people with the guts to openly say what so many of us have only silently wondered, by noting that the enormous ecological cost to construct "a coast to coast shopping mall" (in the immortal words of George Carlin) was virtually entirely wasted to build a monstrosity which is *just plain ugly* anyway! Few things are quite as disheartening as staring at the concrete dungeon which a modern suburban shopping

---

[424] Pentti Linkola, "The Doctrine Of Survival And Doctor Ethics," in *A Collection of Essays by Pentti Linkola 1993 – 2006*, p. 116.

mall is revealed to be once the excitement of buying overhyped junk there wears off like cheap liquor and one can suddenly see the same hideous beast through sober eyes which lack the rosy tint of beer goggle vision. Let alone could one stomach the sight of the countless mini-strip malls lining the highways like so many deformed bastard offspring which have combined being ugly with being boring even more impressively than a real shopping mall could:

> [T]he cityscape is becoming gross and shabby. Beauty is always a central and inalienable value, a value far more important than economy [yet we are squandering it just to get a few more cheap manufactured products][425]

In "Against Highway Crime," he noted the irony that even though the construction of highways was one of the greatest eco-crimes, not to mention one of the costliest infrastructural projects ever devised, they don't actually improve our quality of life in the least:

> An increase in road traffic does not contribute to human well-being. Ninety percent of cargo traffic transports unnecessary and harmful material. Ninety percent of passenger car traffic is either wasteful driving or the kind of travelling that could easily be replaced by public transport (with 50 to 500 people per vehicle).[426]

One could hardly describe being stuck in traffic on a freeway for three hours at a time just to get home from work as a "joyful" experience, nor could one deny that road rage is a demon that possesses perfectly agreeable people and drives them to behave in the most diabolical ways in response to minor conflicts with other drivers. It is deeply troubling to consider how many people have been needlessly killed after the most trivial traffic mishap accelerated to the point of cold-blooded murder, a chilling testament

---

[425] Pentti Linkola, "Sales Season", in *Can Life Prevail?* (Kindle Edition).
[426] Pentti Linkola, "Against Highway Crime," in *Can Life Prevail?* (Kindle Edition).

to eco-crimes' tendency to hijack the human body and drive it to self-destruct in an act of suicide which is unfortunately carrying Nature along with it.

In his 1993 essay "Karelia," Linkola noted that his visit to a village with roads that were inaccessible by car actually proved far more pleasant than a modernized Western city, since the sight of farmers and their wives walking down the paths carrying their bags from the village shop was far more soothing than the blare of noise and the waves of pollution emitting from countless ugly motor vehicles on a suburban highway.[427] In addition, the sound of laughter and stories being told by villagers amidst the hard work of chopping wood to keep the home fires burning offered a glimpse into a way of life which was commonplace just a few generations ago but was traded in for the dull and overpriced experience of paying a high monthly bill for natural gas heating and then using those hours of free time to just idle in front of a television set to passively consume whatever garbage the cable networks happened to deem acceptable for distribution. The ultimate con job lay in convincing people to spend more money and commit more ecological damage just to make themselves more bored and more cut off from the local community, which itself ceased to exist as its functions were all automated away one by one. In fact, he closed the essay by recounting that this experience led him to realize why he despised the way of life which had seized Finland in recent years so much: it was precisely because the project of rationalized technological ordering had succeeded so well there that his nation had been robbed of any lingering traces of mystery. This is arguably even truer of the United States, a country which was "ordered" into one giant suburb and, as a result, was transformed into a single amorphous pseudo-place completely devoid of wonder. Contrary to media caricatures, it is technology which is dull; only Nature can truly fascinate Man, for only Nature is genuinely unpredictable and capable of generating something new.

Language and Apocalypse

---

[427] See Pentti Linkola, "Karelia," in *Collection of Essays by Pentti Linkola 1993-2006*.

Linkola was careful to note that his own warnings of ecological collapse are categorically different from virtually all previous predictions of doom, since the latter have almost always been founded on unverifiable mystical visions or obscure interpretations of religious texts. It is intellectually dishonest to compare groups concerned about the coming ecological catastrophe to John Hagee-style apocalyptic cults centred around claims that the Antichrist has really arrived this time because of so many ad hoc connections between the Book of Revelation and the latest news of violent conflict in Israel, a set of unrelated fragments pieced together with about as much adhesive strength as if one had used bubble gum as a substitute for cement in a construction project. Linkola himself noted:

> While doomsday omens can be said to be old news, in the present century they are based on something other than intuition or revelation: modern forecasts are founded on scientific facts, data, calculations and figures. This kind of news is no more than a century old.[428]

Linkola reiterated his commitment to strict ecological forms over flexible linguistic abstractions in his 1996 essay "Of The Evaluation Of The Book 'Into The Ecological Way Of Life [Ekologiseen Elämäntapaan],'" in which he promised the reader that he keeps his mind "clear" by treating "figures as figures" and "facts as facts" in order to keep all "assessments of the situation" as lucid as possible. Above all, he maintains this high standard of clarity by actively distancing the distorting "eyewash" of "prejudices, attitudes and belief," especially "the most dangerous of them all: empty optimism."[429] Public relations firms whose sole "job" is to inflate

---

[428] Pentti Linkola, "Can We Survive? A Model for a Controlled Future", in *Can Life Prevail?* (Kindle Edition).

[429] Pentti Linkola, "Of The Evaluation Of The Book 'Into The Ecological Way Of Life [Ekologiseen Elämäntapaan],'" in *A Collection of Essays by Pentti Linkola 1993 – 2006*, p. 146.

the latter are, therefore, among the worst of all eco-criminals for their relentless deception of the masses.

Interestingly, Linkola also unearthed a difference in the underlying structures at work in ecological figures and linguistic catchphrases. The very standard of evidence differs for each at the most fundamental of levels. Above all, apocalyptic religious cults simply manipulate language to derive ever more far-fetched results with no need to be held accountable to anything more substantial than a string of words which they themselves made up out of whole cloth in the first place. In the essay "Can We Survive: A Model for a Controlled Future," Linkola noted that human language is hard-wired to allow such abuses because there is quite literally no fixed limit to how twisted its claims might become, especially at the hands of a skilled orator with a talent for scamming the masses. He opened the essay by warning that even though "[n]o natural scientist or serious futurologist believes we have more than thirty or — at the most — one hundred years left" before a catastrophic event, perhaps even human extinction itself, arrives, public relations firms employed by corporate interests are somehow able to completely blot out these undeniable figures by abusing human language's nearly-limitless elasticity to fabricate any contorted linguistic form which will promise to keep the public in a state of mindless consumption to allow their profits to keep growing:

> The human language makes it possible for any twisted claim to be formulated: it is easy to say that the sun rises in the west and sets in the east.[430]

In his "Refresher Course on the State of the World," Linkola repeated this witty absurdity but added that such a person might claim
"that females impregnate and males give birth."[431]

This elasticity inherent in language is strictly out of accord with the physical properties of ecological and natural reality, a fact

---

[430] Ibid.
[431] Pentti Linkola, "Refresher Course on the State of the World," in *Can Life Prevail?* (Kindle Edition).

emphasized especially by the same occultists who acknowledge additional dimensions of existence beyond physical matter. In John Michael Greer's 1996 *Paths of Meaning*, his first published book, he provided something of an "Occultist Phenomenology" by documenting the distinctions among how different types of phenomena appear within consciousness. Whereas entities which appear within imagination and dreams are inherently "stretchy" and can expand, shrink, warp, and fly at will, material beings from the realm of Nature are fixed into stricter forms due to their need to adhere to the Laws of Physics.[432]

In a 2019 *Ecosophia* post titled "The Worlds We Live In" Greer argued that one of the primary errors of materialistic reductivism is that it overlooks a central ambiguity in the term "world." Although it is true that the physical world of scientific materialism "really exists," this outer world is only one of two worlds we always inhabit. In addition, there is an inner world of imagination, emotion, and spiritual motivation. He explained this contrast through comparing how a turkey sandwich would behave in the inner world with how it would behave in the outer world. Whereas a turkey sandwich on the outer world can only appear if somebody actually slaughters a turkey, grows a tomato and a head of lettuce, and grinds rye or wheat flour for bread, a turkey sandwich can appear in the inner world without any of these physical inputs. In addition, a turkey sandwich on the inner world can fly, stretch, change colours, and even vanish at will, while a turkey sandwich on the outer world can only undergo changes and movements if these accord with the strict limits of natural law.[433]

In other words, the morphological fluidity of linguistification is simply a feature transitively borrowed from humans' capacity for imagination and hallucination. It is fundamentally incommensurate with the requirements of a Deep Ecology which has been freed from the contamination of humanistic delusion. Deep Ecology, in fact, might very well be defined as a phenomenological purification that drains out any elements of

---

[432] John Michael Greer, *Paths of Meaning: Cabala in the Golden Dawn Tradition* (London: Llewellyn, 1996).
[433] John Michael Greer, "The Worlds We Live In," *Ecosophia*, 06-03-2019.

imaginative fancy in order to yield ecological law without the slightest humanistic distortion.

In a 2004 interview with Virpi Adamsson conducted at the international book fair at Turku, Adamsson asked Linkola whether, after some forty years of tireless activism for Nature, he felt in retrospect that he had been wrong about anything. Linkola responded that he had almost never made any errors with regard to the data captured in situational surveys or society's mapping and analysis; his only error lay in not purifying the last bits of hopeless humanistic optimism from his interpretation of these models of ecological reality.[434] In other words, Linkola's only regret was that he had not calibrated his own mind to the Mind of Nature even more purely.

In fact, in the same interview he noted that the problem was not that he had abused language to exaggerate in order to awaken audiences from their collective stupor to seize the moment for action, as the interviewer suggested might be the case; on the contrary, Linkola argued that language had indeed been a "barrier" rather than a help, but only because it could not communicate strongly enough how serious the situation was. Only the non-linguistified ecological form itself is fully up to that task.

In "Can We Survive? A Model for a Controlled Future," Linkola explicitly noted the irony that ecologically-impossible ambitions are almost always founded on the crassest materialistic desires and yet, somehow, are defined by a departure from the realm of "concrete, material reality" for the realm of "virtual reality" fiction. He asserted that anyone lucky enough to make "their way back from [the] most ghastly odyssey yet" by surviving the journey from this "absurd world of modern delusion" back to the firm grounding of ecological reality will quickly realize certain things which the Mind of Nature can see clearly but the sleepwalking masses remain unable to see due to a trance of collective linguistic psychosis. Most important of all, such a person would see that he or she must immediately "move all information technology [straight]

---

[434] "Interview with Pentti Linkola 10-2-2004." Available at http://www.penttilinkola.com/pentti_linkola/ecofascism_writings/interview_10-2-2003

into the trash bin of history," on grounds that the failure to do so may very well end in a situation in which "the present bubble will burst, and nothing will remain at the bottom of the bin." In other words, anyone who woke up from the witch's spell over his or her mind would immediately realize the machines have to go before anything else.

He ends this haunting fragment by warning that any "reader who is contently living in the absurd world of modern delusions may think that what has been presented above is only a form of humour — dark humour."[435] Be that as it may, it is not at all clear how humorous the situation will be if there is no one left to get the "last laugh" after the world becomes as devoid of human life as the ghost towns in "Where is Everybody?", the first episode of *The Twilight Zone*.[436]

Because language is inherently contaminated by the quasi-psychotic properties of hallucination and imagination, Linkola categorically rejects the use of open-ended language games to defend his claims of coming catastrophe. Instead, he maintains a faithful commitment to citing scientific figures which are far from malleable, in that they are themselves merely a means to an end to represent real ecological situations which are bound by a set of natural laws which have no obligation to bow down to the whims of Man. The ontological status of non-linguistic ecological forms actively rules out the possibility of the kinds of abuses rampant among groups which only appeal to linguistification.

Dmitry Orlov similarly opened his 2013 classic *The Five Stages of Collapse: A Survivor's Toolkit* by contrasting approaches to the future founded on the methodology of (honest) engineers with approaches to the future founded on the methodology of public relations firms.[437] An engineer who interprets the numerical data regarding resource depletion rates, mountains of unpayable debt, and intrinsically-high international trade costs can't *not* see collapse

---

[435] Pentti Linkola, "Can We Survive? A Model for a Controlled Future," in *Can Life Prevail?* (Kindle Edition).
[436] "Where is Everybody?," *The Twilight Zone*, Season One, 1959.
[437] Dmitry Orlov, *The Five Stages of Collapse: Survivors' Toolkit* (Gabriola Island: New Society Publishers, 2013).

coming, provided he is not being paid a handsome sum by some corporate or government bureaucracy to pretend not to see it.

In one memorable urban legend, Stalin is said to have appointed an architect with the task of overseeing the construction of a massive building on a questionable site which Stalin happened to fancy for aesthetic reasons alone.[438] The architect's fidelity to hard numbers and strict physical limits forced him to break the unwelcome news that the site was totally unfit for such a building project. Stalin is alleged to have promptly ordered that man's execution without any further debate. The next man appointed for the task immediately began work on the construction of the building. While such an act was still somewhat scandalous in the era of Stalin, it has arguably been universalized in our era, as any "technician of empire" interested in keeping his or her livelihood must follow through with orders to construct a doomed project which spans the entire globe rather than a single ill-chosen site in the Soviet Union. Stalin allegedly commissioned self-destruction for a single architectural project; the System today has mandated self-destruction for the Earth itself.

Orlov is careful to note that short of this forced choice between one's money and one's life, one would have to see that at this point collapse is simply hard-wired into the numerical figures themselves. If nothing else, the total amount of debt plus interest that has been issued already far exceeds the total number of dollars that exist, despite the fact that the latter require nothing more than a few keystrokes to be conjured out of thin air! Suffice it to say that once access to fossil fuels drops like a rock, demanding millions of highly-indebted borrowers to pay back money that doesn't exist with real wealth that has already evaporated out of existence is to punish them for failing to do the impossible.

Of course, we almost never hear such inconvenient truths reported because media talking heads, politicians, and public educators do not approach the future from an engineering

---

[438] The author admits he has had trouble locating the source for this urban legend which was passed down to him by oral tradition from one of his high school teachers. Even if it is not historically true, it is still useful as a metaphor for the way that our own System functions.

perspective founded on hard numbers, especially not from a standpoint with any accountability to the impersonal laws of ecological reality. Instead, they work from a public relations standpoint in which linguistic abstraction is abused with the sole interest of artificially raising the public's happiness index by whatever means necessary. Whereas engineering is intrinsically constrained by mathematical procedure and natural limitation, public relations is solely measured by its ability to generate good feelings and suppress bad feelings through broadcasting catchwords and marketing slogans which were designed to play audience's emotions like keys on a piano. Likewise, any appeal to that linguistic chimera of "progress towards a better future" is favoured for emotional reasons alone, even as the cognitive dissonance to repress its contradiction of reality hovers just slightly over the breaking point.[439]

Linkola has similarly emphasized that it is peculiar for professional bureaucrats to continue ignoring the omens of ecological collapse, since one has to wilfully *not* see the hard numbers in order to deny that it is coming. In his 1993 essay "It is Dark in the Woods," for example, Linkola noted that one need not appeal to emotional abstractions (in Orlov's terms, the subject matter of public relations firms) to formulate arguments against the logging industry's devastation of Finland's forests, because the numerical figures alone already indicate that the current project is a failure on technical grounds alone.

For example, he mentions a figure named Lauri Vaara who lacks any explicit ideological commitments to conservationism and who does not even feel the need to explicitly criticise the methods of forestry but who still found himself having to "mathematically emphasise how terribly unprofitable heavily mechanised forest harvesting is in terms of national economy, country trade and employment."[440] In other words, even a person who is not ideologically committed to a stance opposing technology, waste, or industrial overshoot will have to admit that using machines is not

---

[439] Dmitry Orlov, *The Five Stages of Collapse: Survivors' Toolkit* (Gabriola Island: New Society Publishers, 2013).
[440] Pentti Linkola, "It is Dark in the Woods," in *Can Life Prevail?* (Kindle Edition).

even profitable in comparison with using traditional manual labour and employing a human workforce. There is no need to take the public relations path of saying machines are "bad." It is clear from the numbers alone that machines have failed at the job they were appointed to perform.

Linkola has been troubled by this double-loss since at least the 1974 article "Metsäpolitiikka— Suomen luonnonsuojelun ydin," in which he pointed out that the forest industry had somehow combined the (dis-)honours of being both "the most fuel-consuming branch of industry in the country and [also] the one with the worst operating efficiency when it comes to the amount of energy used for a finished product."

By his 1993 essay "The Armoured Idiot," he found that even speaking of "gains" in the industry are misplaced – the only thing which is reliably accumulated in their activities is simply massive losses which easily cancel out any "meagre merits and victories elsewhere."[441] The "final result" of this coordinated madness is therefore clearly in the negative, as far more energy and resources were wasted to accomplish a task which could have been done far more efficiently with human labourers and hand tools. In his 2004 essay "Refresher Course About Forests," he recounted that in the pre-war period, traditional methods provided both an enormous amount of meaningful work for both humans and horses and yet still harvested only a modest amount of timber – a true win-win situation compared to the present dysfunction.[442] Likewise, he favoured changing the modern forestry professional's nickname from the "armoured destroyer" to the "armoured idiot" in order to reflect its true meaning more clearly.[443]

Your Eyes Must be Wrong if They See the Truth

---

[441] Pentti Linkola, "Armored Idiot," in *A Collection of Essays by Pentti Linkola 1993 – 2006*, pp. 9-10.

[442] Pentti Linkola, "Refresher Course about Forest," in *A Collection of Essays by Pentti Linkola 1993 – 2006*, p. 32.

[443] Pentti Linkola, "Armored Idiot," in *A Collection of Essays by Pentti Linkola 1993 – 2006*, pp. 9-10.

As one might imagine, even in cases where the opposition does provide data to bolster the interests of the System, they literally have to fabricate outright lies in one form or another to do so. In "It is Dark in the Woods," Linkola memorably recounted an experience which taught him first-hand how widespread statistical fraud is within the bureaucracies tasked with overseeing forest land in Finland. When he was preparing to purchase some property for the upcoming nature preservation trust, he reviewed the official data before visiting the sites in person. When he arrived, it became all too clear to him that the official information documenting the state of the land was, as he said himself, "not at all accurate."[444] He closed the essay by warning the reader to be sceptical towards any official data whatsoever, as the balance sheet is hard-wired to have been thoroughly manipulated to bolster the interests of the System.

In fact, in his 1993 "New Climate - Greetings To Meteorologists" he noted that meteorologists' contradiction of ordinary people's personal experience has become so common that it had become a point of humour for him and his outdoorsy friends of hunters and fishers.[445] Even as the vastly-overpaid experts ramble into a one-way megaphone to the television audiences without any interest in hearing back from the other side, more and more heretics find that, ultimately, "Man believes what he sees for himself." Linkola recounted that his "own reality has been for the last fifty years in the events of nature; forests, marshlands, lakes and sea archipelagos." Blessed with an "exceptionally good" memory, he could not help noticing that the only problem with the expert's opinions is that they just happen to contradict reality.

This contradiction between first-hand experience and the official narrative of the System was revisited in his 1993 essay "The Green Lie," in which he lamented that almost no one is able to "see" the obvious fact that the invention of the chainsaw has proven absolutely devastating for Finnish forests, despite the fact that this tragic mass murder of trees is so objectively visible that even the electronic eyes of "satellites" which view the Earth from afar are

---

[444] Ibid.
[445] Pentti Linkola, "New Climate - Greetings to Meteorologists," in *A Collection of Essays by Pentti Linkola 1993 – 2006*, pp. 34-6.

able to see it. In fact, anyone who even bothers to gaze outside his or her car window as he or she speeds down the highway in Finland will be greeted with the unwelcome sight of ever-shrinking reserves of wild trees. Sadly, fewer and fewer people are capable of even so basic an activity as seeing what is right before their eyes simply because the "propaganda devised by the forest industry" has proven so effective that almost everyone will continue to favour the bogus statistics spoon-fed to the media by the industry even when it blatantly contradicts their own personal experience:

> [The] propaganda devised by the forest industry has proven amazingly effective. [The decline of trees is visible to both human] eyes and satellites all across the country. And yet, the words spoken by the forest industry about the logging, preservation and growth of state timber reserves [is still reliably] swallowed whole by [the masses] who do not [bother to] explore the woods or even gaze at them from their car windows.[446]

One need not appeal to far-fetched conspiracy theories or even moralistic abstractions regarding "evil" to demonstrate this, as the numbers alone speak for themselves all too clearly:

> [After the introduction of the chainsaw, t]he number of trees [in Finland has] decreased at an inconceivable pace. [In some areas there was] a loss of about two-thirds in just thirty years [and in some cases] the loss was even greater [than that].[447]

In 1993 "From Gunslingers To Environmental Disasters," Linkola affirmed that "industrialization and an efficient economy came with a horrendous cost on nature,"[448] but by his 2004 essay "A Refresher Course About Forest" he had concluded that the concise formula

---

[446] Ibid.
[447] Pentti Linkola, "The Green Lie," in *Can Life Prevail?* (Kindle Edition).
[448] Pentti Linkola, ""From Gunslingers To Environmental Disasters"," in *A Collection of Essays by Pentti Linkola 1993 – 2006*, p. 39.

"efficiency=extermination" is the true meaning of any appeals to those chimeras of "technological innovation,"[449] an equation which proves that the ultimate leap in efficiency would simultaneously kill its host by eliminating it from existence.

In Orlov's terms, the industry has managed to avoid exposing the hard numbers documenting how many trees have disappeared because they have utilized their public relations skills to distract the public from this troubling reality by manufacturing emotional abstractions such as "comfort" and "trust in the authorities" to sedate them out of caring about the catastrophe unfolding in their midst:

> All the media have swallowed the official lies [which were invented out of whole cloth at the first stage of the process]. To my bewilderment, I recently even found the same statistics about forest growth cited in an otherwise detailed and insightful book [which proved that] any claim will be taken to be true if repeated often enough.[450]

In his essay "It is Dark in the Woods," Linkola went slightly beyond Orlov by emphasizing the transitive nature of propaganda. A bogus figure manufactured by one corrupt agency will instantly clone itself as it travels down the chain of subordinate links on the trail of yes-men. The labour invested to produce it is effectively "saved" at each of these later stages, as they'll merely conduct the same electric shock over a single continuous wire without having to generate anything new in the process. He notes that even figures whose intentions are not malicious will still be duped into regurgitating faulty claims simply because of the stamp of legitimacy the statistics hold and because their presence has become so ubiquitous as to be unavoidable:

> How have [these] statistics . . . been gathered? Well, they were compiled by [an institution] whose main duty is to

---

[449] Pentti Linkola, "Refresher Course about Forest," in *A Collection of Essays by Pentti Linkola 1993 – 2006*, p. 31.
[450] Ibid.

> collect data on behalf of the forest industry. [This institution has] nothing to do with unbiased academia, although the masses — and the [media] — often believe it does. The scientific-sounding name of the Department and the appointment of its officials to professorships are nothing but an ingenious bluff. The same holds true for the official title given to forest fellers: "foresters".[451]

Linkola is careful to note, however, that in the rare cases where a responsible researcher will cite accurate figures which contradict the official narrative of industrial interests, he or she will find out the hard way that although he or she is right and the big institutional forces are wrong, he or she simply lacks the raw horsepower to compete in a war of noise against a System which has hijacked the gargantuan strength of Modern Technology to do its dirty work. Linkola laments that even his own efforts must be counted among those of a tiny David standing up against the massive corporate Goliaths who have hijacked the power of the industrial system to advance their own financial self-interests:

> Biologists of course occasionally dare to correct the absurdities delivered by the industry . . . [These] friends of nature, however, soon grow weary: they simply do not possess the resources to wage a constant battle of information. They are but a small minority in Finland and their chirping is easily quelled. My writing, too, will be drowned in the beating of drums.[452]

Any claims to "unbiased academia" among the "professional bullshitters" tasked with justifying environmental damage through disseminating misinformation are laughable when one considers that the ultimate origin for this chain of lies is simply the forest industry itself, an institution for which the drive for profits represents the most grotesque of all conflicts of interests. This drive for profit, while undoubtedly present in past eras, has

---

[451] Pentti Linkola, "It is Dark in the Woods," in *Can Life Prevail?* (Kindle Edition).
[452] Ibid.

proven uniquely devastating at a time in which materialistic greed has effectively been elevated to the status of a state religion:

> The industry, like any major corporation, is only interested in business. Things could not be any different from the way they are now, particularly with regard to morals, as the industry's only gods are the bank and the market: the industry would readily sell its own grandmother.[453]

The term "industrial expert" has become something of an oxymoron in itself, since Linkola noted in his 1993 essay "The Armoured Idiot" that forestry professionals only succeed in forming a "monumental island of foolishness," despite the fact that their job description is literally to be "professional knowers." [454] This "expertise" reliably consists of breaking new barriers to make a horrific situation even worse, yet the common denominator in each act of institutionalized stupidity is the same: driving Modern Technology even deeper into the forests. Their fanatical commitment to "the mobilization of all the enormous machinery" proved so single-minded that they memorably decided to "wipe [the] birch out" with it "just before it arose as the most expensive of valued trees in industry."[455] Nor was their judgment any more impressive when they brought about "equally astounding losses" by means of "kalelointi" which "were used to fell groups of quite young trees there where 'the nursery wasn't even.'" The expert's role in bringing about the "birth of clearfelling" only succeeded in causing "the greatest curse upon Finnish landscapes since the Ice Age."[456] In this essay, Linkola found that even behind such monumental displays of idiocy, there was in fact a general rule dictating what appears to be mindless incompetence: in any case, the only flaw the regulators found with traditional methods was precisely that they did not require help from an "expert."

---

[453] Ibid.
[454] Pentti Linkola, "Armored Idiot," in *A Collection of Essays by Pentti Linkola 1993 – 2006*, p. 7.
[455] Ibid.
[456] Ibid., p. 8.

One can only be shocked by these revelations if one overlooks that any institution which has managed to staff its seemingly-extrinsic regulators with its own insiders cannot be expected to function in any other way, much like Alan Collinge's revelation that the student loan companies exported their own top-level insiders to the Department of Education and other institutions charged with the task of ensuring that "abuses" would not occur within these same companies, an obvious conflict of interest which was normalized as "business as usual" within a uniquely corrupt racket. Collinge memorably noted in his classic *The Student Loan Scam: The Most Oppressive Debt in U.S. History and How We Can Fight Back*: "In many cases, it had become impossible to tell where the universities ended and the student loan companies began."[457]

In "The Green Lie," Linkola revealed a similarly incestuous relationship between industry and its regulators by recounting one of the most shocking "stories about the unscrupulous business of forestry professionals." According to this story, it is simply business as usual to "cook the books" to get around environmental regulations which had nominally been designed to prevent overlogging. For example, one will make it seem as though one is in dire need of revenue to pay rising property taxes on forest land, when in reality one is simply manipulating regulatory red tape in order to justify more logging in the interest of maximizing profits. In other words, the problem is not the lack of any regulation whatsoever, but rather the ease with which current regulations can be abused to violate the same ecological laws they were nominally meant to reinforce. In the absence of a political institution overseen by the Mind of Nature, it is all too easy to allow the humanistic chimera of money to overshadow ecological law.[458]

Signitive Pathway to Truth or Symbolic Dead End?

Arguably, one of the most important themes in Linkola's philosophy lies in the following opposition: while language can be

---

[457] Alan Collinge, *The Student Loan Scam: The Most Oppressive Debt in U.S. History and How We Can Fight Back* (Boston: Beacon Hill, 2008).
[458] Pentti Linkola, "The Green Lie," in *Can Life Prevail?* (Kindle Edition).

systematically abused to affirm the birthmark of ecological impossibility as though it were something real, attention to strict ecological form can unscramble the message embedded within the birthmark to reveal the eco-crime underlying a seemingly credible proposal. This opposition is implicitly founded upon a philosophical belief that any use of language which does not provide a symbolic pathway to access a valid ecological situation is worse than useless; it's deadly. It is no exaggeration to say that the autopsy following after the destruction of life on Earth would read "death by linguistification" if there were anyone left alive to decipher it.

Although Linkola does not usually tend to favour getting deep into the weeds of philosophical speculation as such, it is not difficult to reconstruct a general theory of symbols inherent in his work. Linkola's unexpected affinity with the early Edmund Husserl is sufficiently profound to justify designating his work as a type of Ecological Phenomenology. For this reason, it will be important to briefly consider Husserl's earliest theory of signs in greater detail to fully appreciate Linkola's own stance.

In Husserl's earliest work, particularly in his little-read 1891 text *The Philosophy of Arithmetic*, he contrasted authentic intuitions of numbers with merely signitive intentions of them. Small numbers under ten, for example, can be grasped authentically within intuition, while virtually any other number can only be accessed indirectly through a sign which constructs a bridge to connect the conscious subject to some mathematical object which would remain inaccessible without this intermediary structure.[459] For example, one can grasp the number three directly in an act of seeing three apples but large numbers, negative numbers, and zero can only be "given" indirectly by means of a symbol which can extend the range of contents available for comprehension. The problem is not that we can't grasp these numbers; the problem is that a symbolic pathway is categorically inferior to one which is founded solely on an act of intuition.

Intentionality is a bit like electricity, in that it can travel a vast distance before arriving at a fairly far-fetched destination, so

---

[459] Edmund Husserl, *The Philosophy of Arithmetic* (Dordrecht: Kluwer Academic Publishers, 2003), p. 16.

long as it is provided with sufficient conduction along the way. The symbol which allows this journey to take place, however, is only useful if it actually provides a pathway for consciousness to be directed towards the address for a location occupied by a number which "really exists." While it is not difficult to accept that zero, 300, and -25 are real things despite the fact that they can only be given symbolically, the ontological status of imaginary numbers such as the square root of -1 is far less clear, despite the fact that the signitive pathway to access them seems perfectly legitimate on symbolic grounds alone.

As a general rule, one can argue that any symbol which conducts consciousness to something real is only transitively valuable, insofar as it borrows reality from its referent but lacks any on its own. Any symbol which sends consciousness on a wild goose chase into the abyss is worse than useless; it is suicidal.

In this sense, Linkola's philosophy is essentially Ecological Phenomenology, in that a humanistic chimera, such as "progress towards a better future," can very precisely be described as an empty unit of linguistification misrecognized as a real entity in itself. Linkola has repeatedly dismissed progress as a misnomer, in that the "better conditions" it claims to symbolize don't actually exist. Far from constantly improving people's quality of life, let alone the ecological conditions for Nature, each incremental leap in "progress" actually worsens both considerably.

In his 2004 author's preface to *Can Life Prevail?*, Linkola harshly dismissed the "uncritical worship" of technology, automation, and market economy as delusions which require one to ignore the birthmark inherent in the inconvenient fact that each of these has only made life worse. He went as far as to categorically claim that of *all* the "good and joyful things in life, none of them came from progress."[460]

Linkola explicitly emphasized a connection between "progress" and "madness" in his "Human Nature and History" by warning that any "future [which] is fashioned after a madman's belief and progress and development" will be held hostage to

---

[460] Ibid.

"delusions and science fictions" with as little substance behind them as Oz. If these hallucinations are allowed to serve as models for policy, he warns that "the game is most certainly over."[461] In "The Objection Raised by the Deep Ecologist" subsection of "The ABC of the Deep Ecologist – Part One," he clarified his opposition to the chimera of "progress" by explaining that it is basically just a euphemism for the delusion that man has assumed a "dominating position" over the rest of life, an ecologically-impossible stance which crumbles to dust when one realizes that Man remains fatally dependent upon the stability of the underlying ecosystem even as he actively disrupts it to the breaking point: "The guardian of life, the deep ecologist, will not accept progress as the end of evolution and will reject the dominating position man has assumed."[462] In the same essay, he noted that "progress" in this view is simply leading to "utter devastation." The deep ecologist is by definition the one who responds to the ethical call to "stop" this or at the very least "slow [it] down."[463]

Similarly, Brett Stevens noted in his own 2008 introduction to *Can Life Prevail?* that for Linkola "progress is an illusion" insofar as this word is simply a euphemism for the same economic growth and technological advances which have actually made life far more unsatisfying. He quotes Linkola's own words that: "material prosperity doesn't bring about anything apart from misery." In other words, progress is actually something of a misnomer, since each wave of it just makes life more miserable.

In Linkola's 2004 interview with Virpi Adamsson, Adamsson mentioned that a media controversy had erupted after Linkola proposed that any mention of the word "progress" should effectively be banned. On one hand, Linkola justified this outrageous claim by acknowledging that it would have been better if the kind of technological and economic overshoot symbolized by this term had never occurred.[464] However, Linkola qualified his

---

[461] Pentti Linkola, "Human Nature and History," in *Can Life Prevail?* (Kindle Edition).
[462] Pentti Linkola, "The ABC of the Deep Ecologist – Part One," in *Can Life Prevail?* (Kindle Edition).
[463] Ibid.

stance by warning the audience not to misinterpret his aversion to progress as a belief that all change is in itself bad. In fact, natural change is actually far more fascinating than any of the artificial pseudo-changes pumped out by the System which are just so many spuriously infinite variations on the same bland themes.[465] Nature already provides more than enough change to keep humans' natural desire for it satisfied. For example, experiencing the transition from winter to spring and then from summer back to fall is incomparably more enjoyable than watching Demi Lovato release yet another mass-produced electronic song which sounds not the least bit different from any of her previous dozens but is still praised by the media as a "radically new innovation never thought of before."

In his lengthy interview published in the final issue of the Finnish magazine *Quadrivium* in December 2014, he noted that the world would pretty much be the same if all these pop culture works didn't exist. Not only naturally, but culturally, nothing is gained:

> Most people have no spirited or culture-related interests even as customers, spectators or listeners. Even if you consider all the activities in these towns, they add nothing to the whole. If we didn't have that Äänekoski or Kokkola, the Finnish cultural life would be exactly the same. . . . The only thing gained with these great volumes is the crushing of everything else.[466]

In fact the only change you see in progress is, in fact, change for the worse. In fact, in his 2004 essay "A Refresher Course About Forest," he acknowledged that the only thing which "grows" each day in the forest industry is the brutality of its methods and the

---

[464] "Interview with Pentti Linkola 10-2-2004." Available at http://www.penttilinkola.com/pentti_linkola/ecofascism_writings/interview_10-2-2003

[465] In Hegel's *Logic*, spurious infinity is an endless, linear repetition of the same, while true infinity goes beyond this to grasp the power of true change.

[466] Pentti Linkola interview from *Quadrivium* #6 (2014): abridged version. Available at http://qvadrivivm.blogspot.com/2015/12/pentti-linkola-interview-from.html

damage it inflicts.[467] Similarly, in his *Quadrivium* interview he went on to emphasize that the demand for constant novelty is hard-wired by technology but always makes things worse even on objective grounds of quality:

> We know from the business world that not being able to grow or innovate equals destruction. Mindless lips chant a mantra of renewal, renewal, renewal, renewal, renewal. The level of technological progress being what it is, renewal is always a negative thing, and it's getting crazier all the time. I find the adjective "new" absolutely despicable and horrible. Most of the times, our intention has been to find the perfect way of living, the perfect culture, literature and music. And we know what renewal has led to in music and painting. All the time for the worse and more wicked. Everything has to be new! It's desperate.[468]

In this sense, Linkola's critique of progress holds a good deal of common ground with Julius Evola's own self-proclaimed *Revolt Against the Modern World*. Evola noted that while the linguistic chimera of progress is a fairly recent invention, the underlying structural features which it describes have been well known ever since prehistoric times; these were, however, correctly identified in the past not as progress but as *decline* and *degradation*.[469] Modern progress cannot mean anything except the deterioration of traditional forms of knowledge,[470] spirituality,[471] and social organization,[472] yet this does not bring about the promised liberation

---

[467] Pentti Linkola, "A Refresher Course about Forest," in *A Collection of Essays by Pentti Linkola 1993 – 2006*, p. 33.
[468] Pentti Linkola interview from *Quadrivium* #6 (2014): abridged version. Available at http://qvadrivivm.blogspot.com/2015/12/pentti-linkola-interview-from.html
[469] Julius Evola, Revolt Against the Modern World (Rochester: Inner Traditions, 1995), p. 171.
[470] Ibid., p. 4.
[471] Ibid., p. 247.
[472] Ibid., p. 94.

of humans from the chains of chauvinism. Instead, it only guarantees a total reduction of all existence to a stockpile of material "stuff" ripe for economic exploitation. Evola has noted that the disappearance of spiritual tradition inevitably coincides with a proliferation of machines which are given the green light to ruthlessly exploit the Earth, including all of its people and animals, in order to extract a purely economic standard of value from them.[473] What the delusional madmen drunk on the chimera of "progress" fail to see is that they are themselves included within this subset, insofar as disregard for the ecological totality inevitably leads to the devaluation of human life as well. Evola was one of the few thinkers sufficiently honest to admit the supremely discomforting fact that although the modern world condemns the "archaic views" of work embedded in Tradition, it is ironic that the slavery rampant today is far worse even than the literal slavery which occurred in the world of Tradition.[474] Evola noted, for example, that the Stalinist work camps present in his own era embodied a type of collectivization which, while claiming to be based in secularized materialism alone, is outright satanic in its spiritual nature.[475] Few have the guts to admit that there is something Luciferian about the way that Modern Technology blots out the dignity of life even while claiming to be the great liberator of Mankind.

Nor is progress the only linguistic chimera which actually inhibits one from accessing reality. In his author's preface to *Can Life Prevail?* Linkola acknowledged that many dismiss him as a "a naïve optimist" whose ambitions are hopelessly unlikely to be implemented in a scenario in which "the game can't be changed." He noted that even his own friends dismiss his plans as impossible, simply because they correctly identify their unviability on democratic grounds:

> [W]hen I persistently attempt to erect dams in the way of a devastating flood, most of my friends and many strangers regard me as a naïve optimist. They think that the game is

---

[473] Ibid., p. 156.
[474] Ibid., p. 109.
[475] Ibid.

already over: that the life of our planet is declining; that it is heading at a rapidly accelerating pace toward final suffocation, and there is no longer much we can do about it. Yet, I will still argue against these people.[476]

He warned the reader that even this attitude of learned helplessness is a linguistic chimera with no substance behind it. The very belief that technology, automation, and market economy are "inevitable" is what is truly out of touch with reality, since this implies that humans are not living agents with a free will and the potential for action in the real world but are instead fully-passivized prisoners at the mercy of the System. In other words, it amounts to a denial of our very life force, the ultimate denial of ecology.

The humanistic chimeras of progress and learned helplessness are strictly anti-ecological symbols. It is not even the case that each symbol is interpreted as a reference to some real thing beyond itself and therefore holds instrumental value in conducting attention to it like electricity over a copper wire; rather, one must actively suspend one's awareness of the ecological totality in order to "rise up" to the linguistic chimera, even in the face of outright absurdity. In this case, it is an ad hoc label which effectively refers to nothing at all, a gaze into the abyss of nothingness enabled only through a certain linguistic hack which allows a string of words to overstep the limits of reality and then trick the speaker into believing he or she has settled onto the firm grounding of some new planet when one has only walked over the edge of a cliff. This often takes the form of outright conflict, in which one is forced to choose the symbolic string *over* the ecological form, even when the latter actively rules the former out as impossible.

No Compromise with Morons

For these reasons, Linkola has openly affirmed that a meaningful dialogue between the deep ecologist and the technophile is not

---

[476] Pentti Linkola, "Preface by the Author," in *Can Life Prevail?* (Kindle Edition).

simply difficult; it is impossible. In an old speech he had given at the Jyväskylä summer's environmental protection discussion in 1967, Linkola described a scene from his own life for the audience to illustrate this point: he had been rowing a boat on the open waters of Vanaja in 1957, in what appeared to be the perfect place for a "friend of Nature" to encounter the wilderness without intrusions from the beast of Modern Technology. It was all too good to last, however, as almost immediately the ugly roar of a hundred-horsepower motorboat cut into the air like a chainsaw invading the forest. He recalls realizing at that moment that there could never be any possibility of a "brotherhood" with this sort of man. He vowed to "detest and loathe this kind of person" for the rest of his life.[477]

In "The Forest Covering in Finland Must Be Restored," in addition, he argued that any communication between those who prioritize economic growth and those who value as modest a demand as the survival of life on Earth[478] is arguably comparable to the MU Puzzle in Douglas Hofstadter's *Gödel, Escher, Bach*, a game for which the solution always seems to be just a few turns away no matter how long it goes on.[479] Communicative action is a labyrinth structured around the optical illusion that one is always nearing a solution no matter how deep one gets into a maze with no exit.

In his *Quadrivium* interview, the interviewers admitted that Linkola's reputation as a person with little interest in compromise with other viewpoints is not far from the truth, as they explicitly described him as "very judgemental" and nearly incapable of

---

[477] "Interview with Pentti Linkola 10-2-2004." Available at http://www.penttilinkola.com/pentti_linkola/ecofascism_writings/interview_10-2-2003

[478] Not coincidentally, this is nearly perfectly equivalent to Kaczynski's opposition between progress defined as economic growth and wilderness defined as natural freedom from Modern Technology in his classic 1971 essay "Progress Versus Wilderness."
Ted Kaczynski, "Progress Versus Wilderness," Ted Kaczynski Papers, Labadie Collection at the University of Michigan's Special Collections Library, Ann Arbor.

[479] See the opening chapter of the text for a more detailed explanation of this unsolvable puzzle.
Douglas Hofstadter. *Gödel Escher Bach* (New York: Vintage, 1980), p. 33.

"tolerating any other views of the world besides his own."[480] While this feature makes his writings "exhilarating for fanatics" who rank as card-carrying members within the (alleged) Linkola cult, the interviewers lamented that it is "limiting to those that have a more full-fledged view of the multifarious causal chains of society." In other words, Linkola's writing is the exact antithesis of a Habermasian dialogue with the Other – it is simply an attempt to channel the Mind of Nature in a purified state

The interviewers cited the useful biographical detail that Linkola's writings were not always so stubbornly single-minded in their orientation. According to them, it was only from his 1979 *Toisinajattelijan päiväkirjasta* (*From the Journal of a Dissent*) onwards that Linkola fell down the Thalean well of philosophical madness to become a full-blown "doomsday prophet" with little regard for wasting time running circles around trying to communicate with heretics. At this point, "the weak idealism of his youth starts to disappear, as does the need to suck up to his readers and listeners." He instead became obsessed with voicing absolute truths mined directly from the Mind of Nature without any regard for their contradiction of the cultural code of political correctness or their lack of palatability to the general public: "There is, as he describes it, an embittered authoritarianism in him upon facing total ignorance and foolishness," leading him to acknowledge the President of this "empire of death," Urho Kekkonen, as an "architect of catastrophe" who lacks "wisdom and understanding for the panoramic picture of reality, the biological comprehension of man— everything." According to them, 1979 was the year in which Linkola increasingly expressed frustration over the lack of meaningful response to his writings, a testament to the utter uselessness of dialogue and the possibility that, instead, violence might theoretically find a legitimate role as an "extension of the environmental truth," a leap in seriousness justified by the accelerated pace of industrial and ecological catastrophes mentioned in this text:

---

[480] Pentti Linkola interview from *Quadrivium* #6 (2014): abridged version. Available at http://qvadrivivm.blogspot.com/2015/12/pentti-linkola-interview-from.html

Individual themes he is concerned with in this very private and turgid collection include the amount of "sheet metal tigers" as he calls cars, the spreading of recreational fishing, the spreading of motor water sports and feverish summer cottage building, the pollution and damage caused to surface waters and the shorelines, the sulphuric acid.[481]

By his 1993 essay "Finland Equals Forests," Linkola had lost all patience for allowing heretics to waste our time voicing their arguments in favour of eco-crimes, as he argued that even appeals to the Holy Cow of *employment* could not be cited as a legitimate excuse to continue pillaging the Earth. In this essay, he contrasted a hypothetical official whose sole interest is maximizing employment with a friend of nature for whom even sacred incantations to bring "jobs, jobs, jobs" into existence will fall on deaf ears if they cannot be implemented without violating the Will of Nature: "For a lover of nature the fate of the forest is a matter of life and death. Finland equals forest."[482] Any plea to sell out the forest for a high-paying job with generous benefits is a deal with the devil which will only lead to demise for both the Earth and the fool who signs the dotted line in blood without realizing that a bargain with the "father of lies" will be broken as soon as possible.

Similarly, in 1995 "Vuotos and Suomen Kuvalehti" he mentioned the sacrilegious though obvious fact that this fanatical overemphasis on maximizing employment rates at any cost misses the point by failing to ask whether the work itself is senseless in the first place: "I'm sure we probably could employ the whole populace of Finland and all the people of the world to dig a hole through the crust of earth to China. The question is never about employment or unemployment, but if the work is nonsensical, in vain or harmful." In fact, if the kind of "work" one favours is this sort of unnecessary,

---

[481] Pentti Linkola interview from *Quadrivium* #6 (2014): abridged version. Available at http://qvadrivivm.blogspot.com/2015/12/pentti-linkola-interview-from.html

[482] Pentti Linkola, "Finland Equals Forest," in *A Collection of Essays by Pentti Linkola 1993 – 2006*, pp. 18-9.

waste, even "unemployment is always preferable to doing damaging labor."[483] For this reason, in his lengthy interview published in the final issue of the Finnish magazine *Quadrivium* in December 2014, he asserted that "Employment must never be the reason or argument for anything."[484]

Climbing Down the Rathole

He noted that the futility of climbing down the rathole of dialogue with a clueless technophile lies in a disagreement regarding the most fundamental question of all, that of Man's place in relation to the biosphere. In the most literal sense possible, Ecology determines one's stance towards all other issues, much like how Varg Vikernes noted in his fragmentary prison manifesto *Vargsmål* that the battle against the System must be won on ecological grounds or all other accomplishments will prove futile.[485] Vikernes warned his readers near the end of the text that one can only have the strength to fight if one rejects drugs, porn, junk food, and other artificial slow-killers engineered by the System for nefarious purposes. If one loses the battle on ecological grounds first, nothing else one accomplishes on the political level will truly make a difference in the end.

Linkola goes even further than Vikernes, however, by warning that if a person so much as has the wrong ecological viewpoint, it will not matter what his or her views on any other issue might happen to be. Communication with that person is by definition already ruled out as a waste of time. In his 1998 "Joy of Living Characterizes Life" he noted that one's "relationship with nature is absolutely essential in constructing everyone's worldview." [486] Although the mind of the "arrogant human" has

---

[483] Pentti Linkola, "Vuotos and Suomen Kuvalehti," in *A Collection of Essays by Pentti Linkola 1993 – 2006*, p. 96.
[484] Pentti Linkola interview from *Quadrivium* #6 (2014): abridged version. Available at http://qvadrivivm.blogspot.com/2015/12/pentti-linkola-interview-from.html
[485] Varg Vikernes, *Vargsmål* (unpublished, unofficial 1997 English translation from Norwegian manuscript).
[486] Pentti Linkola, "Joy of Living Characterizes Life," in *A Collection of Essays by*

always tended to incorporate very little "knowledge of nature and the life of animals and plants," this general tendency towards ignorance has been accelerated to the point of absurdity by industrialism: "Nowadays, even that little bit is vanishing to the winds as the interest of the quickly urbanizing man is being concentrated exclusively to mischief between men."[487] Similarly in his "The Forest Covering in Finland Must Be Restored" he asserted that obtaining an ecological worldview holds more than just theoretical value: it determines one's ethical standpoint towards the Earth by revealing whether one understands Man to be its dominator or its caretaker:

> One's outlook on forests is thus linked to the most basic of questions: one's perception of life, humanity and its place in the biocoenosis (i.e. biosphere). For a protector of life, who is moved by the diversity of life (biodiversity), it is unthinkable that the whole Earth should belong only to one animal species, humanity.[488]

It should go without saying that if the disagreement is primarily over whether Man is the "protector of life," the deep ecologist's opponent must by definition support the view that Man is life's destroyer, an ideological stance which the Techno-Industrial System empirically confirms with the most horrifically concrete action on a daily basis.

Linkola noted that anyone who is truly moved by the biodiversity of Nature would find it absurd to claim that the whole earth should belong to only one species because, at the very least, such a person would have to realize that mass extinction, likely including that of humans, is an unavoidable consequence of following such pseudo-logic to its conclusion. Yet even if we only throw the rest of the Animal Kingdom under the bus in order to keep this madness going, Linkola mentioned the uniquely

---

Pentti Linkola 1993 – 2006, p. 53.
[487] Ibid.
[488] Pentti Linkola, "The Forest Covering in Finland Must Be Restored," in *Can Life Prevail?* (Kindle Edition).

unwelcome fact that this defeats its own purpose, as the quality of human life has been so badly diminished as to be almost completely devoid of meaning as a result of these disruptions. Chief among all the ironies, he noted, was that in a certain sense there's been a massive surplus of material wealth as a direct result of automation, yet automation has itself removed any value from the people who were supposed to enjoy its benefits by condemning them to the shame of permanent unemployment or the humiliation of slaving away at meaningless welfare jobs. Yet it is not only our psychological well-being which has been forced to sacrifice itself for the Religion of Progress. The physical deterioration of our bodies has proven so extreme that we have effectively been mandated to perform a pseudo-ascetic "mortification of the flesh" in order to provide human blood for the gods of greed: "The lack of physical work, in turn, has led to widespread physical deficiencies."[489] We have each been forced to re-enact the masochistic self-flagellation practiced by Silas, the wicked monk in Dan Brown's *Da Vinci Code*,[490] by wilfully deforming our bodies through a fanatical adherence to the Cult of Mammon.

For these reasons, Linkola does not mince words at all regarding the uselessness of trying to "compromise" with the unthinking technophiles who lie fundamentally out of reach to rational arguments as a result of having a worldview poisoned down to its roots by a flawed ecological view: "It is absurd to believe that a compromise is possible with the champions of economic growth, whose arguments spell utter doom."[491] He went on to insist:

> [S]ome people believe the highest value to be the economic growth of Finland; others the preservation of life on Earth. No serious exchange of opinions can take place between those holding these two opposite stances: they simply have to settle in delivering separate speeches.[492]

---

[489] Ibid.
[490] Dan Brown, *The Da Vinci Code* (London: Transworld Publishers, 2004).
[491] Pentti Linkola, "The Forest Covering in Finland Must Be Restored," in *Can Life Prevail?* (Kindle Edition).
[492] Ibid.

In the same essay Linkola noted that although people are more or less consistent in physical appearance etc. in opinions they are "light years apart."[493] In other words, our physical accountability to ecological laws has more or less constrained our bodies to fit a strict set of norms, while the infinite elasticity of linguistification has allowed limitless variation in terms of ideology.

More specifically, dialogue is impossible between these two stances because each presupposes a different underlying grid of coordinates to determine the "universe of discourse" under discussion. Whereas the deep ecologist maintains accountability to the strict laws of ecological viability while formulating his or her arguments, the technophile abandons this firm grounding and instead structures his or her arguments on the basis of desire and desire alone.

Linkola's realization that human language and desire operate under one system of laws while natural forms operate under another led him to realize the supremely-controversial fact that it is impossible to solve ecological problems by using the resources of human communication alone, insofar as communication is by definition the use of language and, for that reason, of desire. His tendency to dismiss democratic political systems on grounds that they operate under the laws of "desire" rather than "necessity"[494] might be better understood through the opposition between language and ecology. Linkola decidedly *did not* fall for the Linguistic Turn delusion that Ecology is simply one more language among all the others, on grounds that "everything is language." Ecology is, rather, an independent standard of rationality which ultimately obeys its own laws rather than those which might be applicable to any purely linguistic system.

For one, whereas ecological understanding by definition connects Man to the broader whole of which he is a part, language and desire both provide the raw technical means to disconnect Man from ecological reality because both language and desire borrow the

---

[493] Ibid.
[494] Pentti Linkola, "Can We Survive: A Model for a Controlled Future," in *Can Life Prevail?* (Kindle Edition).

structural resources of imagination and hallucination to normalize the expectation that objects should be free to stretch, warp, fly, and transform at will without any need to provide a bulletproof ecological explanation for why they are able to somehow suspend the Laws of Physics just because we want them to. It is all too seldom realized that the very concept of "infinite progress" is simply one more example of an imaginary object which can defy the Laws of Thermodynamics by expanding endlessly without any need to explain where its resource inputs come from or where its waste ends up. The self-proclaimed hard-core materialist will fail to realize that this is because this ecologically impossible object is a spiritual chimera which lacks a physical body altogether.

Just as the prince in a proverbial fairy tale falls under a witch's curse and then sees a beautiful face where everyone else can only see a hideous hag, we have similarly fallen under the delusion of mistaking the fragile, unsatisfying, and just plain ugly monstrosity of the modern global industrial economy for the spiritual symbol of happiness embodied in the linguistic chimera of "progress." Our inability to distinguish the two has led even the self-proclaimed "scientific rationalists" of our era to openly embrace the absurdity of expecting that a physical object limited by ecological laws should behave in the same way as an object of fantasy by growing forever without ever facing the consequences of doing just that. Our failure to see the witch behind the princess's disguise will lead to nothing except an early death by the same sort of black magic.

For this reason, linguistic communication is basically just a positive feedback loop in which conflicting desires compete with one another for a trophy which effectively just grants one desire the right to dictate what form the next technological project will take. Behind the façade of "serious debate about the real world" lies the reality that these struggles are often as arbitrary as determining whether the next NFL stadium will be built in Toronto, Omaha, or Salt Lake City. Communicative struggle is little more than a bubble-blowing machine in which participants take turns arguing over whose inkblot will be granted a construction permit, without realizing that this transformation from linguistic chimera into material object can only occur through the properly ecological procedure of harnessing the power of Modern Technology and countless natural resources to temporarily satisfy Man's insatiable appetite for weirdness.

Communication, in other words, is inherently pathological. There is no "innocent" form which desire only later invades from the outside, since language is always already the native territory for desire and provides the ideal breeding ground for unreal chimeras to multiply like rats high on Viagra. In this sense, Linkola must be understood as the exact opposite not only of Kant (on the level of individual ethics) but also of Habermas (on the level of collective politics). For this reason, a serious analysis of Habermas's ideas is absolutely necessary to fully appreciate Linkola's own unique disagreements with these stances.

You Can't Communicate Your Way out of a Paper Bag

Although Linkola admittedly does not appear to be particularly concerned with Habermas as an individual, it is still enormously useful to contrast their positions because Habermas himself is little more than an academic spokesman for the ideology which materialized within the System simply as an historical consequence of allowing the trajectory of technologization to run its course. In other words, Habermas largely just followed after this general historical trend which was unfolding on its own and provided an explicit theoretical account for something which had already come to fruition without him.

In fact, the phenomenon of democracy continues to *exceed* even Habermas's most scrupulous attempts to linguistify it into words. Although it is fashionable since the rise of the Linguistic Turn to claim that "all is language" and to deny the very existence of such an excess beyond it, this gap between embodied practice and its formal explanation is recognized even by psychologists working from a strictly neuroscientific perspective. In Jordan Peterson's 1999 *Maps of Meaning*, for example, he noted that most of our knowledge is embodied within behavioural practices which are only ever secondarily and incompletely translated into explicit linguistic explanations.⁴⁹⁵ In other words, we all know more than we can say, since most of our knowledge is not linguistic in nature but is still perfectly legitimate to designate as "knowledge." The process of "linguistifying" this knowledge into words is, in a certain sense, simply the process of science.⁴⁹⁶ It is absolutely vital, however, to recognize that even the most linearly-complicated explanations still lag behind the "real thing" in the race.

In more recent years, Peterson's early work as a psychological theorist has largely been overshadowed by the media spotlight which followed from their utter disbelief that there really could be a professor in the West who was willing to criticize the social justice madness rampant on college campuses. It is quite humorous that he briefly became the world's most famous intellectual simply because he refused to acknowledge that there are 68 genders, or however many the "professional gender theorists" on the university payroll have decided to make up out of whole cloth this time (no doubt, a fine use for all those billions of dollars of student loan funds). Predictably, this media frenzy has led him to be demonized for the thought crime of defending "outdated social institutions" such as the traditional family, yet almost no clueless 18-year-old college student protester who attempted to shout down his message with a flurry of mindlessly-recyclable "---------ist/phobic" catchwords flowing out of a "random attack generator machine" actually understands Peterson's highly-technical explanation for why he upheld these controversial viewpoints in the face of widespread and fanatical opposition.

Above all, Peterson warned that carelessly dismantling established social structures such as the traditional family, a dissolution which was justified simply because "patriarchy" is objectionable on linguistic grounds, is playing with fire, since even though no one can fully explain *why* the family functions (partly, because it required thousands of years to evolve and is an enormously complex empirical reality), we still can say that it *does* function or, at the very least, that it functions far better than the ad

---

⁴⁹⁵ Jürgen Habermas, *The Structural Transformation of the Public Sphere* (Cambridge: MIT Press, 1991), p. 20.
⁴⁹⁶ Jordan Peterson, *Maps of Meaning* (New York: Routledge, 1999), p. 79.

hoc alternatives which have materialized in its place. Few things capture humanistic hubris quite as succinctly as the collective decision in the West to dismantle tens of thousands of years of tradition under the illusion that the latest round of technological gimmicks pumped out by industrial forces driven by their own self-interested profit motives will be sufficient to fill the gap of meaninglessness left in its wake. The utter chaos which has engulfed the West has proven that we collectively sold our souls out in exchange for sleazy corporate marketing tricks which lacked any underlying substance behind their flashy advertising campaigns.

Following Peterson's view, Habermas has simply filled the role of the official "linguistifier" of the System, the academic "social scientist" who translated democratic practice into language without necessarily inventing anything new in the process.

Habermas revolutionized the Frankfurt School of Critical Theory by committing the ultimate academic faux-pas of the 20th Century by openly endorsing rationality at a time when it had become highly-fashionable to just take the easy way out by positing Reason as a scapegoat worthy to take the blame for every social injustice dating back to the time of the mythical figure Odysseus. This is not at all hyperbole, as Adorno and Horkheimer literally extended the blame game of Western guilt all the way back to *The Odyssey* in their highly-overrated book *Dialectic of Enlightenment.*

Habermas defended what was initially a very unpopular stance by revealing that Adorno and Horkheimer's condemnation of Reason was based on a blatant logical fallacy, in that they used a single word to paint several unrelated things with the same broad brush of shame. While it is true that reason *can* be used as something like an intellectual technology oriented towards manipulating the Other to realize one's own self-interested goals, this is a definition applicable only to instrumental reason and is simply inappropriate to apply to the other types.

Nor was Habermas guilty of trying to revive the archaic image of the Cartesian cogito as a single isolated thinker, since, above all, he was interested in the type of rationality inherent in communicative procedures. There is a certain sense in which failing (or, in some cases, refusing) to adhere to communicative rules during discussion is noticeably irrational without necessarily violating the Cartesian rules for valid individual thinking. Although there may not be a mathematical or logical error involved in, say, the violation of a cultural norm during discussion, disregard for the latter nonetheless qualifies as a violation of a communicative rule and evidences a certain type of irrationality in the speaker. Given the limitations of Cartesian models of Reason, Habermas required a baroque new system of criteria to explain how communication could be carried out properly.

Habermas's innovation lay in exposing the extent to which past errors had been defined through a failure to properly distinguish a set of unrelated spheres at work in communication. For example, while it is true that the scientific formulation of indicative statements about empirical states of affairs is a valid use of language, this theoretical dimension is only one of five spheres he identified.

In addition to the theoretical sphere of scientific description, a second dimension was made up by a practical sphere not based on logical validity but rather on cultural normativity. Behaving in accord with the cultural norms which happen to dominate a speaker's lived social context is necessary to remain rational, despite the fact that these norms are of course anthropological contingencies rather than the sort of naturally-existing physical objects which could be investigated through scientific observation.[497]

In the third dimension, rationality was measured by one's ability to use language to form evaluative judgments; examples of these include appraising the aesthetic value of a work of art or the beauty of a person. To say "Bach's Fugue in G Minor, BWV 542 sounds pleasant" or to say "Italian actress Gina Lollobrigida looked beautiful in the films *Solomon and Sheba* (1959), *The Hunchback of Notre Dame* (1956), and *La Romana* (1954)"[498] are not statements

---

[497] Instrumental reason is also situated within the theoretical branch, in that reason can be instrumental insofar as it can be judged on grounds of its own efficacy (whether an act was a failure or a success etc.)

[498] Luigina Lollobrigida played the gypsy girl Esmeralda in *The Hunchback of Notre Dame* and Queen Sheba in the Biblical film *Solomon and Sheba*. Although I am not a cinephile and I categorically boycott contemporary Hollywood films, I

of scientific fact but are still perfectly legitimate uses of language because they are situated within the aesthetic rather than theoretical realm. The criteria of validity for these statements is adequacy of evaluation rather than theoretical truth (i.e., science) or normative rightness (i.e., culture).

In the fourth dimension, one can use language to formulate therapeutic statements about one's own subjective state, such as in the psychoanalytic setting of lying on the couch to express one's psychological condition to the analyst. In this case, the criteria of validity are measured by how sincerely the speaker expresses himself or herself, rather than by scientific correctness, cultural normativity, or evaluative adequacy. This sphere would prove particularly important to Habermas's broader theory, in that Habermas noticed that the truthfulness of the speaker plays a major role in separating the legitimate use of communication from its derivative and abusive forms. If the speaker's motives are transparent, communication can proceed towards consensus without any bias from one participant to skew the results in a pre-determined direction. If, however, the speaker distorts his or her motives, even including to the point of self-deception, this inevitably perverts the dialogue into just another form of manipulation. It really does matter, in other words, whether the speaker believes his or her own arguments or not.

Finally, in the explicative realm, Habermas noted that it is a communicative requirement for one's use of language to be comprehensible on a purely syntactic level. A failure to generate well-formed sentences cannot result in anything except a distortion of the communicative procedure which will fatally inhibit it from reaching the goal of consensus. It is not necessary for the speaker to have any malicious intent for this to be the case either: if I myself were to attempt to communicate with someone in Russian, a language which I have studied only at the most basic level, my incompetence on syntactic grounds alone would be enough to disqualify the discussion from satisfying the minimal criteria for usefulness.

---

admit that these are two of the best films ever made.

With these five spheres properly delineated, Habermas realized that past views of rationality primarily made the mistake of erroneously defining Reason as nothing more than the possession of true knowledge. Descartes, for example, literally posited the rational cogito as a storehouse filled with innate ideas of mathematical truths. Yet this concept alone was insufficient to address Reason's essence on all five levels because it privileged the theoretical level to the exclusion of all the others. Habermas's own broader view of language's possibilities led him to realize that Reason is simply the practice of engaging in communication.

In fact, the old Cartesian view simply clings to dogmatic notions of correctness through fetishizing absolute truths as so many picture cards stamped with the right answer by God himself and then deposited by hand into the subject's intellectual bank account, while the Platonic view simply located this gallery of picture cards in the World of Ideas rather than the inside of the subject's mind. Habermas revealed that this sort of attitude cannot be anything except an impediment to the communicative procedure since it fundamentally contradicts one of its most important requirements. In dialogue, one can only behave rationally if one allows what one says to be open to critique from other speakers. In other words, the very belief in an "absolute content" is inherently irrational.

Under Habermas's view, the archaic notion of papal infallibility amounts to the most grotesque violation of the communicative procedure, since it categorically rules out the possibility that one's own stance might be open to error. Nor is this a problem only in the case of religion. Far from being a system of dogmatic truths, science itself must consist of an intrinsic openness to refutation, not only from human scientists with competing viewpoints but even from the natural world itself, as countless hypotheses once accepted as dogmatic fact were eventually disproven simply through gathering better data from Nature. Habermas's emphasis on communication revealed the irony that science owes its existence to the possibility of communication, rather than the other way around.

With this new definition of Reason in mind, Habermas became interested not only in the ability for individual thinkers to be rational, a problem which countless philosophers before had focused on, but also in the way that entire worldviews can be more or less rational than others. In fact, he argued that there was a broad trend in history for progressively more rationalized worldviews to systematically displace older models. Citing Piaget's stages of cognitive development, Habermas noted that a given society's evolution to a more modern worldview fundamentally devalues its predecessor, leaving no question at all that the two might go on coexisting side by side. The arrival of modernity, in other words, made the mythic and metaphysical worldviews of the past impossible to uphold any longer. This is because, above all, the rationality of a worldview is measured by the extent to which it properly differentiates the five separate spheres of communicative meaning. The problem with outdated worldviews is simply that they tended to confuse several of these spheres without realizing it.

The earliest Mythical Worldview, for example, systematically conflated theoretical science and cultural normativity. On one hand, tribal cultures tend to anthropomorphize natural forces by worshipping animals, meteorological forces, and astrological bodies as gods. On the other hand, they tend to naturalize cultural contingencies by, for example, declaring their own religious beliefs to be "truth" and their own tribe to be "the people" without any further qualification. Even the Ancient Egyptians, a fairly sophisticated civilization, had no word for religion despite having a society steeped in traditional magic. Under Habermas's view, this confusion of spheres negates the very possibility for scientific rationality to develop because one's understanding of Nature is always already mixed up with cultural criteria through an institutionalized failure to distinguish theoretical from practical contents.

Following the Mythical Worldview, the Metaphysical Worldview continued to be marred by irrationality in its tendency to seek out cosmological proofs for the solutions to ethical and political dilemmas. On one hand, this took the form of upholding archaic political systems in which leaders were thought to be divinely ordained by some divine agency which had supposedly established a given royal family as a hereditary line of monarchical power which was not open to dispute from the democratic masses. In addition, the ethical code reflected pre-rational religious biases such as the mandate to punish blasphemy with capital punishment, on grounds that some obscure dogma from a sacred text was beyond even the tamest rational critique.

Above all, Habermas noted that errors of this kind stemmed from a type of metaphysical fetishism. The concept of an ethical code which is thought to be intrinsically true in itself misleads one to neglect crucial communicative procedures, on grounds that some dogmatic content lies beyond dispute even from the highest of worldly authorities. In modern times, this traditional bias remains visible in the tendency for conservative Catholics to harshly warn that even Pope Francis himself lacks the authority to tamper with the established dogmas of the Church, yet Habermas would argue that this is merely a remnant leftover from the Metaphysical Worldview's tendency to withhold the possibility of rational critique even for the highest ranking Catholic in the world.

Habermas noted that such appeals to seek such "absolute contents" within a supernatural order established by God himself systematically conflate pseudo-scientific explanations regarding the structure of the universe as a whole with ethical and political questions regarding how society should be run. The scientific question of the physical constitution of the universe is quite simply not the same thing as the social question regarding who should rule or which religious text should be granted supremacy over all the others.

Finally, the Post-Metaphysical Worldview completed the process of societal rationalization by explicitly suspending the archaic search for that which is "good in itself" or that which is "intrinsically true," dismissing these as optical illusions generated by a primitive fetishism which could no longer be upheld in the secularized universe of modernity. Instead, political and ethical disagreements were finally recognized for what they had always been: opportunities to engage in communicative dialogue in order to reach consensus. In the absence of any need to presume that a single "absolute answer" lies at the end of the road, one could be freed up to instead optimize the process of communication itself.

Crucially, this did not imply any naïve hope that speakers from irreconcilable viewpoints would abandon their own partisan stances at the end of the discussion in order to agree on a single identical viewpoint, the content of which would be acknowledged by both parties as "intrinsically correct." On the contrary, Habermas fully accepted that a far-left pro-choice feminist professor from Berkeley and a conservative pro-life Mormon housewife from Utah would continue to hold irreconcilable views on abortion even after going through the dialogue regarding the topic. However, the very expectation that either one of these views must be "the right one in itself" is simply an illusion from the Metaphysical Worldview which could no longer be upheld in our era. Even if they could never agree on a single answer, they could both acknowledge the legitimacy of a procedure such as voting for candidates to pass legislation on the issue or allowing the Supreme Court to debate the topic in a formal setting.

Carried to the highest level of national politics, this respect for a procedure regardless of its outcome was accepted as legitimate enough even to appoint the "leader of the free world." The fact that any given presidential election was certain to *not* yield an outcome with unanimous support from the populace is simply the ultimate confirmation that this transition to respecting communication as a process rather than getting lost in the pseudo-problem of seeking out the Fountain of Youth of an "absolute content" was precisely the transition to the chief political form of modernity: democracy.

It is quite telling that in the aftermath of the 2016 United States Election, for example, liberal Democrats and social justice leftists faithfully reinforced this Habermasian belief in post-metaphysical democracy by insisting that Russian bots, Macedonian fake news peddlers, Putin himself, 4chan trolls, or *somebody* must have meddled with the electoral procedure itself in order to grant Trump a presidency he could not have possibly won the good old fashioned (a.k.a. the democratic) way. In other words, these people suffered from the ultimate cognitive dissonance by assuring themselves that if the process had been allowed to run its course without interference from some extrinsic malicious agent, it would have certainly yielded the result which they wanted. It is quite telling that those who vehemently rejected the election results realized they had to shift the emphasis to a bug within the procedure rather than fetishize its outcome as "evil in itself" in order to maintain their good standing as citizens of post-metaphysical modernity.

For this reason, it is all the more absurd for Habermasian scholars to portray their hero as some sort of rebel against the System when his theories of Linguistic Turn reductivism and Democracy are simply the official ideologies of modernity. Democracy is the indisputable political correlate to a universe in which everything except language has dissolved into worthless superstition, as the disappearance of an orderly cosmos, an omniscient deity, and even of the transcendental subject itself had left nothing except language to hold the weight of the entire world upon its shoulders, a responsibility which ultimately proved to be far beyond its paygrade.

Democracy and the Post-Metaphysical Worldview

As compelling as Habermas's ideas might be on theoretical grounds, his belief that language's original essence is to provide the communicative procedure for speaking subjects to solve problems through reaching consensus led him to miss the point that language always already embodies its own misuse. Habermas's faith in what language's life was like "before the Fall" of lying, cheating, deceiving, etc. arguably betrays the lingering presence of religious archetypes in a horizon of modernity which has long since banished them to the dustbin of history. Contrary to his view, these misuses are not merely secondary perversions which distort language's inherent goodness but provide a window of insight into the tendency for language to always already be contaminated by pathological desire.

Habermas's flawed view of language ultimately stemmed from the academically-fashionable belief that it was no longer possible to locate rationality within any transcendent structure.

Habermas opened his two-volume *Theory of Communicative Action* by rejecting archaic attempts to locate rationality within the "orderly cosmos" itself (as was the case in the Ancient and Medieval eras) as well as more recent attempts to ground Reason in the faculties of a Kantian or Husserlian subject, as Habermas admitted that neuroscientific advances had fundamentally devalued the pursuit of transcendental explanations of subjectivity by effectively erecting a barrier which philosophers were no longer able to cross without having a passport proving dual-citizenship in some properly scientific department as well.[499] One could only uphold rationality in a Post-Metaphysical Worldview if one located it directly in the structure of language itself, yet this materialistic requirement fuelled the delusion that communication is hard-wired to yield solutions to empirical problems, however challenging they might be. Following Habermas's logic, it is unavoidable to conclude that language is uniquely suited to solve the same ecological crises which, according to Linkola,[500] it had itself created.

Habermas's overemphasis on linguistic normativity was a natural conclusion of his attempts to satisfy the academy's Orwellian, self-contradictory demands to promote materialistic reductivism while somehow still accounting for the problem of human rationality. In his 2014 *Absolute Recoil*, Zizek noted that Habermas got around this challenge by simply making communication into an irreducible horizon which one cannot go beyond for the simple reason that any attempt to break free from it requires one to borrow resources from the same stock of material one tried to transcend. One cannot posit evolutionary biologism as a "deeper" foundation to explain how we communicate on purely physical terms, for example, because scientific explanation itself requires one to utilize the norms of communication in order to be understood.[501]

---

[499] Habermas forbade transcendental accounts of subjectivity near the beginning of the first volume of his *Theory of Communicative Action*.
[500] Pentti Linkola, "Can We Survive? A Model for a Controlled Future", in *Can Life Prevail?* (Kindle Edition).
[501] Slavoj Zizek, *Absolute Recoil* (London: Verso: 2014), p. 57.

Despite Habermas's heated insistence that he remains committed to the highest standard of secularist rationalism, one cannot help but be reminded of the oral tradition among Baptist pastors to tell the joke about the scientist who challenged God to a competition over who could create life from out of nothing faster. As the scientist gathered together the raw materials in the laboratory to conduct the Frankensteinian experiment, God blew the whistle and shouted, "Hey! Get your own raw materials from somewhere else – I created those!"[502] Is not Habermas's insistence that one can't get beyond communication without using communication simply a Linguistic Turn re-enactment of the Southern Baptist urban legend of a scientist who can't recreate God's creation without using God's creation in the first place? Habermas effectively just turns the linguistic community into a new collective deity for which everything that exists is a result of its creative agency, even to the point where the speakers can't uncreate their own creation by reverting to some pre-linguistic layer of meaning.

In fact, Habermas's thought experiment is arguably more radical than the proverbial Baptist pastor's, since he argues that one cannot even opt for scientific materialism anymore without using language to do so. It is all too easy to miss the deeper point, though, that Habermas's fanaticism is just a consequence of the more general requirement for the postmodernist universe to be purged of all transcendent horizons of meaning. Despite Habermas's admitted willingness to criticize Deleuze and other French post-structuralists for falling below the standard of rationality he hoped to uphold himself, his own stance is every bit as constrained by the postmodernist requirement for all explanations to be reduced to a plane of immanence, an ideological mandate which only Julius Evola and a few other thought criminals realized is simply the result of the decline of the fixed forms of Tradition and the rise of institutionalized chaos through Modern Technology.[503]

---

[502] Though I was not raised a Baptist myself, I remember hearing this story while attending a Baptist revival in Amarillo, Texas in 2004 which I had been bussed to with some other kids from my high school.

[503] Julius Evola, *Revolt Against the Modern World* (Rochester: Inner Traditions, 1995), p. 156.

In response to academic industry pressures, Habermas was forced to suspend all transcendent foundations for rationalism, whether in cosmological objectivity (Thomas Aquinas, Aristotle etc.) or transcendental subjectivity (Immanuel Kant, Edmund Husserl etc.), and instead posit communicative rationality as something which is "not an external idea" at all but is rather "immanent to our participation in linguistic intersubjectivity" alone, as Zizek explained in the following quote from *Absolute Recoil*:

> [T]he normativity [Habermas] talks about is not an external idea but is immanent to our participation in linguistic intersubjectivity – when I talk to and with others, I imply that I obey these norms even if I consciously violate them. This pragmatic a priori inherent to language is irreducible (*"unhintergehbares"*: one cannot step behind it) in the strict transcendental sense: one cannot ground it in a "deeper" positivity (to explain, say, through evolutionary biology how the human animal developed intersubjective discursive normativity) since in order to provide such an account, one already has to rely on the argumentative normativity of intersubjective space (since every scientific explanation by definition proceeds in such an argumentative way.) For Habermas, all other uses of language (to lie and cheat, to pretend, to seduce etc.) are derivative: secondary empirical distortions of the inherent normativity, conditioned by relations of power and domination or by the pursuit of private interests.[504]

This mandate to reduce communicative action to a plane of immanence therefore surprisingly reveals Habermas's speaking subjects to be desiring-machines, in a sense fully compatible with the universe of pure immanence depicted in Deleuze and Guattari's writings.

The irony, in other words, is that it was precisely because Habermas felt the need to eliminate transcendent standards of

---

[504] Ibid., pp. 56-7.

meaning (i.e., the cosmos, dogmatic religion, the Kantian subject etc.) from linguistic rationality that he guaranteed that language would always already be contaminated by pathological desires, as the ongoing discharge of the Freudian drives in a universe devoid of any sound except that of Man rambling on to himself about himself would overrun the world as recklessly as the suitors in Odysseus's house did for years on end as he tried to find a way back home to Ithaca.

    Julius Evola once warned that the decline of form following from abandoning the stable realm of Being for the ephemeral world of becoming would not bring about social harmony but, instead, perpetual chaos and unceasing social conflict. Though this prediction fell on deaf ears among the intelligentsia of his era, Evola's prophecy was uncannily realized, birthing the horrid pseudo-world in which we are all inmates. Devoid of any spiritual form of value, the floodgates were indeed opened for the crassest evaluation of materialistic greed to predominate as the only measure of meaning. Even warfare itself devolved into the technological horror in which countless men were mowed down by an impersonal rain of machine gun bullets while stalling over the same tiny sliver of no man's land between the trenches, even as the intelligentsia praised themselves for moving beyond the barbarism which could safely be located only in the distant past.[505] Somehow, removing everything except desire does not bring about liberation, but rather the ultimate nightmare, as this quite literally brings about a universe in which ethics becomes impossible, as pathological desires freely flow with only the conflict of other desires there to impede them on the path to collective self-destruction. In the absence of any standard of accountability to traditional (Evola) or ecological (Linkola) form, desire is set free to wallow in its own pseudo-forms, a set which is somehow both infinite in number and yet endlessly redundant of the same single pseudo-archetype. Suburbia is an explosive tumour which has somehow taken over an entire continent while making every location in the United States exactly

---

[505] Ibid., p. 129.

like any other, a chilling testament to desire's tendency to be both far too large and far too small at the same time.

The New Desiring Machines?

To fully understand the disastrous connection between desire and immanentization which proved to be the Achilles' heel of Habermas's theory, we must first discuss Deleuze and Guattari's *Anti-Oedipus* in greater detail. In this text, they noted that Freud's primary mistake regarding desire lay in his decision to posit the Id as a coherent and singular thing lying somewhere behind the scenes like a mysterious, invisible force which could only ever be reconstructed indirectly from a forensic footprint left behind on visible phenomena such as dreams, weird personal habits, fantasies, etc.[506] On the contrary, they held that this was merely a misunderstanding built on Freud's superstitious belief that desire must be subordinated to some fixed, transcendent structure such as the Oedipal Triangle, a prejudice which Freud himself arguably just borrowed transitively from the archaic Metaphysics of the pre-postmodernist era in which he lived. Freud's insistence on maintaining even the most basic layer of transcendence in the Oedipal Structure was revealed to be totally unnecessary, provided one realized that the Id is not restricted to some extrinsic dimension but is rather immanently present everywhere and is already there on the surface of the same phenomena to which one has direct access. To understand this revolutionary shift, however, one must think of desire in terms of machines.[507]

In fact, according to Deleuze and Guattari, it is not only productive flows which must be rethought as machines— it is also the interruptions of those flows that are machines, insofar as machines never appear as singular entities but are always connected to other ones.[508] The breast, for example, is not the ineffable, inaccessible lost Thing of desire; it is, rather, a machine which is

---

[506] Gilles Deleuze and Félix Guattari, *Anti-Oedipus* (London: Penguin, 1983), p. 1.
[507] Ibid.
[508] Ibid., p. 2.

immanently present, with the child's mouth connected to it as another machine.

For this reason, production is immediately consumption. It is not the case that the two are separate spheres, or even that mediation would be required to bring about this shift, for production is the proper term to describe *any* discharge of desire in a fully-immanentized universe. Understood as a process, this production would overturn all idealistic categories; far from requiring some transcendent structure of mediation, production's relation to desire is revealed to be that of an imminent principle.[509] This emphasis on the immanence of desire proved so radical, in fact, that it was able to accommodate itself to the death drive, a desire which desires its own death without contradicting its own essence as production.[510]

For these reasons, the Oedipal Structure was ruthlessly condemned in this text for the thought crime of challenging the immanence of desire. The Oedipal Triangle is inherently dualistic, since it posits the Father even behind God himself, as Freud explained away monotheistic religion as just one more manifestation of mommy, daddy, and me.[511] Under this view, the subject could no longer be an extrinsic origin beyond desire, but was itself something produced as a residuum alongside the desiring machine.[512]

It is extremely crucial to note, though, that what is produced in any case is intensive in nature. Deleuze was interested over the course of his intellectual career in the way that intensive changes are often misunderstood through applying metaphors from the extensive realm which were simply inappropriate to this area. Leaping from 50 to 100 degrees in temperature or from 50 to 100 miles per hour in speed is not the same as chopping a piece of rope into two smaller segments. An intensive shift is fundamentally different from an extensive shift.

Deleuze's interest in the movement-image in his *Cinema 1* was largely built on this realization that movement itself must be

---

[509] Ibid., p. 4.
[510] Ibid., p. 8.
[511] Ibid., p. 14.
[512] Ibid., p. 17.

understood intensively, insofar as it cannot be divided without changing qualitatively. Ironically, he was able to overturn Bergson's dismissal of cinema as an artificial reconstruction of 24 static frames per second precisely through using Bergson's own theses on movement against him.

In *Anti-Oedipus*, Deleuze and Guttari's interest in privileging schizoanalysis over psychoanalysis lay in their realization that the schizo is simply the one who experiences these intensive shifts in "the pure state, the transition, states of pure, naked intensity stripped of all shape or form."[513] Deleuze and Guttari's stance was so extreme, in fact, that they argued that against the common-sense tendency to describe the schizo's intensive states merely negatively as hallucinations devoid of reality; according to them, this misses the point that the schizo's experiences are more like purified states of immanent intensity than gaps of absence.

Similarly, they argued that we must introduce "desire into mechanism" and "production into desire" in order to overturn Freud's Oedipal structuration by recognizing it as the idealism it truly is.[514] Above all, traditional psychoanalysis's flaw is that it treats desire as something oriented towards acquisition and motivated by a fundamental lack, rather than as an immanent procedure which is strictly productive and knows lack only in the most secondary and derivative sense.[515] The problem with the traditional Lacanian emphasis on lack is that it upholds a Metaphysical dualism by contrasting a Real Thing with an imagined object. This attitude fundamentally misunderstands the makeup of desire, since it holds that the only thing desire actively produces is an imagined object which lacks Being. This Lacanian argument falls to pieces when one realizes that the Real is not quite as inaccessible/impossible as it would seem. For Deleuze and Guattari, the product of desire production is always Real and what desire produces is simply the production of reality. [516]

---

[513] Ibid., p. 18.
[514] Ibid., p. 24.
[515] Ibid., p. 25.
[516] Ibid., p. 26.

Although they did mention a number of different types of syntheses in this text, they were careful to avoid the Hegelian error of understanding these through the metaphors of some transcendental idealism. Although they did admit that speaking of a "sum" in the context of a discussion of synthesis is meaningful, they were careful to note that this is not something which ever succeeds in bringing its parts together as a single whole because the breaks are productive in themselves and are already reassemblies rather than empty spaces of negativity.[517] Against Hegel, they argued that there is neither an original totality which must be restored nor a final totality in the future which brings about a reconciliation and elevation to higher order. For this reason, they went as far to dismiss the Hegelian standpoint as just plain "boring," a "dreary, colourless dialectic of evolution."[518]

Gaps are therefore very important but somewhat deceptive, in that gaps are always affirmative rather than merely privative. Once again, this is the anti-Hegelian view of a fragmented universe in which there is no Law to unite the units into a single Whole; rather there is a mapping out of divergences in themselves.[519] The Whole does not lie beyond, precede, or escape production, since even the Whole itself must be produced. The body without organs, for example, is a whole but is itself something produced without ever unifying its parts, insofar as this set includes the breaks, subject, and other disruptive elements which escape the naïve Metaphysics of a pre-postmodernist worldview.

Freud's obsession with Oedipialization is thoroughly artificial and can only ever result from having analysts coerce their patients to Oedipalize situations needlessly.[520] Freud's enslavement to this dualism led him to miss the point about his own theory, in that the very same partial objects he discovered are so potent that they can blow up Oedipus themselves.[521]

---

[517] Ibid., p. 42.
[518] Ibid.
[519] Ibid., p. 43.
[520] Ibid., p. 45.
[521] Ibid., p. 44.

Democracy as Social Technology of Desire

From Linkola's perspective, this postmodernist requirement to "suspend all dimensions of transcendence whatsoever" in order to reduce the sphere of existence to an ongoing discharge of desire with no standard of order beyond itself simply opens the floodgates to permanently banish the Mind of Nature from the realm of political discussion, as any appeal to a non-subjective set of laws (basically, an ecological equivalent of Descartes's God or perfect cogito) would rank as the very worst form of superstition. Devoid of the Mind of Nature's authority, Man would then be abandoned to the predictable chaos of democratic linguistification, as desire would be allowed full reign to clear a path of destruction with the raving masses remaining too foolish to realize that they were simply setting fire to their own household (οἶκος)[522] in the process.

It is peculiar for Deleuze, Guattari, and Habermas to act as though there is anything new in affirming such a stance, since as early as the 19th Century, Dostoyevsky's *Demons* demonstrated that the Russian appropriation of Western Rationalism similarly banished God and other transcendent "superstitions" from the universe of acceptable discourse. In the aftermath of this "victory of Reason," however, one character could not help but wonder whether this newfound freedom in a fully-immanentized universe had suddenly made him so free that he could kill himself just to prove that God could not punish him in the afterlife for doing so. In fact, he goes as far as to assert the absolute absurdity that shooting himself *will make him God*:

> "I remember that there was something about God . . . you tried explaining it to me once, you know, even twice. If you do shoot yourself, then you will become God. That's how it goes, I think?"
> "Yes, I will become God." [523]

---

[522] One should bear in mind that "eco" is a transliteration from the Greek term for household.
[523] Fyodor Dostoyevsky, *Demons* (London: Penguin, 2008), p. 681.

In Linkola's worldview, similarly, the loss of the Mind of Nature simply leaves us with the most perverse of all freedoms: the freedom to commit ecological mass suicide just to prove that we can.

It is supremely ironic that Habermas formulated his theory of communicative action in order to avoid the instrumental use of reason as manipulation, since Habermas's model for democratic communication is the ultimate social technology in Ellul's sense of the term. Democracy is simply an artificial organization of human activity which is teleologically oriented towards achieving the technical goal of maximizing subjects' pathological self-interests by isolating the pattern of behaviours in which desire alone could be freed up to overwhelm any other (eco-)logical criteria.

[524]Finally, Habermas's proposals to solve ecological crises are unviable for the simple reason that it is extremely perverse to pretend that we haven't *already* reached a unanimous consensus, in that the commitment to technological overshoot, economic growth, fossil fuel industrialism, and historically anomalous lifestyles make up a dogma which virtually *no one* will challenge. The media's growing obsession with denouncing anyone who expresses even the slightest disagreement with these pillars of faith as an "ecofascist" who must by definition be guilty of a range of other unrelated thought-crimes demonstrates that the problem is not at all a lack of consensus, but rather an excess of it.

Not-So-Public Sphere

Habermas argues that democracy represents a more rationalized social form than its predecessors simply because it extends the industrial mandate for financial abstraction to overshadow individual contingencies into a corresponding political mandate for democratic abstraction to overshadow individual contingencies. In other words, just as anyone with money can purchase a product regardless of *who* they are, any citizen of a democratic nation can vote for any candidate on the ballot regardless of who either one of

---

[524]

them is. Comforting as such a thought might appear to be on theoretical grounds, Linkola has noted that it is simply the philosophy that "all lives are exactly the same," a claim which is both preposterous on ecological grounds and which flatly contradicts our common-sense experience of the world. Still, Habermas's obscure claim that this equalization is the defining feature of a rationalized social order shall prove vital to grasping Linkola's radical opposition to democracy on a more sophisticated level than the media caricature of an "ecofascist dictatorship." For this reason, we will require a brief detour into Habermas's well-known *Structural Transformation of the Public Sphere*.

One of Habermas's motivations for writing his lengthy study on the Public Sphere lay in the irony that although Sociology is by definition the study of the public, it remains somewhat unclear even to professional social scientists how to define this public. The only thing that's really clear about it is that if it's public, it is open to all, as opposed to a private sphere which would be closed or would exclude members on the basis of some arbitrary criteria.[525] Although this concept is taken for granted today, an open public is a feature of modernity with a rather short history. Even the German word *Offentlichkeit* itself is not that old, only dating back to the 18th Century.[526] Not coincidentally, it was in this historical period that a public sphere became possible as a sociological phenomenon.

Although Habermas did admit that something like a public-private distinction can be found all the way back in the Ancient Greek opposition between the Koine (common) Polis and the private Oikos (house), he noted that it would be somewhat misleading to equate this archaic notion of a common space with the modern Public Sphere because certain property and class restrictions negated its claim to publicness.[527] The Greek Polis wasn't *really* public because one had to be the master of a house in order to be a participating member. Nonetheless, one can identify some later values of the Public Sphere in this model, though on an

---

[525] Jürgen Habermas, *The Structural Transformation of the Public Sphere* (Cambridge: MIT Press, 1991), p. 1.
[526] Ibid., p. 2.
[527] Ibid., p. 3.

admittedly primitive level. For example, it was a place where equals could interact as equals, and yet still seek to excel within this communicative space because it enabled something like an actualization of one's potential as a human person. Habermas claimed that Aristotle's virtues (i.e., courage, temperance, honour, friendliness, truthfulness, justice etc.) were really meant to define the proper ways to excel within this quasi-public sphere.[528]

The exact opposite of the Public Sphere found its fullest realization in the Middle Ages, a period during which all relations of domination were concentrated in the private space of the lord's household.[529] Although there was a concept of "the commons" in the Middle Ages, such as in marketplaces and fountains, these were not really public as we understand the term today because they lacked any orientation towards the rationalization of communication.[530] In fact, the concept of "publicity" in the Middle Ages was tied to archaic social forms such as how the king had to publicly represent his lordship for the subjects living under his rule to see, yet what he really represented publicly to them in this context was just his own inner life power. Likewise, in the Middle Ages badges, clothing, demeanour, and even rhetoric were considered public along these same lines – as a means of staging the representation of power for some figure thought to possess it simply by virtue of his role within society.

Habermas found this primitive definition of publicness to be something of a confusion of the term and a distortion rooted in an archaic sort of Metaphysical fetishism. This emphasis on staging the power of some royal monarch or high-ranking Church cleric distorted the proper meaning of the term "public," since in this case, publicness was not understood as a social realm (of communication) but rather as a status attribute held by powerful figures.[531] This type of public is flawed for the additional reason that it was inherently defined through its exclusion of the private. Because possessing some reified royal or magisterial power was understood to be a

---

[528] Ibid., p. 4.
[529] Ibid., p. 5.
[530] Ibid., p. 6.
[531] Ibid., p. 7.

condition necessary for publicity, it was by definition restricted to elites. A private soldier fighting for his superiors' interests, for example, could not publicly represent his own power because he had none. This exclusion of privacy also provided the rationale for the Catholic liturgy and Bible to be publicly read in Latin in order to exclude the vernacular language of the private peasant, a figure who was understood to fundamentally lack the ability to publicly represent power because he did not possess it in the first place.[532]

By the end of the 18th Century, this old representative publicness dissolved under the pressures of modernization.[533] In turn, the old Church powers, prince, and nobility either became private or they became public in a new sense of the word. In some ways, the proto-capitalist shift removed the very need for representation, since whereas a medieval nobleman was understood to be what he represents, the modern bourgeois is still understood to be what he produces.[534] A new public sphere of sorts materialized, but one which had nothing to do with the old medieval view of a fetishized representation of royal power.

Crucially, the Bourgeois Public Sphere arose along with early finance and trade capitalism. At least at the beginning, this shift was largely motivated by practical economic needs. For example, in the 14th Century merchant trade required knowledge of distant events.[535] Since this was not yet the era of public newspapers, they disseminated this information through private newsletters, a venue which initially lacked publicness. By the end of the 17th Century, however, one did see the rise of a public news press in the proper sense of the term.

Another major historical shift in the concept of publicity lay in capitalism's gradual expansion from the limits of the town to the nation as a whole.[536] In turn, the modern state arose through tapping into the power of taxation as a source of raising capital. A new sense of "public authority" emerged through newfound powers to

---

[532] Ibid., p. 9.
[533] Ibid., p. 11.
[534] Ibid., p. 13.
[535] Ibid., p. 16.
[536] Ibid., p. 17.

maintain permanent administration, a standing army, and other features familiar today but quite recent in historical origin.

Civil Society as such arose through the depersonalization of state authority.[537] Whereas before the 17th Century the economy largely referred to Oikos (in the literal sense of a household) and the pater familias, after the 17th Century one instead understood the economy to mean the public market rather than the private household. With this economic shift, newspapers' dominance grew to the point that daily journals became common because the news itself somehow became a commodity in the process. In retrospect, this was only to be expected, since selling to more people literally meant making more profit. This naturally drove a tendency towards generating ever-more-massive sales to ever-more-anonymous customers.[538]

As could be expected, the state used the press as transposition of publicity of representation into this new form of the public sphere by manipulating the press to systematically serve state interests, even in the guise of "disinterested journalism." Although the press was formally addressed to the public, it was really just intended for the educated classes. In this case, the term "public" continued to hold a defective meaning, since it could not mean all subjects but rather just the bourgeois professionals.[539]

By the end of the 17th Century, the press had expanded beyond mere dissemination of information to instead provide instruction, criticism, and reviews. The Public Sphere therefore shifted from a function of fetishized public authority to a communicative forum in which private people could compel the public authority to legitimate itself before the collective public opinion. The subject defined as a rational subject required this type of public sphere as a condition for it to emerge, since this represented the historically unprecedented situation in which people were allowed to make public use of reason through communication.

This tension between burgeoning modernization and archaic social forms was clearly displayed by the way that whereas the

---

[537] Ibid., p. 19.
[538] Ibid., pp. 20-1.
[539] Ibid., p. 23.

aristocratic court continued to be a sphere of royal representation, the town had become a public sphere as such. In fact, in England, the two were physically as well as conceptually separated; since the court was located in secluded areas far from the city, the town became an autonomous public space which was freed up to embody modern institutions such as coffee houses. By 1810, in fact, London had over 3,000 of them.[540] In the 18th Century, these coffee houses bridged the gap between the collapsing court publicity and emerging bourgeois public sphere by providing a space in which more or less anyone could come in and discuss literature and art and, later, politics and economics.

Unlike the court, the coffeehouse was inherently democratic, since it was open to craftsmen and shopkeepers rather than elites only.[541] For this reason, it provided a nearly-perfect physical space to realize the ideal of allowing intellectuals to meet on equal footing. In addition, unlike in preceding centuries, intellectuals' minds were no longer rented out to serve wealthy patrons' interests (i.e., Edmund Spenser's obligations to write his poetry in order to advance Queen Elizabeth's political and religious interests etc.) but could finally exercise reason publicly on an autonomous level.

By allowing vernacular discussion within democratic institutions, these participants were made into human beings *and nothing more than human beings*. Reason was now properly identified as something which could only be realized in rational communication by an open public with no restrictions delimited on the basis of archaic social distinctions. Although the sizes of various publics varied, one could still identify a lot of institutional overlap in terms of the communicative procedure involved. These included the requirement that social status be disregarded if communication is to be rational.[542] In addition, participants had to discuss areas which had previously been left unproblematized rather than reiterate established calcified ideologies; only if this were the case could one overcome the Church/state monopoly on knowledge which had persisted for centuries before.[543] Finally, there had to be a shift from

---

[540] Ibid., p. 32.
[541] Ibid., p. 33.
[542] Ibid., p. 36.

the older model of "high culture" to the newer model of a democratic commodity sold to the masses because the public is in principle defined by its level of inclusiveness.[544]

Needless to say, the old court aristocracy failed to meet these demands for rationality since, among other things, they were not even a reading public, let alone one which had optimized the conditions for literary discussion. The rise of a Public Sphere in the proper sense corresponded to a shift from the archaic form of occasional music favoured by the old aristocracy (i.e., music for worship, court, ceremony occasions etc.) to a newer form of music with no purpose defined by the slogan "art for art's sake" which in turn led to a change in the general public's tastes.[545] Similarly, painting shifted from a realm uniquely reserved for judgment by connoisseurs to a realm open to critique even from the most ordinary members of the general public. Although it was true that art critics as such continue to exist even in our era, their only authority lies in having better rhetorical arguments than non-critics, rather than through being naturally endowed with social privilege in some archaic sense of the term.[546] The processes described here are inherently democratic, since their basis is the public use of reason in communication and nothing more.

Interestingly, Addison and Steele's *The Spectator* became something of a literary mirror to this process by allowing the public to directly discuss itself.[547] This tendency to reduplicate the phenomenon of communication into literature led the 18th Century to be defined as the century of letters. The 18th Century best-seller Pamela, for example, was literally a novel filled with letters written by a house servant, nominally to her family but in all actuality to the anonymous masses of the reading public. Letters are therefore literary experiments with subjectivity because a letter always presupposes an audience who reads it. One might argue that subjectivity communicated with itself to gain clarity about itself, yet

---

[543] Ibid.
[544] Ibid., p. 37.
[545] Ibid., p. 39.
[546] Ibid., p. 41.
[547] Ibid., p. 43.

it did so precisely through speaking to an anonymous reader and, in the case of *The Spectator*, using an anonymous narrator to do so.

Yet this rationalization was not restricted to the realm of literary entertainment; within time, even the law itself came to be rationalized on communicative lines. Against the inherent tendency for the prince to have secrecy, critical public debate developed to pursue an overlap between what is right and what is just. At the level of political theory, law eventually came to be related to public opinion as an expression of Reason. While princely sovereignty merely requires legislative competence, abstract rational laws require public opinions. Under these democratic conditions, the universal rules of communicative rationality would take precedence over archaic reifications of rank, social status etc. Only if these conditions were satisfied could we obtain the ideals of liberty and equality, yet this could itself be achieved only if one first derived them from a properly communicative foundation.

France also saw a rise of its own public sphere, as the most widely read newspaper in France in 1763 had some 1,600 subscribers.[548] By the end of the 18th Century, there was a remarkable shift in France in that public communication was formally proclaimed to be a basic human right.[549] This was consistent with a general change in how persons were recognized, as the general status of all legal subjects was no longer defined by estate and birth but rather, increasingly, by the public use of reason in communication.[550]

In addition, the 18th Century was characterized by a shift from natural law to positive law.[551] One sign of "progress" in this regard was that a society governed solely by laws of the free market appeared to be purified of more archaic notions of coercion.[552] Free market transactions, for example, proceed in accord with calculable expectations which will hold consistent regardless of *who* engages in the procedure.[553] From this basis, it was generalized that the laws

---

[548] Ibid., p. 67.
[549] Ibid., p. 70.
[550] Ibid., p. 75.
[551] Ibid., p. 76.
[552] Ibid., p. 79.

of state should be made like the laws of the market – equal for all without any exceptions based on personal bias.

Likewise, an ideal of a legislative procedure based on solving problems through rational agreement rather than through a battle of political willpower would realize this ideal of reason overcoming coercion within the legal realm as well.[554] Crucially, under this view we explicitly find that public opinion is fundamentally misunderstood if it is treated as one more form of "power" among all the older versions of royal or magisterial privilege. The entire point was, rather, to overcome these primitive models of coercion in favour of a procedure which made no presuppositions about the social status of its participants.

In this sense, Kant and Habermas (as well as, to a lesser extent, Zizek) are each "linguistifiers" of modernity, in that each of them noticed the same requirement for abstraction beyond individual context to serve as the very standard of social rationalization. In other words, just as Habermas argued that communication should reduce participants to speakers and nothing more than speakers, Kant recognised that the ethical law could be pure only if it reduced moral agents to nothing more than moral agents, banishing any extra contextual details as pathological contaminants. Similarly, Zizek realized that even Nature itself must be denied the dignity of existence in order for the Cartesian cogito to maximize its emptiness under a bizarre new definition of "materialism without matter." Somehow, however, this all just leads to the absurd conclusion that a society is only as rational as its members are substitutable for one another, since fixating on the unique characteristics of each would come to be seen as an archaic fetishism left over from the Metaphysical Worldview.

In other words, the experiment of modernity is successful only to the extent that it makes us all the same. Of course, perfect democratic equality is an ecologically impossible chimera with no need for accountability beyond the fluid realm of linguistification, so this situation of universal equality can never actually be completed within a world accountable to the laws of ecological

---

[553] Ibid., p.80.
[554] Ibid., p. 82.

reality. Still, the effects of allowing it to serve as a formal mandate have already proven devastating despite its fundamental impossibility. In this sense, Linkola actually does agree that democracy means we are all the same, but that is precisely the problem with it, since few things are quite as absurd on an ecological level as this belief.

All Lives Matter?

Linkola's harshest critics within the media and academic intelligentsia tend to neglect the crucial distinction between his critique of democracy as a concrete political system and his critique of democracy as an abstract philosophy. For this reason, we will profit from examining his stance on the latter in greater detail. One of his most memorable meditations on democracy as a philosophy lay in his "A Refresher Course on the State of the World," in which he contrasted humanistic values not only with ecological reality, but with Reason itself. In other words, he implied that continued affirmation of chimeras such as "progress" required one to outright suspend one's ability to think clearly and logically.[555]

Reason, for example, tells us that an "ecocatastrophe is taking place on Earth,"[556] yet Linkola distinguished himself from the unserious "green campus" activist types by admitting the uncomfortable fact that this crisis is being driven not only by familiar sources such as pollution, food chain disruption, and climate change, but also by excessive medical intervention by doctors. Linkola proved his unprecedented willingness to align his own mind with the Mind of Nature by acknowledging the uniquely unpalatable fact that doctors have made our situation far worse than it had to be by tampering with natural human die-off rates which would have acted as an ecological check to keep our population under control. Unthinkable as it might be, he admits that the drop in traditional infant mortality rates is not an accomplishment to be celebrated but is rather a "deeply depressing" turn of events which

---

[555] Pentti Linkola, "A Refresher Course on the State of the World," in *Can Life Prevail?* (Kindle Edition).
[556] Ibid.

inevitably led to our current mess and should arguably be restored to its previous rate as soon as possible.

Reason alone is also sufficient to tell us that not every sick or injured person is equally worthy of medical attention, yet this is itself indicative of a broader philosophical truth that not every life is equally valuable. Linkola has the guts to openly ask the obvious question how anyone could be so crazy as to think that all human life has exactly the same value, since one could certainly never arrive at such a strange doctrine from just empirically comparing the worst serial child molester in prison with a selfless doctor working to save lives in a god-forsaken Third World war zone. Even from a strictly numerical perspective, though, this makes no sense. In his "Human and Animal Nature," he acknowledged the obvious though unpalatable fact that each time a new baby is born, the value of every other human life slightly decreases, simply as a matter of supply and demand. The grand irony is that the mutually exclusive motifs of unbridled overpopulation *and* democratic equality have been squeezed together into the most blatant form of Orwellian doublethink.

In "The Value of Humans and that of Animals," Linkola doubled down on his insistence that any effort to uphold the chimera of universal human rights will simply legislate a death sentence for all of natural creation.[557] In this essay, he refused to accept the absurdity that there could be any such thing as a set of universal human rights which would have remained unchanged since the beginning of time. Even if such a thing existed, its value could not have remained constant over all of these historical eras, since the rapid increase in population in recent decades has been sufficient on its own to decrease each of our value as individuals. Yet even if this were not a problem on quantitative grounds, it would still be ridiculous to overlook the blatant qualitative differences which are glaringly obvious even in a comparison of any two humans taken at random from the global population:

---

[557] Pentti Linkola, "The Value of Humans and that of Animals," in *Can Life Prevail?* (Kindle Edition).

> [I cannot see why] human rights are seen as being applicable to everyone in the same way. . . I find this kind of thinking truly worthless. I could never find two people who are perfectly equal: one will always be more valuable than the other. And many people, as a matter of fact, simply have no value. Some individuals exceed the "environmental allowance" by a factor of a thousand: they vastly decrease the richness of nature and squander its resource reserves, both through their own way of life and through their influence. There are also plenty of evil people around, who have no moral standards: downright criminals who in extreme cases cause a horrid amount of pain to other members of their species. What mysticism, what black magic can allow such creatures to possess full human rights? What is the philosophy of those who oppose the death sentence?[558]

Despite paying unceasing lip service to the glories of "diversity," the humanistic ideology of modernity is something of an institutionalized blindness to naturally-occurring differences among people. Even the most hardened criminals are assumed to be ordinary folks who naturally should have ended up as the same sort of stockbrokers, lawyers, Ivy League social scientists, or physicians who populate the elites' own circles, as they look from afar upon these unfortunate specimens and conclude that they only ended up behind bars due to a set of preventable sociological contingencies which can just be legislated away through more government control. The very concept of a person who is evil just because he or she wants to be has become so unthinkable that it can only be entertained on the rare occasions that pre-modern Fairy Tales are retrieved from the archives of tradition to entertain children before bed time, despite the fact that, on ecological grounds alone, the world is currently filled with the evilest figures in world history. Far from being a generation of radically positivistic empiricists, the age

---

[558] Ibid.

of "scientific reason" has simply mandated blindness to qualitative differences as a matter of ethical obligation.

In "The Value of Humans and that of Animals," Linkola reaffirmed his controversial stance that the "Animal Rights" fantasy of a world in which every single animal was somehow spared from violence is just another ecologically impossible chimera.[559] However, he qualified his position in this essay by noting the ultimate irony that this is not at all an assertion of Man's "will to dominate Nature" or play God by setting a price on the head of each animal determined on purely arbitrary grounds; on the contrary, not all animals are equal precisely because rare ones rank higher than common ones within a system and wild animals take precedence over domesticated ones. Under these criteria, Man is not the highest within the hierarchy; he is the absolute worst![560] During Linkola's infamous Werstas discussion, he shocked the audience by asserting that if one had to make a choice between killing a 300-year-old pine tree or a random human being, one would unquestionably have to choose the human for elimination.[561]

Man's tendency to drive mass extinction and to meddle in natural environments was bad enough even in prehistoric times, but the current explosion in population figures proved to be the damning evidence for the verdict. Overpopulation has become so excessive that Man has succeeded in breaking all "laws of the food chain" and has effectively transitioned to obtaining the status of an artificial machine implanted into the web of life. Nor is Man's extreme resource waste even limited to meeting legitimate survival needs such as food and water, as he "has even multiplied his burden by indulging on an unscrupulous amount of secondary needs, a massive superseding of other lifeforms," and "impoverishment of nature's affluence."[562] Under this view, he pronounces the grim but

---

[559] Pentti Linkola, "The Value of Humans and that of Animals," in *A Collection of Essays by Pentti Linkola 1993 – 2006*, p. 72.
[560] Ibid., p. 73.
[561] Pentti Linkola interview from *Quadrivium* #6 (2014): abridged version. Available at http://qvadrivivm.blogspot.com/2015/12/pentti-linkola-interview-from.html
[562] Pentti Linkola, "The Value of Humans and that of Animals," in *A Collection of*

unescapable truth that the formula "human rights = [a] death sentence to mankind," a shocking reversal of the stereotypical view that human rights are the guarantee of "life, liberty, and the pursuit of happiness." Human rights are therefore simply a smaller subset of the broader antinomies of democracy, in which the affirmation of life is simultaneously the affirmation of death, and the promise to expand population without limits is paired with the threat of human extinction itself. Linkola admits that even for the most intelligent of minds, these mutually exclusive and self-negating "factors in the concept of human rights will remain incomprehensible until his death."[563] In "The Lone Rider" in reviewing Eero Taivalsaari's book 'Alaston totuus markkinavoimista'" he proposed using one's evaluation of these antinomies as a basic test to determine how credible one's other propositions might be, since one's "attitude to the population explosion, human value, and human rights is the threshold question of the deepest ecological insight."[564] Anyone who fails to comprehend the utter absurdity of the promise to expand the population until it climbs all the way to its final value of "zero" must immediately be disqualified from speaking on any ecological matters, let alone from legislating any formal decisions regarding society's direction.

Nor are these the only contradictions in the modern ideology of democratic humanism. In addition, Linkola noted in "A Refresher Course on the State of the World" that this cult of the "unique and irreplaceable individual" is somehow lumped together with its polar opposite, the ideology of a perfectly-equalized democratic mass. We are told that every life is different from any other that has ever existed, but simultaneously, we are told that we are all the same. This formal requirement to level out any social distinctions and to throw every body (pun intended) onto an indeterminate heap, though fashionable on ideological grounds, has directly facilitated the collective madness of ecological destruction. Linkola argued in the same essay that although the brilliance of

---

Essays by Pentti Linkola 1993 – 2006, p. 73.
[563] Ibid., p. 74.
[564] Pentti Linkola, "The Lone Rider," in *A Collection of Essays by Pentti Linkola 1993 – 2006*, pp. 82-3.

Man does not manifest itself in more than a handful of exceptional individuals, it is precisely when taken as a mass that mankind accelerates its natural tendency towards irrational behavior to levels unthinkable even for the most depraved individual. Contrary to Habermas's philosophy, the democratic mass is not the embodiment of rationality itself but is instead its polar opposite, for it is only when taken as the formless crowd that Man becomes the most destructive.[565] Any attempt to combine universal human rights (which would be the same for all) with a unique value for each person (which would be different for all) is simply one more ecologically impossible situation right alongside the fantasies of universal automation,[566] universal sanitation,[567] and universal veganism.[568]

Fortunately, Linkola provided a direct commentary on his own tendency to recognize subtle contradictions which are virtually invisible to the naked eye in his *Johdatus 1990-luvun ajatteluun* (*An Introduction to 1990s Thinking*), an earlier text which attempted to outline a new world order for the end of the century. He introduced this ambitious plan, however, by warning the reader that "nine out of ten people never think." Even among the people who sincerely believe that they deserve to be called "thinkers," some 90 percent of them fail the test because they think in self-contradictory terms. Yet even passing the test of logical consistency is not enough if one remains too timid to think big, as some ninety percent of those who pass the first test of non-contradiction still lack ambition. Ambition, of course, will itself prove useless if it does not perform the leap of faith to cross over from knowledge to action. The failure to impact reality by hiding in theoretical speculation is just as damning as the other disqualifiers. Likewise, his two dominant values in this text are more like two perspectives on the same content than two separate spheres: intellectual honesty and the continuity of natural

---

[565] Pentti Linkola, "A Refresher Course on the State of the World," in *Can Life Prevail?* (Kindle Edition).
[566] Pentti Linkola, "The Intolerable Misfortune of Technology," in *Can Life Prevail?* (Kindle Edition).
[567] Pentti Linkola, "Humbug," in *Can Life Prevail?* (Kindle Edition).
[568] Pentti Linkola, "A Look at Vegetarianism," in *Can Life Prevail?* (Kindle Edition).

life are more like a parallax of the same One than two distinct notions.

The chimera of the democratic mass which is both completely different and completely the same is, however, far more than a comical stimulant for laughter, as the enormous growth of the human population arguably outweighs any other factor in causing the ongoing collapse of the world. Somehow, even among the thinking minority who realize these things on an intellectual level, a spirit of learned helplessness drives most people to surrender before our current dysfunction as though nothing could possibly be done to change it. This is because the root of the problem is not strictly ecological; it is ideological. The irrational "overvaluation of human life" is the only thing which could lead oversocialized leftists to campaign for the total elimination of the death penalty from the face of the Earth while simultaneously claiming to be "environmentalists." Under this view, even the "most diabolical of criminals" are no longer allowed to be put to death due to political correctness, yet this only means that they will go on consuming resources and generating pollution for what will seem like an eternity under a "criminal justice system" which has somehow been hijacked to perpetuate ecological injustice.

Virtually no one except Linkola seemed to realize that the worst enemy of life is an excess of life, as the increasing burden each new member brings upon Nature has proven devastating even in pre-modern civilizations which lacked fossil fuels or Modern Technology. Humans proved more than capable of altering the biosphere by creating permanent deserts millennia before the first steam engine was invented. Even fewer seem to grasp that the battle for humanistic values which drives this insanity will be completely irrelevant if there is no one to debate it in the first place. It will be the greatest irony of history if the very possibility for ideological values is blotted out, not just through any humanistic value, but that of an irrational overemphasis on human life. In his 1989 *Johdatus 1990-luvun ajatteluun* (*Introduction to the Thinking of the Nineteen Nineties*), the author's preface ends with one of the most famous Linkola quotes:

When the lifeboat is full, those who hate life will try to load it with more people and sink the lot. Those who love and respect life will take the ship's axe and sever the extra hands that cling to the sides of the boat.

Sometimes, the only way to save life, as well as the ability for value to manifest itself hermeneutically to any living being, is to destroy a little life in the process.

Of course, anyone who truly took this matter seriously would realize that there is no alternative to Linkola's stance that reproduction cannot be an individual decision in the hands of families but must instead be deferred to a world council which would grant, at most, one child per fertile woman and, after stabilization, maybe two. He justified this outrageous demand by warning that any dogmatic adherence to the ideology of "equality will only cause misfortune." In the name of Reason alone, even the most hard-core of humanists must agree that anything which fits under the banner of "progress" will ultimately just push us to ecological "ruin."[569] Yet even so obvious a fact as this shall remain ignored even by the most intelligent of minds, as he mentioned that although Man is admittedly a technical genius, he is a mindless animal in every other respect.

Linkola vs. the Antifa Terrorist Manifesto

It was peculiar for the slogan "All Lives Matter" to become a forbidden phrase among leftists during the short-lived run of the Black Lives Matter extravaganza (especially from 2014 to 2015), since the idea that "All lives matter [the exact same amount]" is precisely the official ideology of Modern Technology and of democratic modernity.

In March, 2020, Vanessa Hudgens provoked global outrage when she stated the obvious fact that some people would inevitably die as a result of the coronavirus epidemic which was sweeping the world. Although her delivery was admittedly rather off-putting, it is

---

[569] Pentti Linkola, "A Refresher Course on the State of the World," in *Can Life Prevail?* (Kindle Edition).

peculiar that we live in an era in which the largest source of anger in the midst of a global pandemic could be a Hollywood celebrity who acknowledged an obvious fact that not every life could be saved by the medical system, even as this same crisis was unfolding and empirically confirming this prediction in real-time. We have literally reached the point at which people are more offended by an accidental linguistic contradiction of the dogma that "all lives must be saved" than they are by the System's actual failure to live up to this ideological demand to preserve every human life.

In 2019, chillingly definitive proof was given that "all lives matter" is not at all a blasphemy against the code of democratic modernity and progress but is, rather, so compatible with it that it was explicitly invoked to justify a criminal act of leftist political terrorism. In the United States that year, an Antifa terrorist was shot dead by police while trying to firebomb an ICE facility, apparently under the delusion that he was "liberating concentration camps." Nor were his political motives ambiguous, as he went out of his way to publish a brief "manifesto" explicitly detailing the reasons why he apparently felt the need to seize the moment violently, even if it entailed the risk of harming some lives in order to definitively prove that "all lives matter." It is peculiar that even though he knew his full-length "manifesto" would surely circulate widely after news broke of the crime, it apparently was not worth his time to write more than a tiny handful of random and half-clear ramblings in which even a grammatical demand as basic as capitalizing the pronoun "I" was apparently too much to ask. The entire document, in fact, is little more than two pages long and largely consists of brief slogans which are popular among protesters who pride themselves on being courageous enough to repeatedly shout the exact same thing as hundreds of other people in their immediate vicinity, such as "Keep the faith!" and "Power to the people!" His own claim to be "a black and white thinker" who wants to keep it "simple" and to not "overthink it" is more than sufficiently confirmed by the formal structure of the text itself, not to mention the simple-mindedness of its content!

One of the only explicitly theoretical ideas of the entire fragmentary "manifesto" lies in his conviction that, against the doctrine of moral relativism, there is in fact a strict difference between good and evil, or, as he says himself: "there's wrong and there's right." Given this undeniable fact, he concludes that there is no sense in delaying the battle any longer: "it's time to take action against the forces of evil." Interestingly, he pretty much just defined this "evil" as the idea that "one life is worth less than another." In other words, evil is any disagreement with the philosophy of democracy, however slight, proof that Linkola ranks as arguably the single most controversial Orwellian thought criminal alive today.

It is even more bizarre, however, that the document which mandates agreement with the modern ideology of democracy by threat of bloodshed would also claim to be environmentalist in its ideology, citing "the flow of commerce" which has resulted in "a planet almost used up by the market's greed" as an inevitable outcome of allowing evil to remain unchallenged. His aversion to this "fascist" capitalist state is, in fact, so extreme that he admits that although some of his comrades may opt for less violent methods, the option of "burn[ing] the motherfucker down" will still prove more legitimate than the cowardly passivity of "stand[ing] by" and doing nothing. In fact, he explicitly warns his fellow Antifa thugs to "beware the centrist," for nothing short of extreme measures are required to stop this juggernaut.

Our discussion of Linkola's philosophy has proven just how absurd it is to attempt to have an "environmentalist, modernized democracy in which all lives are the same," since this completely misses the point that democracy *is* the official ideology of Modern Technology and that the environmental crises are precisely the result of allowing this abstract belief to function as a concrete political directive. Most hypocritical of all was this writer's claim that the ideology of Antifa can be condensed to nothing more than a "love for life," one which just happens to espouse the technical conditions to guarantee that this same life will *not* prevail.

For this reason, Brett Stevens noted in his introduction to the English edition of *Can Life Prevail?* that Linkola has argued that the only option is to allow an elite to rule. It is not at all controversial, of course, to claim that only one in 100,000 people has the talent to be a professional athlete. Yet it is somehow unthinkable that a task far more important than catching touchdowns to win a Sunday afternoon football game which will be forgotten by Monday evening of the same week should be reserved for a similarly select group of people. In "A Refresher Course in the State of the World," in fact, he suggested that age must also play a role in qualifying a person to make decisions on behalf of the Mind of Nature. For example, if the minimum age for major decision makers were changed to 80 years old, "many delusions would have been avoided" and "the pace of destruction" would have surely been slowed down.[570] Even the Biblical story of the woman caught in adultery recounts that after Jesus wrote on the ground it was, not coincidentally, the oldest men in the crowd who walked away first, far sooner than young men and teens did, since the wisdom of many years of life experience had led them to realize the folly of stoning a woman to death when they themselves had far worse skeletons in their closets.[571]

Paul Joseph Watson similarly recounts in his video on Extinction Rebellion that the age demographic in the United Kingdom with the greatest disapproval of them were the elderly. Yet this was precisely because they themselves had actually lived through the experience of a lower-energy lifestyle which the protesters claimed to want but did not realize would entail things like using the same water someone else had already bathed in or entertaining themselves without any television, let alone internet. It is all too clear that what most of these "radical environmentalists" really want is for some clever engineer or scientist on the government payroll to find an alternative energy source to let them keep drooling over their social media newsfeeds and video streaming services without feeling any guilt about contributing to global warming.

It is no coincidence, therefore, that the social justice caricatures which claim that all the problems in the world, from global capitalism to global warming, can be blamed on "white privilege" and others' ignorance regarding the current number of genders (68 and counting) are most prevalent among 18 year old

---

[570] Ibid.
[571] John 8:8

kids who have never had to work a job, who survive on student loan funds which they have not the slightest idea how they will ever pay back, and whose sudden interest in political issues just happened to stem from the basest desire to maintain their high school popularity on a college campus regulated by ever-stricter codes of social conformity. Years later, these same figures often look back on their college days with shame and regret after experiencing a different way of life than the two-dimensional puppet show to which the college campus has restricted all life forms.

The New Elitism:
The Mind of Progress and the Myth of the Rule by Majority

Although democracy is officially supposed to be the ideology that "we are all the same," in practice, democracy has still failed to grant political power to the masses on any meaningful level. In his essay "What is the Majority and What is the Minority" Linkola noted the irony that most people actually don't *want* the kind of society which they are forced to live in, despite the fact that it is precisely by nominally-democratic means that these unwelcome changes were brought into being:

> Is society being led in a direction that the majority does not actually approve of? How many actually wish for and support things like strenuous competition, efficiency, rationalisation and renovation [or] rushing to invent new things and abandon the old [for no good reason]? [How many people actually support needless] travelling back and forth to the far reaches of the Earth [or] the shipping of goods to and fro [in unnecessary circumstances]? [What about] adult schooling [and] re-education [for workers who had been laid off due to automation and are then force to] always hurry about as if one's heels were on fire?[572]

---

[572] Pentti Linkola, "What is the Majority and What is the Minority?" in *Can Life Prevail?* (Kindle Edition).

The economic policies which truly matter, such as large-scale international trade and attempts to maximize technological automation (which, in turn, drives this ridiculous need for adults to constantly retrain for new jobs which won't even exist by the time they graduate) are things which only a small minority truly like and that is only because these policies financially benefit them while harming the vast majority of the population through driving unemployment as well as the cost of living well past the breaking point. Linkola distinguished himself as one of the few sufficiently-courageous thought criminals to openly wonder whether "[p]erhaps only a few people set the rules [after all]."[573]

The conditions of modernity are peculiar, since even if this path did not lead to eco-catastrophe (which it most certainly does), it would still be gloomy simply on its own terms:

> How many believe that human well-being, pleasure and happiness diminish the more we follow this path? And that even if this path were not to lead to ecocatastrophe and extinction, it would still be a gloomy [one].[574]

The true enigma of our time, in other words, lies in explaining why (supposedly) empowering the people through democratic universalization of abstract "human rights" has actually just led to a set of living conditions which the vast majority of people find unbearable. Few things are quite as paradoxical as a democratic consensus which no one likes.

Linkola has distinguished himself from other so-called conspiracy theorists, however, in that he has gone as far as to argue that even "those who vote in government" don't actually want these things – they just assume that these are the "Will of the Majority" and vote against their own gut feelings out of a strange feeling of quasi-religious obligation. Interestingly, he explicitly notes that these people vote along with the *consensus*, that humanistic chimera which Habermas claimed would be sufficient to solve all problems

---

[573] Ibid.
[574] Ibid.

but has only ensured that they would be preserved indefinitely despite being disliked even by the politicians themselves:

> It is often the case that after a municipal assembly or a similar event, when a bad decision has been taken, a member of the assembly will privately admit that he was personally against the decision, but voted in favour all the same because he knew it was the position held by the majority and did not wish to shatter the consensus, disturb the easy flow of things, and give rise to unnecessary confusion. Then the same matter is often brought up with another assembly member in private, and again the same words are heard. In the end, it may be that thirty councillors are individually making a decision that is the exact opposite of the one they all just voted for. [575]

This mysterious consensus which is actually not to be found in the people's own preferences is basically just a perverse double of the Mind of Nature, an ideal cogito filled only with humanistic linguistifications and unreal chimeras, a set of pseudo-truths in which the sole criterion for inclusion is precisely that they *violate* ecological law.

This Mind of Progress which is driving our pseudo-democratic society off the cliff of collective suicide is a perverse object, combining "the power and cogency of a shaman" with "the drive of a fanatic, the mysterious, irrational and persuasive strength of an idiot."[576] Somehow, though, this Mind who is nobody and who claims to speak for the democratic totality of voters only ends up promoting the interests of the same minority of elites:

> It is entirely possible that the "opinion of the majority", "the general view" according to which decisions are taken — the opinion of town councils, the parliament and media — in fact only reflects the position of a small but powerful minority. This minority fosters rivalry between individuals,

---

[575] Ibid.
[576] Ibid.

companies and societies in the name of performance, automatisation, production, consumption, exports, imports, the stock market, motorways and fast trains [but only in order to benefit itself].

The abstraction of a mysterious democratic "majority" which somehow wills things which virtually no one on the ground level actually likes is a mere euphemism for this impersonal Mind of Progress which is, in a certain sense, nobody at all.

In Habermas's discussion of Hegel in his *Structural Transformation of the Public Sphere*, he noted that the "realm of enlightenment" was defined by the ideal of allowing "the mind of the nation" to become "aware of itself as public opinion."[577] Ideally, democracy would simply institutionalize the Mind of the Nation's "self-awareness" into official state policy. While it is true that allowing the Mind of Nature to dominate the political realm through a Green Police force would require the Mind of the Nation to be suspended in the interest of serving higher goals, it is arguable that what Linkola demands is already being done for the Mind of Progress. It's *already* the case that the Mind of the Nation has been eclipsed by another pseudo-intelligence which is no one at all. But rather than submit to ecological law we have renounced our agency for the sake of the very worst humanistic chimeras. In other words, the Mind of the Nation has already lost any hope of achieving the enlightenment ideal of self-awareness. It is only a question now of what shall be allowed to take its place.

Unfortunately, the misperception that this abstract collection of dogmas embodied in the Mind of Progress (i.e., automation, suburbanization, bureaucratization, democratization, social justice etc.) is not only a real person but "the majority of them" actually ends up forcing people to support big parties they don't like and to neglect small parties they do like:

> People would like to vote for small, alternative parties, "but it just isn't worth it: they'll get so few votes, they will never

---

[577] Jürgen Habermas, *The Structural Transformation of the Public Sphere* (Cambridge: MIT Press, 1991), pp. 121-2.

make an impact." It is both shocking and absurd, for instance, that while most Finns would ultimately like to vote for the Green Party, they don't. Is Finnish society a tragicomedy, where one doesn't know whether to laugh or cry?[578]

The democratic right to vote is effectively meaningless because any vote cast essentially goes to reinforcing the same set of policies, insofar as all the parties are just surrogates for this Mind of Progress in disguise. In fact, the one candidate which one *cannot* vote for at the democratic ballot box is precisely the Mind of Nature:

> [W]e all have the same right to vote and one's word weighs as much as anyone else's in decision-making. Election after election, the major parties, which are all the same, [all go] on about [the same bland topics of] development, progress and money.[579]

Somehow, people have never been more helpless than after they had been given a symbolic share of political agency under democracy. Despite having the nominal right to vote, for example, farmers simply accept what is dictated to them from above within distant and corrupt bureaucracies. Linkola noted himself in "Life Protection, Utopias, and Agriculture" that:

> I have lived in a farming community for the last fifty years and am increasingly terrified at how farmers surrender, apathetically yielding to what is dealt from above.[580]

Similarly, in his "It is Dark in the Woods," he mentioned that the real reason why the forestry industry has no need to be accurate in

---

[578] Pentti Linkola, "What is the Majority and What is the Minority?" in *Can Life Prevail?* (Kindle Edition).
[579] Ibid.
[580] Pentti Linkola, "Life Protection, Utopias, and Agriculture," in *Can Life Prevail?* (Kindle Edition).

its official figures is because it possesses two overwhelming advantages: a technical means to repeat lies often through the propaganda channels of the media and a group of labourers who will do anything which is dictated to them due to the sheer lack of genuine freedom under these bloated bureaucracies:

> [As far as the industry is concerned,] all its claims are true, provided they are repeated often enough. The industry also knows that it can repeat statements and slogans frequently enough, for it possesses a fair amount of money and . . . a vast army [of] foresters, who do just what they are ordered.[581]

It bears repeating that because Linkola's ontology is basically summed up by the phrase "to be is to be ecological," the Mind of Progress has effectively mandated that the "birthmark" of ecological impossibility be implemented as official state policy. In a strange reversal of Zizek's claim that "Nature doesn't exist,"[582] Linkola has instead shown us that "democracy doesn't exist," for democracy is simply the institutionalization of ecological impossibility. We are quite literally living in a society of institutionalized nothingness in which Being has become a crime. Linkola's ethics is closely linked with his metaphysics, insofar as his ethical mandate for us all "to be ecological" is simply redundant of the metaphysical demand to restore Being over the chimeras of nothingness.

Linkola's Critique of Metaphysics: The Antinomies of Democracy

It is supremely ironic that Habermas's aversion to any standard of truth beyond the materialistic discharge of desiring-production is justified by claims to respect the historical demands of a Post-Metaphysical Worldview by avoiding the fetishism of a "an absolute content which is true in itself," since from a Linkolan viewpoint, Habermasian linguistification is nearly indistinguishable

---
[581] Pentti Linkola, "It is Dark in the Woods," in *Can Life Prevail?* (Kindle Edition).
[582] Slavoj Zizek, *In Defense of Lost Causes* (London: Verso, 2008), p. 444.

from the sort of Metaphysics which Kant had forbidden in his own system. Kant once warned that an illegitimate synthesis which oversteps the phenomenal appearance in order to try to apply the transcendental Notion to the thing in itself does not actually reach it, but rather gets lost in the transcendental illusion where something seems to appear where there is really just nothing. It is precisely because the rational idea goes beyond the black and white nature of the concepts of the understanding that it is capable of providing the temptation to engage in Metaphysics by inducing the subject to want to go beyond itself to talk about the world, for example, as though it were an objective given when "the world" is really just a regulative idea which Reason employs in its search for completeness.

In Book II of his *Critique of Practical Reason*, Kant noted that because legitimate intuitions "cannot be other than sensible," they by definition "do not let objects be cognized as things in themselves but only as appearances," For this reason, the illusion is simply the result of applying the rational idea directly to the appearance as if it were the thing in itself. [583] The resulting antinomy in which both a thesis and its antithesis simultaneously appear to be true with regard to the same thing is therefore simply Reason's conflict with itself misrecognized as a contradiction directly embodied in the object as such.

In his *Critique of Pure Reason*, for example, the first antinomy of space and time proved that if one investigates the cosmos as though it were a real object, one would be led into the contradiction of having to affirm that the world has a beginning in time and limits in space, but simultaneously, that the world has no beginning in time and no limits in space.[584]

Similarly, the second antinomy of atomism leads one into the contradiction of affirming that every composite substance in the world is made up of simple parts and nothing anywhere exists save the simple or what is composed of the simple; but also, that no

---

[583] Immanuel Kant, *Critique of Practical Reason* (Cambridge: Cambridge University Press, 2012), p. 90.
[584] Immanuel Kant, *Critique of Pure Reason* (London: Penguin, 2007), p. 391.

composite thing in the world is made up of simple parts, and there does not exist anything which is simple.[585]

The third antinomy of spontaneity and causal determinism leads one to affirm the type of causality which accords with the laws of nature is not the only kind of causality, because another type of spontaneous causality is required to explain the functioning of all appearances within the world; yet, at the same time, one also affirms the anti-thesis that there is no such thing as spontaneity because every event in the world occurs solely in accordance with the laws of nature.[586]

The fourth antinomy of necessary being leads one to affirm that an absolutely necessary being exists in the world (whether as a part or a cause of that world); but, at the same time, one affirms that there is no such thing as an absolutely necessary being, neither as a part of the world nor as an extrinsic cause to it.[587]

The conflict inherent in each antinomy, therefore, can never be overcome through amplifying one's efforts to investigate the illusion (as one would naively think) but, rather, only through turning inward to investigate Reason itself better. This is the true justification for Kant's thesis that the death of Metaphysics cannot help but follow from Reason's critical investigation of itself.

Under Linkola's view, democratic linguistification is simply the illusory "Metaphysics" which his own critical philosophy opposes, as this illusion is just the institutionalized mandate for its adherents to collectively overstep the limits of ecological reality in order to land on the void of nothingness through a collective misuse of language which will inevitably generate its own "Antinomies of Democracy," in which both a thesis and its antithesis will seem to be equally true at the same time.

For example, democracy is an inherently conflicted pseudo-object in which all citizens must be the same/equal *and* all citizens must be different/unique at the same time. In addition, democracy promises every citizen a voice in determining the direction of society, however unqualified he or she might be, while

---

[585] Ibid., p. 397.
[586] Ibid., p. 405.
[587] Ibid., p. 412.

simultaneously handing over control to the purified Mind of Progress which is *no one at all*; in other words, democracy provides a platform for both everyone and no one to speak. Finally, democracy promises citizens the right to fulfil their desires regardless of any lack of rational justification, yet it simultaneously forces citizens to renounce their desires in order to become martyrs for the chimeras of progress simply because the latter are deemed perfect on abstract, pseudo-rationalistic grounds of linguistification.

One cannot speak about democracy without falling into hopeless and unresolvable contradictions for which the possibility of a dialectical resolution is not even an option, for there is nothing there to be resolved at all, only a gap of nothingness masquerading as a real being. In his essay "Of The Evaluation Of The Book 'Into The Ecological Way Of Life [Ekologiseen Elämäntapaan]'" Linkola noted that it is literally not possible to "picture the contradiction between the population explosion and the value of a human individual in our minds" because the requirements to satisfy one half of the contradiction immediately rule out any attempt to satisfy the other. Even the cliché that "Every human is worth a song" is simply a form of narcissism masquerading as a selfless love for the Other so vast as to cover seven billion strangers. At best, one might be able to "ponder over" one's "own biography," or perhaps a few close friends or family members, but providing a song for the entire global population is beyond the realm of possibility.[588] Even in the most sincere attempt to carry out this madness, one will quickly find that "the pieces of the puzzle do not meet each other - not after man created a human mass out of its personalities, sung billions of songs and with them, covered the surface of the Earth into a suffocating coat."[589]

Bizarrely, this coordinated irrationality of "humanistic illusion" is almost always praised as the model for reason itself. Yet far from embodying a higher, post-Cartesian ideal of "communicative rationality," Habermas's model is simply a

---

[588] Pentti Linkola, "Of The Evaluation Of The Book 'Into The Ecological Way Of Life [Ekologiseen Elämäntapaan],'" in *A Collection of Essays by Pentti Linkola 1993 – 2006*, p. 146.
[589] Ibid.

collectivized solipsism. The only thing speaking subjects are actually "freed up" to do in his public sphere is to talk about themselves, much like how exiled Polish writer Gombrowicz's *Diary* opened with a set of entries consisting of the single word "Me" and then progressed to longer entries which superficially appeared to be about other topics but were really just slightly-encrypted redundancies of these opening entries, embodying his narcissistic fixation on himself in the guise of a dialogue with the outside world. Behind the façade of "selfless accountability to the global community," communicative action is similarly a perversion of human agency into a technology of irrationality, a machine of desire which is hard-wired to inflate the stock values of so many humanistic chimeras in a medium of abstraction where the very need for accountability to Nature would evaporate like so many tears for the dead on the planet Arrakis.[590]

Foucault vs. Linkola on Insanity:
Democracy Doesn't Exist

A perceptive reader might have noticed that Linkola's emphasis on a connection among the concepts of language, unreal chimeras, madness, nothingness, and death is shockingly reminiscent of Michel Foucault's treatment of these same topics in his monumental study of the history of insanity. Foucault's *Madness and Civilization*, a widely-read abridgement of the broader *History of Madness*, has provided one of the most exhaustive analyses of these topics to date and is crucially relevant to any serious discussion of Linkola's own stances on the matter. For this reason, it is necessary to briefly focus on the unexpected relation between Foucault and Linkola in order to gain a clearer view of Linkola's rejection of the "collective madness" of anti-ecological thinking which is currently

---

[590] Paul memorably shed tears for the dead while attending the funeral for a man he himself had to kill as part of his initiation to a higher level of political responsibility. His tears shocked the audience, since even the man's closest friends could not give up moisture on the extreme desert planet of Arrakis. Frank Herbert, *Dune* (New York: Ace Books, 1990), p. 314.

holding the Earth hostage. Linkola's view on madness is, in other words, every bit as nuanced and counter-intuitive as Foucault's was.

Foucault's *Madness and Civilization* largely consists of his attempt to refute the widespread myth that the rise of Modern Psychiatry marked the "happy moment" when madness was properly identified as what it had always been: a neurological "problem" fit only to be treated with (toxic) pharmaceutical drugs prescribed by a medical professional who claimed to have access to a fully-scientized knowledge about the patient's condition.[591] Although such a definition of "mental illness" is so thoroughly taken for granted today as to seem completely obvious, Foucault provided impressively-detailed analyses of previous eras' definitions of madness to show that all of them contradicted this modern stereotype.

For example, at the end of the Middle Ages madness was simply seen as the new leprosy, insofar as the madman was banished to the margins of society in what effectively amounted to de facto "leper colonies."[592] However, the criteria for this exclusion was not yet psychiatric as such, since vagabonds, criminals, and deranged minds were all lumped together in this single indeterminate category of "outsiders."

Crucially, Foucault noted that this early definition of madness did not contain any references to confinement, despite later periods' tendency to automatically associate the two concepts. Even the Renaissance image of the Ship of Fools drifting down the Flemish canals cannot exactly be called an example of confinement, insofar as this was historically situated within an era when the mad were, though banished from the city, still allowed to wander freely in the countryside.[593] Further, unlike later notions of personal responsibility and guilt, "folly" at this stage was seen as a type of unreason which was not understood to be the result of vice or even of disease. It was just a mysterious blot "for which nothing, in fact, is exactly responsible."[594]

---

[591] Michel Foucault, *Madness and Civilization* (New York: Vintage Books, 1988), p. 275.
[592] Ibid., p. 7.
[593] Ibid., p. 8.

In addition, unlike the later Freudian expectation that madness must be humiliated through being placed in the presence of Reason (embodied in the figure of the analyst) and then forced to admit that it was *not* itself Reason, in the Early Renaissance, madness was actually seen as the result of too much learning and too much knowledge: "Madness appears here as the comic punishment of knowledge and its ignorant presumptions."[595] Don Quixote, for example, goes mad not as a result of completely lacking Reason, nor from embodying mental illness as a somatic disease reducible to some chemical makeup in his brain, but precisely from a surplus of knowledge stemming from too many hours of reading books. The following passage from Cervantes' novel itself documents that Don Quixote's brain was rotted out from a surplus of intellectual stimulation accumulated from an excessive devotion to the study of literary texts:

> [H]e became so absorbed in his books that he spent his nights from sunset to sunrise, and his days from dawn to dark, poring over them; and what with little sleep and much reading his brains got so dry that he lost his wits. His fancy grew full of what he used to read about in his books, enchantments, quarrels, battles, challenges, wounds, wooings, loves, agonies, and all sorts of impossible nonsense; and it so possessed his mind that the whole fabric of invention and fancy he read of was true, that to him no history in the world had more reality in it . . . So he went on stringing together these and other absurdities, all in the style of those his books had taught him, imitating their language as well as he could; and all the while he rode so slowly and the sun mounted so rapidly and with such fervour that it was enough to melt his brains if he had any [left].[596]

---

[594] Ibid., p. 13.
[595] Ibid., p. 26.
[596] Miguel de Cervantes, *Don Quixote*, The Unabridged Classic Ormsby Translation. e-artnow. Kindle Edition.

Above all, in this era, madness was understood to stem from a "delusive attachment" to oneself which "generates [one's own] madness like a mirage" in the desert of psychotic isolation.[597] It is no coincidence that Don Quixote's madness was defined not as a lack of logical or linguistic comprehension altogether, but rather a proliferation of unreal chimeras, such as in his tendency to see giants where others see windmills, fair damsels where others see low-class prostitutes, and castles where others see shady inns. The ontological status of these mirages, however, proved notoriously difficult to pin down with any Metaphysics available at that time and became even more problematic in the later phases of madness's history.

Despite his evident psychosis, the madman in this era was not yet seen as someone to be removed from public space. It is crucial to note that efforts to cure Don Quixote of his madness never took the form of transferring him to the "professional care" of an insane asylum, as his would-be saviour within the novel instead tried to beat him at his own game by directly entering the frame of his fantasy and challenging him to a knightly duel consistent with the delusions of his own chimerical pseudo-world. It was believed, in other words, that the only way to exorcise Don Quixote's chimeras was to become one of them.

This lack of any need to confine the madman is attested as well by the fact that in the early 17th Century, the well-known Prince of Fools (i.e., Quasimodo in *The Hunchback of Notre Dame*) was actually somebody who was by definition *a pleasure* to be around rather than a contaminated body or a threat.[598] Under this view, madness was not yet something to be shunned, let alone confined, but rather enjoyed. Foucault cited one quote from the era which went as far as to suggest that the madman was animated "by the inspiration of God and the Angels."[599]

Foucault noted that the "classical experience of madness" was born when Madness was immobilized for the first time, a great

---

[597] Michel Foucault, *Madness and Civilization* (New York: Vintage Books, 1988), p. 27.
[598] Ibid., p. 37.
[599] Ibid.

historical anomaly in itself.⁶⁰⁰ By this era, the days of allowing the mad to freely roam the countryside or sail down canals had come to an end, as the Ship of Fools was replaced by the confinement-space of the hospital. Crucially, the voice of madness would be silenced as well, though the very presence of this voice, with its capability to speak the same language as the sane, posed a considerable epistemological challenge which arguably remains unresolved even to the present day.

Foucault was careful to note that the Great Confinement of the Early Modern era cannot be understood through anachronistic references to an asylum as such, because this movement gathered up the poor, the unemployed, young men who had squandered their family's money, those with no profession, prisoners, and the mad without any need for psychiatric qualifications to justify this act of collective imprisonment. Likewise, the institution in which they were housed was decidedly *not* a medical establishment but was rather a juridical structure, insofar as the goal of such a place was not medicine but order.⁶⁰¹ It is no coincidence that record keeping in this context presupposed that one was measuring the economic value of an inmate's work. In this place, there was no belief that one was monitoring the medical progress of a patient.

This crucial difference in emphasis is also evident in the fact that the primary opposition was understood to lie between idleness and labour, not between illness and health. This emphasis on work provided a perverse incentive to actually imprison an excess of labourers, because it was quickly found that they could provide cheap manpower to do society's dirty work. Beggars, for example, were arrested in large numbers and then forced to work in sewers, proving that an all too utilitarian motivation lay behind claims to disinterested epistemological objectivity.⁶⁰² However, this strategy proved too effective for its own good. Initially, the need for this space of confinement stemmed from the tendency for economic crisis to generate unemployment which created huge masses of idlers and vagabonds with no place to go and nothing to do.

---

⁶⁰⁰ Ibid., p. 38.
⁶⁰¹ Ibid., p. 40.
⁶⁰² Ibid., p. 47.

However, the result of this confinement was itself just another round of economic crisis driven by the inability for paid workers to compete with this army of slaves. Nor was this phenomenon unique to France and other European nations, as Stefan Molyneux has emphasized the little-known historical fact that far from being uniquely responsible for the practice of slavery, lower-class whites in the American South by and large *hated* slavery because it made it effectively impossible for them to compete against free labour and still make an acceptable living.[603]

By the next historical phase of madness, Foucault noted that although confinement was traditionally used to avoid public scandal, such as in cases where an adulteress was placed out of sight to avoid bringing shame to her family, there was, however, one very notable exception to this rule.[604] The mad were confined not to be removed from the public eye, but precisely in order to be displayed like dancing monkeys for the raving masses.[605] This is hardly surprising if one considers that even on an etymological level, a monster is quite literally a thing "to be shown," since *Monstrare* is simply the Latin term for this public de-*monstra*-tion.[606]

In this context, confinement was not yet punishment or rehabilitation, as it would later come to be, but was rather just exhibition in the most literal sense.[607] Far from being a medical establishment, the zone of confinement was basically just a human zoo, a circus for the crassest sort of spectacular entertainment to be staged. Men who lacked reason were seen as animals in a "human stable" and were accordingly defined as sufferers of a natural frenzy stemming from having been reduced to the immediacy of their own animality.[608] Although he had not yet developed his theory of limits to the level of sophistication present in his later work *The*

---

[603] See Stefan Molyneux's infamous YouTube video "The Truth about Slavery: Past, Present, and Future."
[604] Michel Foucault, *Madness and Civilization* (New York: Vintage Books, 1988), p. 68.
[605] Ibid., p. 69.
[606] Ibid., p. 70.
[607] Ibid., p. 71.
[608] Ibid., p. 74.

Archaeology of Knowledge,[609] this early text by Foucault still fell back on the concept of a limit to describe the mysterious relation between the madman and his animality. While death was seen as the limit of life rather than a distinct substantial object in itself, madness was here understood to be the limit of life in the realm of animality and therefore could not be made to fit into the ontological resources of any Metaphysics available at the time.[610]

The need to show the mad to the world was, however, complicated by the fact that madness distinguished itself from other forms of unreason by its ability to speak.[611] The public spectacle of madness was not only something to be seen, but also something to be heard. This relation between madness and language, a crucial item of concern for Linkola as well, would prove even more puzzling in the following phase of madness.

By the era of "passion and delirium," madness was explicitly understood to be a blind surrender to the danger of the passions.[612] In this pre-Cartesian context which did not know any dualism of mind and body as such, passion was seen as the meeting ground of the body and the (Christian) soul.[613] More precisely, passion was understood to be the site where the body and soul had not yet been distinguished, a location uniquely suitable for the explosion of unreason to occur.[614] Passion was understood to be the very presupposition of madness, insofar as madness was seen as a disease affecting the body *and* the soul due to the sinner's failure to keep this explosive energy under control through spiritual repressions of his or her desires. Madness also exposed just how fragile this unity was in the first place, insofar as madness brought about an abrupt suspension of natural law and a cessation of movement within the madman.[615]

---

[609] Foucault, Michel, *The Archaeology of Knowledge* (New York: Vintage Books, 2010), p. 46,
[610] Michel Foucault, Madness and Civilization (New York: Vintage Books, 1988), p. 81.
[611] Ibid., p. 78.
[612] Ibid., p. 85.
[613] Ibid., p. 86.
[614] Ibid., p. 88.

This immobility, however, was thoroughly paradoxical, because the madman's movement had cancelled itself out precisely by its own excess, bringing about an immobility bordering on death through what appeared to be a surplus of its own life force.[616] The madman would then be reduced to a living statue, with the perception of external objects shut off by its own melancholia.[617]

Crucially, however, this cessation of external perception was not simply negative in character, since this merely facilitated the conditions for the madman to become absorbed in fragments of fantasy which would isolate him both from himself and from the external world.[618] Foucault explicitly designated these "chimeras," hallucinations which banished the madman to the emptiness of "the cycle of non-being."[619]

The ontological status of these chimeras was somewhat ambiguous, however, since one would ordinarily assume that imagination, rather than perception, would have to provide the foundation for such fantasies to emerge. However, Foucault noted that madness was not simply rooted in imagination but went beyond its limits as well, in that madness did not recognize these chimeras as empty fantasies by only *pretending* that they were real while knowing full well that they were not. Rather, madness fell for its own tricks by "allowing the image [to take on] a spontaneous value [as a] total and absolute truth."[620] The problem is not simply that the image of the chimera had been birthed by the imagination, but that the madman had affirmed it as something real. The only structure capable of accomplishing such a bizarre feat was, of course, language.

The madman's ability to both imagine chimeras which do not exist *and* speak the language of reason to affirm them as though they did, therefore, had to presuppose a certain asymmetrical relation between these two subjective faculties. Linguistic

---

[615] Ibid.
[616] Ibid., p. 90.
[617] Ibid., p. 92.
[618] Ibid., p. 93.
[619] Ibid.
[620] Ibid., p. 94.

rationality, however linearly-sophisticated it might become, is utterly meaningless if it ever becomes enslaved to a chimerical image whose referent is merely an empty void of non-being:

> The ultimate language of madness is that of reason, but the language of reason enveloped in the prestige of the image, limited to the locus of appearance which the image defines.[621]

Madness is therefore neither completely linguistic nor completely imaginary in nature, but only exists as such in a composite complex of image, speech, and convictions.[622]

In this era, madness was understood to be this delirium which effectively hijacks the artificial unity of language to affirm a false view which could never achieve this level of coherence without this artificial supplement.[623] Foucault noted that "[l]anguage is the first and last structure of madness" because it alone provides the technical resources to allow a gap of nothingness to masquerade as a bulletproof reality.[624] Under this view, paradoxically, language itself "goes mad" by suffering from a delirium which it provided the conditions for in the first place: "It is in this delirium, which is of both body and soul, of both language and image, of both grammar and physiology, that all the cycles of madness conclude and begin."[625] The chimerical image alone, in other words, is not sufficient to constitute madness. It is only in the linguistic affirmation of the false image that madness can embody its true essence as error.[626]

Under this view, madness is literally a nothingness completely devoid of Being, insofar as it "fills the void of error with images and links hallucinations by affirmation of the false" yet still simply generates a false plentitude which is merely "the culmination of the void" in the guise of a substantial reality. Foucault warned

---

[621] Ibid.
[622] Ibid., p. 96.
[623] Ibid., p. 100.
[624] Ibid.
[625] Ibid., pp. 100-1.
[626] Ibid., p. 104.

that "however vividly they are [given], however rigorously established in the body, these images are nothingness, since they represent nothing."[627]

Madness came to be defined as error simply because in "affirming nothing as true or real, it does not affirm at all; it is ensnared in the non-being of error."[628] Madness was now understood to be the nothing which manifests itself, exploding in signs, words, and gestures. Madness became reason dazzled, a reason which looks into the sun and sees nothing but somehow still believes that it sees something real. It is no coincidence, then, that Descartes found he could only break the dazzlement of madness by closing his senses off to allow reason to dialogue with itself in the absence of the delusions manufactured by the Evil Genius.

While classical tragedy used day and night as a pair of reflecting mirrors, this was to be distinguished from madness, in that the madman couldn't let light be the disclosure of clear truth because even in the light he was a confused murmur.[629] Madness was the endless murmur which cancelled both day and night, insofar as "the images of madness are only dream and error, and if the sufferer who is blinded by them appeals to them, it is only to disappear with them in the annihilation to which they are fated."[630] Unlike its status in earlier periods, "madness in the classical world ceased to be the sign of another world," as "it became the paradoxical manifestation of non-being."[631] Death had to be the fulfilment of madness, because both madness and death were forms of non-being in disguise.[632]

With these resources in mind, we can finally attempt to reconstruct Linkola's own theory of madness. Like Foucault, Linkola argued that madness must not be contrasted with linguistic rationality, for madness is *primarily* to be understood as an abuse of the language of sanity to craft impressively-complicated proposals

---

[627] Ibid., p. 106.
[628] Ibid., p. 107.
[629] Ibid., pp. 110-1.
[630] Ibid., p. 113.
[631] Ibid., p. 115.
[632] Ibid., p. 116.

for objects which seem perfectly viable so long as one only evaluates them on linguistic grounds. Linguistic syntax is not sufficient in itself to unearth why a five-headed unicorn with wings is not a real object, since there is no grammatical error as such in this string of symbols. Because discovering that its status as a chimera is false requires something beyond language, the madman is simply the one who has linguistic rationality but has fallen short in another area of reason. The abuse of language to affirm chimeras which are, in themselves, gaps of nothingness and non-being is therefore the definition of madness for Linkola as well.

Linkola goes beyond Foucault's analysis, however, by suggesting that one can only succeed in unearthing these chimeras' unviability if one evaluates them on strictly ecological grounds. Whereas Don Quixote's chimeras (i.e., windmills as giants, barber's basin as helmet, prostitutes as damsels) did not necessarily require ecological analysis to unearth their lack of realness, Linkola insists that universal democracy, universal sanitation, and universal automation can only be fully grasped as gaps of non-existence if one recognizes the specifically ecological reasons why. For this reason, Linkola's understanding of rationality is far more sophisticated than his predecessors', for a vague appeal to "the laws of reality" will always remain incomplete if its ecological meaning is left unrecognized. Quite fittingly, in his lengthy interview published in the final issue of the Finnish magazine *Quadrivium* in December 2014, Linkola's calling in life was described as the coordinated mission of "dissembling the wall of madness brick by brick," something of an inverse operation to Pink Floyd's construction of insanity which once occurred on stage "another brick in the wall" at a time.[633]

Language and Ontology

One might argue that the ultimate antithesis to Linkola is, therefore, simply the Linguistic Turn philosophy which enables this madness

---

[633] Pentti Linkola interview from *Quadrivium* #6 (2014): abridged version. Available at http://qvadrivivm.blogspot.com/2015/12/pentti-linkola-interview-from.html

to go on by providing the underlying structure to make even the most absurd humanistic chimera pass not only as something real, but as the embodiment of the highest standard of Being itself. Although fundamentally misguided, the Linguistic Turn fad is a theory which must be addressed on a serious level, since this perversion seduced some of the finest minds of the 20th Century, even including the later Heidegger himself, to fall under the spell of linguistification. Nowhere is this conflict between ecology and language more apparent than in Gadamer's Hermeneutics, which makes up something of the ultimate antithesis to Linkola's thought process. We can only understand Linkola fully, in other words, if we descend into the belly of the beast to examine the exact opposite to his thought process first.

Like the early Heidegger, Gadamer downplayed Cartesian models of a private stream of experience and instead argued that anything which has fallen short of being disclosed publicly within a common space has always already failed to live up to any meaningful definition of Being. Yet Gadamer proposed an even more radical ontological standard even than the early Heidegger's Dasein by insisting that the ultimate commons is not merely spatial exteriority and other naïve definitions of outsideness, but is rather language itself. The same physical space might be utilized by more than one person, or even by a set of non-human animals and things, but only a linguistic meaning can truly be *shared* in the proper sense of the term. Any model positing meaning as a private content trapped on the inside of a single mind had to be abandoned if one hoped to cast off the chains of solipsism and release the prisoners of the Cartesian cave back into the blinding light of Logos once again. In his sprawling 2012 work *Less Than Nothing*, Slavoj Zizek went as far as to synopsize Gadamer's hermeneutical philosophy as a new Linguistic Turn ontology: "to be is to be understood."[634]

Likewise, Gadamer found traditional hermeneutical models to be fatally flawed, since all too often the problem of interpretation was understood through a model in which a single subject worked to reconstruct the author's intended meaning in his or her own mind

---

[634] Slavoj Zizek, *Less Than Nothing* (London: Verso, 2012).

one step at a time until the last piece of the puzzle was recovered and the original picture was reduplicated. Nowhere was this Cartesian bias more damaging than in the work of Schleiermacher, Gadamer's chief intellectual enemy, who basically argued that the meaning of the text could be contained in a single event which only occurred once at the moment of inspiration. Under this view, the novel *Demons,* for example, only "really happened" when Dostoyevsky himself wrote it in the 19th Century. Any reader who approaches the text after the fact can only hope to approximate this original event by laboriously building up a forensic reconstruction of it, much like a detective who tries to piece together a cryptic homicide on the basis of so many fragments of evidence.[635]

Gadamer found this approach to be entirely unnecessary for the simple fact that interpretation is never a procedure executed by a single mind on its own. On the contrary, anything worthy of the term "understanding" is always already on the outside in a public medium which is common to all.[636] This is the case not only in great works of art, such as Cervantes' *Don Quixote* or Balzac's *La Comédie Humaine*, but is at work even in the most mundane of conversations. Gadamer noted that the very notion of a "conducted conversation" is inherently contradictory, since a conversation can only be genuine if it is by definition something which is not controlled by any given subject, let alone by both participants at the same time.[637] A conversation is not so much an activity which one "does" as it is an event which "happens." The word for this virtual common space in which an event of understanding takes place is simply language itself. Likewise, the ontological definition of Being had to change from objective presence to hermeneutical understanding.

We might argue that achieving a shared meaning could never occur simply through coordinating both minds to execute an identical algorithmic procedure in unison, an approach which would effectively treat hermeneutical participants as slaves who must be

---

[635] Hans-Georg Gadamer, *Truth and Method* (New York: Continuum, 1989), p. 166.
[636] Ibid., p. 388.
[637] Ibid., p. 383.

induced to row in perfect conformity to the vocal demands of the author who would be elevated to the status of a metaphorical master at the helm of a ship. A shared meaning is not simply the result of coercing multiple minds to yield the exact same return value in some technological sense that would reduce the mind to a very fancy biological computer.

Gadamer was careful to note that any appeal to private execution of a procedure misses the point that shared meaning can only be achieved through a fusion of horizons, a paradoxical illustration of language's status as both on the outside and only ever imperfectly shared.[638] Interpretation is an open procedure precisely because a "closed horizon" is an inherent contradiction in terms; a horizon is only a horizon if it is indeterminately disclosed and always open to newness.[639] For this reason, interpretation can always admit of further improvements, which themselves can only be obtained through repeating the cyclical movement of traversing the hermeneutical circle, yet this is precisely because it is a fusion of openings to the outside rather than a fixed entity bound by the limits of ontological closure which would be applicable to a stone or some other lifeless object.

For this reason, Gadamer insisted vehemently that freedom is impossible without language.[640] Ecology alone is not sufficient to make one free, for even entities which exhibit a biological life force still lack true agency if the foundation of their activity is ecological rather than hermeneutical. A honey bee, for example, might appear to the naïve viewer to act spontaneously in accord with a free will, but a closer analysis will reveal that its activities are all determined by its hard-wired instincts and by the naturalistic constraints of its environment. Under this view, Nature basically holds the status of a giant composite stimulus which induces predictable reactions from the organism on the basis of evolutionary conditioning which is hard-wired on a physical level alone.

In his early lectures on *The Fundamental Concepts of Metaphysics*, Heidegger similarly dismissed animal instinct as a

---

[638] Ibid., p. 306.
[639] Ibid., p. 304.
[640] Ibid., p. 473.

poor imitation of freedom, in that he cited a zoological experiment from his era which proved that a honey bee will continue to suck nectar from a flower even after its abdomen has been cut off, leaving the nectar to leak out into the abyss as the bee executes the infinite loop of instinctual response to the stimulus, lacking the freedom even to become aware of how pointless its own activity is. Under this view, executing Nature's hard-wired instructions is the exact antithesis to freedom. The most conclusive form of slavery is slavery to environment and biological makeup alone.

It is not hard to imagine Gadamer and Heidegger condemning Linkola's call to revert to the Mind of Nature to be nothing more than an institutionalized destruction of freedom and, indeed, of the possibility of the disclosure of Being itself. Although this characterization has already been thoroughly proven to be unfair, it is nonetheless important to acknowledge that Linkola's philosophy does not represent a minor disagreement with Heidegger's and Gadamer's views but rather a total reversal of them. Linkola's ontology is roughly the idea that "to be is to be ecological." More precisely, anything which cannot be instantiated in some concrete ecological form has no Being at all; it is merely an empty concept, a linguistic label with no corresponding object. Under this view, humanistic chimeras don't just have less Being than real ecological situations; they have no Being at all. Contrary to Gadamer's thesis, even achieving public commonness is useless if the thing one is talking about is impossible to correlate with a valid ecological form, as an ecologically impossible object is not a flawed being, but no being at all. Language cannot bear the burden of providing an ontological foundation for Being on its own, since language is merely secondary to an ecological standard of truth which is far more primordial. Ecology is not just one more language among all others in a universe which lacks any other standard of Being; rather, ecology is the set of true forms which will always override the set of pseudo-forms generated by the madness of linguistification.

Deep Ecology as Linkola's Ethical Code

While madness can be defined as the affirmation of nothingness through falling for the delusion of linguistification, sanity is simply to be defined as the stance of Deep Ecology itself. Linkola's own understanding of the term Deep Ecology, however, differs in some very significant ways from Arne Naess's original vision for this idea. A thorough discussion of their contrasts shall therefore be necessary before concluding the present study of Linkola's philosophy.

Norwegian philosopher Arne Naess's vision for Deep Ecology is particularly significant, in that he was the one who first coined the term itself. According to Alan Drengson, Naess's first known public reference to Deep Ecology occurred in 1972 when he attended the Third World Future Research Conference in Bucharest, Romania. In his own talk at this event, Naess introduced the term in order to contrast this new "deep" approach to ecology with more traditional models which were all "shallow" in comparison. Among other things, whereas a shallow approach was restricted to the specialized knowledge indigenous to one academic discipline, his proposal for a deep view would instead favour a total view of the situation limited to no one academic department in particular.[641]

In addition, he responded to the need to distinguish a deeper view "respecting nature and the inherent worth of other beings" regardless of their utilitarian value for humans with a shallower approach which risks treating ecology as an engineering problem oriented towards "fixing bugs" within the System only insofar as they advance human projects and meet human needs.

Whereas the shallow view is limited through its need to utilize established systems of knowledge in order to solve problems which are defined with humanistic prejudices, the deep view is freed up to instead question all fundamental values in themselves.[642] Shallow Ecology is inherently anthropocentric because it remains enslaved to human-first value systems, while Deep Ecology performs the leap of faith to suspend these same systems' claims to certainty. Naess argued that the result of performing this reduction

---

[641] See Alan Drengson's introduction to Arne Naess's collection of essays *Ecology of Wisdom*, p. 25.
[642] Ibid., p. 26.

cannot be anything except a change of heart to recognize the inherent worth of *all* living beings, not only those which happen to be useful or even aesthetically pleasing to humans.[643]

In addition to this negative emphasis on suspending inhibitions from the shallow attitude, Naess defined Deep Ecology positively by deducing the following eight proposals. First, one must favour the flourishing of life on Earth and one must conceptualize it as having inherent value independent of any questions of its usefulness for us. Second, one must posit the richness and diversity of natural life as values in themselves. Third, one must acknowledge that people have no right to reduce this richness and diversity except to satisfy vital needs. Fourth, one must accept that this requires a significant decrease in human population. Fifth, one must admit that present-day levels of human interference in Nature are excessive. Sixth, one must recognize that our current policies must be radically changed rather than slightly modified. Seventh, one must change the emphasis to increasing the quality of life rather than focus on traditional measures of "standard of living" which are measured in purely quantitative terms. Eighth, one must take up the obligation to participate in concrete attempts to implement necessary changes rather than remain stuck at the level of empty contemplation.[644]

Naess has emphasized that the ethical implications of this conversion to Deep Ecology cannot be anything except pacifistic. Rising up to the task of recognizing the gap between the current status of human theory and the totality of ecological knowledge which vastly transcends it, one cannot adopt any stance *except* to be moved to reject violence against any living being within this system. Naess has repeatedly insisted that the ecological preservation of Nature must be combined with a pacifist project to end violence, as well as with an agenda for social justice to eradicate poverty and other sociological evils.[645] Far from only increasing one's appreciation for plants, fungi, and non-human

---

[643] Ibid., p. 27.
[644] Ibid., pp. 111-2.
[645] Arne Naess, "The Three Great Movements," in *Ecology of Wisdom* (London: Penguin, 2008), p. 81.

animals, Deep Ecology also builds a stronger foundation for one to feel empathy for one's fellow humans. In fact, Naess has gone as far as to define "ecosophy" precisely as a "philosophy of ecological harmony or equilibrium."[646]

Naess insists that Deep Ecology can only strengthen harmony, not only among distinct species but even among humans from different viewpoints, yet he justifies this ambitious claim through paradoxically arguing that Deep Ecology is not, in fact, the deepest layer of meaning accessible to an embodied ecological subject. In "The Basics of the Deep Ecology Movement," Naess insisted that Deep Ecology is inherently a trans-cultural movement compatible with a number of different ultimate worldviews such as Buddhism, Christianity, Hinduism, and even secularist naturalism. This is because the principles of Deep Ecology do not form an ultimate worldview in themselves.[647] In other words, according to Naess, Deep Ecology is *not* metaphysics or religion and does not provide its own ontological answers or its own ultimate definition of Being.

In fact, it is impossible to establish the principles of Deep Ecology without presupposing some deeper foundation of meaning and a grounding worldview because, within Naess's own original hierarchy of layers, the principles of Deep Ecology are located only within level two and must presuppose some other system of meaning below them in level one, the proper layer for metaphysical and religious systems. Like Bertrand Russell and Aristotle, Naess argued that disagreements among speakers often stem from a failure to properly distinguish levels of meaning; philosophers' role is therefore largely to make these distinctions explicit in order to help clarify communication among participants in dialogue.[648]

For Naess, this means unearthing the differences not only between these two layers but among the four total spheres which are always at work in thought and communication, even if they have been left unrecognized before his own work brought them to light.

---

[646] Ibid., p. 32.
[647] Arne Naess, "The Basics of the Deep Ecology Movement," in *Ecology of Wisdom* (London: Penguin, 2008), p. 106.
[648] Ibid., p. 109.

Determinate actions, for example, are situated within the shallowest layer (level four) but can only be executed within this surface layer if one has already presupposed a foundation in each of the three deeper strata. Such an action in the fourth level will be informed by each of the following deeper layers: guidelines for lifestyles and policies, which make up level three; platform principles for movements, which make up level two; and finally, verbalized fundamental philosophical and religious worldviews which form level one and terminate this hierarchy.

Once again, within this model, Naess argued that Deep Ecology is a set of level two principles rather than a system of ultimate metaphysical truths.[649] Likewise, it is not at all a problem that supporters of Deep Ecology cannot agree on the ultimate fundamentals which they import from the various religious and metaphysical worldviews which they bring to the movement from afar; on the contrary, this diversity is actually a good thing which Naess explicitly praises as a strength rather than flaw of the community.[650] In fact, this disagreement is more apparent than real, since Deep Ecology's status as a level-two system makes it intrinsically compatible with many different religions and philosophies, each of which can ground it equally legitimately.[651]

Naess has argued that Deep Ecology is not merely an intellectual exercise pursued in order to make a person "smarter" like, say, Mathematics, but is rather a means of personal transformation which can lead a person to reach a superior level of subjective realization. In his essay "An Example of a Place: Tvergastein," he argued that industrialism has inhibited this self-realization by removing the traditional milieus in which people once existed. There is "no place for a place" amidst the universal conversion of locations into identical and mutually substitutable urban and suburban pseudo-spaces. All sense of "home" has been lost as people no longer live off the land, yet this concept of "home" was not just an exterior container in which the body was situated but was, rather, always a deeper part of oneself. While the modern

---

[649] Ibid., p. 108.
[650] Ibid., p. 115.
[651] Ibid., p. 117.

self simply takes this homelessness for granted as the norm, the ecological self can only be achieved if it is grounded in a home within a "place" worthy of the name.[652] Much like Linkola, Naess noted the irony that although waste has increased dramatically within these pseudo-spaces, this enormous ecological cost was doubly tragic because it did not actually improve our quality of life in the least.[653]

In contrast with the cardboard prison cells of modernity, Naess has written about his experiences retreating into Nature to dwell in traditional buildings which lack technological distractions. One notable difference between the two is that whereas the former is merely a venue for "stimulation," the latter allows one to experience the "presence" of things, especially Nature.[654] In other words, one can only obtain the mindset of Deep Ecology if one actually immerses oneself in a genuine place of presence and abandons the pseudo-spaces of stimulation. In his own journey to the place of Tvergastein, for example, Naess recounted that the deep ecologist there will realize that even the mice there have different personalities and exhibit a richness and diversity of natural life which would go unnoticed to the urban attitude that would merely treat them as identical pests to be exterminated at once.[655] In addition to realizing that mice are not vermin but are natural creatures with a legitimate right to exist in their natural habitats, Naess insisted that the deep ecologist will also realize that it is "improper and shameful language" to claim that any place *is* harsh or extreme. The real ecological question is, rather, what does a given place require of me? What sort of lifestyle is possible in a given place, and which ones are not?[656] Tvergastein, for example, is a place which fundamentally rules out modern suburban pseudo-lifestyles, as it forces one to confront the ecological absurdity of heating 99% of the air in a building when one only inhabits some

---

[652] Arne Naess, "An Example of a Place: Tvergastein" in *Ecology of Wisdom* (London: Penguin, 2008), p. 45.
[653] Ibid., p. 48.
[654] Ibid., p. 50.
[655] Ibid., p. 51.
[656] Ibid., p. 54.

1% of it at a time. In addition, it forces one to acknowledge that it takes more energy to melt snow than it does to carry water, so the labour invested in personally fetching the water by hand must be preferred over taking the "easy way out."[657]

Likewise, a place is not a neutral grid of coordinates with a purely quantitative meaning; rather, it qualitatively determines your likes and dislikes when you are situated within it. Naess insists that there is no Cartesian dualism to separate a self from the place in which it is grounded.[658] He even goes as far as to argue that a place is like the Freudian superego: it can give orders. The deep ecologist, in other words, is simply the one who can "hear" Nature speak, largely through recognizing the birthmark of ecological contradiction which a given place will forbid vehemently from being carried out.[659]

Because a place is only a place if it determines the details of one's life, Naess argued that one cannot help having inconsistent thoughts with someone who is not of that place.[660] This is because the deep ecologist does not merely "use" the Earth as a piece of technology; instead, the deep ecologist communicates with nature, even though this is not done through words.[661] Contrary to expectation, Naess insists that this communication is not reducible to traditional ideas of Romantic aestheticism, since the poet inspired to sing the praises of Nature or the painter driven to capture it in images will only admire one particular fraction of Nature, and will base this preference only on grounds of aesthetic appreciation. This one-sided gaze at Nature misses the point of allowing Nature itself to speak without any regard for our humanistic prejudices. For this reason, Naess argued that the tendency to dismiss scientific approaches to Nature miss the point that the responsible scientist really does try to view the whole rather than fixate only on the sections of it which are appealing on aesthetic grounds. For this

---

[657] Ibid., p. 56.
[658] Ibid., p. 57.
[659] Ibid., p. 57.
[660] Ibid., p. 60.
[661] Ibid., p. 61.

reason, he warns his readers that they must not speak of science and research in merely negative terms.[662]

In his "Modesty and the Conquest of Mountains," Naess reiterated the limitations of aesthetic prejudice by noting that the widespread stereotype that the mountains and mountain peoples are "rough" miss the point that their lifestyles simply disregard urban luxuries yet this is simply because the place itself dictates this lifestyle for them.[663] Above all, one must resist the urge to take up the "Civilized Man's Burden" and import urban values into this place in order to "modernize" it. Because each place speaks for itself, this would only create a mismatch between place and value which will only damage the people's connection with their home.[664]

In "The World of Concrete Contents," Naess grappled with the problem of "objectivity" towards Nature by revisiting Galileo's traditional distinction between primary and secondary qualities: Galileo argued that water, for example, is neither hot nor cold in itself; these are secondary qualities which only make sense as sensations for us. In itself, water has only primary qualities which are to be expressed in mathematical notation rather than through references to human sensations.[665] Naess argues that although Galileo's distinction might sound quite logical, it cannot help leading to absurdity and is especially incompatible with the stance of Deep Ecology.[666]

The grand irony he notes is that it is precisely when the environmentalist talks in terms of his or her feelings that the environmentalist actually succeeds in talking about reality. There is no absolutist "Thing in Itself" which would remain after purging these terms, because the primary qualities Galileo once sought out do not really exist. Galileo's theory falls apart at the moment when it is absolutized.[667]

---

[662] Ibid., pp. 62-3.
[663] Arne Naess, "Modesty and the Conquest of Mountains," in *Ecology of Wisdom* (London: Penguin, 2008), p. 66.
[664] Ibid., p. 67.
[665] Arne Naess, "The World of Concrete Contents," in *Ecology of Wisdom* (London: Penguin, 2008), p. 70.
[666] Ibid., p. 71.

Naess finds the very belief in primary qualities to be epistemologically problematic, because the entire point of primary qualities is to disconnect the object as such from our experience of it. Under this view, it inevitably becomes just another resource for us, since any feelings of empathy or value are simply illusions which must be wiped out to gain an "objective view" of the matter.

In fact, this treatment of the object as a resource for subjective use is hard-wired even into our attempts to describe our approaches to it in scientifically neutral terms. Because it was eventually proven that colours don't really exist, Whitehead noted the unavoidable conclusion that if the rose isn't red in itself, it was only my brain which made it red through its own processing. It is patently absurd, therefore, to claim that primary qualities allow one to grasp the contents of reality as such.[668] Even contemporary physics is not oriented towards grasping these contents, since its subject matter has been reduced to a fully abstract structure.

Naess argues, though, that it is meaningful to speak of concrete contents of experience. A tree within a place is not an illusion, yet it is also not something which the subject must cross a gulf of separation to reach from the outside; instead, both the subject and the tree are always part of a total.[669] Any talk of a subject being placed into an environment is therefore an error. [670]

Likewise, questions of value affirmation are there from the start, even in what appear to be declarative sentences formed by an objective speaker, because the world is inherently something encountered at the level of content rather than structure. Even the scientific project of deducing the abstract structures of Physics, however well-founded it might be, must respect the fact that even if the world "has" such structures, it does not actually reveal them.[671] The realm of content-revelation is therefore not an imperfect glimpse into the realm of abstract structure but is an independent

---

[667] Ibid., p. 72.
[668] Ibid., p. 74.
[669] Ibid., p. 76.
[670] Ibid., p. 77.
[671] Ibid., p. 78.

venue in which feeling and experience are to be valued on their own terms.

In his "Self-Realization: An Ecological Approach to Being in the World," he further developed this thesis that Deep Ecology leads to self-realization by affirming that the "I" is far more than the "ego" in the traditional, narrow sense of the term.[672] Rather than speak of the ego as a single determinate object, Naess revisits a traditional model in which there is a set theoretical group of concentric circles, of which the ego is the smallest member. One level higher, the broader social self is situated, while the metaphysical self makes up the largest circle. Naess's main objection to this configuration is simply that it leaves out Nature. He introduces the ecological self as the broadest level to make up for this. This shift is necessary for the additional reason that emphasizing the human community is too limiting since the ecological context is far more than a social realm.

With these resources at his disposal, Naess affirmed that self-realization is unique for each of us, insofar as the self is not simply a synonym for the physical body.[673] Although such a claim will offend the materialist reductivism which has become the official doctrine of "professional thinkers" today, he noted that if the two were actually synonyms, one could simply replace one term for the other without modifying the meaning of the same statement. Sentences substituting "my body" for "I" just don't work. "My body knows Mr. Smith" is not simply a paraphrase of the sentence "I know Mr. Smith," just as "My body likes Beethoven" fails to capture the meaning of "I like Beethoven."

For this reason, Naess insisted that one has fundamentally misunderstood the self if one attempts to treat it as a substance. It is, instead, a process of identification.[674] Likewise, Deep Ecology enriches the self because it aids the process of identification through building empathy with the natural world, even with creatures as seemingly insignificant or annoying as fleas (his own example.)[675]

---

[672] Arne Naess, "Self-Realization: An Ecological Approach to Being in the World," in *Ecology of Wisdom* (London: Penguin, 2008), p. 81.
[673] Ibid., p. 82.
[674] Ibid., p. 83.

Likewise, the conservation of Nature actually does serve one's own self-interests, because it is only through this pathway that one can obtain a more genuine self.[676]

Because the self is a process of identification rather than a fixed and static object, self-realization is the active procedure of realizing inherent potentialities. In his passionate readings of Spinoza in the original Latin, Naess asserts, much like Bronze Age Pervert, that fixating on survival alone misses the point that allowing a creature to "persevere in his being" is more than simply maintaining existence. He argues, "The expression persevere in his being in the quotation from Spinoza is better than [the more commonly used phrase] 'preserve his existence,' since the latter is often associated with physical survival and a struggle for survival." Instead, Naess proposes the unconventional translation "persevere in his being" as a much more faithful glimpse into the meaning of the phrase *perservare in suo esse* in the original Latin: "This has to do with acting from one's own nature. Survival is only a necessary condition, not a sufficient condition for continued self-realization."[677]

The loss of place is therefore simply the loss of this personal identity, since the self is not a lump of matter which can be transplanted from one location to another without changing its character. Against Descartes, Naess asserts that the self is not on the inside.[678] The ecological self is, rather, wide and deep; defending its place is literally an act of self-defense for this reason.[679]

Naess's insistence that Deep Ecology must also be a pacifist movement stemmed from his belief that Ghandi's commitment to non-violence was a natural conclusion of Ghandi's interpretation of his own religious principle that self-realization is not the individualization of the narrow ego but deals instead with the Atman of Hinduism. Non-violence is a necessary conclusion from the oneness of all life.[680] In addition to obvious example such as

---

[675] Ibid., p. 84.
[676] Ibid., p. 85.
[677] Ibid., p. 86.
[678] Ibid., p. 89.
[679] Ibid., p. 88.
[680] Ibid., p. 90.

unjustified killings, the deep ecologist will realize that the rejection of unnecessary commodities must be a part of this broader rejection of violence.[681] In other words, Naess's ethics is basically the same as "the philosophy of Michael Jackson" from his 1987 album *Bad*: "You're just another part of me":

> This is our planet
> You're one of us
> We're sendin' out a major love
> And this is our message to you
> The planets are linin' up
> We're bringin' brighter days
> They're all in line waitin' for you
> Can't you see?
> You're just another part of me

Because self-fulfilment deepens the self to embrace all life forms, Naess argues that a person who progresses on this path will see that the traditional Latin terms alter and ego form a false binary which disappears as the self is progressively widened.[682] Revisiting Kant's distinction between a moral act (which is performed out of duty and without joy) with a beautiful act which is performed out of a love for doing good, he claims that anyone who obtains this wider self will achieve the Kantian beautiful act, in that such a person will naturally want to do what's right for the broader whole of which he or she will realize he or she is an integrated part. Against Linkola, Naess affirms that what we need right now is not to be forced to sacrifice but, rather, to celebrate the joy of wilfully choosing to do the right thing without coercion.[683] This is because joy is not on the inside of a Cartesian mind but is rather only possible on the outside: joy simply *is* this wider self.[684]

Likewise, Naess remains committed to joining Deep Ecology with the agenda for social justice. In "The Three Great

---

[681] Ibid., p. 91.
[682] Ibid., p. 92.
[683] Ibid., p. 93.
[684] Ibid., p. 94.

Movements" he lists ecological crime alongside the elimination of war and poverty as the three great venues of ethical action in our era.[685] Yet there is a deeply intimate connection among the three concerns. For example, Deep Ecology requires significant changes in both rich and poor countries in order to satisfy the goal to protect life's richness and diversity for its own sake. For this reason, he affirms that there can be no Deep Ecology victory without corresponding peace and social justice victories.[686] Because an ecosystem is more than a human environment, one of industrialism's greatest crimes is that it impedes self-realization by inhibiting the ecological self through submitting it to economic exploitation.[687] It is self-contradictory to seek out ecological solutions without also fighting for a victory in the realm of social justice. Nor are these problems disconnected, since an ecological fix will simultaneously alleviate social problems as well. For example, implementing necessary "green changes" would simultaneously lower the unemployment rate, as there is no shortage of real work required to retrofit the whole world into a green form.[688]

In "The Place of Joy in a World of Fact," Naess therefore asserts that stereotypical beliefs that joylessness is a requirement to implement the Deep Ecology agenda miss the point that joy is precisely "of Nature!"[689] For this reason, he affirms Spinoza's and Thomas Aquinas's archaic beliefs that there is no such thing as evil. Evil is simply the privation of the good.[690] Restoring Nature cannot result in anything except the realization of happiness and the satisfaction of the ethical code as well, since all three are redundancies of the same positive essence of Being.

At the risk of needlessly overemphasizing their differences, it must be noted at the outset that Linkola's vision for Deep Ecology

---

[685] Arne Naess, "The Three Great Movements," in *Ecology of Wisdom* (London: Penguin, 2008), p. 81.
[686] Ibid., p. 100.
[687] Ibid., p. 102.
[688] Ibid., p. 101.
[689] Arne Naess, "The Place of Joy in a World of Fact," in *Ecology of Wisdom* (London: Penguin, 2008), p. 124.
[690] Ibid., p. 126.

overlaps with Naess's definition in many ways. Linkola's agreement with Naess's insistence that joy can only be achieved in Nature, for example, was important enough to merit its own essay in his 1998 "Joy of Living Characterizes Life." In it, Linkola asserted that Darwinist clichés reducing all activity to "the struggle for survival" miss the point that a bird can often meet a whole day's feeding requirements with only about half an hour of work, a plain fact which anyone who has actually spent time observing them in the wild would know. In fact, most of their time is simply spent enjoying themselves and relaxing: "an enormous part of the common gull's day is spent with lackadaisically sitting beside the partner and visiting neighbours; tens of times a day in clamorous welcoming rituals, in hours' worth of floating over the home bay by wind's buoyancy."[691]

Likewise, Linkola exposes that the rigid "functionality" which professional biologists and evolutionists claim is omnipresent in nature is actually just an academic fiction which is flatly contradicted by birds' behaviour in the wild. Much of life there "is an act of pure fun," as birds spend remarkably little of their time in anything like the human conception of "work."[692] Seeking out "deeper motivations" proves futile: their activity is often just sheer emotion, dreaming, and meditating pleasure.[693]

In this sense, Linkola essentially agrees with Naess that Augustine and other archaic thinkers pretty much got it right when it came to the difference between good and evil: as Augustine said in *The City of God*, "evil has no positive nature; [it is only] the loss of good [which] has received the name 'evil.'"[694] Evil is not a something in itself at all, for it is merely privative with regards to the good, insofar as the phrase "to be good" is redundant – Being is already in itself the good! Because only the good holds the status of Being, evil is merely negative, the absence of Being. Linkola goes further than Augustine, however, by specifically emphasizing that

---

[691] Pentti Linkola, "Joy of Living Characterizes Life," in *A Collection of Essays by Pentti Linkola 1993 – 2006*, p. 54.
[692] Ibid., p. 55.
[693] Ibid., p. 56.
[694] See *The City of God*, XI, Chapter 9.

Being is not any material configuration whatsoever, but only one which is ecological, almost like a total inversion of Gadamer's thesis that something can lay claim to the status of Being only if it has been disclosed publicly through the medium of linguistic communication. Contrary to expectation, Deep Ecology's rejection of linguistification does not amount to the self-enclosure of individual solipsism but rather affirms the ultimate "public sphere" through establishing requirements for intersubjective reality which go far beyond the limits of language alone.

In addition, Naess shares Linkola's preference for maintaining simple technologies and resisting the temptation to buy into the cult of "the new" simply because market pressures and clever advertising induce one to update to some newer product. In Naess's "Lifestyle Trends Within the Deep Ecology Movement," he mandated the use of simple means and the avoidance of unnecessarily complicated methods as the first principle in a list of lifestyle practices for the deep ecologist.[695]

Linkola espouses the Deep Ecology principle that natural diversity is a good in itself which must never be subordinated to humanistic judgments of utilitarianism or aesthetic beauty. In his 1993 "Finland Equals Forests," he defended the preservation of Finnish forests by warning the reader that, in addition to producing oxygen and adjusting the climate, this would be necessary to maintain biodiversity within the nation as a whole.[696] Only if this "immeasurably rich biocenose of thousands of species of plants, mushrooms and animals" is maintained as a "sanctuary where man won't rage and ravage" could any hope of biodiversity preservation remain.[697] Similarly, in his "Preservation Of Traditional Landscape And Nature," he mentioned that one of the most fitting aliases to designate modern industrial man is the "scoundrel" which impoverishes nature's variety through an idiotic commitment to monoculture.[698]

---

[695] Arne Naess, "Lifestyle Trends Within the Deep Ecology Movement," in *Ecology of Wisdom* (London: Penguin, 2008), p. 140.
[696] Pentti Linkola, "Finland Equals Forest," in *A Collection of Essays by Pentti Linkola 1993 – 2006*, p. 19.
[697] Ibid., p. 18.

In his *Quadrivium* interview he defined environmentalism as the stance in which one "considers nature as an environment for people" while conservationism is defined as the stance in which one "sees nature as a thing in and for itself." For this reason, he affirmed that "Nature exists for nature" and does not depend upon humanistic evaluations of utility or beauty to maintain this value. His decision to rename the stereotypical forestry professional as "The Armored Idiot" in his 1993 essay of the same name ultimately stemmed from the idiocy of failing to recognize Nature for what it really is. In the essay, Linkola explicitly claimed that "a forester doesn't comprehend anything about the essence of [a] tree nor the wholeness of [a] forest," yet this is not due to a lack of scientific data. It is rather their failure to understand "how they feel, their demands, or what they tolerate" on their own terms. Above all, the failure to recognize that diversity is willed by the forest itself defeats any claims to expertise: "a forest having only one type of tree is usually insane to even try [to] think about."[699]

Linkola similarly shares Naess's insistence that Deep Ecology must be explicitly contrasted with Romantic notions of aesthetic appreciation, as Linkola noted in his 1995 "The Masterpiece of Owl Men" that people's aesthetic judgment is so arbitrary that the same birds considered pests or killed a generation ago in Finland have suddenly become so fashionable that Finns feed them expensive sunflower seeds and publish books about them. He was careful to note, however, that this was not due to gaining a clearer view of Nature in itself but was based solely on the most arbitrary whims of aesthetic fashionability. Just as we suddenly find out that we love this one part of Nature, we go on damaging less fashionable parts of Nature all the same.[700]

In his 1997 "The Landscapes Of Sääksmäki," he echoed Naess's claim that it is foolish to consider anything in Nature as

---

[698] Pentti Linkola, "Preservation Of Traditional Landscape And Nature" in *A Collection of Essays by Pentti Linkola 1993 – 2006*, p. 52.
[699] Pentti Linkola, "Armored Idiot," in *A Collection of Essays by Pentti Linkola 1993 – 2006*, p. 9.
[700] Pentti Linkola, "The Masterpiece of Owl Men," in *A Collection of Essays by Pentti Linkola 1993 – 2006*, p. 76

being intrinsically ugly, though Linkola qualified this argument by assuring the reader that such descriptions are perfectly applicable to technology. While no bush, tree, or plant can be dismissed as messy or unkempt in itself, it is perfectly legitimate to designate man-produced waste and junk, as well as wretched, desolate buildings as ugly – because they are! Even buildings widely considered to be masterfully constructed will still stick out as a "flaw in the scenery" when contrasted with the natural landscape in which they are introduced.[701] Paradoxically, however, suspending the Romantic gaze of beauty towards Nature does not reduce it to so much dead matter to be processed industrially, but rather frees one up to connect to a given location as a *place* in Naess's sense of the term. In Linkola's 1995 "A Letter to Hannu Hautala" he condemned the industrial relation to the forest in which one has "no personal ties" at all to the land, as the only connection one cares about is "the dividend coming to [the] bank."[702]

Arguably, the single most important point of disagreement between the two deep ecologists lies in Naess's faith that rising up to the achievement of realizing the ecological self will necessarily lead people to embrace social harmony and to spontaneously do the right thing simply because they want to (i.e., the Kantian beautiful act.) One can only suspect that Naess's promise is simply an attempt to incorporate the Habermasian ideal of a public sphere in which coercion is progressively squeezed out as society is rationalized, yet Linkola has demonstrated that this is simply a euphemism for the ecologically impossible object of a democratic mass which votes to "do the right thing" by choice. Linkola reiterated his scepticism that this could ever be done, let alone that it has any place within the movement of Deep Ecology, during his 2011 interview with Francisco Martinez and Larissa Vanamo, in which he asserted that force and oppression are necessary precisely because life as such is a value. The Deep Ecology stance will lead one to realize this even more radically, since "life" would include

---

[701] Pentti Linkola, "The Landscapes Of Sääksmäki," in *A Collection of Essays by Pentti Linkola 1993 – 2006*, p. 99.
[702] Pentti Linkola, "A Letter to Hannu Hautala," in *A Collection of Essays by Pentti Linkola 1993 – 2006*, p. 22.

not only human life, but all animals and plants and fungi as well. In other words, life is far too valuable to be trusted to the whims of a democratic procedure which always promises that the solution is just one election away, no matter how many decades or centuries pass without progress in any ecologically-meaningful sense of the term.

Even as early as his 1989 title essay for the collection *Johdatus 1990-luvun ajatteluun* (*Introduction to the Thinking of the Nineteen Nineties*), Linkola reiterated that if one actually obtains a genuine respect for life on Earth, one's proposals for how to maintain it must begin with the words, "We have to . . ." His own commitment to formulating plans with reference to necessity (in Naess's terms "coercion") led him to refuse to gamble on allowing people to mystically evolve themselves to the angelic status of doing the right thing simply because they *want to*. Naess's certainty that this far-fetched goal can be achieved anytime soon is arguably just as misguided as Martin Luther's belief *some five centuries ago* that the corresponding religious revolution in which believers would do good works without any coercion from the Law was just around the corner – not to mention Paul's hope for ostensibly the same thing in his epistle to the Romans some two millennia ago!

Likewise, Linkola used this 1989 document to urge readers to forget about humanism, social issues, freedoms, and rights, in order to recognize that the primary concern of our era is not the communicative dialogue among people, but the relation of Man to Nature. Deep Ecology is the exact opposite of communicative action, as Linkola contradicted public opinion in his *Quadrivium* interview by remarking that few things anger him as much as receiving praise for "arousing so much debate" through functioning as a "professional polemicist." Far from valuing discussion as a good in itself, Linkola harshly asserted in this interview that adjusting opinions is worthless if one cannot link it with any real actions. Of course, the kind of "real actions" he praised in this context cannot mean anything except forceful changes in legislation which cannot help but appear as "coercion" to the oversocialized and those with feelings of inferiority. However, any appeal to preserve "individual freedom" will prove meaningless if there is no one left alive to enjoy even the artificial front which currently passes as liberty within an ever more tightly regulated System of technological control:

> Of course, changes in legislation can be made by force. Just as people don't cross the streets when the lights are red and don't surpass speed limits, they should be made unable to violate the environment. If you try to suggest that, people will tell you it is violating our individual freedom. It's senseless.[703]

Somehow, we can only be free if we allow the Mind of Nature to force us to be free. It remains uncertain whether life will prevail, but reinforcing this life-force against all odds is the sole reliable catalyst which can be trusted to somehow provide its own conditions of self-fulfilment.

---

[703] Pentti Linkola interview from *Quadrivium* #6 (2014): abridged version. Available at http://qvadrivivm.blogspot.com/2015/12/pentti-linkola-interview-from.html

Printed in Great Britain
by Amazon